CITY

CITY

A GUIDEBOOK FOR THE URBAN AGE

P. D. SMITH

BLOOMSBURY

LONDON · BERLIN · NEW YORK · SYDNEY

To Susan, for sharing my love of cities

First published in Great Britain and the USA in 2012

Bloomsbury Publishing Plc, 50 Bedford Square, London WC1B 3DP
Bloomsbury USA, 175 Fifth Avenue, New York, NY 10010

A CIP catalogue record for this book is available from the British Library.
Cataloging-in-Publication Data is available from the Library of Congress.

UK HARDBACK ISBN 978 1 4088 0191 8
UK TRADE PAPERBACK ISBN 978 1 4088 2443 6 (EXPORT EDITION)
US ISBN 978 1 60819 676 0

First Edition

10 9 8 7 6 5 4 3 2 1

www.bloomsbury.com
www.bloomsburyusa.com

All papers used by Bloomsbury Publishing are natural, recyclable products made from wood grown in well-managed forests. The manufacturing processes conform to the environmental regulations of the country of origin.

Printed in China by C & C Offset Printing Co Ltd

What is the city but the people?

William Shakespeare, *Coriolanus*

Contents

Chicago from the Willis Tower (formerly the Sears Tower). (following page)

INTRODUCTION

As a species, we have never been entirely satisfied with what nature gave us. We are the ape that shapes our environment, the city builders – *Homo urbanus*. Cities are our greatest creation. They embody our ability to imagine how the world might be and to realise those dreams in brick, steel, concrete and glass. Today, for the first time in the history of the planet, more than half the population – 3.3 billion people – are city dwellers. Two hundred years ago only 3 per cent of the world's population lived in cities, a figure that had remained fairly stable (give or take the occasional epidemic) for the last thousand years. By 2050, 75 per cent will be urbanites.

The experience of living in cities is universal. As one historian has written: 'A town is always a town, wherever it is located, in time as well as space.'[1] The first city builders were the Sumerians, who lived in the fertile land between the rivers of the Tigris and the Euphrates in the south of Mesopotamia. Today, this is part of Iraq. For the Sumerians seven thousand years ago, Eden was not a garden but a city. In their legends the first city was called Eridu and it was created by the god Marduk. He wanted to give his people a place of shelter, a refuge to protect them from a natural world that could be harsh and unforgiving. The Sumerians did not long for some mythic rural idyll, an unobtainable Arcadia. They believed the city was the place where all their dreams would be realised. By about 2000 BC, 90 per cent of Sumerians lived in cities such as Ur.

When the first city builders set out on their urban experiment, they created far more than a new man-made environment built of mud bricks. In many respects, they were laying the foundations of modern urban life. Civilisation as we know it today began in the city.

City dwellers also created a new way of being. Humanity was reinvented in these pioneering cities. Urban communities formed a revolutionary social and moral order that broke free from the rigid structures – tribes and clans – of the rural world. According to a medieval German saying, 'Stadtluft macht frei', city air sets you free. In a city, you could liberate yourself from feudal bonds and become an individual. The city allows you to be whatever you want to be. In *The Great Gatsby*, when Nick Carraway glimpses the skyline of mid-town Manhattan, with 'its first wild promise of all the mystery and the beauty in the world', he tells himself: 'Anything can happen now ... anything at all.'[2] For thousands of years, people arriving in the city have uttered these words.

From ancient Memphis to Manhattan, the intense experience of urban life has turned cities into magnets attracting the most talented people from the surrounding lands. Whether you were a Chinese peasant passing through the city walls of Nanjing in the third century AD, a Muslim pilgrim entering bustling Baghdad a thousand years ago, or a European immigrant arriving by ship in New York in the early years of the twentieth century, those first impressions of the city are overwhelming: the crowds of people filling the alleys and streets; the din of the traffic, whether horse-drawn carts, automobiles or street-cars; the bitter-sweet smell of humanity living cheek by jowl; buskers and beggars competing for your attention and your money; hawkers offering freshly cooked food; and shop windows stacked with goods from the four corners of the world, at never-to-be-repeated prices.

Two and a half thousand years ago, the Greek poet Alcaeus praised cities as being places of opportunity and vision, where dreams are made and desires fulfilled. Cities were successful because they became centres of trade, creating work and wealth for their inhabitants; because they were safe and secure places in which to live; and because they offered an intense social and cultural life. In its essentials, life for the inhabitants of the first cities was not so very different from today. Indeed, while writing this book I have often been struck by the remarkable continuity of urban life across time and space.

Cities bear the traces of countless past lives. 'All cities are geological and three steps cannot be taken without encountering ghosts', as the proto-Situationist Ivan Chtcheglov has rather beautifully put it.[3] The awareness of these ghosts as you walk through the city is – for me at least – one of the most important aspects of the urban experience. Cities are rich storehouses of human history. Even the structure of a new city harks back to earlier urbanisms and age-old dreams of a shining city on a hill. Amidst constant change and flux, there is profound continuity.

Above all, what motivated me to write *City* was a desire to explore and celebrate what is undoubtedly humankind's greatest achievement. When you have spent all your life in cities, it is easy to forget the exhilarating sense of awe felt by those who encounter the city for the first time.

When the German poet Heinrich Heine first saw London in 1827 he was 'astonished' by what he described as 'the greatest wonder which the world can show'.[4] Poets, like great photographers, make the world anew through their work, so that we see it as if for the first time. They make the stone stony, in Viktor Shklovsky's memorable phrase.[5] If this book manages to reawaken in you, the reader, something of the sense of wonder that Heine felt on seeing London for the first time, then it will have succeeded.

* * *

As Iain Sinclair has rightly said, 'walking is the best way to explore and exploit the city'.[6] To really understand a city, you need to walk its streets and read its geography through the soles of your feet. The book you are holding is designed with this in mind, as a guidebook to an imaginary 'Everycity'. It will accompany you on your way around those many features of urban life and geography that have been present in cities since the beginning and have become part of our urban genetic code.

You can start on page one and read all the way through to the end if you want. But I have tried to create a book in which you can wander and drift. The elements of surprise and discovery are important, just as they are when you explore a real city. Open the book anywhere and begin – there are no set routes here. From the Central Station you could strike out to Chinatown or the House of God. Then you could grab some Street Food to eat in the Park before making your way to the Department Store. In the evening you could explore the City and the Stage, or stroll through the Red-Light District, and then head back to your Hotel or Downtown apartment for the night. As in a real city, you can follow any number of pathways through this book. And don't worry about getting lost. Some say it's the only way really to experience a city.

Christ the Redeemer overlooking Rio de Janeiro, Brazil. (following page)

1 ARRIVAL

The City in the Lake

On 8 November 1519, Europeans caught their first glimpse of Tenochtitlán, the Aztec capital and the centre of the greatest empire ever seen in Mesoamerica.[1] 'We came to a broad causeway,' recalled a twenty-three-year-old Spanish soldier, Bernal Díaz del Castillo, 'and when we saw all those cities and villages built in the water, and other great towns on dry land, and that straight and level causeway leading to [Tenochtitlán], we were astounded.'[2] It was an extraordinary moment for the Spaniards and for the Aztecs, a moment when two great civilisations that had grown up in complete ignorance of each other suddenly collided. The sight of men mounted on war horses was deeply unsettling for the Aztecs, who had never even seen a donkey let alone such powerful beasts of burden. For Díaz and his five hundred or so comrades, led by Hernán Cortés, it was a moment of real fear as they approached the huge metropolis. But there was also wonder and awe at the sight of this strange yet beautiful city in the lake.

Tenochtitlán was built in a valley, high up in the mountains, on the site of today's sprawling Mexico City. Sheer volcanic peaks rose around it like jagged teeth. Water cascaded down from the mountains into a series of five lakes which were spread out along the valley. On their banks were countless small towns and villages built beside the clear water. The largest of these was the magnificent city

A man climbs the Malwiya minaret of the Great Mosque in the medieval city of Samarra, Iraq. Built in the ninth century AD by the caliph Al-Mutawakkil, the top of the 55-metre-high minaret was badly damaged in 2005 during fighting between American soldiers and insurgents.

of Tenochtitlán, the Venice of the New World. It stood on an island in the corner of the biggest lake, Lake Texcoco. Causeways, each 'as wide as two cavalry lances', according to Cortés, led into the city from north, south and west, stretching up to eight kilometres across the lake from the shore to the city.[3] A cloud of jostling dugout canoes laden with goods swarmed around it like bees round a hive. For Díaz, the sight of Tenochtitlán rising out of the glittering waters of the lake was 'like an enchanted vision' from some magical tale. 'Indeed,' he added, 'some of our soldiers asked whether it was not all a dream.' Even forty years later, as he began to write his memoirs in what is today Guatemala, words still failed him: 'It was all so wonderful that I do not know how to describe this first glimpse of things never heard of, seen or dreamed of before.'[4]

Cortés and his men were the first Europeans to enter Tenochtitlán. Their motivation was both sacred and profane: their ships had left Cuba nine months before to claim these unexplored lands for the Spanish crown and for the Roman Catholic Church. But they were also driven by greed, by the desire to find the mythic city of gold, El Dorado. As they marched across the causeway to the city of Tenochtitlán, as magnificent as any in Europe, Díaz and his comrades must have thought they had found the city of their dreams. They saw houses draped with exotic flowers and above them the towers of magnificent palaces and temples to strange gods. 'With such wonderful sights to gaze on,' Díaz wrote, 'we did not know what to say, or if this was real that we saw before our eyes.'[5] The Aztecs rushed to see these emissaries from another world. 'Who could now count the multitude of men, women, and boys in the streets, on the rooftops and in canoes on the waterways, who had come to see us?'[6] recalled Díaz.

The Aztec ruler, known to us as Montezuma (his name was in fact Motecuhzoma), greeted them at the end of the causeway. Around him were his lords and chieftains arrayed in brilliantly coloured cloaks. Montezuma was, said Díaz, about forty years old, with a short black beard, a cheerful face and 'fine eyes'.[7] He was standing beneath a rich canopy of green feathers, decorated with gold work, silver, pearls and semi-precious stones hanging from a border. As Montezuma stepped forward, his lords threw down their cloaks so that his feet would not touch the ground. As they did so, none dared look at his face. Montezuma greeted Cortés with fragrant garlands of flowers. In return, Cortés offered a necklace of glass beads. Then the conquistadors marched on into the city of Tenochtitlán.

Later, Montezuma invited his foreign visitors to climb the steps to the summit of the Templo Mayor, or Great Temple, the highest and most sacred structure in the city. At the top, the *tlatoani* (literally the 'speaker' or ruler) of the Mexica people took Cortés by the hand and, writes Díaz, 'told him to look at his great city and all the other cities standing in the water, and the many others on the land around the lake'.[8] The two men stood with one of the greatest cities in the world at their feet. For this was not just a meeting between the peoples of two continents. It was a meeting between two great urban civilisations.

Despite the linguistic and cultural barriers separating them, the Spaniards could not fail to be impressed by a people who were able to build a city as great as Tenochtitlán. The city in the lake was a triumph of organisation as well as of craftsmanship and engineering. From their vantage point they saw the causeways leading into the city and the aqueducts bringing freshwater. They saw a flotilla of canoes laden with provisions and cargo. In the city itself they noted that all the houses had flat roofs, many converted into roof gardens, and that most could only be reached by canoe or across a drawbridge. And among the private residences they saw temples and shrines rising 'like gleaming white towers and castles'. It was, said Díaz, 'a marvellous sight'.[9]

What they saw then from the Great Temple, and discovered later for themselves while exploring on foot, astonished the Spanish soldiers. Some of them had visited great cities like Constantinople and Rome, but this was on a different scale. In his dispatches to the king of Spain, Cortés prefaced his descriptions of the city with the warning that his reader would find it 'so remarkable as not to be believed, for we who saw them with our own eyes could not grasp them with

A reconstruction of Tenochtitlán by Mexican artist Miguel Covarrubias (1904–1957).

understanding'.[10] The 'great city' had many fine streets and squares, one of which was arcaded and served as a vast market. This was the great market of Tlatelolco, once part of a separate island city, now absorbed into the metropolis. The Spaniards had 'never seen a market so well laid out, so large, so orderly, and so full of people'.[11] Each day sixty thousand people came to buy and sell. Here were goods from every corner of the Aztec empire, goods which Cortés itemised for his imperial master, who was eager for news of the wealth of his new lands.

The market was divided into sections like a modern department store. One part offered live animals: 'chickens, partridges and quails, wild ducks, fly-catchers, widgeons, turtledoves, pigeons, cane birds, parrots, eagles and eagle fowls, falcons, sparrow hawks and kestrels … rabbits and hares, and stags and small gelded dogs which they breed for eating'. There were brightly coloured fruits and vegetables – from cherries and plums to onions, leeks, garlic, watercress, borage, maize and artichokes. In another part of the market fresh flowers filled the air with a heavy fragrance. Elsewhere cooked food was for sale, such as chicken and fish pies, tripe, as well as sweet foods, like honey cake and chocolate. Finely crafted goods were also on offer, including ornaments made from gold, silver, bone, shell and feathers. In his account, Díaz mentions seeing the skins of tigers, lions, otters, jackals, deer and badgers being traded. In the textile market, there was a greater range of spun cotton in all the colours of the rainbow than in the famous silk market at Granada, according to Cortés. Beyond the great market were streets where only herbalists or apothecaries traded, selling and prescribing herbal medicines.

When Cortés and his men entered Tenochtitlán it was a thriving city covering about five square miles and, with a population of at least 200,000 people, bigger than any Spanish or, indeed, most European cities. (In 1551 London's population was about eighty thousand.)[12] At a time when the streets in European cities were often open sewers, choked with stinking rubbish, Tenochtitlán's wide streets were kept spotlessly clean by a workforce of a thousand men. Indeed, the city provided people with public toilets (reed huts) on all the roads where they could – as Díaz so delicately phrased it – 'purge their bowels unseen by passers-by'. The excrement was collected 'for the manufacture of salt and the curing of skins'.[13] It was also used as fertiliser.

Like the Dutch, the Aztecs had become extremely skilled at

reclaiming swampland both for construction and for cultivation. Their reclaimed *chinampas*, or floating gardens, produced at least two harvests a year, their fertility boosted by regular treatments with human manure collected in the city. Each day a flotilla of perhaps fifty thousand canoes – each cut from a single tree trunk – swarmed to and from the great metropolis carrying produce from these hydroponic gardens and from further afield, the life blood of the city. But as well as food, clean water was essential, as it is for any city. Skilfully engineered aqueducts brought fresh water in from the surrounding mountains. Canoes then dispensed the water to individual residences.

The city itself was divided into four by grand avenues which converged on a central walled complex of palaces and temples. Out of this soared the stepped pyramid of the Great Temple, sixty metres high, on which were two shrines: to Tlaloc, the rain god, and to Huitzilopoctli, the fearsome god of war who was the Mexica's patron deity. It was to this god, identified with the sun, that the Aztecs sacrificed human beings, typically prisoners of war. Cortés estimated that between three and four thousand victims a year were sacrificed. Díaz described how the priests 'strike open the wretched Indian's chest with flint knives and hastily tear out the palpitating heart which, with the blood, they present to the idols'.[14] To the Mexica, their city was 'the foundation of heaven', literally the political and religious centre of the universe.[15] It was their responsibility to offer 'precious water', or blood, as nourishment to the deities so that life could continue in this harsh world.[16]

Beyond the central complex were many other smaller temples as well as markets, private residences and Montezuma's fabulous palace with its water gardens, aviaries and menageries. Some of the private residences were two storeys high and had roof gardens. In these walled compounds two extended families lived, each home having access to the street and the canal, a fact that helped make this a socially mobile society: 'Even commoners could achieve high rank through military service or the acquisition of great personal wealth.'[17] The wealth of a family was apparent from the external decoration and ornamentation of their homes. The craftsmanship was superb. 'It could not be bettered anywhere,' said one Spanish eyewitness.[18]

The Spaniards were astonished by Tenochtitlán. It was a remarkable creation, a wonder of the world at that time, in many respects excelling the cities of Europe, a fact grudgingly acknowledged by Cortés: 'these people live almost like those of Spain, and in as much harmony and order as there, and considering that they are barbarous and so far from the knowledge of God and cut off from all civilized nations, it is truly remarkable to see what they have achieved in all things'.[19]

But this meeting of worlds was to be a fateful moment for Montezuma and his people. Within three years, Cortés had conquered the Aztec empire and the great city of Tenochtitlán had been destroyed. In 1520, a terrible epidemic of smallpox swept through the city, reducing the population by at least a third.[20] Then, in April of the following year, Cortés returned to the city with an army. At the final siege of Tenochtitlán, Cortés had a mere 1,300 Spanish soldiers. However, he cleverly enlisted the help of rival states. At least 100,000 indigenous warriors supported the Spaniards in the attack on Tenochtitlán. The city's defenders fought valiantly, but, weakened by disease and lack of food and water, they had no hope of victory against the gunpowder and steel of the Europeans. There was vicious house-to-house fighting. In the end Cortés could only take the city by systematically destroying it.

The First Metropolis of the New World

The Mexica city of Tenochtitlán was by no means the first great city in this region. Forty kilometres north-east of today's Mexico City lie the impressive ruins of Teotihuacán. From 300 to 100 BC this became an important economic, political and religious centre, expanding rapidly to more than 40,000 inhabitants. Over the next six centuries Teotihuacán became the capital of an empire that controlled much of central Mexico. The city eventually covered twenty square kilometres and may have had as many as 200,000 inhabitants, making it one of the most significant cities in the world at this time, second only to cities such as Constantinople or Chang'an in China.

Visitors must have been overwhelmed by the scale and grandeur of the city and its structures. A five-kilometre-long central avenue, known as the Street of the Dead, ran through the city, connecting the Pyramid of the Moon in the north to the Temple of the Feathered Serpent, Quetzalcoatl, in the south. To the east of the Pyramid of the Moon lies the Pyramid of the Sun. At more than 200 feet high, this intimidating building is today recognised as the third largest pyramid in the world. For merchants, pilgrims and traders approaching the city, these pyramids would have been clearly visible on the horizon.

Any visitor arriving for the first time in this city and walking down the main street could not fail to be inspired and awed by this

The proud people of Tenochtitlán surrendered on 21 August 1521. Their once great city was in ruins. As Díaz put it, 'today all is overthrown and lost, nothing is left standing'.[21] A Mexica poem, 'Flowers and Songs of Sorrow', expresses rather more eloquently the grief felt by the people of Tenochtitlán, or Mexico as it is translated here:

Nothing but flowers and songs of sorrow
are left in Mexico and Tlatelolco,
where once we saw warriors and wise men.

[...]

We wander here and there
in our desolate poverty.
We are mortal men.
We have seen bloodshed and pain
where once we saw beauty and valour. [22]

man-made environment. Teotihuacán was carefully planned and laid out in a grid. It contained hundreds of smaller pyramids, as well as nearly two thousand residential compounds, and numerous workshops. On the Street of the Dead was a huge marketplace and the walled palace of the ruler. Little is known about the people who lived in this city. Even their writing has yet to be deciphered. Teotihuacán's importance owed much to a nearby source of rare green obsidian, used for tools, and the existence of a deep cave in a lava tube beneath the Pyramid of the Sun. This was undoubtedly an important religious shrine for people in the region. But in the eighth century the city fell into decline. The reason for this is still unknown although archaeologists have speculated that climatic variations may have contributed to the fall of one of the world's great urban communities.[23]

Reconstruction of the Pyramid of the Sun, Teotihuacán.

The Golden Door

'About four or five o'clock in the morning we all got up. The whole boat bent toward her because everybody went out – everybody. She was beautiful with the sunshine so bright – and so big, and everybody was crying. The captain came over and said, please everybody, we should move a little bit to the center, but nobody would move.'[24] For immigrants like Sarah Asher, here recalling her arrival in America, the Statue of Liberty was their first glimpse of the New World. From 1886 the colossus welcomed people arriving in New York Harbour with the promise of a new beginning. Emma Lazarus put this promise into resonant poetry:

> 'Give me your tired, your poor,
> Your huddled masses yearning to breathe free,
> The wretched refuse of your teeming shore;
> Send these, the homeless, tempest-tost to me,
> I lift my lamp beside the golden door!'[25]

At the end of the nineteenth century, a tidal wave of immigration swept out of the Old World, flooding into America and particularly the city of New York. Between 1880 and 1920, some twenty million Europeans arrived in the United States, four out of five of them passing through the port of New York. By 1900, the city's population exceeded three million. Two-thirds were born abroad. New York's Lower East Side soon became the most overcrowded slum area in the Western world with more than 520 people per acre. As Henry Roth wrote at the start of his great novel about the immigrant experience, *Call It Sleep* (1934), the ships delivered the new arrivals 'from the stench and throb of the steerage to the stench and throb of New York tenements'.[26] By the beginning of the century, steel-hulled ships such as the *Olympic* or *Vaterland* could carry as many as three thousand steerage passengers. After one to two weeks at sea they arrived at the Hudson River piers on Manhattan Island. Here the first- and second-class cabin passengers were inspected on board by officials. When they had disembarked, the steerage passengers were herded on board ferries for the trip downriver to the federal immigration station on Ellis Island.

Initially, immigrants were processed in Castle Garden at the

The Main
Building on
Ellis Island,
1905.

bottom of Manhattan Island, where the first Dutch settlers had landed and where they established the colony of New Amsterdam in 1625. But from 1892, when the federal authorities took over immigration control, they were dealt with on Ellis Island. In the years to 1919, no fewer than twelve million people passed through this gateway to America. Nearly half settled permanently in New York City. It has been estimated that almost 40 per cent of Americans have an ancestor who passed through Ellis Island.

The first federal immigration station on Ellis Island burned down in 1897. When the award-winning new building reopened in 1900, the press declared it to be 'the model immigration station of the world'.[27] Eventually there were thirty-four buildings covering fourteen acres on what was mostly reclaimed land. One immigrant recalled that it was 'like a whole city'. He added: 'I almost felt smaller than I am.'[28] It was, indeed, a city in itself, with its own power station, restaurant, post office, telegraph station, laundry, bath house, 125-bed hospital, a police force and fire brigade.

Impressive though the facilities were, the station was never quite up to the task of examining and sorting the vast tide of humanity that swept through the island. Thousands of people arrived every day. In the 1890s, there were never more than half a million a year landing at New York.[29] But in the peak year of 1907, more than a million people arrived at Ellis Island, including 11,747 immigrants on one day alone.[30] Immigration officials working here felt as though they were manning a factory assembly line. Henry James visited what he called 'the terrible little Ellis Island' in 1907. The urbane novelist was appalled. The immigrants were, he said, 'marshalled, herded, divided, subdivided, sorted, sifted, searched, fumigated'.[31] Unsurprisingly, one Norwegian immigrant found the experience profoundly dehumanising. He said he felt like 'a commodity to be processed'.[32] Stephen Graham sailed from Liverpool in 1913. He recalled feeling like 'a hurrying, bumping, wandering piece of coal being mechanically guided to the sacks of its type and size'.[33]

Nobody forgot the day they arrived at Ellis Island. One person described it as being like a 'second birth'.[34] At busy times of the year, people had to wait for hours on packed barges off Ellis Island. When they were finally allowed to disembark the anxious immigrants waited in line under a canopy at the front of the building. Most chose to keep their few precious belongings with them rather than trust them to the baggage room. The new arrivals were easy targets for thieves and con men.

By the turn of the century the traditional immigrant nations – Germany, Ireland, England and the Scandinavian countries – had been supplanted by Italy, Russia, Poland and Hungary. Wherever they came from, everyone tried hard to look their best as they waited, not an easy task after many days in steerage. Henry Roth described the motley appearance of the immigrants, 'the vivid costumes of other lands, the speckled green-and-yellow aprons, the flowered kerchief,

H. G. Wells Visits Ellis Island in 1906

'All day long through an intricate series of metal pens, the long procession files, step by step, bearing bundles and trunks and boxes, past this examiner and that, past the quick, alert medical officers, the tallymen, and the clerks; at every point immigrants are being picked out and set aside for further medical examination, for further questions, for the busy little courts, but the main procession satisfies conditions, passes on. It is a daily procession that, with a yard of space to each, would stretch over three miles . . . On they go, from this pen to that, pen by pen, towards a desk at a little metal wicket – the gate of America. Through this metal wicket drips the immigration stream – all day long, every two or three seconds an immigrant, with a valise or a bundle, passes the little desk and goes on past the well-managed money-changing place, past the carefully organised separating ways that go to this railway or that, past the guiding, protecting officials – into a new world. The great majority are young men and young women, between seventeen and thirty, good, youthful, hopeful peasant stock.

embroidered homespun, the silver-braided sheepskin vest, the gaudy scarfs, yellow boots, fur caps, caftans, dull gabardines'.

Fear was etched in all their faces, the nagging fear that they would be sent back. For them home often meant poverty, persecution and hopelessness. A reporter from the *New York Tribune* visited the island in 1896 and was struck by what he saw in their faces: 'it is pitiable indeed to watch their longing looks, hoping against hope as they do, for freedom.'[35] For those who were turned away, this little island in the shadow of Lady Liberty became the 'Island of Tears'.

The immigrants' ordeal began with a cursory medical examination at the top of a flight of stairs. A quick but efficient eye examination came first. Doctors pulled up their eyelids with a crude metal buttonhook to check for trachoma. Anyone with this incurable disease was sent back immediately. On busy days examiners had less than six seconds to detect any of sixty conditions. Chalk was used to mark the clothing of those suspected of medical problems requiring more detailed examination – L for lameness, H for heart conditions, EC for eye problems, an X for suspected mental impairment, and so on.

Once past the medics, they were allowed to take their place in the high-ceilinged Registry Room on the second floor. This was the largest room in the building, measuring 200 by 100 feet. On one side a large window looked out across the harbour to the skyline of

Immigrants waiting to be questioned at Ellis Island, 1904.

They stand in a long string, waiting to go through that wicket, with bundles, with little tin-boxes, with cheap portmanteaus, with odd packages, in pairs, in families, alone, women with children, men with strings of dependents, young couples. All day that string of human beads waits there, jerks forward, waits again; all day and every day, constantly replenished, constantly dropping the end beads through the wicket, till the units mount to hundreds and the hundreds to thousands…'[36]

Manhattan – the promised land, as the journalist and photographer Jacob Riis (a Danish-born immigrant from the Castle Garden days) described it in 1903. They were so near and yet so far. The hopefuls waited here for hours, penned between metal railings like cattle, anxiously waiting to be called.

Then the questioning began. Each inspector saw between four to five hundred people a day, leaving him about two minutes in which to decide the fate of each nervous immigrant. Name? Place of birth? Where are you going? What is your occupation? How much money do you have? Have you been in jail? Have you been an anarchist? The last three questions were crucial. There was no room for paupers, criminals or anarchists in the land of the free.

Louis Adamic, a Slovenian who arrived in 1913, never forgot the experience: 'The day I spent on Ellis Island was an eternity. Rumours were current among immigrants of several nationalities that some of us would be refused admittance into the United States and sent back to Europe. For several hours I was in a cold sweat on this account … The first night in America I spent, with hundreds of other recently arrived immigrants, in an immense hall with tiers of narrow iron-and-canvas bunks, four deep … I shivered, sleepless, all night, listening to snores and dream-monologues in perhaps a dozen different languages.'[37] A Siberian convict who spent eight nights in the dormitory said it was 'very much worse than a Russian prison', apart from the fact that he was not beaten and the food was slightly better.[38]

Although Adamic was detained overnight, he was eventually granted permission to enter America. The immigrants' fears were real enough, but in reality few were excluded, about 2 per cent at most.[39] If you were very lucky you would only spend a few hours on the island. But they would have been the longest hours in your life as you were passed from one official to another, until eventually with a curt nod from a stern immigration officer you were allowed to continue your journey into the United States of America. Many who passed through Ellis Island chose to settle within sight of this island where dreams were made and broken. For New York City – also built on an island – was a mere fifteen-minute boat ride away. By the beginning of the twentieth century, it was becoming the metropolis against which all other cities were measured. This was the city of everyone's dreams.

Skyline

The skylines of the first cities were defined by high-walled citadels and imposing religious buildings such as the great ziggurat of Babylon, the legendary Tower of Babel, described by Herodotus. In Tenochtitlán, the pyramid of the Grand Temple dominated the urban landscape as well as the surrounding lakes. Above the tiled rooftops of medieval European cities soared baronial tower-houses, as in Bologna, and church towers, like that of Bern's late Gothic Münster, Switzerland's highest and most beautiful spire. In the nineteenth century, the smoke stack towered over industrial cities, belching noxious fumes.

It seems scarcely believable today but New York's skyline was also once dominated by church towers. For almost two hundred years the spire of Trinity Church at the head of Wall Street rose gracefully above the other buildings on Manhattan Island. Rebuilt three times, Trinity's steeple rises some 280 feet above the sidewalk. But in the mid-1880s, the city of New York began to change. As American corporations sought to exploit the growing financial significance of Wall Street, they began moving their headquarters to Lower Manhattan. On this granite island, where space was at a premium, they vied with each other to build the highest and most distinctive skyscraper, towers that would stamp their corporate identity on the city. As Henry James

Manhattan from Brooklyn Bridge, 1946.

The Tower of Babel

Herodotus, the father of history, seems to have visited Babylon about 450 BC. Babylon was the greatest city of ancient Iraq, built on the Euphrates River. It rose to prominence about 2000 BC and its fame lives on in the stories of the Tower of Babel and the Hanging Gardens. The biblical story of the Tower of Babel is believed to be based on the ziggurat at Babylon, Etemenanki. This was an enormous square, brick tower, made of stages of decreasing size, like a step pyramid, with a temple on the top. It was dedicated to Marduk, the god of the city. At well over seventy metres high on a base ninety-one metres square, it was not quite 'a tower that reaches to the heavens', as it says in Genesis, but it was one of the largest buildings in the ancient world and would have dominated the skyline of Babylon. Today it has vanished completely.[40] All that remains is the description of Herodotus:

'In the midmost of one division of the city stands the royal palace, surrounded by a high and strong wall; and in the midmost of the other is still to this day the sacred enclosure of Zeus Belus, a square of two furlongs each way, with gates of bronze. In the centre

lamented in 1904, Trinity Church was left 'so cruelly overtopped and so barely distinguishable … in its abject helpless humility'.[42]

The use of 'skyline' to refer to buildings on the horizon dates from 1876.[43] It was in the mid-1890s that the term skyline came into common use to describe New York's rapidly changing profile. Journals and guidebooks, such as the *New York Standard Guide* or *Valentine's Manual*, no longer pictured the city's harbour. Instead their photographers headed out into New York Bay to focus their cameras on its soaring skyline. New Yorkers followed in their wake, catching the Staten Island ferry to George Washington Bridge to view their city's soaring silhouette and to identify the highest buildings. Skyscrapers such as the Woolworth Tower (1913) became high-profile trademarks for their corporate owners, advertisements in stone and steel visible from miles around. But collectively New York's skyscrapers proclaimed the dynamism and success of the city and, indeed, of America itself. For critic Mary Fanton Roberts, writing in 1907, New York's skyline represented 'the first absolutely genuine expression of an original American architecture'.[44] Two years later, a writer for the popular journal *The Living Age* rightly predicted that this 'towered city' would soon be imitated around the world: 'the towers of New York will be reckoned as characteristic as the minarets of a Mohammedan city, as of this enclosure a solid tower has been built, of one furlong's length and breadth; a second tower rises from this, and from it yet another, till at last there are eight. The way up to them mounts spirally outside all the towers; about halfway in the ascent is a halting place, with seats for repose, where those who ascend sit down and rest. In the last tower there is a great shrine; and in it a great and well-covered couch is laid, and a golden table set hard by. But no image has been set up in the shrine, nor does any human creature lie therein for the night, except one native woman, chosen from all women by the god...'[41]

Fall of the Tower of Babel by **Cornelis Anthonisz** (1547).

the bell towers of Russia, as the pillar-towers of India ... or as the campaniles of Italy.'[45]

In the twentieth century, the skyline became a signature, an expression of urban identity. And no skyline was more emblematic of the modern metropolis than that of Manhattan. Unlike Babylon, this futuristic cosmopolis did not just have one great tower, but dozens forming a vertical city. From *King Kong* (1933) and *On the Town* (1949), to *Manhattan* (1979) and *Batman* (1989), Hollywood transformed New York's soaring towers into an immortal celluloid skyline.[46] In the late twentieth century, the most iconic of its skyscrapers were the Twin Towers of the World Trade Center. Although not universally popular (Jan Morris described them as 'those enormous blank obelisks'), the unprecedented act of terrorism that destroyed them in 2001 left a gaping hole in New York's skyline as well as in the city's psyche.[47] Mohammed Atta, who flew a Boeing 767 into the North Tower, was studying town planning in Hamburg and had a degree in architecture from Cairo University. More than anyone, Atta understood the power of a skyline to define a city and, indeed, a nation.

The Victoria Terminus, Mumbai, which was renamed the
Chhatrapati Shivaji Terminus in 1996. (following page)

The Central Station

'Train journeys are about possibilities,' says Ram, the Mumbai 'Slumdog Millionaire' of Vikras Swarup's novel. 'They denote a change in state. When you arrive, you are no longer the same person who departed.'[48] There is no better way to arrive in a city than by train. As soon as the door of the train opens, you step out into the heart of the metropolis and become part of the urban crowd.

A city terminus is where countless journeys begin or end. Its platforms are the stage on which many personal dramas unfold every day – tearful separations, joyful reunions and brief encounters. Loved ones departing to fight in wars, perhaps never to return; families laden with luggage off to a seaside holiday; newly-wed couples – confetti still in their hair – with a honeymoon and the rest of their lives ahead of them; lovers hurrying to a rendezvous under the station clock; migrant workers arriving for the first time in an unfamiliar city, trying not to think of their distant home and family; parents waving goodbye to children about to start a new term at boarding school; travellers catching the Orient Express or with a passage booked on a slow boat to China. The central station is a place of constant motion and emotion: 'The grief and pain of separation, the hopes, the fears, the loving care, the prayers, the joys, the trust!'[49]

The coming of the railways in the first half of the nineteenth century allowed people from all over the country to visit the city with relative ease. In 1850, *The Times* claimed: 'Thirty years ago not one countryman in one hundred had seen the metropolis. There is now scarcely one in the same number who has not spent the day there.' Railway termini became the modern gateways into the city, echoing the ancient gates of the earliest cities. Euston, built 1835–9, was the first inter-city station in London. An inter-city line had run from Liverpool to Manchester since 1830 but it was mainly used for freight. Architect Philip Hardwick worked with Robert Stephenson to build Euston Station. Unlike previous stations, it had platforms for both arrivals and departures. As if to express the idea of the station as city gate, in front of Euston they erected an imposing propylaeum, a seventy-two-foot high monumental gateway like Berlin's famous Brandenburg Gate. Inspired by the ancient entrance to the Acropolis in Athens (propylaeum means 'before the gates'), the Euston Arch

– one of the biggest such structures ever built – faced the city of London. 'When Euston was first built,' recalled one Victorian, 'it was regarded not as a railway station but as a spectacle. Visitors used to flock to it in omnibuses and examine it with the careful scrutiny of sightseers.'[50] The four tall classical pillars at the front of Hardwick's Curzon Street Station in Birmingham (1838) echo the design of the Euston Arch.

Ten years later a 126-foot entry hall built in the classical style, with a flight of stairs leading up to the booking office, was added behind the Euston Arch, separating the trains and platforms from the street. From this design came the model for stations everywhere, with an entry hall at the head of the railway lines.[51] By 1838, the line from London Euston to Birmingham Curzon Street was fully operational. It was a great engineering achievement. Some contemporaries compared it to the construction of the Great Pyramid at Giza, others to the aqueducts of Rome.[52] It had taken twenty thousand workers five years to build, including nine tunnels and three long, deep cuttings. The journey between the two cities lasted six hours and a one-way, first-class ticket cost £1 10s. (£1.50, or about £100 adjusted for inflation). A second-class fare was £1 (£67) but passengers had to brace themselves for a journey in open wagons, exposed to the elements and flying cinders from the engine.[53] Today the West Coast Main Line runs from Euston to Glasgow. It is one of the busiest lines in the world, carrying seventy-five million passengers a year and 40 per cent of the country's freight on its 640-kilometre route.[54] A ten-year upgrade on the line was completed at the end of 2008, costing an estimated £9 billion.

Until King's Cross was built in 1852, Euston Station was the gateway to the north. But for those travelling south it was the entrance to London, the megalopolis of the modern world. The demolition of Euston's station and arch in 1962 was an act of municipal vandalism. Today's station has been accurately described as 'an all-purpose combination of airport lounge and open-plan public lavatory'.[55] But its triumphal arch lives on in the façades of other stations, such as Budapest's Ost Bahnhof (Julius Rochlitz, 1881), and, indeed, Lewis Cubitt's King's Cross station, the vaulted sheds of which are considered to be 'among the finest ever erected'.[56]

In 1875, *Building News* described railway stations as the representative buildings of the age: 'Railway termini and hotels are to the nineteenth century what monasteries and cathedrals were to the thirteenth century.[57] Indeed, for G. K. Chesterton, walking through a great railway station in the age of steam was a religious experience akin to 'the quietude and consolation of a cathedral ... dedicated to the celebration of water and fire, the two prime elements of all human ceremonial'.[58] The railway station was not only the most distinctive architectural form of its time, but also the first which was truly global. From China (where they burnt down the first railway station and replaced it with a temple) to the high Andes, the construction of stations testified to the imperialism of steam. Parisian writer Théophile Gautier (1811–72) saw them as the focal points of urban modernity: 'These cathedrals of the new humanity are the meeting points of nations, the centre where all converges, the nucleus of huge stars whose iron rays stretch out to the ends of the earth.'[59]

By 1869 railways spanned the United States. Between 1830 and 1950, Americans built 140,000 stations. Civic pride transformed these from mere transport hubs into masterpieces of architecture that freely sampled Gothic, classical and baroque styles. Berlin's Anhalter Bahnhof (1872–80) was as much a celebration of the importance of this emerging world city as a temple to steam. Its huge iron and glass train shed could easily accommodate forty thousand people. Today all that remains after the post-war demolition of the bombed structure is the brick entrance portico to the east of Askanischer Platz, a sad reminder of one of the world's greatest railway stations. In Paris, stations such as Gare de l'Est (1847–52) and Gare d'Orsay (1897–1900) were admired and imitated around the world. At Gare d'Orsay the smoky train shed was dispensed with thanks to a new technology – electric trains. Entry was through enormous glazed archways into the concourse and waiting rooms. From here travellers could look down through open wells on to the trains waiting at the underground platforms.

Gare d'Orsay, which has been splendidly converted into a gallery of predominantly Impressionist art, was the model for New York's Pennsylvania Station (1906–10) and Grand Central Terminal, or Station as it is popularly known (1903–13). Pennsylvania Station's lofty vaulted main waiting room, with grand staircases on four sides, was modelled on the Roman Baths of Caracalla and described by one architectural historian who saw it as 'an awe-inspiring space'.[60] Incredibly, this wonderful building was demolished. Grand Central

Station almost met the same fate but was saved from demolition in the 1970s by a landmark ruling of the US Supreme Court. This classical palace transported into the modern metropolis has been described as one of the finest interior spaces ever created. The three monumental arches in its façade evoke the triumphal gates of Roman cities. The 125-foot-high ceiling of its vast concourse is decorated with Paul Helleu's murals of the constellations in which sixty electric light bulbs provide the stars with that extra twinkle. Its record number of sixty-seven platforms could handle seventy thousand outward-bound passengers an hour. Grand Central was also designed for electric engines which allowed railway tracks to be sunk below ground. All trains approaching New York had their steam engines exchanged for electric ones at outlying stations.

As an imperial power and a pioneer of the railways, Britain left an enduring legacy of stations in cities across the world. In India they built grand stations at Madras (1868), Howrah (1906) and Calcutta (1862;

The main concourse of Grand Central Station, New York, in 1929.

now Kolkata). But the most remarkable of all is Victoria Terminus in Mumbai, still known locally as the VT despite being renamed in 1996 the Chhatrapati Shivaji Terminus, after the seventeenth-century Maratha king. John Murray's *Handbook for Travellers in India, Burma and Ceylon* described it in the 1890s as the finest railway station ever built. Since 2004 the station has been a UNESCO World Heritage Site.

Designed by British architect F. W. Stevens, working with local craftsmen, the station is an exuberant fusion of East and West, a fantasy of domes, turrets and spires, pointed arches and rose windows glittering with stained glass, a Gothic Saracenic cathedral to steam. Stevens spent ten months touring railway stations in Europe before deciding on his final design. It took ten years to build and was opened by the Great Indian Peninsula Railway on Queen Victoria's Jubilee day in 1887 at a cost of £300,000 – a vast sum at the time. In the gables were panels depicting 'Engineering', 'Commerce' and 'Science'.[61] For the Victorians, a railway station was an essential attribute of the modern scientific city. Today, in this vibrant international port, it is one of the busiest stations in India and is used by about 2.5 million travellers every day.

Mark Twain spent ten days in what was then Bombay in January 1896. The city enthralled him: 'Bombay! A bewitching place, a bewildering place, an enchanting place – the Arabian Nights come again!' At that time it was, he said, a 'vast city' of a million people.[62] Today, Greater Mumbai has some nineteen million inhabitants. Twain departed by train and the experience clearly made a powerful impression on him:

'What a spectacle the railway station was, at train-time! It was a very large station, yet when we arrived it seemed as if the whole world was present – half of it inside, the other half outside, and both halves, bearing mountainous head-loads of bedding and other freight, trying simultaneously to pass each other, in opposing floods, in one narrow door . . . Inside the great station, tides upon tides of rainbow-costumed natives swept along, this way and that, in massed and bewildering confusion, eager, anxious, belated, distressed; and washed up to the long trains and flowed into them with their packs and bundles, and disappeared, followed at once by the next wash, the next wave.'[63]

It was at just such a teeming Mumbai railway station that V. S. Naipaul became overwhelmed by the fear that he 'might sink without a trace into that Indian crowd'.[64] In Paul Theroux's novel *The Elephant Suite* (2008), a Western traveller, Alice, experiences something similar when she goes to the Victoria Terminus to meet a friend: 'Inside it was a nuthouse, and it stank.' It is as though the whole of human life and experience is crammed into the station. The experience is overwhelming. She sees people quarrelling loudly, others sleeping on the floor. A security guard stops her and demands to see her ticket. And everywhere there are beggars, a familiar sight in this city of slums.[65]

Central stations are microcosms of the cities they serve. The poverty in a city known as the Manhattan of the East, where apartments are among the most expensive in world, is indeed shocking. On the platforms of Victoria Terminus there is misery, but hope, too. For the whole of life is here. Young army recruits wait patiently with their kitbags. Mothers prepare a meal for their families, cooking on portable stoves while their children squat on the ground. Holy men, their chests bare, stand alongside businessmen in crisp white shirts. The cries of tea sellers – 'Chai, garam chaaai' – mingle with the more or less incomprehensible announcements over the loudspeakers. Despite the misery that is undeniably present, despite this – as Émile Zola insisted in 1878 – 'a station is beautiful'.[66]

A vast station such as Victoria Terminus is a community, almost a city in its own right, inhabited by a transient population of millions. There is money to be made and there are people to be served: stalls, shops and other facilities offer travellers everything they need from tickets and the recovery of lost property, to lavatories (London's Waterloo Station once had the finest 'gentlemen's court' in Europe, an 800-foot underground area with marble floors, bathrooms, boot cleaning and barbers, as well as toilets), to newspapers, books and, of course, bars and restaurants. The Oyster Bar in Grand Central Station has been open since 1913 and has a well-earned reputation for mouth-watering seafood dishes. Phileas Fogg dines at a less well-known restaurant at Victoria Terminus in Jules Verne's *Around the World in Eighty Days* (1873). At the recommendation of the chef he orders 'a certain giblet of "native rabbit"', but is far from happy with his meal, suspecting the meat has a decidedly feline origin. Walter Salles's film *Central Station* (1998) begins with Dora (Fernanda Montenegro) writing letters for illiterate Brazilians at Rio de Janeiro's largest railroad station, the Central do Brasil. As they were filming,

Today's Terminals

Le Corbusier believed that 'a city made for speed is made for success', and at the centre of his vision for the Modernist city of the future was a station with a landing platform on its roof.[67] In the age of megacities, an efficient transport system is indeed essential and urban railway stations must be designed to cope with vast numbers of passengers. The busiest is Tokyo's Shinjuku Station, which was used by an average of 3.64 million people each day in 2007. One of the best-designed stations of the second half of the twentieth century was the Stazioni Termini, Rome (1951). Carroll Meeks describes it as 'the finest modern station to date', and architectural connoisseur Nikolaus Pevsner claimed it was 'the best European station of the last half century'.[68] It was also the subject of the first movie to be filmed entirely in the main station of a capital city – Vittorio De Sica's *Terminal Station* (1953, rereleased as *Indiscretion of an American Wife*), partly scripted by Truman Capote and starring Montgomery Clift and Jennifer Jones.

In the twenty-first century, railway stations are increasingly imitating the design of airports. Shanghai's ultra-modern South Railway Station (2006), which took four years to build, is the first circular railway station anywhere in the world. The roof covers about 60,000 square metres, with a diameter of 255 metres, and is capped with a translucent dome. The French architects, AREP, designed it to be a 'gateway to the city'. At night, illuminated from within, the station becomes a shining beacon in the heart of Shanghai. 'It is a stunning building; it really looks like a UFO,' an enthusiastic commuter told the *People's Daily*.[69] Also opened in 2006 was Berlin's new Hauptbahnhof, which replaces the Zoo Station and the Ostbahnhof as the central station of the now unified German capital. Built at a cost of €700 million on the site of the Lehrter Bahnhof, it is Europe's largest two-level railway station, designed to be used by about 300,000 people every day. Some have complained that the 151-foot (46 metre) steel and glass structure dwarfs the nearby parliament buildings of the Reichstag and the Chancellery. But Jan Morris is full of praise for 'Europe Central', describing it as a 'marvel': 'It is as though Piranesi designed it, with a help-

Shanghai's South Railway Station (2006).

ing hand from Maurits Escher. Wherever you look inside its gantry-like construction, sleek trains are sliding one way or another, above your head, below your feet, miraculously disappearing.'[70] For Chancellor Angela Merkel, its design perfectly expresses the cosmopolitan outlook of today's Germany and its capital city: 'The new transparent central station is a symbol of a modern country that is open to the rest of the world.'[71]

real people approached her to write letters for them and some of these were included in the film.

Like cities, stations also have a shadowy underclass, a shifting population of those at the fringes of society, beggars as well as 'dossers, derelicts, drifters, drug addicts, the homeless and the friendless'.[72] A criminal underworld preys on these vulnerable people, as do pickpockets on the unsuspecting travellers. In the impoverished years following the First World War, Fritz Haarmann picked up teenage boys hanging around Hanover Station. He would sexually abuse and then murder them. He sold their clothes and it is rumoured he even sold their flesh to butchers unable to obtain meat. Haarmann was caught in 1924 and confessed to at least twenty-four murders. Fritz Lang's film about a serial killer, *M* (1931), starring Peter Lorre, was inspired in part by Haarmann's crimes. The film *Christiane F.: We Children from the Zoo Station* (*Wir Kinder von Bahnhof Zoo*, 1981), based on the actual experiences of Christiane Felscherinow, a fourteen-year-old Berlin drug addict, vividly depicted this dark underside to the life of a city railway station. With a soundtrack by David Bowie, the film shocked audiences with its bleak depiction of the lives of the teenage prostitutes and addicts at West Berlin's largest station, the Berlin Zoological Garden Station, known locally as Bahnhof Zoo. The film is a stark reminder that, for some, the city's central station can indeed become a terminal station.

The ruined Inca city of Machu Picchu, Peru, inhabited by about 1,000 people, *c*. AD 1440–1530. (following page)

2 HISTORY

Origins

In the beginning was the city. Before mankind existed, before even the primeval sea had fully receded from the land, Marduk, the creator of everything, made the city. The gods settled in the city and found it to be 'the dwelling of their hearts' delight'. Then Marduk created man to serve the gods and to share the city. The name of that first city was Eridu.[1]

This ancient creation story was found on a clay tablet dating back 2,500 years. The text was written in Babylonian as well as in the older Sumerian language and would have been read aloud during a cleansing ritual in the temple. The tradition that Eridu is the oldest city can be found in the earliest written texts in existence, tablets from the late fourth millennium BC, and historians believe it may be far older than even writing itself.

Eridu was a real city. It is now known as Tell Abu Shahrain, and lies some 200 kilometres north-west of the modern city of Basra in southern Iraq. But today all that remains of this once great city are seven mounds of rubble and dust. Such mounds are common in this arid landscape and are known in Arabic as a 'tell' or ruin heap, reminders of past urban glories. In the first mud-brick cities, when houses became dilapidated, they were levelled and new ones built on top of the compacted remains. Over many hundreds of years of habitation, the ground on which these cities stood gradually rose, a visible sign of a settlement's age and importance. When a team of Iraqi archaeologists excavated Tell Abu Shahrain in the late 1940s, they dug

The stone wall of Great Zimbabwe was probably built between the thirteenth and fifteenth centuries AD, part of a city that may have had as many as 19,000 inhabitants.

down through eighteen layers of collapsed mud-brick buildings representing millennia of urban life. At the bottom they came to a sand dune and on it was built a simple, hut-like structure, three metres square, made of sun-dried bricks some 6,800 years old. Facing the door of the building stood a pedestal and in one wall was a niche. The archaeologists realised that they were looking at the temple of the first and most sacred city, the home of the gods of Eridu.

Eridu was part of an urban revolution that swept across what was then the fertile land of southern Mesopotamia, through which flowed the ancient rivers of the Tigris and the Euphrates. The first cities were built by a people we now know as the Sumerians. Their language was unique and their origins remain shrouded in mystery. According to archaeologist Charles Gates, 'the Sumerians stand alone in human history. Their language has no known relatives and their architecture and artifacts do not indicate ethnic ties with cultures of other regions.'[2] The name Sumer comes from the ancient Akkadian name for this region: 'Shumer'. They described themselves as 'the black-headed ones'.[3] Nobody knows where these people came from, but they and their gods created the world's first urban civilisation.

At the heart of their distinctive civilisation were independent, self-governing cities, beginning with the first city: Eridu. The Sumerians believed that each city had been built by a god or goddess as their own dwelling. The temple was therefore at the centre of city life, a focus of ritual and economic activity. The god entrusted each city to the care of a king, or 'lugal' in Sumerian. For Sumerians, civilised life was city life. They did not pine for some lost idyllic Garden of Eden, a perfect realm from which (according to the Judaeo-Christian tradition) mankind was expelled by a wrathful God. Instead the Sumerians believed their gods had given them the city – a place of plentiful food and water, a place of society, of family and friendship, and a centre of civilisation. They were at home in the city. It was where they believed all their dreams would be realised.

Remarkable though the Sumerian civilisation undoubtedly was, cities – with or without the help of the gods – did not rise out of the Mesopotamian landscape in a single generation. In Sumer, cities developed over two millennia, from c. 5500–3500 BC.[4] But the city's roots go deeper still. Archaeology is now revealing tantalising glimpses of the Neolithic origins of modern urbanism. Lewis Mumford, whose monumental work *The City in History* remains a classic study of urbanism, notes that 'the embryonic structure of the city already existed in the village. House, shrine, cistern, public way, agora – not yet a specialised market – all first took form in the village.[5] As Neolithic people increasingly gained control over food production, creating surpluses that could support specialist craftsmen, their villages gradually grew into a new kind of community. These Neolithic towns have been discovered at Çatalhöyük in Turkey and Jericho in the West Bank of the Palestinian territories.

The walled oasis town of Jericho in the valley of the Jordan River began to be inhabited on a seasonal basis about 11,000 years ago.[6] Between 8500 and 6000 BC a permanent settlement was established, including a defensive ditch and stone wall 3.6 metres high. The Book of Joshua tells how the famous walls of Jericho were supposedly destroyed by Joshua and the Israelites, who circled the city seven times, blowing rams' horns. At the seventh blast the walls came tumbling down.

An imposing circular tower has also been unearthed inside the town, nine metres in diameter at its base and eight metres high. Internal stairs lead up to the top, which it is thought was used for religious purposes. The earliest houses found in Jericho were round and made of hog-backed, sun-dried mud bricks. The scale of the building here, especially the wall and tower, are impressive evidence of a community (about three thousand people) working together to achieve large-scale projects.[7] In later periods, the walls inside the houses were painted red or pink and the floors plastered with gypsum, before being covered with reed mats. Beneath one floor, human skulls have been discovered. Each has a face lovingly recreated from plaster, with shells for eyes, evidence perhaps of ancestor worship.

It is from these tender Neolithic shoots that the urban revolution in southern Mesopotamia grew and flowered. After 3500 BC the climate of Mesopotamia became cooler and drier. The south had been swampy, but now more fertile land became available for farming crops such as wheat, barley and dates. Several harvests a year became possible, generating an abundance of food. There was also a constant flow of traders moving between the Fertile Crescent in the north and the Persian Gulf, bringing goods made of obsidian, metal and pottery. By 3200 BC, this region became the most densely populated farming area in the world. These were the conditions that brought about the rise of cities here before anywhere else. Across the region dozens of cities sprang up, most of which (including Eridu) were within a day's walk of each other. By 2800 BC, city-states stretched from the Persian Gulf to just south of modern Baghdad.[8] Eventually almost all the population moved into cities which, with their increasingly impressive fortifications, offered security and the promise of prosperity. Cities became magnets drawing skilled people and goods from surrounding regions.

Uruk ('Warka' in Arabic) was the dominant city of early Sumer. In 3200 BC, it covered 100 hectares. The other largest city in the region was half this size. People flocked from the surrounding territory to Uruk, making it the largest city in the world, with at least fifty thousand inhabitants by 3000 BC.[9] In 2800 BC its mud-brick city walls were ten kilometres long, with nearly a thousand semi-circular towers. For traders and farmers arriving at its gates for the first time it must have been an awe-inspiring sight. Soon Uruk had expanded across an area of some 550 hectares.[10] In AD 43, Jerusalem covered just 100 hectares and even Emperor Hadrian's Rome – the first metropolis with more than a million inhabitants – was only twice the size Uruk had been three thousand years before.[11] Writing was invented here in about 3500 BC, probably by priests tasked with recording and administering

The ruins at Ur, photographed in 1932.

the affairs of the teeming city-state. The central figure in the ancient poem *The Epic of Gilgamesh*, the world's oldest epic, is Gilgamesh, the fifth king of the First Dynasty of Uruk, who is thought to have reigned during the period when the city's soaring walls were built.

However, as the climate became drier, Sumer's farmers grew increasingly dependent on irrigation. The cities had the manpower and the organisational skills to create impressive irrigation schemes. Unfortunately, as the land here drains poorly, over the years salts accumulated in the soil and, although the Sumerians grew salt-resistant barley, soon even that withered and died. Here in the cradle of urban civilisation, the city faced – and ultimately lost – its first environmental crisis. The dusty tells dotting this sun-baked landscape are the only reminders of the area's once great urban civilisation.

The fundamentals of human life in these first cities did not differ greatly from ours today. From the love of good food expertly cooked and enjoyed with friends and family, to the need to work and the pleasures of shopping, their daily lives mirror ours. The Sumerians gave us the first cities, the first irrigated agriculture, the first written language. They also gave us our measurement of time: sixty seconds to every minute, a sexagesimal system rather than a decimal one (at Uruk they, in fact, used both systems).[12] But with urban civilisation also came the need to protect the wealth and power that had been achieved. In these cities we also see the first standing armies, consisting of professional soldiers. As resources, especially water, became scarce armies were needed to defend the cities and their territories. The Sumerian city-states applied their considerable skills and manpower to the conduct of warfare. War became an annual feature of life in the region, for as the cities became more successful, populations grew and more food and water were needed.

By 2000 BC, as Mumford has said, 'most of the major physical organs of the city had been created'.[13] These were recognisably cities in the modern sense of the word. They would have looked like a walled North African city, with narrow alleys no more than eight feet wide (offering shelter from the blinding midday sun), white-washed, mud-brick houses of one or two storeys, with flat roofs and inner courtyards. The skyline of a Sumerian city would have been dominated by a steep, stepped ziggurat, a man-made mountain to the glory of their gods. Uruk's magnificent ziggurat (modelled on Eridu's) was some twelve metres high and was surmounted by the imposing White

The First Cityscape

The Neolithic town of Çatalhöyük in the Konya Plain, Anatolia, was discovered in the late 1950s. It was excavated in 1961 by James Mellaart, who found spectacular wall paintings inside the remains of the houses. Since 1993 an international team of archaeologists, led by Ian Hodder, has continued this work. Twelve building levels have been uncovered in the two adjacent mounds (*höyük* is Turkish for 'mound'), all that remains of this important town that was home to some eight thousand people in the period 7000–5500 BC. There were no streets in Çatalhöyük. The houses (offering a maximum of 30m² floor space) were clustered together like a honeycomb and people walked across the rooftops, entering through holes in the roofs, and climbing down ladders into their mud-brick homes.

The people of Çatalhöyük were superb artists, producing paintings, reliefs and sculptures, including striking female figurines. Some house walls have as many as a hundred layers of plaster, any of which could hold paintings. On one wall archaeologists have found

Temple. The names of the other great Mesopotamian cities are now part of the urban story of our species – *Homo urbanus*. They include Ur, Agade, Nineveh and Babylon – the Mesopotamian city to the north that in the second millennium became the dominant city in the region and the largest metropolis of its day. The legends of this city's greatness – its Hanging Gardens and the Tower of Babel – live on even today.

After the first cities appeared in Sumer, elsewhere in the world other cities began to emerge as regions experienced their own spontaneous urban revolutions. In the third millennium BC, there was the city of Mohenjo-daro, a sprawling community of 250 hectares north-east of modern Karachi in the Indus Valley, with its gridiron street plan as well as an advanced system of covered drains and clay water pipes. From the second millennium, urban communities began appearing in the Yellow River and Wei valleys of China, the country with the longest urban tradition of any culture – some four thousand years of city building. By the end of the first millennium, there were significant cities in Mesoamerica, such as Teotihuacán. A tide of urbanism swept the planet, eventually reaching every continent, a tide that seems to reflect a universal human instinct to build cities. The urban dream, the vision of that shining city on the hill, flows through our blood. And as the cities grew and flourished, so too did human what may well be the oldest map and, indeed, the oldest painting of an urban community. It appears to show the town spread out beneath the distinctive twin horns of the nearby volcano of Hasan Dağ. These people were also fine craftsmen, making pottery, textiles and metal goods. Çatalhöyük was at the centre of a flourishing and extensive trade network: its inhabitants traded local obsidian and their own craftsmanship for valuable items from afar, including shells from the Mediterranean and turquoise from Sinai.[14]

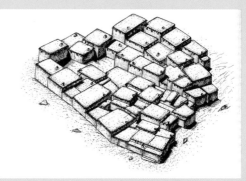

Reconstruction of houses in the town of Çatalhöyük, Turkey, 7000–5500 BC.

creativity and ingenuity: the plough, the potter's wheel, the sailing boat, the draw loom, copper metallurgy, abstract mathematics, precise astronomical observations, the calendar, writing and methods of making permanent records – all these are advances that accompanied the rise of the city five to six thousand years ago.[15] Our move to the city produced an unprecedented flowering of culture, commerce and technology. The city became the cradle of modern civilisation.

The Greek poet Alcaeus praised cities 2,500 years ago: 'Not houses finely roofed nor the stones of walls well built nor canals nor dockyards make the city, but men able to use their opportunity.'[16] The city is a place of ambition and vision, where dreams are dreamed and desires fulfilled. The city has always attracted people with new ideas, perhaps because it is here that the great motivating forces of human society – economics, politics, science and religion – can best be harnessed. From its beginning as the home of the gods, the city became the inspiration for mankind's dreams of Utopia.

Early cities timeline

10,000 BC	last glaciers recede; beginnings of agriculture
8500–6000	permanent settlement at Jericho
7000–5500	Çatalhöyük, Turkey. The first painting of a town in its landscape
5500–3500	origins of urbanism in Mesopotamia, modern Iraq
3500	first examples of writing, Uruk
3000	Nanjing, China, occupied since about this date
3000–1500	Stonehenge, England
2800	city-states stretch from the Persian Gulf to south of modern Baghdad
2600	Great Pyramid, Cheops, Egypt
2350	King Sargon of Akkad conquers the Mesopotamian city-states
2600–1900	Indus Valley cities (modern Pakistan), Harappa and Mohenjo-daro
2004	fall of last Sumerian dynasty
1792–1750	King Hammurabi's reign in Babylon, the centre of urban power in Mesopotamia for a thousand years or more
1600	emergence of Shang Dynasty urban civilisation in China
1100	alphabet invented in the Phoenician cities
650	Nineveh becomes world's largest city (120,000), near Mosul, Iraq
753	legend of Rome's founding
447–438	construction of Parthenon, Athens
332	Alexandria founded (300,000 free citizens by 60 BC)
200	Chang'an becomes capital of Han China and 100,000 families relocated here
100	Teotihuacán becomes dominant city in Mesoamerica (c. forty thousand people)

The Ideal City

In Italo Calvino's *Invisible Cities*, Marco Polo entertains the Great Khan with evocative tales of cities he has visited or imagined: 'With cities, it is as with dreams: everything imaginable can be dreamed . . .' Cities are not just utilitarian structures, agglomerations of houses and workplaces. As Marco Polo tells the oriental emperor, 'Cities, like dreams, are made of desires and fears, even if the thread of their discourse is secret, their rules are absurd, their perspectives deceitful, and everything conceals something else.'[17] We imbue our built environments with meaning. In the course of human history, our desires and fears, our dreams and nightmares have all been given urban form. Even as the first town was rising out of the dust, an ideal city was already glimmering in men's minds, a mirage on the horizon, beckoning from afar, inviting them to construct the future.

Cities have always been deeply symbolic. The design of streets and squares, temples and palaces – all have been used at one time or another to project ideas about man's place in the universe. From the beginning, the city was a celebration of the cosmos, man's homage in wood, mud brick and stone to the gods who created him. For at least four thousand years, Chinese imperial cities were consistently designed as four-sided walled enclosures with twelve gates, three in each side. As the earthly residence of the Son of Heaven, the imperial city was seen as a microcosm of the celestial realm: the universe was believed to be square, and therefore the emperor's city had to reiterate that cosmological fact. Courtly geomancers decided where to site the imperial city. Unfortunately, because their esoteric computations were subject to change without notice, large cities sometimes had to be relocated within a few years of their founding.[18] Extreme measures, perhaps, but necessary ones if they were to avoid disturbing the cosmic order. As the Chinese saying goes: 'Rites obviate disaster as dikes prevent inundation.'[19]

The Chinese cosmological city survived until the twentieth century, an astonishingly long-lived example of the attempt to use cities to create an ideal equilibrium between nature, the state and the cosmos. But China was not alone in attaching cosmic significance to the square as an ideal urban form. It found favour in India and the Near East as well. According to traditional Jewish beliefs, rooted in the ancient myths of Mesopotamia (Ur was, after all, the home

of Abraham), the Holy City of Jerusalem was square, reflecting the shape of the sacred Temple within it.[20] Likewise the Heavenly City, as described in the Book of Revelation, from the first century AD. In a striking case of synchronicity, like the Chinese imperial city it also had twelve gates. John saw 'the holy city, new Jerusalem, coming down from God out of heaven' and this spiritual city shone 'like unto a stone most precious, even like a jasper stone, clear as crystal'. The 'foursquare' city had foundations garnished with precious stones – sapphire, emerald, amethyst – and Jerusalem itself was made 'of pure gold, like unto clear glass'.[21] The Heavenly City of Jerusalem became a celestial ideal in medieval Christian Europe, but one which at the time few earthly cities could equal.

The quest for the ideal city has intrigued philosophers, architects and artists since antiquity. It has become the Holy Grail of architecture and town planning. Ideal cities are the ultimate aspirational location. Their plans are an expression of the geometry of living, forming the perfect physical environment, a union of aesthetics and functionality that serves a social, even an ethical, purpose. For the very structures and spaces of the ideal city instil a sense of order and fulfilment in their inhabitants. They are optimistic, progressive cities that teach you

The Ideal City by Fra Carnevale (*c.* 1445–1484). Apparently commissioned for the palace of Duke Federico da Montefeltro of Urbino, this painting would have seemed like a window on to the perfect Renaissance city.

the good life with every step you take upon their pristine pavements.

One of the first urban visionaries was Plato. His *Republic* (from about 380 BC) is one of the most influential, if flawed, attempts to define the ideal city. Plato's 'Kallipolis' (in Greek, beautiful or noble city) is a rigidly hierarchical state governed by philosopher-kings, the Rulers. The population was strictly policed and controlled. There was censorship: writers and artists were only allowed to portray noble characters, and there was no place for poets in the ideal city. Doctors practised eugenics and euthanasia, removing from society those judged not to be of sound mind or body. In this communistic state, private property and even families were banned. Admittedly Plato had a noble aim in devising this authoritarian state, namely to eliminate greed and self-interest. But the cure was worse than the disease and Plato's city seems far from ideal today. What is valuable, however, in this urban thought experiment is the realisation that cities bring together a wide range of different people, who have diverse needs and desires, and that for everyone to live in harmony a framework of law and traditions is essential.

The Renaissance was an age when men turned their minds to reforming society. Creating ideal cities became a kind of philosophical game, an exercise in urban fabulation not unlike that pursued so beautifully by Calvino. Many Renaissance designs for geometrically perfect city plans – *città ideale* in Italian – derive from the seminal writings of architect and theorist Marcus Vitruvius Pollio – known simply as Vitruvius – who lived in Rome in the century before the Christian era. His *De Architectura Libri Decem* is the only surviving work by a practising Roman architect. Although most Roman towns were square or rectangular with gridiron street plans, Vitruvius favoured the radial city. The Florentine sculptor and architect Antonio di Pietro Averlino (*c.* 1400–69), who used the Greek name Filarete ('lover of virtue'), was inspired by Vitruvius to design Sforzinda, 'the first fully planned ideal city of the Renaissance'.[22] At about the same time, Pope Pius II tried to transform the village of Pienza into an ideal city in 1463, yet never lived to see his grand designs completed. Some regard its fine city square, with its palace, cathedral and city hall, as 'the cradle of Renaissance urban design'.[23]

Star City

Antonio di Pietro Averlino, aka Filarete, was a student of the great Florentine architect, philosopher and artist Leone Battista Alberti. Filarete's Sforzinda (1457–64) was dedicated to his patrons, the powerful Sforza family of Milan. He described it in his *Trattato d'Architettura* (Treatise on Architecture, 1461–4), which was written in the form of a novel in dialogue. Sforzinda is in the shape of an eight-pointed star, a design formed from two squares superimposed diagonally inside a Vitruvian circle: 'the outer walls should form a sixteen-sided figure and their height should be four times their depth. The streets should lead from the gates to the centre of the town where I would place the main square, which ought to be twice as long as it is wide. In the

middle of it I would build a tower high enough to overlook the whole surrounding district.'[25]

Filarete designed his urban vision as part of the landscape and for this reason it has been described as probably the first instance of combined town and country planning.[26] It was an exercise in civic pride, a humanistic and progressive city. Sforzinda contains a ducal palace, a cathedral, separate schools for boys and girls, and a prison. Unlike Vitruvius, Filarete considered the needs of ordinary people, too, in his ideal city, providing houses for workers and merchants. One remarkable feature is the 'House of Vice and Virtue'. This ten-storey square building rose from a socle and was surmounted with a statue to Virtue. It was dedicated to the moral perfection of the citizens. On the ground floor was a brothel, while on upper floors were a university and lecture

Leonardo da Vinci (1452–1519) became fascinated by designs for ideal cities in about 1487. His notes and drawings reveal plans for a geometric city of piazzas, tunnels, canals and loggias. Part of his city was to be underground. The upper level consisted of pedestrian precincts and residences, while below ground were underpasses and subways for goods and animals: 'All carts and loads for the service and convenience of the common people should be confined to the low-level roads,' he wrote.[24] But Leonardo's city was only ideal for the aptly named upper classes. The 'common people' live below ground, an idea that anticipates the socially divided city of H. G. Wells's futuristic urban novel *The Sleeper Awakes*. At the time he was writing, Leonardo was living in Milan, a city stricken with bubonic plague. Perhaps for this reason his brilliant mind was focused on sanitation and particularly toilets: 'The seat of the latrine should be able to swivel like the turnstile in a convent and return to its original position by the use of a counterweight. The ceiling should have many holes in it so

rooms, with an observatory and facilities for the study of astrology on the top floor. Filarete distributed important buildings equally among the three central squares of Sforzinda – 'the first germinating idea of what developed later as multi-focal planning'.[27]

Filarete is also renowned for designing what is arguably the first modern hospital, Milan's Ospedale Maggiore (1456), in which patients could be isolated in wards. Unlike his hospital, the city of Sforzinda remained in the realm of the ideal. It did, however, influence the design of the most perfect radial city ever built – Palmanova. But this star-shaped fortified town near Venice, built in 1593, though visually stunning, proved so unpopular with residents that, in 1622, Venice had to offer pardons to criminals to entice them to move to the city.[28] Living in a garrison town surrounded by high

walls did not appeal to people, though. It was, perhaps, too much like a prison.

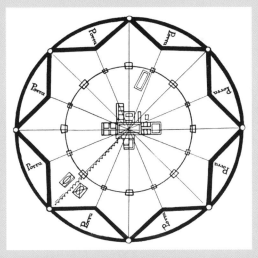

Filarete's plan for the ideal city of Sforzinda (1457–64).

that one can breathe.'[29] He also proposed a system of adjustable and moveable houses – the first prefabricated buildings.[30]

Artists have always been intrigued by ideal cities, from Ambrogio Lorenzetti's *The City of Good Government* (1337–9) in the Palazzo Pubblico, Siena, to Giorgio de Chirico's haunting *Mystery and Melancholy of a Street* (1914). Albrecht Dürer turned his talents towards town planning in his later years, developing both circular and square fortified cities. Indeed, it has been suggested that his design for a circular fortification, published in 1527, may have been influenced by plans of Tenochtitlán which had been published a couple of years earlier in Europe.[31]

Three years before the first Europeans entered the city of Tenochtitlán, the English humanist scholar Thomas More finished his social satire, *Utopia* (1516). Inspired by Plato's *Republic*, his title is a pun, derived from the Greek *ou* (not or no) *topos* (place), a play on *eu-topos* (good place). Unfortunately, this witty coinage meaning 'nowhere' has stuck, and now we think of ideal cities and states as unattainably utopian rather than eutopian. More's Utopia was an island of more than fifty cities, all within a day's walk of each other and all built according to the same pattern: 'whoso knoweth one of them knoweth them all'. The main city is Amaurote. It is 'almost four-square in shape', with identical rows of houses: 'The streets be appointed and set forth very commodious and handsome, both for carriage and also against the winds. The houses be of fair and gorgeous building, and on the street side they stand joined together in a long row through the whole street, without any partition or separation. The streets be twenty foot broad.' The houses are of three storeys with flat roofs, mostly glass windows, and each has a large back garden, 'so pleasant, so well furnished, and so finely kept', with vineyards, fruit trees, herbs and flowers.[32] As in Plato's Kallipolis, More's Utopia is governed by strict laws and has been described as the first surveillance society. It has the same austere communistic traits, too: there is no money, private property, or even competition between people. Houses are chosen by lots every ten years. Everything is shared equally and all live in harmony with one another. Whether More meant his nowhere-city to be taken seriously is a matter that scholars are still debating five hundred years later.

It was Plato who first wrote down the story of Atlantis, the urban civilisation that was destroyed 'in a single dreadful day and night' by 'earthquakes and floods of extraordinary violence'.[33] In the seventeenth century, the Atlantis legend was one of the inspirations for ideal cities, such as Tommaso Campanella's *The City of the Sun* (1602). A free-thinking Dominican monk imprisoned and tortured for heresy by the Inquisition, Campanella's urban eutopia is built on a hill with seven concentric walled circles, the middle ones rising up above the outer rings. The design was influenced by Pieter Bruegel the Elder's famous 1563 painting *The Tower of Babel* with its seven ascending concentric levels. Just as in Bruegel's painting and in the original ziggurats on which it was based, the City of the Sun has at its centre, on the summit of the hill, 'a great temple of marvellous workmanship'.[34] The temple is round and its dome is decorated with sparkling star maps, as well as astrological verses. Indeed, the city functions as an encyclopaedia of natural and esoteric knowledge, each circle being decorated with illustrations from the sciences – trees, herbs, metals, as well as real and fantastic animals. This is the city as classroom, where the inhabitants absorb enlightenment by osmosis, as they go about their daily lives.

Campanella's ideal city influenced many British architects involved in the Garden City movement at the start of the twentieth century, such as C. R. Ashbee, designer of the abortive Ruislip Garden City (1910), who apparently liked to drop the phrase 'City of the Sun' into conversations.[35] Campanella's book was not published until 1623, four years after another account of an ideal city, Johann Valentin Andreae's *Christianopolis* (1619). Andreae was a German Protestant theologian and founder of the Rosicrucian secret society. He described an ideal Christian community on the island of Caphar Salama that was square, surrounded by impressive walls and towers, with parallel lines of terraced, three-storey houses within. Francis Bacon drew on both texts when he wrote his *New Atlantis* in 1626, an account of a Utopia called Bensalem. The 'fair city' his travellers discover is, however, not the focus of Bacon's interest, which is to demonstrate the advantages for society of a scientific research institute, known as the House of Salomon and dating back almost to the time of Plato.

Most ideal cities remained pipe dreams, blue-sky thinking confined to the drawing board. Karlsruhe in Germany, founded by Margrave Carl Wilhelm of Baden in 1715, 'came closest to having the essential characteristics of the ideal city'.[36] Vitruvian in inspiration, this elegant city uses the sector as a city plan, the streets fanning out from the stately *Schloss* behind which stretch gardens and parkland. But ideal cities are very much the product of their own ages. Designed as complete urban statements, they bear the unmistakable imprint of their own culture and world view in every street and building. And yet to be successful a city has to be open to continuous development, free to evolve and grow with the demands of new times. Like science fiction accounts of the future, ideal cities quickly become outmoded.

For a time in the optimistic eighteenth century, it seemed that progress in science and technology would lead to the construction of the ideal city, as Louis-Sébastien Mercier predicted in his science fictional *The Year 2440* (1771). But instead of improving, in the nineteenth century conditions in cities became worse than had ever been experienced before. Social reformers and visionaries, such as Canon Barnett (*The Ideal City*, 1893) and Ebenezer Howard (*Garden Cities of To-morrow*, 1898), stepped forward to show how the urban future could be improved. Le Corbusier's 1925 design of a *ville contemporaine* – a redesigned Paris consisting of glass skyscrapers surrounded by open countryside – was an ideal city of sun and fresh air that harked back to the Heavenly City itself, built 'of pure gold, like unto clear glass'. For a world desperate to escape the overcrowding and pollution created by industrialisation, this radical architectural vision became the ideal city of the mid-twentieth century, although not always with ideal results.

New Town

Most cities emerge across time, developing organically with the ebb and flow of population, self-organising systems that evolve to meet people's needs – new schools, roads, suburbs.[37] But some cities – such as St Petersburg, built in Russia in 1703 – are born fully grown. The new town, *Neue Stadt* or *città nuova*, emerges from its scaffolding shell at a single moment in history.

The urban planner's craft can be compared to that of a storyteller.[38] Building an invisible city in the mind is like writing a novel made up of many narrative strands – national identity, local history, trade and commerce, culture, religion and architectural traditions. All these threads must be tightly woven, leaving no loose ends. Despite the claims of some of its practitioners, designing cities will always be more of an art than a science. New towns may begin as a fantasy, a vision of gleaming towers, but cities cannot survive long in the ideal realm. They need to be lived in. The stuff of dreams must be translated into concrete and steel, forming tangible expressions of what we are and what we want to become.

The desire to improve the layout and design of cities dates back to the first urban civilisations. An ancient text from Ur warns: 'If a house blocks the main street in its building, the owner of the house will die; if a house overhangs or obstructs the side of the main street, the heart of the dweller in that house will not be glad.'[39] When it comes to designing cities from scratch, the plan that has proved universally popular is the gridiron. Such orthogonal plans, where streets in both directions run parallel to each other, have been used to create cities across the world, from the four-thousand-year-old city of Mohenjo-daro in what is today Pakistan and Chang'an in China, to Philadelphia in the New World and the expansion of Barcelona in Spain according to the Cerdá Plan in 1860.

Egyptian civilisation, that created the world's most spectacular houses for the dead, designed some of the earliest gridiron towns. The inflexible grid plan of the pyramid town of Kahun (2670 BC) speaks powerfully of ancient Egypt's tightly regulated, class-based society and its sophisticated administrative system. The scribe was central to this bureaucratic culture. Using papyrus as his ground, he drew the plan of Kahun and other new towns with a grid of streets and two types of housing unit, each very similar yet intended for different social strata.[40] Across nearly five thousand years, the grid has continued to appeal to administrators and technocrats looking for an efficient and rational solution to urban design.

In ancient Greece, the city of Miletus was rebuilt after 479 BC, having been destroyed by the Persians. A strict grid plan was imposed, with a central marketplace and associated public facilities. For the first time, a city's residents (some ten thousand at Miletus) were divided up between three residential neighbourhoods. The Greek architect and pioneering urban planner Hippodamus of Miletus, whom Aristotle credited with discovering the 'divisioning of cities',[41] was one of the first to realise that the structure and layout of cities could create a social order. Chequerboard cities existed before Hippodamus, but for Aristotle he was the man who 'invented the art of planning cities'.[42]

An early version of the
Commissioners' Plan,
New York.

He was the intellectual ancestor of modern urbanists like Le Corbusier or Richard Rogers, designers 'capable of combining abstract social, political, philosophical, religious, and natural principles in the form of a single plan'.[43] The geometric order of the Milesian gridiron plan also brought the street fully into existence for the first time. Streets were no longer merely narrow, winding passageways created by the disordered positioning of buildings. Streets would become the vital human arteries of the city.

In China the ancient city of Suzhou was given a complete makeover during the Song Dynasty (AD 960–1279). Designed as a walled rectangle, 4.5 miles long by 3 miles wide (about 10 by 5 kilometres), the city's streets and canals were laid out in an orthogonal pattern – six canals running north to south, and fourteen east to west. Thanks to Suzhou's grid plan, it is easy to navigate this city of walled gardens in which stands of swaying bamboo can be glimpsed through latticework windows. Cecilia Lindqvist, a historian of Chinese culture, considers that Suzhou, with its waterways and hundreds of camel-hump bridges (Marco Polo erroneously claimed there were six thousand), is so beautiful 'that Canaletto might have wept with sorrow at wasting his life in Venice'.[44] The grid was imposed here less dogmatically than it was at Chang'an, planned in AD 580 during the Tang Dynasty (618–907). The chequerboard layout of this vast administrative capital – for a time one of the largest cities in the world and a model for Japanese cities such as Heijokyo (Nara) – was a clear visual expression of a society in which political power and hierarchy were rigidly enforced.[45]

For colonial settlements and military camps the grid was an obvious choice, a plan easily adaptable to suit every terrain. As the Roman Empire expanded inexorably in the first century AD, gridded towns appeared across Gaul, Britain and North Africa, reflecting the geometry of their army camps. One of the best preserved is at Timgad in Algeria.[46] When Europeans discovered the New World, they, too, chose the grid for their settlements. Spain imposed a grid plan with a central open plaza for its colonial towns in the Americas. The Spanish built more than 350 cities in the Americas beginning with Santo

Domingo (1493). Philadelphia, founded by William Penn in 1682, also had a gridded plan. 'Settle the figure of the town,' directed Penn, 'so that the streets hereafter may be uniform down to the water from the country bounds … only let the houses be built in a line, or upon a line.' The city that would become America's busiest port was, said Penn, to be 'a green country town'.[47]

Ironically, the city of New York, one of the most famous urban grids, began life in the seventeenth century as an organically evolving colonial town. Nearly two hundred years later, the city's dynamic mayor, De Witt Clinton (described by some as 'the greatest New Yorker of all time'),[48] founded a commission to come up with a development plan. The Commissioners' Plan was unveiled in 1811, a single map of the island over eight feet long. It was a bold blueprint for the future at a time when this city of under 100,000 people had barely filled the southern tip of Manhattan Island. The commissioners drew a grid across the entire island – twelve 100-foot-wide avenues running north to south and 155 narrower streets from east to west leading to the rivers. This plan created more than two thousand blocks and anticipated a future city of more than a million people. The world had never seen such an ambitious grid as this one. According to architect Rem Koolhaas, it was 'the most courageous act of prediction in Western civilisation: the land it divides, unoccupied; the population it describes, conjectural; the buildings it locates, phantoms; the activities it frames, nonexistent'.[49]

Science fiction was one of the main inspirations for the Garden City movement. In *Looking Backward* (1887), Edward Bellamy had imagined Boston in the year 2000 as a utopian city of broad tree-lined streets and large open squares, untroubled by pollution and overcrowding. The novel made a powerful impression on Ebenezer Howard, who sought to cure the problems of the city by bringing town and country together: 'out of this joyous union will spring a new hope, a new life, a new civilisation'.[50] In *Garden Cities of To-morrow*, Howard envisaged a network of new cities spread across the countryside (similar to Thomas More's island of Utopia, with fifty cities all within walking distance), each with its own light industrial base and having no more than thirty thousand inhabitants, with individual homes provided for every family. These were clean, green cities, built on a human scale, in stark contrast to the sooty, stinking megalopolis that was London in the nineteenth century.

Howard's decentralised vision was immensely influential on twentieth-century urban planning. The garden cities of Letchworth (1903) and Welwyn (1920) were the direct result in Britain but his idea inspired new towns across Europe and America in the 1930s.[51] In the post-war era, too, many new towns were built, such as Milton Keynes in Britain and Brasília in Brazil. But it has been in the suburbs that people have tried to realise the garden city dream for themselves. Thanks largely to the motor car, in the twentieth century suburban sprawl spread out like an oil slick from the edges of cities across the world, creating conurbations that are the very antithesis of Howard's decentralised vision.

The person who had the greatest influence on urban design in the twentieth century was the Swiss-born architect Charles-Édouard Jeanneret-Gris, better known by his pseudonym Le Corbusier. He was an urban revolutionary who argued that the problems of the nineteenth-century city could only be solved by starting anew, with a blank slate. He especially disliked the traditional urban street: 'although we have been accustomed to it for more than a thousand years, our hearts are always oppressed by the constriction of enclosing walls'.[52] His radical 1925 plan for central Paris, the 'Plan Voisin', involved demolishing

Brasília

Brasília was a heroic attempt to realise the Modernist urban theories of Le Corbusier and the CIAM. Somewhat hubristically, the new Brazilian capital was inaugurated on 21 April 1960, the day celebrated as the legendary birthday of Rome, once the greatest city on earth. Thirty-eight tons of fireworks were detonated and 150,000 people crowded into the new city to witness the moment of its birth. The Pope even conducted a special Mass by radio. Brasília was constructed on a vast plateau, 3,500 feet above sea level. Its planner, the architect Lúcio Costa, described the landscape as 'like an ocean, with immense clouds moving over it'. But such was his commitment to preserving the purity of the design that he refused even to visit the site where this city for half a million people was to rise from the empty scrubland.

It was one of the largest construction projects in human history. Many of the individual buildings are strikingly beautiful, designed by one of Le Corbusier's disciples, Oscar Niemeyer. The main structures are the National Congress, the Ministries, the National Theatre and the cathedral, all designed by Niemeyer. Architecturally and as a display of national pride, Brasília was a success. But as an attempt to create a dynamic urban centre, it was a a vast swathe of the historic Right Bank and replacing it with a grid of eighteen sixty-storey tower blocks and expressways set in parkland. Although Corbusier's schemes – described in *Urbanisme* (1925) and *La Ville Radieuse* (1935) – were not adopted, his attempt to re-imagine the city inspired planners and politicians around the world. Unfortunately, when such plans were realised his utopian Towers in a Park quickly degenerated into Towers in a Car Park. Regarded by many as an urban prophet, Le Corbusier's ideas and those of the International Congress of Modern Architecture (CIAM), with which he was closely associated from its founding in 1928, have transformed the urban landscape in the post-war period.

Today the impact of Le Corbusier and the Modernist movement on town planning is widely seen as little short of a disaster.[53] The urban theorist and historian Richard Sennett has accused Modernists of impoverishing the art of urban design and of undermining the complex social fabric of the city. In particular, the vertical city destroyed street life, an essential urban experience for thousands of years, one created by many hands, from builders to architects: 'The London street has "citiness". It is incoherent. Incoherent is good.'[54] For Sennett and Jane Jacobs, the Modernists' scientific plans eliminated

failure. Costa described it as the capital of the 'autostrada and the park'. He brought together the bucolic ideal of the English garden city

The Congresso Nacional (National Congress), Brasília, designed by Oscar Niemeyer, 1960.

with the technology that did most to determine (some would say destroy) the shape of post-war cities everywhere: the motor car.[55] Indeed, the city is designed around a motorway, the Eixo Rodoviário, with its eight lanes of high-speed traffic. Pedestrians are made to feel as though they are second-class citizens, forced to cross the road in dirty and dangerous subways.[56] But, as Simone de Beauvoir pointed out after the inauguration, 'what possible interest could there be in wandering about? … The street, that meeting ground of … passers-by, of stores and houses, of vehicles and pedestrians … does not exist in Brasília and never will.'[57]

the sources of density, diversity and even disorder that are vital to the creation of dynamic urban communities. Instead, from Moscow to Chicago, what Sennett terms the 'overplanning' of post-war cities has produced a 'dystopia' in which high-rise housing estates have become warehouses for the poor.[58]

Deyan Sudjic, director of London's Design Museum, also believes that the inhabitants of today's cities are 'witnesses to the many soured urban utopias' of the Modernists.[59] A city is shaped by many people, from speculators to visionaries. But it is also a complex system, subject to almost organic laws of development, a system largely created by those who use it – us. The urban blueprints of many post-war architects and planners occluded that most essential part of any city: their inhabitants. They forgot that in the walkways and tower blocks they were designing, children would play, people would go to work, fall in love, and eventually grow old. Technology allows planners to design and build virtually any city, even self-sufficient eco-cities like Norman Foster's ambitious Masdar City in Abu Dhabi, being constructed with a budget of $22 billion.[60] But even the most visionary plans must allow for change over time and, most importantly, for the needs of their inhabitants. As Sudjic says, 'successful cities are the ones that allow people to be what they want; unsuccessful ones try to force them to be what others want them to be'.[61]

Necropolis

In 1878, archaeologists discovered a crudely made sarcophagus while excavating a site in the rue Pierre-Nicole, Paris. The 1,800-year-old stone coffin was found in one of three burial grounds situated outside the walls of what was then the Roman town of Lutetia. Inside the sarcophagus was the corpse of a young child, between twelve and fifteen months old. Lying next to it was a finely made glass milk bottle.

This remarkable discovery was one of just three sarcophagi found in what was a very large cemetery. Some of the bodies had been placed in wooden coffins but most had been buried straight into the ground. Burial in a costly sarcophagus was rare. But the one found in the rue Pierre-Nicole contained something rarer still: an impression of the dead child's face. One of the archaeologists, Eugène Toulouzé, recalled that the child's head 'was partly covered by a layer of fairly thick cement. After carefully removing it, how great was our surprise to see that the cement had formed a kind of death-mask over the head, thus conserving intact for us, after eighteen centuries, the face of the child. Perhaps as the coffin was being sealed, the cement had become stuck to the lid, and had become detached, fixing itself on the child's head and receiving its imprint.[62]

The necropolis – the silent city of the dead – is older than the bustling city of the living. The landscapes inhabited by footloose prehistoric tribes were marked by barrows and cairns housing their ancestors: 'the dead were the first to have a permanent dwelling'.[63] For both the ancient Greeks and the Romans, the dead were ritually unclean and cemeteries were therefore sited beyond the city walls. Travellers to Athens and Rome would have passed through a city of the dead before they reached the alleys and habitations of the living. In the Kerameikos cemetery at Athens, to the north-west of the city, graves were marked with amphorae almost the height of a man. Holes in them allowed liquid offerings to trickle through on to the ground, nourishing the departed. Whether they came from the east, west or north, travellers to Roman London would have passed funeral monuments along the main roads before reaching the city. There were both walled cemeteries and family plots, some with tombstones or wooden markers, others with impressive stone mausolea. Visitors to these ancient cities were introduced to the ancestors before the current inhabitants.

I now live in Winchester, south-west of London, a city that began as the Roman military settlement of Venta Belgarum. If I had walked out of what was then the North Gate of the city 1,700 years ago, I would have seen a large cemetery spread out along the eastern side of the Roman road to Cirencester (Corinium). Indeed, one of the nearby roads, Worthy Lane, was known in the Middle Ages as 'Bonestraete' because wherever people dug they unearthed Roman bones. Today, the whole area is covered by roads and houses (including my own). It's a reminder that in a city the traces – and even remains – of your predecessors are never far away.

In Çatalhöyük nearly eight thousand years ago, people buried the bones of their relatives beneath the floor of their homes, once the corpses had been picked clean by vultures. After the fall of Rome, Christianity brought the dead back into the heart of the city. From the time of Pope Gregory I in the late sixth century, the leading members of the community – bishops, abbots, priests and select lay church members – were interred within churches, while ordinary people were buried in the surrounding churchyard. In the Christian era, you could tell how important someone had been by where they were buried: everyone wanted to be as near as possible to the holy bones of the saints entombed in the churches, in anticipation of the Day of Judgement, when the dead were reunited with their souls and resurrected. In Winchester, which became the capital of England under King Egbert of Wessex in 829, the bodies of saints, monarchs and other influential figures were interred inside the Saxon Minster in the centre of the town, while commoners had to make do with burial in the churchyard.

However, as cities grew steadily larger this practice became unsustainable. Cities had always experienced higher death rates than rural areas. With its cramped houses and narrow, filthy alleyways, Athens – one of the most creative cities in history – was not a healthy environment in which to live. Its people fell victim to regular epidemics. Indeed, more Athenians died from disease than from war. In 430–28 BC, one epidemic – probably smallpox – killed a quarter of their armed forces. In seventeenth-century London, disposing of the corpses of plague victims became a major health issue, even for a city with more than a hundred parish churches within its walls. On 30 January 1666, the diarist Samuel Pepys was concerned 'to see so many graves lie so high upon the churchyard' at St Olave's, near where he lived in Seething Lane. Already some 146 corpses had been buried on top of each other in its tiny graveyard. Unsurprisingly, a contemporary of Pepys noted that the stench was 'offensive and unwholesome'.[64] Local residents beseeched the authorities to spread lime on the graveyard as bodies continued to be buried there. (Due to the number of burials, the churchyard remains banked up to this day.) Another diarist, John Evelyn, condemned 'that superstitious custom of burying in churches' as neither 'decent nor sufferable'.[65] But old habits die hard: people insisted on being buried next to other family members. After all, their eternal life was at stake.

Paris had been burying its dead in the Cimetière des Innocents since 1186. In 1780, people living in the apartment buildings next to the cemetery were terrified by a loud rumbling coming from their basements. This was followed by a truly dreadful stench that spread throughout the buildings, causing many residents to be taken ill, some seriously. When officials investigated the cause, they found that the walls in the basements had collapsed under the weight of the over-crowded graveyard, sending more than two thousand decomposing bodies tumbling into the bottom storey of the buildings.

Up until then, the living and the dead had existed side by side in Paris. The Cimetière des Innocents – the place of burial for 10 per cent of the city's corpses each year – stood next to a major market, Les Halles. But not everyone was happy to spend their lives in such close proximity to a burial ground. Since at least the 1760s, there had been attempts in the name of pub-lic hygiene to prevent the dead being buried in the city centre. The disaster at Cimetière des Innocents eventually forced city officials to act. In 1786, the six hundred-year-old cemetery was finally closed and the bones moved to the catacombs at the site of the Tombe-Issoire in southern Paris. The site was then turned into a vegetable market.

The cemetery of Père-Lachaise, Paris, opened in 1803.

Catacombs are found in many places throughout the Mediterranean, the most famous being around Rome. Dating from the first to the fifth centuries, all are outside the city walls and near the old Roman roads. The word comes from the Greek 'katà kymbas' ('near the hol-lows') and it was first used to describe the catacombs of St Sebastian in AD 354.[66] Rome's catacombs form a mysterious labyrinth beneath the living city. Their full extent is unknown, but they are thought to be hundreds of kilometres in length. They were dug out of the soft volcanic tufa by the 'fossores', or grave diggers. The underground gal-leries can be more than six metres high and generally about a metre wide. Tiers of niches run along the walls. Bodies were wrapped in a sheet before being placed in a niche, which was then sealed using stone and lime. The name was often inscribed on the stone, together with a date. Relatives would sometimes also pay for decorative frescos. By the seventh century, pilgrims arriving in Rome were visiting the catacombs, and guidebooks were even written about them.

The nineteenth-century Paris catacombs were an attempt by the now imperial city to outshine the Eternal City and to create a new visitor attraction. From 1809, the remains of some two million Parisians, from the Cimetière des Innocents as well as from other churchyards and charnel houses, were arranged in macabre displays in existing tunnels beneath the city. The neatly stacked tibias and other bones fill just one-eight-hundredth of the total underground passages beneath Paris.

It was not just the new catacombs that people wanted to visit in Paris. The beautiful cemetery of Père-Lachaise also quickly became a popular tourist attraction. One of three new municipal cemeteries created outside Paris in 1803, Père-Lachaise lay to the east of the city, at Mont-Louis, and was built on the estate of François d'Aix de

The Urban Graveyard Effect

Cities were once decidedly bad for your health. Until the beginning of the twentieth century, more people died in cities than were born in them, a situation referred to as the 'urban graveyard effect'. It was Thomas Malthus, in his *Essay on the Principles of Population* (1803), who first described the urban graveyard effect. He calculated that half of all children born in Manchester and Birmingham died before the age of three. Malthus put this high mortality rate down to the 'closeness and foulness of the air'. In 1861, the life expectancy of a male baby born in Liverpool was twenty-six years compared to fifty-six for one born in the rural community of Okehampton, Devon. Death rates from disease and malnutrition during the first part of the nineteenth century in Manchester were three times that of rural areas.[68]

Conditions in working-class areas of Manhattan were little better at this time. Rates of infant mortality here doubled between 1810 and 1870. Without a continual influx of migrants from the countryside, cities could not survive. Moving to the city was a high-stakes gamble, but one many were prepared to take in order to find work. If you were lucky and you didn't catch something fatal, your future prospects were better than those of someone who remained in a village.

Diseases thrive where humans live in crowded conditions. In cities, the build-up of refuse and human waste, together with high population density, all encouraged the spread of diseases. Most air-borne acute infectious diseases (such as measles) require a city of around 500,000 to maintain the virus, or it simply dies out. Similarly, classic crowd diseases, like smallpox (also spread through the air), are diseases of urbanisation. First recorded in ancient Egypt, smallpox thrives in slum conditions, and regular waves of the disease swept through cities killing a third of victims and scarring or blinding others for life.

The experience of these epidemics must have been terrifying for city dwellers. In the sixth century AD, a terrible plague struck

La Chaise, who had been King Louis XIV's confessor. The French described it as an 'anglo-chinois' garden cemetery, for, like many of the new urban parks that would soon grace European and American cities, it was inspired by the naturalism of both Chinese imperial parks and English landscape gardens. Its tree-lined walks and picturesque views impressed everyone, including an American visitor in the 1830s who observed that 'it is impossible to visit this vast sanctuary of the dead, where the rose and the cypress encircle each tomb, and the arborvitae and eglantine shade the marble obelisk, without feeling a solemn yet sweet and soothing emotion steal over the senses'.[67] In time, the hill in Père-Lachaise became a famous vantage point from which to view the city.

Constantinople. In the course of a year a quarter of the population was wiped out. At its height, ten thousand people a day were dying, more than the city's inhabitants could bury. It was the first epidemic of bubonic plague in Europe, spreading for the next two hundred years before mysteriously disappearing. When the Black Death struck London in 1348 it wiped out half the city's population of sixty thousand. Renaissance Europe was also devastated by plagues and the great trading cities of Italy – Milan, Venice and Florence – suffered very badly. In three centuries their populations fell by a half.

Cities may have been dangerous places to live but they also had some of the first hospitals, such as Filarete's Ospedale Maggiore in Milan. The introduction of piped, clean drinking water and sewage systems in the late nineteenth century helped free industrialised cities from the scourge of water-borne diseases such as cholera. As well as improvements to urban infrastructure, twentieth-century advances in medical treatments helped eradicate some urban diseases (smallpox) and reduced the threat from others (TB, measles). However, new viruses – such as SARS or the H5N1 influenza virus – continue to pose a real threat to the densely populated megacities of the twenty-first century.

'Father Thames Introducing His Offspring to the Fair City of London', by John Leech, published in *Punch* on 3 July 1858, during what became known as the Great Stink. Among the 'offspring' of Father Thames are Diphtheria, Scrofula and Cholera.

Père-Lachaise 'was the first continental cemetery to allow middle-class families to purchase perpetual burial rights'.[69] It offered a permanent resting place for the dead. In the old churchyards after as little as six years the remains were usually exhumed and placed in a charnel house. Now the middle classes had a place where they were free to commemorate their ancestors with permanent and often impressive monuments. But this garden city of the dead soon became a victim of its own success: it proved so popular with the French bourgeoisie that within fifty years it was almost as full as some of the old city graveyards.

Père-Lachaise represented a revolution in the design of cemeteries and it was widely admired and imitated across the world. In the United Kingdom, it was the model for St James's Cemetery, Liverpool (1825–9), the Necropolis, Glasgow (1831–2) and, among many in London, Highgate (1839) and Abney Park (1840), which boasted 'one of the most complete arboretums in the neighbourhood of London'.[70] Within a nine-mile radius of central London there are 103 cemeteries, some three thousand acres in all. In America, Père-Lachaise inspired the rural cemetery movement, beginning with Mount Auburn Cemetery (1831), outside Cambridge, Massachusetts, which served the Boston area. Designed by Henry Alexander Scammel Dearborn, Mount Auburn owed its name to the 'sweet Auburn' of Oliver Goldsmith's poem *The Deserted Village* (1770). Its arboretum and beautifully landscaped grounds were meant to provide a contrast to the busy streets of Boston and it soon became a popular place to stroll through nature. Visitors flocked there in their thousands.

Within twenty years, other American cities had built rural or garden cemeteries, including Portland, Maine, and St Louis, Missouri. Some sixty thousand people a year went to New York City's Green-Wood Cemetery (1838) and enjoyed a scenic tour among its monuments and the views across Upper New York Bay.[71] Guidebooks directed people to the most scenic routes and inspiring vistas. Cemeteries had become part of a new 'national culture', one created by 'the new urban citizens of America'.[72] Among their winding, leafy paths, people forgot the habitual cares and troubles of the city and their thoughts turned to more profound matters, such as the meaning of life and human mortality.

In the twentieth century, the memorial park became the preferred burial ground for an increasingly suburban nation. The first of these was Forest Lawn, Glendale, California (1913), designed by Hubert Eaton. In the new century, death had become big business in America. The new memorial parks promised grieving relatives that they would take care of the whole traumatic process, albeit for a price. By 1929, Forest Lawn covered 200 acres, contained thirty thousand interments and had sales of \$1 million a year. It employed four hundred people and handled 3,600 interments a year. They even held weddings there. Half a million visitors came to Forest Lawn each year. It quickly became the model for cemeteries across America and, by 1935, there were more than six hundred memorial parks in the United States.

In his 'Builder's Creed' (1917), Eaton said – somewhat immodestly – that he aspired to create 'God's garden': 'I shall try to build at Forest Lawn a great park, devoid of mis-shapen monuments and other customary signs of earthly Death, but filled with towering trees, sweeping lawns, splashing fountains, singing birds, beautiful statuary, cheerful flowers.'[73] With its wide roads, carefully manicured lawns and ornamental flowering shrubs, the memorial park was thoroughly suburban and for many Americans this final resting place felt just like home.

The Berlin Wall, photographed in 1986 by French artist Thierry Noir at Bethaniendamm in Berlin-Kreuzberg. In 1984, Noir and Christophe Bouchet had painted this stretch of the Wall, becoming the first artists to use it in this way. (following page)

The City Wall

Walls create the spaces in which we live, separating the public from the private, protecting us from the elements and other people. The walls of buildings guide our route – sometimes straight, sometimes meandering – through the city, shaping the pattern of our urban lives. As we pass through cities we are travelling between the walls of other people's lives. Between four walls you can be whatever you want to be: your apartment becomes the theatre of your dreams. From Beijing to Berlin, in our seven-thousand-year love affair with cities, walls have – at different times and different places – imprisoned people and helped set them free.

Whether they are made of glass, brick or concrete, walls are the defining structures in cities. 'The wall is, probably, the greatest of all inventions,' says the narrator of Yevgeny Zamyatin's novel *We* (1924). 'Man ceased to be a wild animal only when he had built his first wall.'[74] For D-503 (numbers have replaced names in Zamyatin's future society), the crystalline Green Wall that surrounds his city is the guarantor of civilisation. Like butterflies under a bell jar, he and his fellow Numbers live in an artificial bubble of rationality and mathematical order protected from the chaos of nature by the Green Wall. But, like all inventions, walls can be used for good or evil. Their beloved wall, the bulwark of D-503's utopia, cuts people off from the world and from reality. Ultimately, the Green Wall does not protect Zamyatin's ideal city from a hostile world, but traps people in a ruthless authoritarian state.

More than any other structure, the fortified city wall has shaped urban communities around the world. 'Polis', the ancient Greek word for city, originally meant a citadel, such as the crown of a hill surrounded by a ring wall. From the earliest times up until the eighteenth century, the defensive wall was the city's most prominent and visible feature. The first city dwellers felt the presence of their defensive wall even when they could not see it. It became a wall in the mind. Subtly and gradually, the city wall changed the way people saw the world. Although it protected populations against real or imagined threats from outside, it also united the enclosed community, binding them with a common sense of identity and shared purpose. The wall made people into citizens.

But the same wall that protected people from wild animals and enemy invaders was also a structure of control. The first walled communities could easily have become prisons, holding camps for forced labour. The ghetto, first named in Venice in 1541, is an example of how walls can be used to control urban populations. But the kings and priests who governed the earliest urban communities didn't need to force people to stay in cities. There were clear social and economic advantages and people wanted to live there. It seems that from the very beginning we had an elective affinity for cities. Like Enkidu in the ancient *Epic of Gilgamesh*, we are destined to leave the wide-open plains for the walls of the city.

The city wall gave communities a physical structure and identity, as well as moulding the character of city dwellers. Within its protective embrace people gained a new sense of security and self-confidence. But by cutting its citizens off from the outside world, walls also created fertile ground in which seeds of suspicion and even paranoia could grow. Pride and arrogance turned the first cities into what Mumford has called pockets of insolent power.[75] Despite the impregnable walls, people became fearful, suspicious of neighbouring cities. Rivalry between cities became intense and warfare a fact of life. Plato was right when he said, 'in reality every city is in a natural state of war with every other'.[76] In the modern world, warfare between urban tribes has segued, apparently seamlessly, into weekend football matches between cities. A leather ball has taken the place of more lethal missiles.

Elaborate fortifications turned early cities into military machines – soaring watchtowers, gates protected by symbolic lions and bulls, battlements, walls wide enough for three chariots, ramparts, moats and ditches. Remarkable Assyrian bas-reliefs survive, such as those in the British Museum in London, vividly depicting the first walled cities and the techniques used to besiege them: engineers tunnelling under walls to create cavities beneath the foundations which would be shored up with timber and then fired to bring about a catastrophic collapse; giant battering rams assaulting brazen gates; and infantry using flimsy ladders to scale ramparts.[77] But before the invention of gunpowder (and unless you had a god on your side, as did the Israelites at Jericho), the advantage lay with the defenders. From the walls they dropped everything they could find on to attacking armies: boiling liquids, pots of scorpions and even beehives.[78] The stakes were high:

if the walls were breached, no mercy was shown to the defenders. In about 1100 BC, the Assyrian king Tiglath-Pileser gloated about his ruthlessness in destroying the city of Hunusa: 'their fighting men I cast down in the midst of the hills, like a gust of wind. I cut off their heads like lambs; their blood I caused to flow in the valleys and on the high places of the mountains ... That city I captured, their gods I carried away. I brought out their goods and their possessions, and I burned the city with fire. The three great walls of their city which were strongly built of burned brick, and the whole of the city I laid waste, I destroyed, I turned into heaps and ruins and I sowed crops thereon.'[79]

Civilisation owes much to the humble brick. The walls of the first Mesopotamian cities were made of mud brick. In the ancient world, sun-dried bricks were bedded in wet mud so that the whole wall became a solid mass. Fired bricks began to appear about five thousand years ago in Mesopotamia. The Sumerian word for brick, *sig*, also meant building, city and the god of building.[80] The act of building, of creating a man-made environment, was deeply symbolic. Creation was, after all, the preserve of the gods. Mere mortals needed to tread carefully lest they upset the divine authorities. In a powerful ceremony the king himself would make and then lay the first brick, known as 'asada', or the 'invincible one'. It is described in this contemporary account: '[the King] put the blessed water in the frame of the brick mould ... He set up the appropriate brick stamp so that [the inscribed side] was upwards; he brushed on honey, butter and cream; he mixed ambergris and essences of all kinds of trees into a paste. He ... acted precisely as prescribed, and behold he succeeded in producing a most beautiful brick ... He struck the brick mould; the brick emerged into daylight ... The sun god rejoiced over [his] brick, which he had put in the mould, which rose up like a swelling river.'[81]

Uruk was almost certainly the largest settlement in the world five thousand years ago, with as many as eighty thousand inhabitants. From around 2800 BC its mud-brick walls enclosed 494 hectares, a vast area for its time, equivalent to about 345 modern football pitches.[82] Uruk's inhabitants believed that the gods themselves had helped create this immense city, with 'its great wall touching the clouds'.[83] *The Epic of Gilgamesh* tells how the brick wall of Uruk was built by King Gilgamesh. It praises 'ramparted Uruk' and its walls 'which none can equal'.[84]

When Babylon became the dominant city in the region, its defences were legendary. Herodotus visited in about 450 BC and was awestruck by its wall. He described seeing a 'deep and wide moat' surrounding the entire city, and an immense wall eighty-nine kilometres long, built of bricks made from earth excavated from the moat.[85] These were fired in a kiln and cemented with a mortar of hot bitumen, reinforced with a course of reed mats added after every thirty layers of brick. 'On the top, along the edges of the wall, they built houses of a single chamber, facing each other, with space enough between for the driving of a four-horse chariot. There are an hundred gates in the circle of the wall, all of bronze, with posts and lintels of the same.' Herodotus described the wall as the city's 'outer armour', part of an impressive defensive system that included a secondary wall running along inside the first one and a royal palace also surrounded 'by a high and strong wall'.[86]

In China cities are synonymous with walls. The Chinese character for 'wall' is the same as the one for 'city' – *cheng*, written as a square with two or four attached gates.[87] Chinese towns have been surrounded by walls since the beginning of recorded history. The walled city is 'the most profound declaration of Chinese urbanism', says Nancy Steinhardt, a historian of Chinese cities.[88] The Neolithic settlement of Chenziyai, in Shangdong province, is a perfect example. Its wall consisted of layers of pounded earth, a technique known as *hangtu*. This became the standard method of wall building for thousands of years in China because of the shortage of stone. The construction of large walled cities began here more than three thousand years ago. The Shang capital, Ao, near today's Zhengzhou, reveals evidence of a square walled city from the second millennium BC, with a pounded-earth outer wall 6,960 metres long. The use of earth for walls and wood for buildings has meant that China's cities have proved extremely vulnerable to both fire and weather. Today little of China's urban history remains for archaeologists.[89]

Chinese cities have always been meticulously planned. According to Chinese cosmology, the universe was square and imperial cities – as the home of the divine emperor – also had to be four-sided, with the walls oriented on a north–south axis. The town planning principles contained in the ancient *Zhouli* (the *Rights of Zhou*) decreed that Chinese city builders should begin with the defensive wall. In practice, however, other buildings would often be finished before the outer fortifications were complete.[90] This was the case at Chang'an (today Xi'an), which had nearly 26 kilometres of walls around it made of yellow rammed earth. The wall, which was 12 metres high, and 12–16 metres thick, narrowing to the top, took five years to build.

China's capital, Beijing, offers ample evidence of why the character for 'city' and 'wall' is the same. Until a few decades ago the great wall of the city, with huge watchtowers and gatehouses, towered over all other structures. Indeed, the Chinese character for 'high' depicts a tall building, possibly an imposing watchtower or gatehouse on a wall.[91] Sadly, this wall has now been demolished to make way for apartment blocks and roads choked with traffic. But sinologist Cecilia Lindqvist remembers the wall when it was still standing in the 1960s. She recalls how 'it felt safe' living inside Beijing's walls: 'The wall was not only the visible boundary between the city and countryside, but also gave the city a definite form and the people a sense of being looked after: One knew one's place in the world.'[92]

Behind a high red wall at the very heart of Beijing lies the Forbidden City, once home to the emperor. This walled city, within what was once itself a walled city, is a labyrinth of courtyards, pavilions and official buildings, symmetrically arranged along a north–south axis according to the rules of the geomancers. The complex measures 960 metres from north to south and 750 metres from east to west, a perfectly proportioned rectangle within a chequerboard city. The layout of Beijing's distinctive single-storey courtyard houses (*siheyuans*) echoed that of the Forbidden City with a main entrance in the south wall. From the outside these walled enclosures appear austere, but inside they were havens of tranquillity from the noise and bustle of the city.

In the sixth century AD, Beijing's government offices were also walled off from the rest of the city. This was known as the *huangcheng*, the administrative city (literally, and rather confusingly, the imperial city). This was distinct from the *gongcheng*, the palace city where the emperor lived and which was also hidden behind walls.[93] This city of walls was itself protected by the most famous of all walls: the Great Wall of China, defending the country and the imperial city from northern invaders. Begun in the first millennium BC and made of pounded earth, it was the most extensive wall ever built, 8,850 kilometres (5,500 miles) long.[94] To walk along this remarkable structure is a truly unforgettable experience and a powerful reminder of humankind's faith in walls.

The Bavarian market town of Frickenhausen am Main. The town wall dates from the late medieval period.

In Europe, defensive walls resulted in round rather than rectilinear cities, a practical rather than a symbolic design decision: 'a circular wall system enclosed the largest amount of town for a given amount of stone and brick'.[95] By the early Middle Ages, city walls had become defining features of European cities, in the same way that art galleries and town halls were in the nineteenth century.[96] From the eleventh century, Europe experienced an urban revival. As populations grew, city walls had to be extended. In the early twelfth century, Perpignan built a new wall enclosing an area six times greater than the previous one. Florence began building its second circuit of walls in 1172, enclosing eighty hectares. This rose dramatically to 630 hectares when the city's defences were expanded in 1333. A third of Germany's city walls were built between 1100 and 1300.[97]

Until the fifteenth century, city walls were an essential part of the European townscape, proudly displayed on maps and civic seals as well as in the background of portraits of the leading figures of the day. In Giovanni Bellini's exquisite painting *The Madonna of the Meadow* (c. 1500), behind the Virgin and child lies a beautiful walled Italian hilltop town, complete with tower houses. The town gate was the point where two worlds met, the interface between urban and rural cultures. The locking of the town gates at sundown helped forge a common sense of civic identity in medieval cities. As the point where goods and people entered the city, the gate was also where the economic quarter of the city was often located. There were storehouses and inns here and nearby you would find the homes and workplaces of craftsmen and merchants. Walled towns were often granted economic privileges, such as being able to hold markets. As in ancient Greece, those who came to buy and sell would be protected by the Market Peace, symbolised by the market cross: 'here a new class got protection against theft and arbitrary tribute, and began to settle down permanently, at first just outside the walls: the merchants.'[98]

In 1453 the walls of Constantinople, which had resisted several previous sieges, were breached by the Turks armed with huge bombards, cannon used to destroy fortifications. The age of gunpowder had arrived in Europe. Until then besieging towns had been a slow and uncertain process, with the defenders having the upper hand. But the new artillery introduced in the late fifteenth century meant that cities were vulnerable as never before. Stone or iron cannonballs were brutally effective at demolishing walls. Beginning in Italian

The City of Darkness

The Walled City of Kowloon, also known as the City of Darkness (in Cantonese *Hak Nam*), was one of the densest urban slums on the planet. It was also a unique city within a city. Measuring just 200 by 100 metres, the Walled City rose up abruptly out of residential Hong Kong, its ramshackle buildings as high as fourteen storeys. Some 35,000 people lived there, most of them refugees from the People's Republic of China.

The Walled City was an anomaly, its existence due solely to a legal and diplomatic loophole. It was built on the site of the oldest inhabited part of Hong Kong. Originally it was a walled garrison town designed according to the principles of traditional Chinese urban planning, facing southwards and with its back to the great Lion Rock to the north. According to the 1898 convention by which Britain gained control of Hong Kong for ninety-nine years, the Walled City remained Chinese territory. When the Japanese captured Hong Kong during the Second World War, they demolished its granite walls. After the war, refugees from China's civil war flooded into the area. As the Walled City lay outside the jurisdiction of the British colony, they could live there without paying taxes. There were also no policemen or government officials to interfere with their lives. The Walled City became 'the closest thing to a truly self-regulating, self-sufficient, self-determining modern city that has ever been built'.[100]

Unsurprisingly, in this anarchistic society the triads flourished, running brothels and selling drugs, beyond the reach of the long arm of the law. But if the inhabitants of the Walled City kept on the good side of the gangs, they were cities such as Perugia, engineers now took control of the redesign of city walls that became ever more complex and expensive to construct. With their outworks, salients and bastions designed to withstand artillery, fortifications became a straitjacket, restricting the expansion of cities. Open land within city walls was developed instead and, as populations increased, so, too, did the height of buildings. In the seventeenth century, tenement buildings in Geneva and Paris rose five or six storeys. In Edinburgh they soared eight or ten storeys. As people continued to flock to the cities, rents also went sky high.

Modern weapons and armies made fortifications increasingly redundant. By the eighteenth century, as cities were forced to expand and modernise, old town walls and gates were being demolished across Europe to make way for wider streets and new housing: 'the circuit of town walls was no longer seen as a defence of a city's cultural identity but rather as an obstacle to cultural progress'.[99] At the end of the century in Paris, the construction of a customs wall proved so

free to get on with their lives: 'Every afternoon the alleys were alive with the throb of hidden machinery and the clacking of mahjong tiles, while up on the roof, in cages not much smaller than some of the City's homes, cooed hundreds of racing pigeons, joined there by children playing after school.'[101] The resourceful citizens drilled 300 feet underground to create some seventy wells for fresh water. They also hijacked Hong Kong's electricity supply. The narrow streets were permanently bathed in the glow of fluorescent lights as sunlight never penetrated the closely packed tower blocks. Like every aspect of life in the Walled City, building was unregulated. Fires were a constant threat.

Following agreement between Britain and the PRC, the Walled City was demolished in 1993. Today it has been transformed into the Kowloon Walled City Park. Within it still stands the Yamen, the last remaining remnant of the original Walled City – a brick and granite building that was the headquarters of the military officials who governed the original garrison town when it was built in 1847.

The Walled City of Kowloon, China, before it was demolished in 1993.

unpopular that it helped to trigger the Revolution. After millennia, the age of the city wall had come to an end.

One hundred and seventy years later the construction of a new wall in the heart of a European capital city provoked an international outcry. Indeed, it could have sparked a world war. This was not a defensive wall or a customs barrier. It was a wall built by a state to control its own people, rather like Zamyatin's fictional Green Wall.

The Berlin Wall was erected by the authoritarian rulers of the German Democratic Republic to isolate West Berlin and to prevent its own citizens escaping to the West. It is without question the most infamous wall of the twentieth century and perhaps of all time. The 165-kilometre wall encircled West Berlin, cutting it off from the German Democratic Republic for twenty-eight years, from the day construction began on 13 August 1961 until it was dismantled by Berliners armed with pickaxes and sledgehammers in 1989. During this period, 125 people were killed trying to cross the Wall into West Berlin. Described by the East Germans as 'an anti-Fascist protective barrier' (*antifaschistischer Schutzwall*) it was initially a barbed-wire fence, but was eventually converted into a concrete wall some four metres high. It became the most visible and chilling symbol of the Cold War, raising tensions between the superpowers to unprecedented levels.

Before 1989, graffiti appeared only on the west face of the Wall, as soldiers shot on sight anyone approaching the eastern side. In the west, the Berlin Wall became famous for its graffiti and artworks. Large lengths were entirely covered in brightly painted murals and slogans, such as *Irgendwann fällt jede Mauer* ('Eventually every wall falls'). The graffiti humanised an utterly inhuman structure that divided families as well as a city. Today, after the collapse of the East German regime, little is left of the Berlin Wall. The longest remaining stretch has been turned into a 1.3-kilometre art gallery, the East Side Gallery, at a cost of some €2.2 million.[102] It was opened in 2009, on the twentieth anniversary of the Wall's fall. The year before, a Berlin auction house sold a section of the graffiti-covered Wall for more than €7,800 (£6,150). It was bought for display in the foyer of an office building. The United Nations, the CIA and the Vatican all own pieces of the Wall, as do millions of ordinary people, myself included. But most of the Wall was ground down to make 310,000 tons of gravel to build the roads necessary to link the eastern and western halves of the city after unification. Thus a structure that divided the city for decades eventually helped bring it together again.

What Germans called the *Mauer im Kopf*, the 'Wall in the head', was once thought to be an obstacle to unification. Now it is an unforgettable part of European cultural history.

The Temple of Hathor and Nefertari, Abu Simbel, southern Egypt, *c.* 1275-1225 BC. (following page)

3 CUSTOMS

Writing

'More than any other single invention, writing has transformed human consciousness,' wrote the cultural historian Walter Ong.[1] The Sumerians had a story about the birth of writing. The lord of Kulab dispatched a royal messenger to a faraway land. But the journey was long and arduous and the man arrived utterly exhausted, incapable of passing on the message he had committed to memory. Fortunately his lord and master had anticipated this eventuality. In the words of the story, he had 'patted some clay and set down the words as on a tablet'. The lord of Kulab's message was delivered after all, despite the incapacity of the messenger. For the first time a dispatch was not spoken but read, the words having been transcribed into symbols and scratched into soft clay with a slender reed. 'It verily was so,' the story-teller claims piously, conveniently eliding the thorny issue of how the foreign lord could read the first written message.[2] But one thing is clear from this ancient tale: the written word endured despite human frailty. Indeed, the story itself only survives today because it was written down, cut into cool clay which hardened into permanence, a message to us from the distant past.

It was in the cities of southern Mesopotamia during the fourth millennium BC that the revolution occurred and writing was invented. We no longer know whether it was an individual or a group of people who made this momentous discovery: the answer is lost beneath the dusty tells of Iraq. In the Upper Paleolithic period (15,000–10,000 BC), notched bones had been used for recording events. From 8000 to 4000

Preparations for the Palio, a medieval horse race held
twice each year in the Piazza del Campo, Siena, Italy.

BC, people used tokens, often enclosed in a ball-shaped clay envelope known as a 'bulla'. On the outer surface, markings recorded the contents and the bulla functioned as a tally or bill of lading. It is a 'lovely irony', says the historian of reading Maryanne Wolf, that writing may have begun 'as an envelope for the world of numbers'.[3]

Writing did indeed develop in the service of economics. In the city of Uruk – believed to be the birthplace of writing – priests used the new invention to keep accounts in the temples from about 3300 BC. The earliest clay tablets found in Uruk contain a combination of numerals and pictographic symbols, some easily recognisable today – a fish, a man's head, a loaf of bread.[4] These early attempts at writing were made by pressing a reed stylus into soft clay, creating holes and fingernail-like impressions. Unlike stone or wood, clay was abundant in the region and provided the Sumerians with a beautifully responsive medium on which to record the prosaic details of their urban lives, details which to us, five thousand years later, seem immensely evocative and even poignant.

Over time, as Mesopotamian cities grew and the demands of administration required ever more detailed records, so their writing evolved, becoming increasingly abstract. Single strokes replaced curved, freely drawn representational signs. Symbols for grammatical structure were invented, as scribes struggled to put complex spoken language on to clay. Writing became less pictographic and more logographic, directly conveying the concepts in the oral language. It also began to represent syllables, a double function known as logosyllabary. Modern Chinese writing is logosyllabic and, like Sumerian, it does not use an alphabet.[5] From the middle of the third millennium BC, Sumerians developed what we now know as cuneiform script, from the Latin *cuneus*, meaning wedge-shaped, because of the narrow V-shaped wedge that was the basic constituent of the symbols. To modern eyes these haunting, enigmatic marks look like the tracks of a bird across river mud. But they are the origins of our written culture, for out of this ingenious system of urban accounting came all of history and literature, from Herodotus to James Joyce.

For nearly three thousand years, cuneiform script was the principal writing system in the Near East. Thousands of cuneiform tablets have been unearthed, a priceless treasure trove of social, economic and historical information. The whole story of Sumerian life and culture is fixed in these tablets – their myths and stories, how they governed their cities, details of their laws and tax systems, what they needed to build a house or a boat, and how they trained a craftsman or a scribe.[6] All was committed to clay by a scribe writing with a cut reed.

Learning to read and write is never easy. Sumerian students spent years copying the many hundreds of characters in their writing system in order to learn the secrets of cuneiform. They were taught in an 'e-dubba', or tablet house. The teacher would write a passage or a proverb on the tablet and the student would carefully copy it on to the back of the tablet. Excavations at the city of Ur, home to 35,000 people some four thousand years ago, have uncovered thousands of clay tablets used by children to learn multiplication tables and to practise writing. Some tablets show the clumsy marks of children starting out on the road to literacy; others show the work of advanced students.

Cuneiform inscriptions at Persepolis, Iran, transcribed by Carsten Niebuhr (1733–1815).

Such texts on clay tablets are our earliest records of what life was like for the first city dwellers. Their timelessness is particularly striking. In a Sumerian letter some 3,700 years old, a father complains about his son's lack of diligence at school. He has been excused from working in the fields, but instead of practising his writing, the boy wanders the streets and hangs out in the city square with his friends.[7] Cities rise and fall, but, as these texts show, the very human concerns of their occupants remain much the same, a red thread running through the skein of our history.

Writing was invented independently at different times and places around the world. In Egypt the earliest hieroglyphic writing appears in about 3100 BC. In the Indus Valley a fully developed script (still undeciphered) emerged around 2500 BC. On Crete, writing appeared c. 1900 BC and in China seven hundred years later, although it is believed the origins of Chinese writing are much older. It is a measure of the success of cuneiform that at least fifteen peoples adopted the Sumerian writing system. However, by 1600 BC no speakers of Sumerian remained and Akkadian was then the dominant language.

But it was to cuneiform writing that Akkadians turned in order to transcribe their language, creating seminal texts on science and law, such as All Things Known in the Universe and the Code of Hammurabi.

The next revolution in writing also took place in a city. It was in Ugarit, near modern Ras Shamra on the north coast of what is today Syria, that the alphabet began to be used from 1400 BC. This heavily fortified city covered fifty-two acres and it was a thriving trading centre with goods arriving from Mesopotamia, Anatolia and further afield. Shipwrecks reveal they were trading in goods such as copper, glass ingots, faience and amber beads, ceramics, jewellery, textiles, tools and timber.[8] Like all successful cities before and after, this was a diverse and vibrant community where ten languages were spoken and five different scripts were in regular use. The dominant script had been Akkadian cuneiform. But at some point the people of Ugarit decided to begin using an alphabet – perhaps in order to find a more fluid and precise way of writing their native language. Just as they imported goods from far and wide, so they took a foreign idea – the alphabet from Canaan in the south – and adapted it to their urban needs. The cuneiform alphabet they created has been described as a 'stunning accomplishment'.[9]

More than a thousand tablets have been discovered in the ruins of Ugarit since 1929, including administrative and business records written using just thirty signs of the alphabet, and religious or literary texts – hymns, myths, poems – for which they used a mere twenty-seven signs. Abecedaries have also been found here, tablets listing the signs of the alphabet in a fixed order similar to the one we use 3,500 years later. Although Ugaritic script disappeared following an invasion in 1200 BC, the alphabet had proved its worth as a more efficient and expressive writing system. Within a century or so it had been adopted by another civilisation built on the power of trade – that of the Phoenicians.

The Phoenicians were the greatest navigators and traders of the ancient world. From the port cities of Tyre, Byblos and Sidon on the Mediterranean coast of what is today Syria and Lebanon, they sailed their black ships down the coast of Africa and north to the British Isles. Their cities were the predecessors of great trading centres such as Venice and Osaka. One of the most important items they traded was the purple dye from the 'murex' snail. Indeed, Phoenician is a

The Code of Hammurabi

King Hammurabi (1792–1750 BC) made Babylon into the most important city of what is today central Iraq and the capital of one of the world's great empires, with a common government and language. The Code of Hammurabi is one of the oldest written legal codes. The Code was inscribed on several stone stelae which were set up in Babylon and across the empire in about 1760 BC. One seven-foot tall, black basalt stele has survived and it is now in the Louvre, Paris. At the top is an image of the Babylonian king paying homage to a god, possibly Marduk, the national god. Below it, inscribed in Akkadian cuneiform, are nearly three hundred laws by which the inhabitants of Babylon should live, 'just decisions which Hammurabi, the able king, has established and thereby directed the land along the course of righteous behaviour and proper conduct'.[10] They govern every aspect of life from criminal law, through marriage and divorce, to the rules of commerce. Punishments were harsh: 'If a man has harboured in his house a fugitive slave or bondmaid belonging to the state or to a private citizen, and not brought him out at the summons of the public crier, the master of that house shall be slain.'[11] Nevertheless, the Code was also enlightened in its attempt to protect women and children from mistreatment. The Code literally set in stone the rules by which the peoples of Babylon should live their lives, rules which rose above tribal or religious customs, and which were meant to last for all time. 'In future time,' proclaimed Hammurabi, 'through all coming generations, let the king, who may be in the land, observe the words of righteousness which I have written on my monument.'[12]

The Law Code of Hammurabi, a basalt stele erected by King Hammurabi of Babylon (1792–1750 BC) probably at Sippar, city of the sun god Shamash, god of justice.

Greek word – first used in Homer's *Iliad* – for 'dealer in purple'.[13] It is in Byblos – the Greek name for the ancient Phoenician city of Gebal – that the earliest example of the Phoenician alphabet has been found, dating back to the eleventh century BC.[14] The Phoenicians also took the radical step of abandoning cuneiform and adopting twenty-two simple and convenient signs. By doing so, 'they inaugurated a script that continues to be found all around the Mediterranean for the next millennium and more'.[15] The Phoenician writing system was easy to memorise and wonderfully adaptable. It became the foundation for the Hebrew, Greek, Latin and most Indo-European alphabets. The Greek letters *alpha* and *beta* are derived directly from the Phoenician *aleph* and *beth*. Indeed, Herodotus called the alphabet 'phoinikeia grammata' – 'Phoenician letters'.[16]

Street Language

In our cities we have created unique environments. Even the birds sing differently here. City birds, such as great tits, sing at a higher pitch than their rural cousins. Scientists believe they do this to make themselves heard above the constant hubbub of the city. But as a result, rural birds have trouble understanding their urban relatives. 'Tit townies don't respond as strongly to the country boys' song, nor do the country boys respond as strongly to the townies,' says Dr Rupert Marshall, who led the research at Aberystwyth University.[17]

It's not just birds that sound different in the city. From Wenzhou (population 865,000) in China's Zhejiang province, to Venice, Italy,

Venetian

From a small settlement of wooden houses in the tenth century, Venice quickly grew into a major Mediterranean power. By 1400, it was Europe's fourth city with a population of 110,000. Its unique language – 'venexian' – is still spoken by the city's 63,000 native inhabitants. The influence of Venice was felt across Europe and the Mediterranean, as can be seen from the number of Venetian words still used in English.

'Ballot', which appears in English in 1549, comes from 'balota', the ball used in Venetian government elections. 'Lotto' is a Venetian word, as is the origin of 'giro', an Italianised version of the Venetian word 'ziro' (to circle or spin, hence the circulation of money), used in the name *Banco del Ziro* (later *Bancoziro* or 'Girobank'), in the Rialto business area of Venice. The Venetian word 'casin' (gaming house) is the source for 'casino', first used in English in 1789. The English word for newssheet, 'gazette' (1605), comes from the Venetian 'gazeta de la novità', meaning 'a penny worth of news', which is what you would have paid for a urban dwellers speak distinctive dialects that are often incomprehensible to people elsewhere in the same country. Wenzhou Chinese has even been described as an entirely separate language from Mandarin. Similarly, Venetian differs from Italian to a greater extent than Italian does from Spanish. Far more than a mere 'dialetto', Venetian is believed to be much older than the national language itself.[18]

The divide between urban and rural cultures began to widen across Europe in the seventeenth century as levels of literacy increased and publishers flourished (by the 1660s, London chapbook publisher Charles Tias had a remarkable ninety thousand titles in stock). At the same time, urban dialects became distinct from those elsewhere and the metropolitan classes began to look down on people in the countryside as being backward – the beginning of centuries of mutual town–country derision.[19]

Every country has its urban dialects. In the teeming, polyglot environment of cities, languages flourish and grow like plants in a hothouse, absorbing foreign words and accents, evolving rapidly to match the fast-moving pace of urban life. In Britain many cities have their own unique ways of speaking – Brummie in Birmingham, Geordie in Newcastle, Scouse in Liverpool and cockney in London, to name but a few. The roots of London's street language stretch back hundreds of years to Essex and the East Saxons. But it bears the mark of

The front page of the *Gazzetta Veneta*, from February 1760.

seventeenth-century newspaper in Venice. The city played a leading role in the development of journalism and was renowned for its paper the *Gazzetta Veneta* in the eighteenth century.

This major trading city also gave the English-speaking world the word 'quarantine', first used in 1609, from 'quarantena', a forty-day maritime isolation period. Such measures were common in Venice from 1403. Some words and concepts have a darker past, though. Infamously, Venice created the word 'ghetto'. Originally the Venetian word for foundry ('gheto'), it became the name of the district in Cannaregio to which Jews were confined in 1516. Despite its inauspicious origins, to this day it remains a vibrant centre of Jewish culture.[20]

foreign tongues, too. The voices of countless merchants and immigrants from far afield continue to resonate in the sound of London: Yiddish gave Londoners words like 'kosher' and 'shtumm'; from Romany they borrowed 'cushty', meaning very good; and still more phrases and words were taken (or 'half-inched' as a Cockney might say) from Dutch, Spanish, Arabic, Italian and German. Out of this Babel chorus emerged cockney English, which for half a millennium or more has been the language of the London street – of costermongers, oyster sellers and innkeepers – the distinctive voice of Britain's most populous city.

Originally, before the fourteenth century, a 'cokeney' (or the Chaucerian 'cokenay') was a misshapen egg, a cock's egg, or alternatively a derisive term for a pampered child or a 'milksop'.[21] But from the sixteenth century, it began to refer to city dwellers, albeit in a far from flattering way, suggesting a puny and generally inadequate individual in contrast to the hardier and worldly-wise country folk. Within a century it was being used to describe specifically Londoners. It's said that a young Londoner was visiting the countryside for the first time when he heard a horse neigh. What is this sound, he asked his father, who replied: 'The horse doth neigh.' When he then heard a cock crow, the Londoner is said to have asked innocently: 'Doth the cock neigh too?' This no doubt apocryphal story about the origin of 'cockney' was first told by Shakespeare's contemporary, John Minsheu, who also gave the word its modern definition – someone born near St Mary-le-Bow church in Cheapside.

Cockney stands accused of being a lazy dialect. According to one scholar: 'Cockneys avoid movement of the lips and jaw as far as possible.'[22] However, a historian of cockney language and life, Julian Franklyn, points out that the Cockney's 'normal speech speed is so great that the stranger, even when able to understand the accent, finds it most difficult to follow.'[23] Others have attacked its sound for being ugly, even vulgar. A London County Council report on the teaching of English concluded in 1909: 'The Cockney mode of speech, with its unpleasant twang, is a modern corruption without legitimate credentials, and is unworthy of being the speech of any person in the capital city of the Empire.'[24] Fortunately, such elitist attitudes to dialects are less common now. London novelist and historian Peter Ackroyd looks to the city itself for an explanation: 'If the Cockney voice is indeed "harsh", it is perhaps because Cockneys have always inhabited a harsh and noisy city where the need to be heard above the roar of "unresting London" is paramount.'[25] It seems that, like city birds, Cockneys and other urban dwellers have adapted their ways of speaking to fit the environment.

Although some aspects of the cockney dialect have disappeared, such as pronouncing 'W' as 'V' ('Vestmynster' rather than 'Westminster', as Sam Weller says in Dickens' *Pickwick Papers*),[26] many cockney phrases and words are still in use that date back to before the sixteenth century, such as 'sav'd 'is bacon' (rescue someone from danger), 'bouze' (drink), 'poppet' (girl), and 'elbow grease' (energy).[27] Other characteristic ways of speaking also remain, for example the frequent use of the glottal stop, as in 'Bri'ish' (British) and 'bu'er' (butter), as well as dropping the 'h', as in 'eye o ben' (High Holborn) and 'th' as in 'bruvver'. Swearing has always played a major role in cockney speech, 'bloody' and 'bleedin'' being 'veritable nails that hold a cockney sentence together'.[28] Cockney rhyming slang emerged in the nineteenth century – 'apples and pears' for stairs; 'trouble and strife' for wife; 'butcher's hook', or just 'butcher's', for look. Today, the influence of cockney has spread across the whole of England as the dialect segues

Sam Weller in an illustration from Charles Dickens's *Pickwick Papers*, 1837.

into what is known as estuary English, a way of speaking popularised by the mass media and in particular TV programmes such as the soap *EastEnders*, set in the fictional London borough of Walford.[29]

Languages and dialects are never fixed and in the twenty-first century the sound of London is once again changing. As estuary English becomes familiar throughout the country, on the streets where cockney originated migrant communities are forging a new London dialect. Indian, Jamaican and West African ways of speaking have merged with cockney English to produce what is variously known as Jafaican or – in the obscure dialect spoken by today's academic linguists – Multicultural London English (MLE). Typically, 'th' is pronounced with a hard 't' or 'd', so that 'thing' becomes 'ting', while 'this' and 'that' become 'dis' and 'dat'. Vowel sounds are opened up: 'why' becomes 'wae' and 'like' is now 'laek'. In this new London dialect 'choong' means 'good looking', 'fo shizzle' is 'for sure', and 'nang' is 'very good'.[30] Urban music such as grime, a sub-genre of rap music that began in London housing estates, and hip hop from 1970s New York, has helped to spread this rolling, jazzy dialect among teenagers. Now, whether you live in London or Birmingham, for fans of east London's grime rappers such as Dizzee Rascal (born in Bow) and Kano (from Newham), this ultra-cool street slang is *de rigueur*.

'Kilroy was here'

Graffiti embraces a wide range of mostly urban markings – lovers' names cut into brick or wood, symbols chalked on walls by hoboes or tramps for one another indicating whether a town was safe or dangerous,[31] the names of gangs marking the bounds of their territory, slogans ('Brahms not Bombs'),[32] obscene or obscure words scrawled drunkenly on walls overnight, 'Kilroy was here' (a graffito that probably originated in the chalk marks of an American shipyard inspector named James J. Kilroy during the Second World War),[33] the names of the famous, such as Lord Byron, who carved his mark into a pillar at Château de Chillon on Lake Geneva, and cryptic tags (a graffiti writer's signature), as well as the dynamic designs of wildstyle graffiti and street art.[34]

Graffiti is certainly not a new kid on the urban block. In ancient Pompeii, houses were brightly painted in reds, yellow and blue, ideal surfaces for everything from electoral slogans and advertisements to spontaneous graffiti. One popular piece of doggerel, found on at least three walls in Pompeii, indicates the popularity of graffiti writing among city dwellers: 'I am amazed that you haven't fallen down, O wall / Loaded as you are with all this scrawl.'[35] Walking through the streets of Pompeii, you would have seen syrupy lover's rhymes, such as this: 'I wish I could be a ring on your finger for an hour, no more …' While on another wall, you could spot the kind of obscene boasts familiar to all city dwellers throughout history: 'Here I fucked loads of girls.' And, inevitably, the natural results of such behaviour also appeared: 'Atimetus got me pregnant'.[36] Roman graffiti writers were also keen to show off their literary as well as their libidinous

interests and over fifty quotations or allusions to Latin literature have been found in Pompeii, including lines from Virgil, Ovid, Propertius and Lucretius.

Graffiti as we know it today – modern aerosol culture – began in the late 1960s and early 1970s in the streets and subways of Philadelphia and New York. It was the era of civil rights and Vietnam. 'Black is Beautiful' and 'Power to the People' were among the slogans appearing in American cities at the time. In 1973, hip hop's founding father, Kool Herc, was spinning records in the basement of his South Bronx apartment building. He had been a 'graf' writer and hip hop would soon become the soundtrack to graf culture in cities everywhere. Journalist Richard Goldstein said in 1973 that graffiti was 'the first genuine teenage street culture since the fifties'.[37] Kids would hang out in subway stations, watching the tags sprayed on the stainless steel subway cars pass by. (The activity was known as 'benching' after the hard wooden benches they sat on in the stations.) Sacha Jenkins, who as a teenager from Queens tagged – or 'bombed' – subway cars, has described how the New York transit system became the precursor to the information superhighway: 'Buses and subway cars with thousands of [nick]names sprayed and dripped all over 'em reached out to

Work by Banksy at the Cans Festival, Leake Street, London, 2008.

a "global" community that raced from Manhattan to the Bronx and from Brooklyn to Queens at very high speeds.³⁸

Aerosol culture soon distinguished itself from the graffiti of earlier ages by its awareness of style. The creation of a distinctive style, a graphic voice, is what transforms words written on a wall into art, as one graf writer explains: 'When I began writing, I thought the only thing needed to get famous was to go around writing my name. I still see trash cans and phone booths with old tags of mine on them, but I'm ashamed of them now. Ashamed of them because they had no style.'³⁹

Modern graffiti is subversive, a way of saying 'up yours!' to the Establishment, as well as an assertion of individuality amidst the anonymity of the metropolis. Although some cities provide surfaces for graffiti ('permission graf'), generally it is illegal, a crime against property. In 1972, New York Mayor John Lindsay declared war on graf. In the following year he spent $10 million combating graffiti. But for some people, graf was more than mere vandalism. In 1974, Jon Naar and Norman Mailer's seminal book *The Faith of Graffiti* was published. Mailer interviewed graf writers like Japan 1 and Cay 161 (tags included a nickname and the street number of writers).⁴⁰ At this time, graf was in a transitional phase between tagging and 'piecing' (a tag

The Faith of Graffiti

In 1973, Jon Naar was commissioned to photograph New York graffiti for *The Faith of Graffiti*, written by Norman Mailer. Naar was surprised to find that the first graf writers he met were children of nine to twelve years old. But, as he points out, 'they were, of course, *New York* children, wise beyond their years in their knowledge of the ways of the city's streets, subways, and public places'. In two weeks he took over three thousand Kodachromes, of which just thirty-nine were used in the book. (In 2007 he published more of his remarkable images

in *The Birth of Graffiti*.) Naar was one of the first professional photographers to document American graffiti extensively and he gained a certain notoriety for celebrating what many thought of as vandalism.⁴² The book is now a classic. Naar had been photographing the 'palimpsest of writings and marks on walls' since 1955 and he says his interest in graf is 'political, in the Greek sense of engagement with the life of the "polis", or city-state'. The graf writers he met and whose work he documented came from run-down districts such as Harlem and the Bronx. Their work was a 'cry for change from the ghetto'.⁴³

outlined in a different colour, derived from 'masterpiece'). Soon graf would evolve into something far more complex, involving cartoon characters, arrows, stars and a whole visual grammar of other signs.

Meanwhile, the war continued. In the mid-1990s, Mayor Rudolph Giuliani renewed the campaign against graffiti as part of the so-called 'broken windows' approach to tackling inner-city crime. Cleaning up neighbourhoods was hailed as the way to prevent more serious offences. Even in 2002, some 250,000 'graf hits' were being removed from New York City's subway cars each year and three million square feet of graffiti cleaned from bridges and other public structures. According to the current Mayor of New York, Michael Bloomberg: 'Graffiti poses a direct threat to the quality of life of all New Yorkers . . . It's not just an eyesore. It is an invitation to criminals and a message to citizens that we don't care.'[41]

Like New York's mayor, many regard graffiti as an antisocial activity, indeed a crime. But to others it is part of a dynamic urban culture that should be celebrated not condemned. Books, like Fabienne Grévy's *Graffiti Paris* (2008), the result of a fifteen-year project, document this striking yet ephemeral street art form. The work of graffiti artists, like Banksy, has now gained international acclaim. Claes Oldenburg began as a graf writer and Keith Haring described the subway as

Graffiti on the base of a statue of Lenin in Kiev, Ukraine.

his 'laboratory'. In 2008, Tate Modern mounted London's first public museum display of street art, inviting six artists from around the world to create new works on the gallery's brick façade overlooking the River Thames and Christopher Wren's St Paul's Cathedral. In the same year, the Cans Festival brought together the work of graffiti artists in Leake Street, a tunnel near London's Waterloo Station.

Street art is a more visual urban art than the text-based graffiti, and one that potentially speaks to a wider audience. Among the artists who displayed at Tate Britain were Blu from Bologna, Italy, Nunca (Never) and Os Gêmeos (The Brothers) from São Paulo, Brazil, and Sixeart from Barcelona, Spain. Nunca began as a graf artist on São Paulo's streets at the age of twelve, working in the city's unique 'pichação' style of tagging.[44] His current work is inspired by indigenous Brazilian art and by the urban experience itself. Using spray paint and acrylic, the city's walls become his canvas as he depicts the faces of people in the streets. With their distinctive black hatching, his haunting images are reminiscent of traditional woodblock prints. Their vivid primary colours – the hues of the body paint used by Brazil's indigenous people – burn with a fierce brightness in the concrete jungle of São Paulo.[45]

The Voice of the Street

Streets are the arteries of the city, channels for the city's life blood: its people. Night and day, the main streets pulse with life as vast numbers of people move through the city in vehicles or on foot – commuters and idlers, tradesmen and pickpockets, hoodies and civil servants. A man in a black suit frowns as he hurries to a meeting, mobile pressed close to his ear. A shopper pauses, dazzled by the glamour of a window display; the tide of people flows past her like a river round a rock. At a table outside a café, a man briefly lowers his newspaper and glances at a young woman passing by. For a moment, it looks as though he remembers something long forgotten; then he looks back at yesterday's news.

Streets guide you through the heart of the city, but they are also places to see and to be seen. For the street is a stage and all the people on it are players. Most perform cameo roles, walk-on parts in the minor domestic dramas out of which lives are made. But occasionally something far greater is at stake. Then people come together on the streets where they play a part in performances of great communal power – demonstrations, rallies and revolutions, as well as parades, festivals and ceremonial processions. Demonstrations and parades were a means of mass communication in the days before the modern media. In the city there is always an audience – its thoroughfares are thronged with people from all ranks and classes, for the street is the most democratic of spaces. Here the beggar rubs shoulders with the businessman. Whatever your social standing, it is impossible not to stop and stare when people join together and walk through the streets, singing songs and waving banners.

The reasons for taking to the streets are legion: to proclaim membership of a guild or union, to celebrate a religious holy day, to display pride in a rich ethnic tradition, to protest, demonstrate, or to riot, as happened first in London and then other English cities in the summer of 2011. In New York, the city's Irish community has been holding a St Patrick's Day parade for more than two hundred years.[46] May Day demonstrations have been held since 1890 to celebrate working-class internationalism.[47] Gay Pride marches began in 1970 and are now regular events in cities around the world. But there are tragedies played out on the streets, too. On 30 April 1977, the Mothers of the Plaza de Mayo, in Buenos Aires, began walking silently around the square where Argentinian independence was declared in 1810, carrying photographs of their missing children, the 'disappeared', victims of the junta's security agents. They still perform their silent protest every Thursday afternoon more than three decades later.[48]

Now a global phenomenon, organised urban street demonstrations were largely a nineteenth-century invention. The word demonstration (in the sense of a public meeting) entered the English language in the 1830s.[49] In August 1872, *The Times* reported that organising a demonstration 'appears to be becoming a recognised branch of industry in this country'.[50] By the beginning of the twentieth century, the march had become a key weapon in the armoury of protesters in Europe and America, where 'the right of the people peaceably to assemble' was enshrined by the First Amendment of the US Constitution.[51]

Protest marches generally take place in cities and last two or three hours, concluding with a rally, often in front of a landmark building such as a city hall or a symbolic monument. It was at the end of the 1963 March on Washington for Jobs and Freedom that civil rights leader Martin Luther King stood on the steps of the Lincoln Memorial and told a gathering of a quarter of a million people, 'I have a dream.' It was, said one eyewitness, 'the greatest assembly for a redress of grievance that the capital has ever seen'.[52] Despite fears about violence (thousands of troops were on standby in case the demonstration turned into a riot), the march remained peaceful. Indeed, there was less crime than usual on that spring day in Washington, DC.

The Lincoln Memorial stands at the western end of the National Mall, a broad, two-mile-long stretch of parkland in the centre of Washington, originally designed by Pierre Charles L'Enfant in 1791. At the eastern end stands the United States Capitol where Congress meets. Also rising from the Mall is the Washington Monument, the world's tallest stone obelisk (over 500 feet high), built in honour of the founder of the American Republic. This is the political heart of the United States of America. Indeed, for the first time in 2009, the Mall was opened during the presidential inauguration allowing an estimated 1.8 million people to witness Barack Obama's swearing in. Because of its symbolic importance, the Mall has been the site of countless protest marches and rallies. Other historic demonstrations here include the suffragette parade of 1913 (organised by the National

British suffragettes marching to what was described as a 'monster meeting' in Hyde Park on 21 June 1908, holding a banner referring to Prime Minister Herbert Asquith. It was one of the largest demonstrations that had yet been seen in Britain.

American Woman Suffrage Association) and the Million Man March of African Americans in 1995. In 1967, 100,000 people rallied at the Lincoln Memorial for the March on the Pentagon in order to protest against the Vietnam War. In what became one of the defining moments of the anti-war movement, they walked the short distance to the Pentagon where an attempt was made by a collective act of will to levitate the implacable headquarters of the United States Department of Defense. Over the sound of a long sustained 'Ommmm', marchers chanted 'Out, demons, out! Out, demons, out! Out, demons, out!' But despite their best efforts, the Pentagon remained firmly fixed to the ground.[53]

In Britain, people have been marching on London from the provinces to seek redress for their grievances since the Middle Ages. London marches traditionally converge either on Trafalgar Square or Hyde Park. From 1905, unemployed men from industrial cities such as Leicester, Nottingham and Manchester began marching to the capital to draw attention to their plight. There were six marches in the 1920s, and ten in the 1930s. In 1936, one newspaper described such protest marches as 'an old-established practice in this country'. In that year, the most famous of these, the Jarrow 'crusade', left Northumberland in the north-east of England and arrived after nearly a month's march in Hyde Park on 1 November. The *Daily Herald* said 250,000 turned out to greet the two hundred marchers; the police put the figure at no more than ten thousand. The marchers were successful in drawing attention to their desperate situation. As George Orwell wrote, 'after all, even the middle classes – yes, even the bridge clubs in the country towns – are beginning to realise that there is such a thing as unemployment'.[54]

At Easter in 1958, some three hundred marchers left Trafalgar Square for a three-day walk to the British atomic weapons research laboratory at Aldermaston. The Easter march became a regular event in CND's struggle to raise awareness about the threat of nuclear weapons. But after 1958 the direction of the march was reversed, concluding with a rally in Trafalgar Square, a public space that formed the perfect theatre in which to draw attention to the movement's concerns.[55] By 1962, 150,000 people massed in the square, making it the largest London turnout since VE (Victory in Europe) Day, when countless thousands thronged the capital's streets in a spontaneous and ecstatic celebration of the defeat of Hitler.[56] On 15 February 2003, people again took to the streets of London to protest against war, this time in Iraq. As many as two million marched that day. In Barcelona 1.3 million protested, as did at least ten million people in cities around the world from San Francisco to Rome and Sydney in what was one of the largest displays of public protest the world has yet seen.[57]

In 2003, the French prime minister angrily dismissed public protest, asserting confidently, 'the street does not rule'.[58] History reveals a somewhat different story, particularly in France, where the *rue* has long played a role in toppling regimes. Indeed, if any city can claim to be the capital of protest, it is Paris. Over the centuries, the blood of Parisians has regularly been spilt on its streets. From at least

Tahrir Square and the Arab Spring

Tahrir Square was created 140 years ago by Isma'il Pasha, who ruled Egypt from 1863 to 1879. While visiting the Exposition Universelle in Paris in 1867, he was astounded by Haussmann's transformation of the city. On his return, he was determined to turn Cairo into 'the Paris of the Nile'.[59] The square – *midan* in Arabic – was named Isma'iliya Square, after its creator.

Following the 1952 revolution which swept King Farouk's monarchy from power, President Gamal Abdel Nasser changed the names of many landmarks in Cairo, including Isma'iliya Square, which became Tahrir – or Liberation – Square to commemorate Egypt's liberation from British colonial rule. In 1970, Tahrir Square became the focus of a national outpouring of grief when Nasser died suddenly. Many hundreds of thousands of people gathered there to mourn his passing.

Centrally located in Cairo and bordered on one side by the River Nile, Tahrir Square has today become a vast traffic roundabout, with more than twenty streets leading into it, constantly jammed with cars and buses.

On 25 January 2011, after three decades of authoritarian rule by Hosni Mubarak, revolution returned to the streets of Cairo. Inspired by the Tunisian people's ousting of their ruler on 14 January, Cairenes marched to Tahrir Square but were soon dispersed by the police. Under Mubarak, even small gatherings of people in a public space could lead to immediate arrest. On 28 January, a larger crowd of some 30,000 people returned to the square. The security forces responded with rubber bullets, tear gas and live ammunition. But after two days, the people managed to occupy the square, which soon became known as the 'free people's republic of Tahrir'.[60]

For two weeks, despite attacks by plainclothes policemen and even men mounted on camels, Cairenes remained in Tahrir Square, keeping the flame of democracy burning on behalf of all Egyptians. They set up checkpoints to keep out the undercover police and the square became a tent city, a microcosm of Cairo, filled with people from all classes and the sixteenth century, French kings lived in fear of the rebellious Parisians. In 1789, their worst fears were realised as the city was consumed by violent revolution. In that year, aristocrats and politicians across Europe wondered if their cities would be next to be engulfed in revolutionary fervour. On 5 October 1789, three months after the storming of the hated Bastille fortress and prison in the city (the event that marked the beginning of the Revolution), working women from the markets of Les Halles marched through Paris to the palace at Versailles as a protest about the shortage of bread. Some sixty thousand people joined the dignified but desperate procession, eventually forcing the royal family to return to Paris together with wagons of

religions, men and women, young and old. Although there was a constant fear of attack, there was a carnival atmosphere. People opened food and drink stalls, doctors offered free medical clinics and a pharmacy was set up, as well as a kindergarten. They brought portable toilets to the square, designated an area for rubbish, and created a news service by pasting up newspapers on the shutters of a shop so that everyone could read the latest reports. Bloggers in the square uploaded stories and images to a world hungry for news. It was a remarkable popular expression of the desire for change, 'the biggest spontaneous event of community-organizing and nation-building the country had ever seen'.[61]

Egyptians in Cairo's Tahrir Square hold aloft a Syrian flag with the slogan 'God, Syria and freedom only' in support of anti-government protestors in Syria, on 8 April 2011.

After 18 days of protest, Mubarak finally resigned. The announcement on 11 February was greeted with scenes of wild jubilation in Tahrir Square with celebrations continuing throughout the night. Egyptians and Cairenes had not just won back control of their streets, but of their entire nation. The events of Tahrir Square showed that even in the age of Facebook and Twitter, you still need people on the streets of a city to bring about a political revolution.

Cairo's Tahrir Square has become synonymous with the Arab Spring, but there are also Liberation Squares in Tripoli, Damascus and Sana'a. These and other public spaces have become the stages on which the voice of the Arab street — so long suppressed — is finally being heard.

wheat and flour. It was an inspiring display of collective power by ordinary Parisians, who realised that power now lay not with those in the palaces but with the people on the streets.[62]

In the mid-nineteenth century, French authorities became so fearful of the power of the streets that Napoleon III commissioned Georges-Eugène Haussmann to redesign the historic centre of Paris. The dense networks of medieval streets were demolished and replaced with broad, straight boulevards. As one contemporary complained, they had 'all the subtlety and intelligence of a cannon-ball'.[63] Which was precisely the point, for the narrow, winding streets had proved too easy for revolutionaries to barricade and defend against government forces. The new boulevards allowed the military to deal swiftly with insurrections. Ironically, as Eric Hobsbawm has pointed out, they also provide the ideal stage for mass demonstrations, such as took place in 1968 when students led an uprising in the Latin Quarter that nearly toppled the government.

The two hundredth anniversary of the French Revolution became a year of urban uprisings on an unprecedented scale. As Rebecca Solnit wrote in her wonderful history of walking, '1989 was the year of the squares – of Tiananmen Square, of the Alexanderplatz, of Karl-Marx-Platz, of Wenceslas Square – and of the people who rediscovered the power of the public in such places.'[64] The 1980s had seen vast demonstrations against nuclear weapons and as the Cold War ended, people took to the streets in Communist countries to display their desire for rapid social and political change. Like Paris, Beijing was a city whose wide boulevards had been designed (in the 1950s) to allow for the rapid movement of military forces. In Tiananmen Square, Chinese tanks brutally crushed protesters on the night of 3 June, killing many hundreds of people.

In Eastern Europe, peaceful protest was more successful. Throughout October 1989, East Germans marched through Leipzig's streets, gathering in Karl-Marx-Platz (now Augustus-Platz) in a display of opposition to Erich Honecker's regime. At the beginning of the month there were ten thousand people in the square, the largest demonstration in East Germany since 1953. By the end of October, half a million were marching in Leipzig and in cities throughout East Germany. In Leipzig they chanted 'Wir sind das Volk!' (We are the people!) There were real fears that the police would open fire. But thankfully this was to be the first successful revolution in German history, one achieved without bloodshed. On 4 November, 500,000 marched in East Berlin, converging on Alexanderplatz to demand elections. Within five days the barriers on the Berlin Wall had been raised, and East Berliners were free to walk the streets of West Berlin, many of them for the first time in their lives.

In Czechoslovakia, people were given hope by the fall of the Berlin Wall. Prague's Wenceslas Square became the stage for their Velvet Revolution. At the centre of the city, this kilometre-long square was where people gathered every day after they had finished work, gaining confidence as their numbers grew, sharing information and news (the public media were not to be trusted), reading the many colourful posters plastered on walls, and – the final act of each day – singing the national anthem. Alexander Dubček, the hero of Czechoslovakia's last uprising, the 1968 Prague Spring, stood with the protest leader and playwright Václav Havel on a balcony above the crowded Wenceslas Square. Later, Dubček – who had been silenced by the authorities for twenty-one years – addressed another Prague rally. The government, he said, 'is telling us that the street is not the place for things to be solved, but I say the street was and is the place. The voice of the street must be heard.'[65] Within weeks the regime had fallen. Once again, the voice of the democratic street had triumphed.

Carnival!

'Revolutionary moments are carnivals in which the individual life celebrates its unification with a regenerated society', said the Situationist Raoul Vaneigem.[66] When large numbers of people gather on the streets for a common purpose, they can rewrite the rules of everyday urban life. And they can have fun.

The spring festivals out of which Carnival emerged are probably as old as civilisation itself. Indeed, the first large settlements may have originally developed out of the human need to socialise, drawing people together from across the land in temporary camps to share alcoholic drinks brewed from grain – a pre-urban Oktoberfest.[67] From these gatherings and other now forgotten rites of spring emerged celebrations such as the City Dionysia of Athens in ancient Greece at the end of March, which involved cultic processions, feasting and revelry, as well as the Roman festivals of Bacchanalia and Liberalia, also in March, and Saturnalia in December. More recent influences on Carnival include the medieval tradition of the Feast of Fools, celebrated at the end of December, a festival of inversion in which a mock bishop curses rather than blesses the congregation. The Church regularly condemned this subversive festival but Christianity has proved adept at absorbing such religious legacies. Fortunately, even after the theological rebranding exercise, Carnival has remained an intoxicating mix of pagan disorder and religious piety, growing into a global urban phenomenon.

Although it is invariably urban in its setting, Carnival is bigger than any one city or religion. Its ebullience and dynamism is a natural florescence of dense communities. During Carnival, usually sober streets explode in a joyous riot of colour, music and dancing. For a few days, outrageous imagination rules the public spaces of the city. The air throbs with rhythms from marching bands and sound systems. People don brightly painted masks and fantastic costumes. For a while, life's disappointments and inequalities are forgotten as people hide their everyday personas. For you can be whatever you want to be in Carnival – a vamp, a buffoon, a devil, or a queen.

Traditionally, Carnival is held in the days before Lent. First used in Roman Catholic texts from the tenth century, the Latin origins of the word reveal its role in Christianity: 'carne' means meat, and 'levare' is to lift up or to remove. In the Christian calendar this was the last chance for people to use up meat and other rich foods before Lent, a period of fasting and abstinence before Easter. As no parties were allowed during Lent, the days before Ash Wednesday became one big street party in Catholic countries such as Italy, where the tradition of Carnival began.[68]

But which are today's Carnival cities? Rio de Janeiro hosts one of the largest, but there's also Mardi Gras in New Orleans, 'Fasching' in Munich, and the Carnival at Rijeka in Croatia. Venice has had a carnival for most of its history.[69] The English diarist John Evelyn noted in 1646 that Shrovetide was 'when all the world repair to Venice, to see the folly and madnesse of the Carnevall'. Masquerade, or the wearing of masks ('vólto' in Venetian, with the same meaning as 'persona' in Latin), is an essential part of the Venice *Carnevale*. The masks are beautifully made, often from papier mâché. Masquerade is part of the inversion of the everyday order of life that was celebrated in early folk culture, a subversive spirit that still runs through carnivals

everywhere. In some cities laws that otherwise prohibit the wearing of masks in public places are suspended during Carnival. Masquerade allows citizens to forget their daily cares and to adopt a new identity for a few hours – in Venice that means becoming Harlequin or Pantaloon or Colombine – colourful characters that stem from the *commedia dell'arte*, Italy's traditional street theatre. Venetian novelist Tiziano Scarpa says that 'the carnival spirit is rooted within the urban population'.[70] City dwellers understand the need for masks. Daily life, spent cheek by jowl with neighbours you never really know or want to know, is a performance. Some might say it's a charade, but it's a necessary one.

Other Catholic nations followed Italy's example and adopted Carnival – first France, Spain, Portugal, then Germany's Rhineland cities. Cologne's 'Karnival' is rooted in pre-Christian folk traditions. In the Middle Ages, it was often a wild and riotous affair. The city authorities and the Church made repeated efforts to regulate the behaviour of the revellers, largely in vain. In the eighteenth century, the 'Redouten' were introduced, fancy-dress balls in Venetian masquerade, principally for the upper classes. In 1823, the *Festkomitee Kölner Karneval* (Cologne Carnival Celebration Committee) began

95

The Battle of the Oranges

Many towns and cities around the world have evolved their own unique festivals, parades and celebrations which have grown out of a past history most of its inhabitants have long since forgotten. Few are more unusual than that practised by the inhabitants of Ivrea in Italy.[71] This Piedmont town to the north of Turin was where Adriano Olivetti, owner of the typewriter business based in the town, once planned to build an ideal city for his workers.[72] It is also the setting for the Battle of the Oranges. For three days, beginning on the Sunday before Lent and ending on Fat Tuesday, some three thousand inhabitants, on foot and in carts drawn by decorated horses, pelt each other mercilessly with oranges, until the streets are coated with the slippery pulp of the fruit and the gutters run with juice. The Battle of the Oranges is part of the town's Carnival, but it commemorates a rebellion against Ivrea's rulers in the thirteenth century. Each year a schoolgirl is chosen to play the role of a courageous young woman who, in medieval times, refused the amorous advances of the town's aristocratic ruler. The orange throwing concludes with a silent procession on the night of Fat Tuesday. By then the streets are covered with eight inches of golden citrus gore.[73]

organising the festivities. Traditionally the season is declared open at eleven minutes past eleven on the eleventh of November ('am elften elften elf Uhr elf'). But the main festivities commence with the 'Tolle Tage' (Crazy Days) which begin on the Thursday before Lent and end on Ash Wednesday. Men wearing ties be warned: if you are in Cologne on the Thursday then it is likely that a woman will approach you with a pair of scissors and cut it off. For this is what is known in the Rhineland as 'Weiberfastnacht' (women's carnival night). Since 1823, 'Rosenmontag' (Rose Monday) has been the climax of celebrations and the parade regularly attracts over a million people. During Carnival, people on the streets wear masks and greet each other with the phrase 'Kölle Alaaf!', which is 'Kölsch' (Cologne dialect) for 'Long live Cologne!'[74]

Spain and Portugal exported their tradition of Carnival to South America and the Caribbean. The island of Trinidad was discovered by Columbus in 1498, but also colonised by the French and the British. Its Carnival, held in Port of Spain, remains one of the most vibrant in the region. In the eighteenth century, Carnival was the preserve of white people and Africans were banned from taking part in the street festivities. But in their compounds, the slaves developed their own traditions

The Battle of the Oranges, Ivrea, Italy.

and, after emancipation in 1838, they took over the Carnival, creating an African-inspired festival with masquerade, dancing, stick fighting, and scenes mocking the whites and memorialising the experience of slavery.[75] The whites responded by trying to ban Carnival, attacking it for being immoral and even obscene. Thankfully, they failed. Today, Carnival processions stretch for miles in Port of Spain and the event generates US $60 million in increased commercial activity each year, while tourists spend some $200 million.[76]

It is certainly lucrative, but some believe it has become too commercialised. Indeed, there are now two carnivals – 'fancy mas' ('mas' is short for masquerade) and 'old mas'. Fancy mas is a lavish and spectacular display. Thousands of marchers – members of large 'fancy bands' – take part in the main parade, enacting topical themes. Traditionalists accuse it of prettifying Carnival for tourists, creating a Disneyfied pageant and removing allusions to slavery. Max Harris, who has participated in carnivals around the world and studied their history, says it is a largely middle-class event, like 'the aristocratic Carnival of slaveholding days'.[77] He argues that the pursuit of spectacle and profit has triumphed over authenticity.

Old mas is rooted in the village traditions of Africa and draws on the experience of slavery. A man in charge of a Carnival float in the old mas tells Harris: 'Mas is really a form of protest, showin' the masters of this time, or the Establishment, that you was not pleased with certain things that they was doin'.'[78] Traditional masquerades include the Moko Jumbie, a stilt walker who towers twelve feet or more above the street. Dressed in brightly coloured clothes, he dances giddily to the sound of drums and flutes. In the Congo, a 'moko' is a diviner and 'jumbie' means ghost or spirit. The Moko Jumbie was believed to be able to protect villages, his great height allowing him to spy approaching evil spirits. (Stilt walkers, or 'Gilles', also star in the Carnival at Binche, Belgium. Dating from the sixteenth century, they wear Inca costumes and ostrich-feather headdresses.)

Another 'mas' in Trinidad's Carnival is the Jab Molassie. 'Jab' is French patois for 'diable' or devil, 'molassie' means molasses. This devil (one of many evil spirits in the Carnival) is daubed with red or blue dye and wears a mask and horns. He is kept chained to a group of imps who play music, to which he dances or 'wines' ('wining' means winding your hips, or 'winin' yo' behin'', often while in contact with one or more people). Other mas include Midnight Robbers (complete with sequinned capes and toy pistols), the Grim Reaper, a Satanic Bookman writing down sins in a large book, Minstrel Boys, American Indians and assorted spirits glistening ghoulishly with white paint. White skulls are painted on the backs of their heads so that they look as though they are walking backwards.[79]

Perhaps more than any other city, New Orleans lives for its Carnival. Preparations begin as early as 6 January. Historian Carol Flake wonders, 'how can a city so ostensibly Catholic celebrate with such pagan gusto? How can a city so poor concoct such extravagant displays, year after year?'[80] Before the disastrous events of 2005, when Hurricane Katrina devastated the city, more than thirty thousand people worked on the staging and planning of Carnival. In 2004 it generated $150 million in economic activity.[81] In 2006, despite apocalyptic scenes in much of the city, New Orleans still celebrated Mardi Gras (Fat Tuesday in French). With its broad avenues divided by tree-lined grounds, New Orleans is a city apparently designed for Carnival. The organised masquerade parade in carriages began in 1837. The civic stage for Mardi Gras was originally the Vieux Carré, Garden District, and Uptown areas and the main parade route was along St Charles Avenue. But eventually Canal Street became the epicentre of the parade. At the end of the nineteenth century, temporary viewing stands festooned with colourful banners were erected above the sidewalk, from where wealthy white people could watch. Working-class whites, including Sicilians, Irish and other Caucasian immigrants, watched the parade from the sidewalk. However, blacks were not even allowed on Canal Street.[82]

Europe's biggest street festival is the Notting Hill Carnival. It was first held in 1964 when it attracted just five hundred people. Today some two million flock here (watched by more than ten thousand police), making it the second largest street festival in the world. Rooted in Trinidad's Carnival, it has a gloriously Caribbean flavour and every August Bank Holiday weekend the streets of this part of west London – Westbourne Grove, Ladbroke Grove and Kensal Road – are packed with dancers and food stalls, while the air vibrates to the sound of calypso music and steelpan bands. Floats and elaborately costumed dancers wind their way through the streets as the capital of a nation once famous for its reserve lets its hair down in style.

Jerusalem, from Hartman Schedel's *Liber Chronicarum* (*Nuremberg Chronicle*), 1493. (following page)

The House of God

Cities are built on top of earlier cities. Beneath our pavements and cellars lie countless layers of urban history preserving the compressed traces of past lives and structures – ossified timbers, shards of glass and pottery, beads from broken necklaces, paths and boardwalks leading nowhere, soles of shoes, clumps of oxidising metals that were once knife blades and tin cans. The concrete piles of today's buildings stretch down like an inverted forest through the remains of old structures. Streets that once thronged with people are cleared to make way for new walls and walkways. All the spaces in the city have been occupied before. Old maps and paintings reveal a ghostly virtual city of which only fragments remain, underground or tucked away down forgotten alleyways. Urban territory is leased to each generation. Residents and buildings are all temporary. What is permanent is the idea of the city.

In Iraq, the cradle of urbanism, the landscape is littered with the artificial hills, or tells, where cities once stood. Generation after generation built here, one on top of another. Today, these mud-brick metropolises have all collapsed into the landscape out of which they emerged, like so many deserted termite mounds.[83] London, too, is raised up on the detritus of its long history. Archaeologists have to dig down through some six metres of the city's rubbish and building debris before they reach the remains of Roman Londonium. It is, perhaps, the entropic fate of all cities to end up as an inconspicuous hill, a modest landscape feature on a future horizon.

This sense of living on top of the past was brought powerfully alive for me in Rome. The twelfth-century basilica of San Clemente lies a few minutes' walk to the east of the Colosseum. Although the medieval church has fine mosaics, its real treasure lies deep beneath them. In an annexe now used as a souvenir shop there is an unremarkable wooden door which opens on to a flight of stone steps leading down under the church. They take you back some 1,600 years. Archaeologists have discovered that the church at street level stands on top of a much earlier one, built before AD 385. Today you can walk down its nave and admire the beautifully fluid frescos on its walls, painted with colours that remain bright and vibrant. But beneath the nave of this ancient subterranean church lie yet more layers of Rome's history.

An echoing labyrinth of narrow passages and stairways leads you down to a deeper level where you can walk on the streets of first-century Rome. A house and the rooms of an official building have been excavated, as well as a narrow alleyway between them. What is still more remarkable is that here, beneath a church where pious Christians have prayed for nearly two millennia, a pagan shrine has been found. It is a mithraeum, a temple to Mithras, a god of wisdom and light once honoured in ancient India and Iran. The celebration of the mysteries of Mithras became popular in Rome around AD 100. This shrine is well preserved. It is a long chamber, like a cave, and on both sides smooth stone benches await worshippers whose bones have long since turned to dust. At the far end, now bathed in pallid fluorescent light, stands an altar with a relief of Mithras slaying the primal bull. There are, apparently, stars on the vaulted ceiling, although it was too gloomy to see them when I visited. Outside, at street level, the temperature was a suffocating 35° Celsius, but down here the air is always cold and damp. The constant noise of Rome's modern traffic is replaced by the roar of an underground river flowing just beneath your feet into the River Tiber.

Standing in front of this ancient temple, many metres below street level, the city's past is made powerfully present. The continuity between the Christian worshippers in the pews above and those who once sat on the stone benches in the mithraeum below is striking and, indeed, strangely moving. Although over time we may discard our gods, the city is always with us, irrevocably part of our soul.

The congruence of these three sacred places is a reminder, too, that religion has always been at the heart of urban life. The first glimpse travellers would have had of the ancient Egyptian city of Memphis was of the golden tips of hundreds of temple flagpoles rising up into the clear blue sky. At least a third of that city consisted of temples.[84] Similarly, the skylines of the earliest Mesopotamian cities were dominated by those imposing man-made mountains, the ziggurats. At seventy feet tall, the ziggurat at Ur – dedicated to Nannar, the Moon God – would have been visible for miles around in the flat landscape. At Babylon, Nebuchadnezzar built an even bigger ziggurat, Etemenanki, some seventy metres high, the inspiration for the myth of the Tower of Babylon.[85] Such sacred structures gave the first city builders a sense both of divine protectedness and of their connection to the cosmos.

When the city was in its infancy, living in this new man-made environment was an act of hubris that risked divine retribution. To prevent this, the first urbanists made their cities into homes for their gods. Mesopotamians believed that Babylon was the place where the gods had come to earth and it was known as Babi-ilani, or 'the Gate of the Gods'. Such foundation myths gave people divine authority to build: it was as if the gods themselves had granted a lease on the land to mortals. Other city builders sought cosmic authority in the symbolism of their urban plans. Beijing's four-square design reflected what they believed was the shape of the universe, a plan repeated in other Chinese imperial cities. Like a sun, the divine emperor sat on his throne in the Hall of Supreme Harmony (the Taihedian), in a city within a city, his divine aura radiating out across this city of walls. During the Ming and Qing dynasties, the Taihedian was the tallest building in China, because no one was allowed to build higher than the emperor. In China, city, society and cosmos were all structured alike, creating a divine harmony.

On the other side of the world, the Aztecs also believed that their great city of Tenochtitlán reflected the structure of the cosmos. Its pyramid, which was dedicated to the gods Huitzilopochtli and Tlaloc, rose like a holy mountain out of the centre of the lake. The pyramids at the earlier sacred city of Teotihuacán were still more impressive. Creating such awe-inspiring structures gave the first city builders a sense of their own power. Humankind's imperial dreams began in these urban celebrations of the divine.

From the beginning, cities were never just fortuitous concentrations of people. They were sites of deep symbolism, and their plans reflected the divine scheme of things. Their message was loud and clear: humankind was destined to live in cities. From China to Central America, to walk into a city was to move through a simulacrum of the universe.[86] Cities had cosmic significance and their inhabitants believed God, the first architect, had ordained and underwritten their urban way of life. To live in the city was to be part of this sacred purpose.

Some of the most beautiful urban structures in the world are temples: for example, the dazzling seventeenth-century Lutfullah Mosque in Isfahan, Iran, the acme of Persian architectural mosaic work;[87] the Angkor Wat temple complex in Cambodia, part of Angkor Thom, the Khmer empire's sacred 'City of the Gods' (built 1181–1219);[88] and the Temple of Amun at Karnak, Egypt (begun *c.* 2000 BC), with its vast hall in which some of the massive columns have a circumference of over thirty feet and are nearly ninety feet tall. But the most famous urban structure built to celebrate the gods is the Parthenon in Athens. Constructed between 447 and 432 BC, it is one of the most lauded examples of architecture and sculpture anywhere in the world. 'There has been nothing like it anywhere or at any period,' enthused the urban idealist Le Corbusier.[89] Many visitors have been reduced to tears by its symmetrical perfection. Its power is such that, after her visit, Virginia Woolf observed that 'our minds had been struck inarticulate by something too great for them to grasp'.[90]

The Parthenon rises above Athens like a crown on a proud but aged royal head. It is built on the Acropolis, known locally as 'the Sacred Rock'. This was originally the site of an ancient fortress, but since at least the eighth century BC it was the most sacred place in Athens, littered with countless shrines and statues of gods. The Parthenon itself stands on the remains of a far older temple destroyed during the Persian occupation. Indeed, recent restoration works revealed an ancient altar and shrine hidden in the north colonnade. Sacred sites, like cities, are architectural palimpsests, rewritten by each generation.

With eight columns at the front and seventeen along its sides, measuring some 230 feet long by 98 feet wide, the Parthenon is larger than other Greek temples. The magnificent sculptures that originally decorated the temple gables (or pediments) and the sculpted frieze that ran around the entire building, celebrated the citizens of Athens themselves. They depicted scenes from Athenian myths (such as the birth of Athena, on the front gable), their struggles with supernatural beasts and their ultimate rise to cosmic grandeur. The floor inside was of the finest polished white marble, laid in giant slabs, ten feet square. The marble wall panels at the east were thin enough to let the sun shine through with an ethereal translucence.[91]

Inside towered a forty-foot statue of the city's virgin goddess: Athena Parthenos. She was built using a wooden frame overlaid with a skin of ivory and a garment of gold. Such chryselephantine constructions (as they are known) were not uncommon at this time and classical writers joked that these hallowed but hollow statues provided ideal homes for mice. Athena was also known as 'the Champion' and she was portrayed as a goddess of war. She wore a helmet on which was a sphinx and two griffins, and on her breastplate was emblazoned the hideous head of the gorgon Medusa. In one hand she carried a spear, while in the other she held the figure of the goddess Victory.[92] In front of Athena was a reflecting pool. The statue must have overwhelmed visitors with its size and splendour – the Statue of Liberty of her day.

But the Parthenon was not a conventional temple: there were no priests and no rituals took place here. There was not even the customary altar outside. Built on the easily defended Acropolis, the Parthenon also served as a very secure treasury containing the city's reserves, as well as thank-offerings to the goddess. In its long history, the Parthenon has been transformed into a Christian cathedral – rededicated to another sacred maiden, the Virgin Mary – and, from the fifteenth century, a mosque. The Parthenon had survived intact until 1687 when, in a gross act of cultural vandalism, Venetian armies bombarded it with cannon fire, igniting gunpowder stored there by the Ottoman Turks. The central parts and half of the columns were completely destroyed. One of the world's greatest buildings was reduced to a ruin. The ancient structure then fell prey to Athenians scavenging building materials and others hunting for souvenirs. Lord Elgin's now infamous removal of the sculptures from the exterior at the beginning of the nineteenth century (half of which still remain in the British Museum) was described by an eyewitness as 'insensate barbarism'.[93]

Today, after extensive reconstruction works during which every block of stone has been bar-coded and its history meticulously recorded, the Parthenon rises once again above Athens, a haunting reminder of the achievements of one of the world's most influential urban cultures. For ancient Greeks, the 'polis' was not just a city but, as Richard Sennett has said, the 'place where people achieved unity'. For the citizens of Athens, as well as being a sacred structure, the Parthenon was an 'icon of unity', visible across the city.[94] Far more than a temple, it became a monument to the Athenian people themselves, to their urban dreams and aspirations.

According to one historian, 'the most interesting of all urban phenomena' is the holy city.[95] Every city has sacred places – shrines, temples, churches – but a holy city is one that contains a sacrum of such spiritual power that it attracts people not just from the city's hinterland but from a vast area, potentially from the whole world. The city of Kyoto, for example, is the focus of a pilgrimage network that extends throughout Japan and even further afield. The capital of Japan from AD 794 to the mid-nineteenth century, it contains no fewer than 1700 Zen Buddhist temples and 300 Shinto shrines. There are also some two hundred exquisite gardens, including those at the largest Zen temple complex, Daitoku-ji, where you can contemplate the raked, white gravel of the 'Sea of Nothingness'. In northern India, Varanasi (or Benares as it was once known) is the most ancient city on the River Ganges and is known as the 'city of temples'. It is sacred for Hindus, Jains and Buddhists and over a million pilgrims come here each year. When he visited at the end of the nineteenth century, Mark Twain was awed by Varanasi, describing the teeming, shrine-packed city as a 'religious Vesuvius': 'Benares is older than history, older than tradition, older even than legend, and looks twice as old as all of them put together … Yes, the city of Benares is in effect just a big church, a religious hive, whose every cell is a temple, a shrine or a mosque, and whose every conceivable earthly and heavenly good is procurable under one roof, so to speak – a sort of Army and Navy Stores, theologically stocked.'[96]

For Hindus, Varanasi is the most important place of pilgrimage. As the sun rises, thousands of Hindus descend the many stone steps (or 'ghats') to bathe in the sacred Ganges, cleansing their bodies of sin as they have done for centuries. Along the banks of the river smoke rises from the many pyres on which burn the remains of Hindus on their final pilgrimage. To die in this ancient holy city will, they

The Sacred Mosque, Masjid al-Haram, in Mecca, during the Hajj.

believe, enable them to escape the eternal cycle of death and rebirth. For millennia, Varanasi has been a way station for the faithful on their journey from this world to the next.

There can be no doubt, however, that the two most famous holy cities are Mecca and Jerusalem. Mecca, in the Red Sea region of Hejaz, western Saudi Arabia, is the holiest city in Islam. According to Sarra III, in the Koran: 'The first house established for the people was that at [Mecca], a place holy, and a guidance to all beings. Therein are clear signs – the station of Abraham, and whosoever enters it is in security. It is the duty of all men towards God to come to the House a pilgrim, if he is able to make his way there.'[97] Home to the world's largest mosque, Masjid al-Haram, up to four million Muslims flock here during the Hajj. Today, whole swathes of the city around the mosque have been razed to accommodate these vast numbers of people.

In 1326, Abu Abdallah ibn Battuta described travelling to Mecca as part of a 'hajj' caravan of some twenty thousand people. Before entering the city they ritually cleansed themselves, and donned a special garment ('ihram') signifying their state of consecration.[98] They then proceeded to the Sacred Mosque (the Haram, or Sanctuary). At the centre of this stands the Ka'ba, the holy stone structure, kept shrouded in a black veil, around which hajjis have to circumambulate, walking seven times anti-clockwise while praying. It is a profound religious experience for pilgrims. Ibn Jubayr visited in 1183. 'The contemplation of the venerable House,' he wrote, 'is an awful sight which distracts the senses in amazement, and ravishes the heart and mind.'[99] Non-Muslims are forbidden from entering Mecca. Richard Burton risked his life by disguising himself and visiting the mosque in 1853 and was immensely impressed by the experience. 'The view was strange, unique,' he said. 'Of all the worshippers who clung weeping to the curtain, or who pressed their beating hearts to the stone, none felt for the moment a deeper emotion than did [I].'[100]

The Ka'ba is a windowless building some fifty feet high with a single door seven foot above the ground. Inside, three wooden pillars support the roof. Lamps of silver and gold hang down above a copy of the Koran. In the eastern corner of the outer wall is embedded the sacred Black Stone, about twelve inches across, which is believed to have fallen from the skies and to have been kissed by the Prophet. It is a 'betyl' (a sacred rock embodying a deity) which was once carried around by nomads (rather like the Israelite's Ark of the Covenant) and

Cathedral City

For religious zealots, urban life has often appeared to be a threat to spirituality. The cities of Sodom and Gomorrah, apparently destroyed by God for their sinfulness, exemplify this perceived danger. In the fifth century AD, Augustine's *The City of God* depicted Rome as the 'earthly city', a place of wickedness that deserved to be punished by God. He wanted Christians to turn their eyes from short-term material gain to the spiritual world, and to the ideal city of God.[101]

Jerusalem has had a profound impact on religious architecture in European cities. The geometrically perfect celestial city of the Book of Revelation became 'the lodestone of the medieval image of a holy city'.[102] The New Jerusalem was the city of the saved after the Last Judgement. It symbolised the spiritual perfection to which Christians aspired: 'there is no eternal city for us in this life but we look for one in the life to come.'[103] Made of gold and precious stones, this fantastical four-square city inspired the architecture of Christian churches. The great European cathedrals became 'the figure of Jerusalem'.[104] With their jewel-like stained-glass windows and typically three entrances in the west front – which, as at Chartres, sometimes bore no relation to the

The west front of Chartres Cathedral, France, begun in the twelfth century.

layout of nave and aisles – cathedrals echoed the design of the New Jerusalem, with its three gates in each wall.

The Holy Roman Emperor, Charlemagne, kept St Augustine's *City of God* beside his bed and sought to realise the Holy City in the architecture of his religious buildings. His abbeys, such as Saint-Denis, north of Paris, were miniature holy cities, symbolising his divine right to rule, in the same way as the imperial cities of China. Charlemagne's abbeys became the models for the Gothic churches of the High Middle Ages, their stained-glass windows evoking the jewel-encrusted walls of the New Jerusalem.

In the twelfth century, the adviser to the French crown, Abbot Suger, was responsible for the influential redesign of Saint-Denis. Walking into the rebuilt church was, he said, like entering Jerusalem itself. Churches were no longer to be mere receptacles for relics but passages into a new, spiritual world. The devout left the city of man in the street outside and, once inside the cathedral, they entered the city of God. Indeed, many European cathedrals at this time had a labyrinth design traced on their floors with Jerusalem at the centre, so that penitents could make a spiritual pilgrimage to the Holy City on their knees.

originally housed in a Bedouin tent. When they settled in Mecca it was placed in the Ka'ba. Muslims believe the original Ka'ba was built by God for Adam, destroyed in the Flood and rebuilt by Abraham.[105] Muhammad, a successful merchant in this desert trading city, lived here in the seventh century. Then it was a frontier town, just forty acres of unexceptional mud-brick houses. But in the following century, Mecca doubled in size and has never stopped growing, thanks to the pilgrims – a testament to the way religion can transform the fortunes of a city.

Inhabited for the last five thousand years, Jerusalem has the good – some might say bad – fortune to have become the focus of veneration for three of the great monotheistic religions that have shaped the course of human history. Jews, Christians and Muslims – the spiritual descendants of Abraham – all claim the city as their own. Temple Mount is said to have been where Abraham prepared to sacrifice his son, Isaac. When it was captured in *c.* 1000 BC by David, the first Judaean king, it was known as Zion. After King David's death, his son, Solomon, built the famous Temple, a four-square building of cedar wood and unhewn stone, in which was placed the sacred Ark of the Covenant. Solomon's Temple was destroyed by the Babylonian king Nebuchadnezzar in 586 BC but rebuilt, first in 516 BC and then again, by Herod the Great, from AD 20 to 62. This was the Temple that existed during the life of Jesus Christ. But it stood for just eight years before being destroyed again, this time by the Romans. The Wailing Wall – part of the second temple – is the holiest site in Judaism. Jews recite the words of their sacred texts here and push written prayers into the cracks between the historic stones. They believe that one day the Temple will be rebuilt with the coming of the Jewish Messiah.

The Dome of the Rock (Qubbat al-Sakhra) on Temple Mount is the city's holiest Muslim shrine (built 691). It marks the spot where Muslims believe Muhammad ascended into heaven. A shrine rather than a mosque, it is 'a marvellously sophisticated and elegant building' with an ambulatory for the liturgical 'tawaf' (circling) of a sacred rock, as at Mecca.[106] The Al-Aqsa Mosque is also on Temple Mount.

St Paul regarded Jerusalem as the home of the first Christian congregation. The Roman Emperor Constantine the Great built the Church of the Holy Sepulchre (*c.* 335) over the rock tomb where Christ was believed to have been buried and to have risen from the dead. It is at the heart of the Christian city. For medieval Christians,

Jerusalem was the *axis mundi*, the centre of the world. As access to the real city of Jerusalem became increasingly dangerous after the seventh century, when it came under the control of Muslim forces, European Christians created alternative pilgrimage sites.

In the Middle Ages, one of the most popular European sites was Santiago de Compostela, attracting 15,000 English pilgrims alone in the fifteenth century.[107] Since the fourth century, Rome, the Eternal City, had attracted Christian pilgrims. In the sixteenth century, Pope Sixtus v designed an ambitious street plan for Rome to allow pilgrims to visit different basilicas corresponding to the 'stations' of Christ's life. In Sixtus's master plan of 1589, roads linked the seven main churches and shrines that pilgrims needed to visit in a day. Sixtus was creating a holy city, turning Rome into 'a single holy shrine'.[108] The idea was that one could travel on foot, by carriage or on horseback virtually in a straight line to visit all the sites of devotion. During his brief time as Pope (1585–90), Sixtus transformed Rome. The change was so sudden and complete that a priest returning after the death of Sixtus remarked: 'Everything seems to be new, edifices, streets, squares, fountains, aqueducts, obelisks.'[109] The historian of architectural Modernism Sigfried Giedion describes Sixtus as 'the first of the modern town planners'.[110] He transformed Rome from a city of narrow medieval streets into a triumphal capital city of squares and broad avenues. But the great achievement of Sixtus was also to create a holy city, one where the sacred became part of daily life.

Chimneys on the Casa Milà (1906–10) in Barcelona, designed by Antonio Gaudí. (following page)

4 WHERE TO STAY

Downtown

For many years, downtown was the vibrant heart of the American city. Every city had one – a pulsing commercial centre where you would find the banks, businesses, hotels, department stores and theatres. Downtown was the economic powerhouse of the city and the region, and every day a tidal wave of workers, clients and shoppers would sweep in and out of it, a human ingress and egress that became known as rush hour. Downtown was where businessmen came to make deals, where ladies came to buy the latest fashions, and where foreign visitors came to marvel at the astonishing vigour and dynamism of America's commercial life.

If London was the city that defined urban expectations in the nineteenth century, then New York was the iconic metropolis of the twentieth. London's geography created the idea of the fashionable, upper-class West End and the *déclassé* East End. Similarly, it was the physical layout of New York that produced the now global concept of 'downtown'. To go downtown in nineteenth-century New York meant to go downstream of the rivers, to make your way south down the island of Manhattan, until you passed Houston Street. Uptown was the suburban north of the island, specifically the avenues either side of Central Park. However, it is possible that London may also have helped inspire the idea of a commercial downtown. After the Great Fire of 1666, London was rebuilt according to the former medieval street plan, much to the disgust of Christopher Wren, who had drawn up a grand design for its rebuilding in the style of sixteenth-century

Interior of the Burj Al Arab hotel (2000), Dubai. At more than 300 metres high, it is one of the tallest hotels in the world.

Rome. But the way it was used changed: its business section – known as the City – became distinct from surrounding residential districts: a commercial hub at the centre of the teeming metropolis and an antecedent of the modern downtown.[1]

By 1830, New York was America's largest city with a population of 250,000, a figure that would soar to 1.5 million within a mere forty years.[2] As the city became increasingly successful, New Yorkers began using 'downtown' to refer specifically to the booming business district. Here, as firms moved in, so well-to-do families moved out, eager to escape the hustle and bustle of the centre for quieter districts. In 1851, the word 'downtown' had its first literary outing in Herman Melville's *Moby-Dick* in a passage about Manhattan: 'Its extreme down-town is the battery, where that noble mole is washed by waves, and cooled by breezes, which a few hours previous were out of sight of land.'[3]

By the 1870s, 'downtown' was used across America to denote the urban core where men went to work and women to shop.[4] As the new century dawned, every American city had its own thriving downtown. Chicago was probably the fastest growing city in the world at this time and its downtown, also known as The Loop, was as busy as the floor of the New York Stock Exchange during trading, according to one journalist.[5] In the early 1900s, the word 'downtown' began appearing in dictionaries. It was a word and a place that was uniquely American. In England people referred to the city centre, and in France to 'le centre de ville'. For Spaniards it was 'el centro', for Germans 'das Zentrum', and Italians 'il centro'.[6] Today, the idea of downtown has gone global and is heard everywhere from Baghdad to Shanghai. The boomtowns of the New World redefined our way of describing – and thus understanding – the urban environment. There is an irony in this, though, for the story of downtown in America during the second half of the twentieth century was one of decline.

In their heyday, downtowns were the engines of the economy: a busy downtown represented not just a healthy city but symbolised the vitality of America itself, at a time when the country was becoming an economic and political player on the world stage. All the city's financial institutions were located here, as were most professional offices and also – at least until the end of the nineteenth century – some light industries. Bankers, insurance brokers, lawyers, realtors, architects, engineers, accountants, office workers, salesgirls, as well as craftsmen and labourers – all streamed into downtown each day to work. Courts and government agencies were here, as well as hotels and restaurants. There were cultural institutions, too, such as museums and galleries, as well as theatres, music halls and other places of entertainment. People also came downtown to shop in the great department stores – on Market Street in Philadelphia, State Street in Chicago and in New York on Broadway. One observer in 1893 remarked that Fulton Street ('the Broadway of Brooklyn') was a vision of 'what Eden might have been were Adam and his part in life dispensed with'.[7] But downtown was not just the economic heart of the city – it was at the centre of people's lives. Jack Thomas, a columnist on the *Boston Globe*, recalled that as a child downtown was where you first visited Father Christmas, where your mother came to help her daughter choose her wedding dress, where you bought furniture for your first home, and where, 'with a sense of the cycles of life, you returned so that your own daughter could visit Santa'.[8]

Congestion in Philadelphia in 1897, as horse-drawn wagons and carriages, an electric streetcar and pedestrians share the same street.

Downtown generated the wealth of the city. In 1897, says historian Robert M. Fogelson, 'more trade was done in downtown Chicago than in the rest of the city combined'.[9] But although downtown was economically vital, it was geographically tiny: Chicago's covered just three-quarters of a square mile in a city of 169 square miles. Even in the 1930s, it was still no more than a square mile. New York's downtown was somewhat bigger, but still smaller than Central Park. And you could stroll round Boston's downtown in an hour (a three-mile walk). As their influence grew, downtowns expanded vertically rather than horizontally. Soon you could find downtown simply by looking at a city's skyline. Downtown was where the tallest office buildings were located, rising some ten to fifteen storeys by 1890. Chicago's twelve-storey Rookery Building was completed in 1888 and stood 181 feet high. It was described as 'a little city in itself', containing everything a businessman could need, from banks and restaurants, to barbers and bootblacks.[10] With the introduction of steel-framed buildings, the sky itself became the limit for downtown architecture.

117

Even by the 1880s, at least half a million people were flooding downtown in New York each morning. Hundreds of thousands more crossed the East and Hudson rivers from Brooklyn and New Jersey. What later became known as 'rush hour' in New York occurred from 7 to 9 a.m. and 5 to 7 p.m. A Parisian visitor to the city was astonished: 'Neither the boulevards, the Strand, nor the Corso of Rome in carnival time can give an idea of this tumultuous movement.'[11] This human ebb and flow centred on downtown occurred in cities across America. As many as 80 per cent travelled by street railway, horse-drawn carriages that ran on tracks, first introduced in the 1830s. These were the arteries of the city, conveying hundreds of thousands of people into downtown. The American streetcar system was unrivalled anywhere in the world. By 1890 (when lines were being electrified), nearly eight hundred companies operated more than 32,000 streetcars on six thousand miles of tracks. They carried some two billion passengers, twice as many as in the rest of the world combined. Unsurprisingly, the streetcars were all overcrowded. 'People are packed into them like sardines in a box, with perspiration for oil,' complained one commuter in 1864.[12]

New Yorkers spent more than two hours each day commuting. The streets were jammed with traffic and if the sidewalks hadn't been equally packed it would have been quicker to walk.[13] On one day in the 1880s, over 22,000 vehicles passed the intersection of Broadway and Fulton Street between 7 a.m. and 6 p.m. – that's one every two seconds. Traffic was often at a standstill for ten minutes or more on Broadway. One eyewitness described the chaos in the 1880s: 'for those who are not obliged to cross the choked-up thoroughfare, the scene is full of a brief amusement – hack-drivers, truckmen, omnibus drivers, swearing vehemently at each other, or indignantly railing at the delay, and police officers yelling and waving their clubs in their attempts to get the machinery of travel again moving smoothly'.[14]

From the 1870s, New Yorkers could also travel on the elevated railways, or 'els', an innovative though controversial attempt to resolve the problem of congestion. In 1898, Boston opened the first American subway, a 1.5-mile stretch for streetcars running under Tremont Street, the centre of the retail district. After years of opposition, the New York subway opened in 1904, running for twenty-one miles under Broadway and up the West Side. Both systems proved popular and in New York the subway was soon carrying hundreds of millions of passengers a year. In contrast to public transport systems in European cities, those in America were designed specifically to take people downtown.

As downtowns became ever busier and more congested, fewer people wanted to live there. The rising price of land tempted many homeowners to sell up to commercial property developers. By the end of the nineteenth century, the population of downtown was falling steadily at a time when the overall population of cities was rising. People were escaping what one newspaper editor described as 'the moral and physical miasma of the metropolis'.[15] Downtown's loss was suburbia's gain. For this was the beginning of America's enduring love affair with suburbia, the dream of a semi-rural bourgeois utopia. For the middle classes this meant a single-family home surrounded by trees and a white picket fence. Suburbia transformed the metropolis in America: as the nineteenth century drew to a close, there was a clear separation of homes and businesses. Soon every American city had two hearts. A British visitor to Chicago described the radical difference between the two: 'In the one – height, narrowness, noise, monotony, dirt, sordid squalor, pretentiousness; in the other – light, space, moderation, homelikeness.'[16] And there was no doubting where most Americans wanted to live.

Up to the 1920s, downtown remained 'the city's vortex', as Chicago sociologist Harvey Warren Zorbaugh described it. On a typical weekday in 1927 about 825,000 people commuted into downtown Boston, more than the entire population of the city and a third of the population of the metropolitan district. Nearly three million flooded into downtown New York. If you lived in a big city in America at this time, the chances are that you went downtown every working day. But the role of downtown was changing. The flight to the suburbs had 'transformed the landscape of urban America' by the late 1920s.[17] People began to talk about the 'central business district' rather than downtown in the 1930s. For on the fringes of the city, new business districts were emerging that began to compete with downtown for shopping and for office space. As the *Atlanta Constitution* observed in 1929, more than one of these outlying districts had become 'a complete city within itself'.[18]

One of the main factors driving the emergence of these new business centres and the growth of suburbia was the internal combustion engine. In 1915, the millionth Model T Ford was produced at

Highland Park, in Detroit, Michigan.[19] By 1920, there were eight million private cars in America. In 1930, that figure had risen to twenty-three million. More than 100,000 cars came into downtown Chicago each weekday and more than 250,000 into Los Angeles, where there was now one private car for every two people. By 1941, more than 50 per cent of Angelinos were using their own cars to get into town. Only in New York did the use of public transport remain high, with less than 20 per cent going downtown by car. The car accelerated the fall of downtown, speeding the flight of middle-class refugees from the big city and leaving behind an urban underclass living in increasingly run-down residential areas. A spiral of decline set in: as the wealthier classes chased the suburban dream, the infrastructure of the urban core became neglected. Dilapidated buildings and worsening social problems in the inner city only hastened the haemorrhage of the middle classes to the urban fringes.

By the 1950s it seemed as if Los Angeles – the world's most decentralised metropolis – was the model for the city of the future. Across America, suburbs were growing four times as fast as the central cities. Once people had been thrilled by going downtown. Now the prospect of packed sidewalks and traffic jams, as well as the noise, dirt and an increasing fear of crime meant that most people regarded going downtown as an ordeal. Falls in retail sales at this time in downtowns reveal the trend: people were staying in their own suburban neighbourhoods.

Even as a location for business, downtown began to lose its appeal. In 1969, 11 per cent of the US's largest companies had their headquarters in the suburbs. By 1994, as many as 50 per cent had moved out of town.[20] In the last quarter of the twentieth century downtown was in crisis. Some cities had experienced a dramatic hollowing out of populations and a near-terminal decline of downtown areas. In 1900, the future of downtown Manhattan seemed rosy: a newspaper depicted downtown New York in 1999 as a towering commercial metropolis, its huge skyscrapers linked by elevated walkways with flat roofs for airships. Bridges and tunnels linked Manhattan Island with its residential districts, channelling the flood of people into the hive of commercial activity that was the future downtown.[21] But the reality was that, by the 1980s, crime and social deprivation had turned New York City into a place of fear. John Carpenter's film *Escape from New York* (1981) depicted a future city that had been abandoned by its ordinary citizens and turned into a vast prison camp. This was downtown as every suburbanite's worst nightmare.

The decline of downtown, or the central city, was a troubling feature of late twentieth-century urban life around the world. In the 1970s and 1980s, British cities appeared to be following the example of the United States. 'White flight' to the suburbs had left hollowed-out inner cities populated with low-income, ethnic minority families, struggling with run-down housing, high crime and other social problems. London's population had been 8.5 million in the 1940s, but it had dropped as low as 6.7 million by 1986.[22] In South Africa, Johannesburg's central Hillbrow district was home to the city's major financial institutions, such as the stock exchange, until the end of apartheid in 1994. But now most have relocated to the suburban centres of Sandton and Rosebank, 'surrounded by a fast expanding sea of walled shopping centres and gated residential communities, inhabited by white families and the emerging class of economically empowered blacks'.[23] This flight to the suburbs has left a city centre full of deserted hotels and office blocks and a population consisting of an impoverished urban underclass. Other cities have coped better. Osaka used to be the most densely populated city in Japan, but although central Osaka has also experienced a dramatic hollowing out of its residential population, the downtown remains a vibrant centre for business and entertainment. Here suburbanisation has not meant the death of downtown.[24]

In the twenty-first century, despite the fact that the majority of Americans now live in the suburbs, there are signs of a revival in the fortunes of downtown. For the first time, people – mostly young professionals – are beginning to move back into the centre, even in such a decentralised city as Los Angeles, where 450,000 commuters travel into downtown every day. Living in a downtown loft apartment means you can avoid the city's appalling traffic congestion. Indeed, since 1999 the Los Angeles authorities have encouraged the conversion of old office buildings – many of which were standing empty – into residential use. This has revitalised downtown, which comprises Chinatown, the Civic Center, the Artists District, South Park, Little Tokyo and the Old Bank District. According to a photographer who has moved back into downtown Los Angeles, 'there's energy here compared with the rest of LA, which is much more laid back'.[25]

Other American cities are following Los Angeles' example and now urban populations are growing again after decades of decline. At the same time poverty rates have been falling in cities.[26] This drift back to the cities is happening at a time when concerns about climate change are highlighting the benefits of living in dense population centres. Cities have a smaller carbon footprint than the dispersed communities of suburbia. The need to reduce car dependency has also led to a renewed interest in public transit systems in American cities.

Tourism is helping to revitalise downtowns too. Residents and visitors are being drawn back into the city centre to enjoy cafés and restaurants, as well as arts and music venues.[27] The meaning of downtown is once again changing, from an economic hub to a historic city centre, a focus of cultural and civic activity, giving America's downtowns a more European flavour. At long last, it appears that an urban renaissance is spreading across America and Europe. In Paris, for example, it has been estimated that 10 per cent of the city's residents are 'urban nomads', part-time city dwellers who come for the cultural events that only a big city can support – opera, theatre, art exhibitions as well as international sporting events and conferences.[28]

On the Waterfront

As the dominance of the central city has waned in the post-industrial era, so new urban centres have emerged. The waterfront is one of these. Some of the most important redevelopments of the 1980s and 1990s were waterfront revitalisation projects, transforming areas that had become industrial wastelands, including London's Canary Wharf, New York's Battery Park City, Sydney's Darling Harbour, San Francisco's Mission Bay and Vancouver's Granville Island.

In the nineteenth century, the waterfront was one of the busiest parts of the city, where goods manufactured locally were shipped out and foreign products imported. It was the city's interface with the world. In the second half of the twentieth century, container transport meant that many of these historic port facilities had to be abandoned, leaving large derelict areas in the city centre. The redevelopment of such sites has allowed the city to rediscover the water's edge and even to forge a new urban identity, attracting new industries. This happened in the 1990s in Bilbao, Spain, with the transformation of the industrial Abandoibarra district and the building of the visually stunning Guggenheim Museum (Frank Gehry, 1997). The port city of Shanghai has also experienced an astonishing revival. The historic Bund has been reconstructed and the Pudong district on the opposite side of Huangpu River transformed from farmland into China's

Cities have changed significantly over the last century and downtown is not the place it used to be. People no longer commute en masse to the downtown, and neither do they do their shopping exclusively there. Thanks to new transport and communication technologies, cities have become amorphous structures, with new urban centres emerging on the peripheries amidst the ubiquitous suburban sprawl. 'In its present incarnation,' writes Deyan Sudjic, 'the old centre is just another piece on the board, a counter that has perhaps the same weight as the airport, or the medical centre, or the museum complex. They all swim in a soup of shopping malls, hypermarkets and warehouses, drive-in restaurants and anonymous industrial sheds, beltways and motorway boxes.'[29] This is the age of the Edge City and 'the hundred-mile city', where the old distinctions between urban and suburban are being demolished and the central city is being eclipsed by the new, expanding 'exopolis'.[30] But downtown has not disappeared as some predicted. The bright lights of the big city centre are still burning. The excitement of earlier years may have faded, but the heart is still beating.

premiere financial and commercial hub with a soaring skyline.

The redevelopment of Baltimore's Inner Harbor in the 1960s was a pioneering waterfront project. It was a direct response to the suburban flight that occurred in the 1950s. The Charles Center-Inner Harbor Redevelopment Program was one of the first public–private partnerships of the post-industrial era. From 1960 to 1995 some twelve million square feet of floor space was created, more than $3 billion invested in construction, and 15,000 jobs generated. Some property values in blocks in the Inner Harbor increased by an astounding 600 per cent. The redevelopment created a lucrative tourism industry, with 6.5 million visitors spending $3 billion in 1999.[31] As well as

Baltimore's, among the most successful waterfront schemes are those in Boston, San Diego, Cape Town, Vancouver and Yokohama.

Houses at Granville Island, Vancouver, Canada.

Chinatown, Little Italy and the Ghetto

'The air is laden with the fumes of smoking sandalwood and strange odours of the East; and the streets, swarming with coolies, resound with the echoes of an unknown tongue. There is hardly room for us to pass; we pick our way, and are sometimes curiously regarded by slanted-eyed pagans.'[32] This was written in 1901, by the American author Charles Warren Stoddard. He was describing his experiences not in the streets of Shanghai or Beijing, but in an American city: San Francisco.

San Francisco's Chinatown was, says historian Yong Chen, 'the first permanent urban settlement that Chinese pioneers established in the New World'.[33] The Chinese came to San Francisco initially during the Gold Rush of 1848, but over time it became the largest Chinese American community in the United States. Despite being levelled in the devastating 1906 earthquake and subsequent fire, San Francisco's Chinatown rose again like a phoenix from the ashes to become the social and cultural capital of Chinese America. Today it is home to more than 150,000 Chinese Americans, some 20 per cent of the total number in the United States, and it boasts one of the largest Chinese New Year parades outside Asia, featuring a 200-foot Golden Dragon carried by a team of a hundred people.

San Francisco's Chinatown began life as a gateway between Old and New Worlds. Hundreds of thousands of people flowed in and out of the city, mostly from the south Chinese port of Canton (now Guangzhou), in the Pearl River region. Between 1848 and 1876, 233,136 Chinese arrived in San Francisco, while in the same period 93,272 left America through the city to return to their homeland. Wherever they were, this migrant population referred to San Francisco's Chinatown as 'dabu', meaning 'the big city' or 'the first city', to distinguish it from the smaller Chinatowns emerging in other American cities.[34]

At first, in the 1850s, there were just two to three thousand Chinese living in what became known as 'Little China', occupying two blocks between Sacramento and Jackson Streets, and Kearny and Stockton Streets. But after 1860, the Chinese population here rapidly increased and within a decade there were 12,000 living in San Francisco, representing 8 per cent of the city's population – the largest Chinese community in America. The vast majority were men: there were just 1,410 women, of whom records suggest some 1,132 were prostitutes and eighteen brothel keepers.[35] Because there were so few women in their community, Chinese men in San Francisco regarded prostitution as indispensable. The number of brothels as well as the popularity of opium dens and gambling in Chinatown meant that the area soon became associated with criminality in the minds of many Americans.

Racism and hostility towards Chinese immigrants was widespread in America. Few white landlords would rent rooms to Chinese people, which meant that they had no alternative but to live in Chinatown. By the end of the 1870s there were thirty thousand Chinese living in San Francisco. By now Chinatown had expanded to almost eight blocks; within ten years it grew still further, to twelve blocks. Although the Chinese were effectively forced to live in this area by the prejudices of the majority population, Chinatown was not what we might now think of as an impoverished ghetto. On the contrary: it always had a dynamic, thriving economy. Indeed, the industriousness of the Chinese earned the respect even of white Americans: 'Other laborers clamor for a working-day of eight hours. The Chinaman patiently works seventeen, takes care of his relatives in China, looks after his own poor in America, and pays his bills as he goes along.'[36] Many Chinese worked in laundries and manufacturing, especially garment making. The original economic heart of Chinatown, with some forty-six Chinese businesses in 1856, was Sacramento Street. In the Chinese community this was known as 'Tangren Jie' (the 'street of Chinese people') and this has now become a synonym for Chinatown itself, a measure of its importance.[37]

There were Chinese-language newspapers in the city from as early as 1854, when *The Golden Hills' News* became the first American paper with a Chinese section. Articles often focused on practical aspects of life in the New World, such as how to survive in America, or 'the Flowery-Flag Country' as the Chinese called it.[38] Chinese theatres played a vital role in maintaining the community's cultural identity. There was a regular Chinese dramatic company in San Francisco from 1852 and by 1875 there were no fewer than eleven troupes, each with at least twenty-eight actors, many of them women. There were four regular theatres (on Jackson and Washington Streets), each employing forty to fifty people. Troupes often came to San Francisco from the province of Guangdong and they generally performed Cantonese operas, with their casts of larger-than-life characters and historical stories with strong moral messages. In 1896, a writer for

Century Illustrated Magazine described the Chinese actor as 'the very embodiment of dignity, while the quintessence of etiquette marks his manners. He endeavors to conceal rather than betray emotion.'[39] The daily and nightly performances were watched by thousands of people, some of whom went more than once a day. Theatres were even known to waive the entry charge for those most hard up.

As well as being poignant reminders of home, these performances were social events, a chance to meet and exchange news with people from China and cities across America. For many years, San Francisco's was the only Chinatown with theatres. From the end of the nineteenth century, white tourists began coming to Chinatown for a glimpse of the Orient. In about 1900, Joseph Carey observed, 'no visit to Chinatown would be complete without an inspection of its theatre and study of the audience'. But few white Americans found the noisy Cantonese operas to their taste ('the performance goes on amid a hideous beating of drums and gongs') and, sadly, most of them left perplexed, even vaguely appalled, by this experience of an unfamiliar culture.[40]

Today you will find a Chinatown in nearly every great city, from Auckland in New Zealand to Yokohama, near Tokyo. Tourists flock to them, if not to visit Chinese theatres then certainly to their restaurants

A shop in San Francisco's Chinatown in the 1890s. The original caption states that 'a trip to Chinatown is an essential feature of a visit to the Pacific coast'.

to eat the delicious steamed and deep-fried dumplings known as dim sum. In London, Chinatown had been located around the Limehouse docks area since the early nineteenth century. Concerns about drug-taking and prostitution led the council to begin clearing the area between the wars. The Blitz finished the job, levelling the area, and after the war restaurants began opening in what is today's Chinatown, centred on Lisle and Gerrard Streets, in central London.[41]

Migrants have always been essential to the success of cities. The unique dynamism and creativity found in cities stems in great part from their cultural and ethnic diversity. As well as a Chinatown, large cities may also have a Little Italy, a Kleindeutschland (Little Germany), an Irishtown, a Poletown, a hispanic *barrio* (in North America), a Little India, or a Banglatown. Brick Lane in London's East End was home to Huguenot refugees in the eighteenth century, to East European Jews in the nineteenth century (when it was known as Little Jerusalem) and Bengali immigrants in the second half of the twentieth century. Today it is known around the world as Banglatown. It is the setting for Monica Ali's novel *Brick Lane* and in Salman Rushdie's *The Satanic Verses* it is called 'Brickhall'. There is even a road named after Brick Lane in Dhaka, the teeming capital of Bangladesh from where many of the area's most recent arrivals originated.[42]

While walking through a city you might come across shop signs written in an unfamiliar script – Hebrew lettering around the Pletzl in Paris's Marais or in Rome's Jewish Ghetto, for instance. This is often the first indication that you have crossed into another part of the world. There are no visible borders in the city but if you turn down one street you might find shops selling filled bagels and pastries, while in another there are Balti houses, and round the corner you will see roasted Peking ducks hanging up in the windows of Chinese restaurants. Not only does this make the metropolis a gourmet's delight, but this seamless tapestry of cultures is integral to urban life. Jacob Riis, writing at the end of the nineteenth century, wonderfully captured the multicultural mix of that most cosmopolitan of cities – Manhattan: 'A map of the city, colored to designate nationalities, would show more stripes than on the skin of a zebra, and more colors than any rainbow. The city on such a map would fall into two great halves, green for the Irish prevailing in the West Side tenement districts, and blue for Germans on the East Side. But intermingled with these ground colors would be an odd variety of tints that would give the whole the appearance of an extraordinary crazy-quilt.[43]

A city is like a country with many provinces. But the map of its diversity is constantly changing shape and colour, as national and global pressures create waves of migration that flow through cities like a blush across a cheek. To use the phrase coined by Israel Zangwill in his 1909 play of the same name, the modern city is in some senses a 'melting pot' of nationalities. And as international travel has become easier, the city has increasingly turned into a microcosm of the planet: the city of nations has become a reflection of the global village.

By the beginning of the twentieth century, New York City was home to more Italians than were living in Genoa, Florence and Venice combined. Most of the 5.3 million Italians who emigrated to the United States came through New York City (via Ellis Island). Today this is still where the greatest concentration of Americans of Italian descent live. Indeed, New York has been described as 'the Italian-American capital of the United States', and has been the inspiration for countless novels and films, such as Mario Puzo's *The Godfather* (1969) and Sergio Leone's *Once Upon a Time in America* (1984), as well as the TV series *The Sopranos* (1999-2007).[44]

Manhattan's Little Italy dates back to the second half of the nineteenth century. Within the space of a few years street life was transformed as immigrants, mostly from southern Italy, brought Mediterranean culture to the New World. There were noisy (and not always welcomed) organ grinders on street corners and colourful religious processions, such as the one H. C. Brunner came across in 1893. 'Six sturdy Italians struggle along under the weight of a mighty temple or pavilion, all made of coloured candles,' Brunner wrote, 'the great big candles of the Roman Church, mighty candles, six and eight feet tall, around a statue of the Virgin … And before and behind them are bands and drum-corps and societies with banners, and it is all a blare of martial music and primary colors the whole length of the street.[45]

Little Italy, where the first Italians settled in the 1850s, was originally called the Five Points. This notorious area contained some of New York's most overcrowded buildings, including the city's first five-storey tenement, and was the subject of Herbert Asbury's 1928 crime book *The Gangs of New York*, the inspiration for Scorsese's 2002 film. Located just below 'Kleindeutschland', Little Italy was near what is today Columbus Park. Eventually it expanded east to the Bowery, west to Lafayette Street and north almost as far as Houston Street. Although today Little Italy has been absorbed by New York's Chinatown (centred on Mott Street), Mulberry Street remains the historic heart of the Italian area. In the early years Little Italy itself reflected the different regions of Italy – Neapolitans on Mulberry Street, Genoese on Bleecker and Baxter Streets, and Pugliesi on Hester Street. On some blocks, families from one Sicilian village would live in adjoining apartments, recreating an ancient community in a New World tenement. A priest recalled how Italian women used to say 'I have been down to America today', which meant they had ventured a few blocks outside the streets of their Italian community.[46] But as *Harper's Magazine* reported in 1881, 'the idyllic life of an Italian hillside or a dreaming medieval town is but poor preparation for the hand-to-hand struggle for bread of an overcrowded city'.[47] Life was indeed very hard for the new arrivals, as it always is for migrants trying to start a new life in a strange city. Many of these European immigrants swapped the grinding poverty of rural life for the squalor of the tenements.[48]

The ghetto is the dark flipside of the cosmopolis. It is Venice that has the dubious distinction of having invented the ghetto. In 1516, Jews were confined to an island in the *sestier*, or district, of Cannaregio which was until 1390 a foundry, or 'gheto' in the Venetian dialect.[49] At night its gates were locked and guarded by Christians. The Venetians – who never missed a trick when it came to money – even made them pay the wages of their guards. During the day they could travel around Venice, but they had to wear a yellow, circular badge or (for women) a yellow scarf. Although they were barred from certain trades, they were free to deal in used cloth, to lend money and to practise medicine. Indeed, Jewish doctors were allowed to leave the ghetto at night, but only to treat Venetians. Even today, the Ghetto Nuovo looks architecturally different from other parts of Venice. Buildings in the ghetto were not allowed to be more than a third higher than elsewhere, and as a result each storey was reduced in height in order to squeeze in the maximum number of floors. In this overcrowded area, seven storeys were not uncommon.

Concentrations of Russian Jews in run-down urban areas began to be termed 'ghettos' in America at the end of the nineteenth century. Jews soon became the largest immigrant group in New York. Some

400,000 of them were crowded into the tenements of the Lower East Side. But in the modern era, racism has made the ghetto an indelible part of the experience of black Americans. 'All the major scourges of American society come together in the Black ghetto with a special virulence, accentuating one another,' says Aidan Southall. 'The ghettos are the complement of the suburbs, occupying the space the suburbanites left behind.'[50] African-American scholars described segregated communities as ghettos as early as the 1890s. But it was after the publication of Gilbert Osofsky's seminal study, *Harlem: the Making of a Ghetto* (1963), that the word became commonly used to refer to African-American communities.

Louis Wirth pointed out in 1928 that the ghetto 'is not so much a physical fact as it is a state of mind'. Both in the mind and on the city street, the ghetto still traps an urban underclass of some two million people, principally young black Americans, condemning them to a life where crime is often the only way of earning money and respect

Harlem

Harlem was once a largely Italian and Jewish area of Manhattan, a middle-class commuter suburb just north of Central Park. But in the first half of the twentieth century, this area – whose name came from the original Dutch settlers in the 1650s (Haarlem) – became the black capital of America. African Americans – New York's second oldest ethnic population – started moving to this fifty-block area at the start of the twentieth century, leaving their old tenements on the middle and lower blocks of the West Side. By 1919 there were 100,000 African Americans here and within a decade the majority of residents were black. Indeed, it was one of the biggest black urban communities in the world.[52] The heart of Harlem is 125th Street. According to the Jamaican-born poet and writer Claude McKay, once you cross Fifth Avenue you enter 'the Negro capital of the world'.[53]

Harlem's golden age was in the 1920s and 1930s, a period known as the Harlem Renaissance. For these years it was one of the most creative and culturally innovative places on earth. Artists, musicians and writers streamed into Harlem, creating works that inspired the city and the nation. The poet and novelist Langston Hughes arrived from Cleveland in 1921: 'More than Paris, or the Shakespeare country, or Berlin, or the Alps, I wanted to see Harlem, the greatest Negro city in the world.'[54] This was the Jazz Age, the era of the flapper and *The Great Gatsby*. Musicians and singers like Duke Ellington, Bessie Smith and Count Basie played to packed clubs. By 1924 there were over 125 licensed cabarets and clubs. Some, like the Cotton Club and the Apollo Theater on 125th Street, have become in their community. They make up an alienated and largely forgotten urban group, invisible to middle-class society, until riots or extreme acts of violence bring them into the headlines.

In Europe, the word ghetto evokes the terrible history of the Holocaust. In the Warsaw Ghetto from November 1941 until its liquidation in May 1943, the Nazis walled in half a million Jews, subjecting them to starvation, disease and random killings.[51] In 1942, they began deporting Jews to concentration camps. The complex of camps at Auschwitz was the largest. The Nazis had even planned to build a New Town nearby, a model German settlement in the east for ethnic Germans. Instead, the Auschwitz concentration camp became a Necropolis, an industrial city of death, while the slogan over the entrance, *Arbeit macht frei* (work sets you free), was a grotesque perversion of the medieval German saying *Stadtluft macht frei* (city air sets you free).

legendary music venues. Le Corbusier visited New York in 1935, and was blown away by the trumpet playing of Louis Armstrong: 'Hot jazz … like the skyscrapers is an event … The jazz is more advanced than the architecture. If architecture were at the point reached by jazz, it would be an incredible spectacle … Manhattan is hot jazz in stone and steel.'[55]

Sadly, the party had to end. After the Second World War, the romance of the Jazz Age faded and Harlem eventually became the most impoverished district of New York, a city which at the time had more black inhabitants (one million) than any other in the world.[56] Half of all families in Harlem were below the poverty line. Riots in 1935 and 1943 had scared off the white clubbers. After the war a new wave of immigrants arrived. By the late 1970s, a quarter of a million Puerto Ricans were living in East Harlem, and now Spanish Harlem – aka El Barrio – reaches as far south as East 96th Street. Today, after difficult times, Harlem's star is once again rising, and people are talking of a second renaissance.[57]

A couple photographed in Harlem, 1932, during what became known as the Harlem Renaissance.

Slum City

Twenty-first-century Mumbai, the capital of the Indian state of Maharashtra, is one of the world's great megacities, with a total population of some nineteen million and rising. In the next few decades, Mumbai is expected to grow into a hypercity of more than thirty million people, perhaps even exceeding Tokyo, which is currently the largest city on the planet.[58] Mumbai's government has ambitious plans, hoping to transform their booming city into one of the world's leading financial centres. Already it is a place of fantastic wealth, with property prices rivalling midtown Manhattan in some areas, sums unimaginable for most Indians. And nowhere is the widening gulf between rich and poor more dramatically visible than in the heart of Mumbai, near to the financial centre. Built on what is now some of the most expensive land in the city is Dharavi, one of many areas marked on local maps with the letters 'ZP' for 'zopadpatti' – slums. Indeed, glitzy Mumbai has the dubious distinction of being the slum capital of the world, with about half of its population living in shanty towns. That's a slum city almost the size of London.[59]

Mumbai's Dharavi slum has become internationally famous after featuring in Danny Boyle's movie *Slumdog Millionaire* (2008), appropriately, perhaps, in a city also known as Bollywood. Mumbai has some of the highest population densities of any city and Dharavi is one of its most crowded slums. Nearly a million people are crammed into less than one square mile. It is not unusual to find three generations of a family – a dozen or so people – living in a single room of ninety square feet, less than an average American car-parking space. Indeed, over half of India's city dwellers live in a space smaller than three square metres (ten square feet); the average American has 900 square feet.[60]

The land on which Dharavi is built was originally a mangrove swamp inhabited by fishermen. In the twentieth century, migrants began arriving from all over India. As ever in the history of cities, people were escaping the grindingly hard life in traditional rural communities. From Gujarat came the Kumbhars, settling in a part of Dharavi now famed for its pottery; Tamils came and opened tanneries, and people from Uttar Pradesh arrived to work in the textile industry. These migrants built two- or three-storey structures to live in, known as 'hutments', *bricolage* buildings made of whatever discarded material they could lay their hands on: corrugated iron, plastic or asbestos sheets, cardboard and concrete. Today Dharavi is a thriving city within a city, a dense labyrinth of narrow, dark alleyways and closely packed hutments, which – like a microcosm of Mumbai itself – is divided into distinct neighbourhoods.

It has been estimated that 80 per cent of Mumbai's places of employment are in the slums, many of them in 'kaarkhanas', or sweatshops.[61] There are some 15,000 businesses in Dharavi alone, generating an astonishing turnover of around $1 billion annually. One of the biggest industries here is recycling. Mumbai's rubbish dump used to be next door to Dharavi and, for many residents, 'ragpicking' – salvaging anything that can be resold from rubbish – is their only source of income. Each day Mumbai produces 6,000 tonnes of rubbish and this is raked over by an army of 30,000 ragpickers.[62] In Dharavi alone there are some four hundred recycling units and they recycle about 80 per cent of Mumbai's plastic waste. (In the UK only 20 per cent of plastic waste is recycled.) As well as shredding plastics, they crush glass, collect paper and disassemble electronic goods, stripping copper from electrical wiring and reclaiming scraps of precious metals from circuit boards. In this city of contrasts – of wealth and poverty, glamour and squalor – virtually everything has a price and these people who have so little endure terrible working conditions to salvage every fragment of saleable material.

The slums of other cities have also turned recycling into an industry. The sprawling slum settlement of Manshiet Nasser stands on the slopes of the Muqattam Hills which form the eastern boundary of Cairo, the largest city in Africa and the Middle East, with a population of about seventeen million. On top of the hills is the community of the Zabbaleen, known as Garbage City. Descendants of poor farmers from Upper Egypt who migrated to the capital at the end of the nineteenth century, these seventy thousand people collect and recycle the city's rubbish (their name is derived from the Arabic word for garbage). Even after the city authorities recently contracted the rubbish collection to multinational cleaning companies, the Zabbaleen are still collecting rubbish door to door in their donkey carts, often subcontracted by the new companies. The Zabbaleen recycle about 80 per cent of Cairo's rubbish, collecting more than 6,000 tons a day, painstakingly sorting the refuse by hand into categories – plastic, metal, glass, paper, rags, organic waste.[63]

Whether you call it a slum, an informal settlement, a migrant city or a squatter community, Dharavi is a paradox.[64] In many ways it is a successful part of Mumbai, with distinct and close-knit communities, all of which enjoy high levels of employment and low crime rates. In this sense Dharavi is a model urban neighbourhood. But the living conditions here would not be accepted anywhere in the developed world. For, as well as being overcrowded, Dharavi is a public health nightmare. The first thing people in the now-popular guided tours of Dharavi notice is the smell. A noxious mix of sewage and chemicals runs through the alleys outside the hutments. There are rats everywhere, scurrying in and out of the rubbish and people's homes. Hundreds of people share a single toilet which may be little more than a shed with a hole opening into a stream. Pipes for drinking water run through open sewers and contaminated water causes diseases such as diphtheria and typhoid. Yet despite such appalling conditions, the inhabitants of Dharavi are proud of their homes and community. Some have even become wealthy businessmen. One Dharavi resident bought his plot of land in the 1950s from the crime gangs that used to run the slum for $7.50. Today his garment factory is worth $250,000 on Dharavi's informal property market.[65]

Slums are not just a problem for Mumbai. In 1900, about one in ten people lived in cities. Today more than half the inhabitants of the world are urbanites. In forty years' time, three-quarters of people will be city dwellers.[66] Urbanisation has been increasing dramatically in the developing world for decades. Lagos, the commercial heart of Nigeria, is one of the world's fastest growing megacities. Its population is expanding at 8 per cent a year. Every day some six thousand people move to this city of nine million and the UN expects its population will rise to well over sixteen million by 2030.[67] The average annual urbanisation rate of most European cities during the peak growth years of the Victorian period was 2.1 per cent. In the developing world during the period 1960 to 1993, it increased at an astonishing 3.8 per cent per annum. However, unlike during the nineteenth century, urbanisation is now generally decoupled from industrialisation. The result is rapidly expanding cities without economic growth. What Mike Davis has called a 'perverse urban boom' often occurs against a backdrop of rising unemployment, falling wages and declining agricultural productivity.[68]

Throughout history, the growth of cities was a sign of increasing average wealth. This is no longer the case. In countries such as Sierra Leone and Chad, more than 90 per cent of urban populations are slum dwellers. There is a fissure running through our brave new postmodern world with its cities the size of nations. On one side are the wealthy minority in their gleaming towers and gated communities. On the other are the slum cities of the poor, the ragpickers and the recyclers. Urbanisation may have reduced absolute poverty, but the urban poor are increasing steadily. There are well over a billion slum dwellers in the world today – nearly one in six of the population.[69] The age of the megacities is also that of the megaslum. Out of the top twenty megacities, fifteen are in developing countries. Today, one in three city dwellers is living in a slum.[70]

Of course, there have always been slums in cities. The Romans complained about the ramshackle shacks that appeared on the outskirts of their cities and which were rebuilt almost as quickly as they were demolished. Throughout the Middle Ages in European cities like Paris, slums formed a major part of the urban landscape. In the eighteenth century, London's rookeries were notorious centres of crime and destitution. They included St Giles, Holborn, where (according to contemporaries) forty people could live in 'small houses of not more than ten feet square': 'In St Giles one feels asphyxiated by the stench: there is no air to breathe nor daylight to find one's way.'[71] In the New World, San Francisco was built by squatters. One 1855 survey estimated that 95 per cent of the property holders in the city 'would not be able to produce a *bona fide* legal title to their land'.[72] There were extensive shanty developments around the fringes of American cities throughout the nineteenth century. In the 1930s, cardboard shanties, or Hoovervilles, appeared on the outskirts of cities across America, the last resort of the desperate victims of the Great Depression.

Today's shanty towns in the developing world evoke the conditions in the earliest cities. Their *bricolage* hutments and narrow alleyways, where people live cheek by jowl, working, sleeping and eating in the same room, surrounded by the sounds and smells of neighbours, offer glimpses of how life must have been in the first cities. In Dharavi or Kibera (a Nairobi slum about the size of Dharavi) the dark, fetid underside of the city is exposed. Yet even here hope is never quite extinguished – the hope for a life better than that in rural villages or in the shanties. Out of that hope great cities are built.

In contrast to the megaslums of today, most of which are on the outskirts, nineteenth-century slums were often in inner-city areas. The poor had no choice but to rent rooms in tenement houses. These were buildings subdivided by landlords to contain as many small units as possible, to maximise profits. They quickly became overcrowded, filthy and dilapidated. In the late 1850s, a New York state legislative committee described the 'hideous squalor and deadly effluvia' in the city's tenements: 'the dim, undrained courts oozing with pollution; the dark, narrow stairways, decayed with age, reeking with filth, overrun with vermin; the rotted floors, ceilings begrimed, and often too low to permit you to stand upright.'[73]

Tenants shared a single water supply. Few had hot water and even fewer bathtubs. There were one or two privies in each building, in the hall or out in the yard. As the front door was rarely shut, the staircases and hallways would fill up at night with the homeless.[74] Whole families (and sometimes more than one) lived in a room often smaller than ten by ten feet. In the daytime, the women would work in the same room – ragpicking, sack-making, or rabbit pulling. Walter Besant found that in Spitalfields, east London, beds were rented out during the day to men on night shifts.[75] Tenement dwellers had less space than those in prison or the workhouse. The population density of New York as a whole was seventy-six people per acre. In the 450 blocks of the Lower East Side – described in 1899 as 'a picture of human misery unparalleled in the world'[76] – the density was 300–700 per acre, and in one area it reached an astonishing 1,000 people an acre, more crowded than the worst parts of London, Paris or even Bombay.[77]

In the nineteenth century, one answer to the problem seemed to be slum clearance. 'The poor we shall have always with us, but the slum we need not have,' wrote Jacob Riis, author of the seminal exposé of tenement life, *How the Other Half Lives* (1890).[78] This and works such as Andrew Mearns' *The Bitter Cry of Outcast London* (1883) spurred reformers to campaign for the demolition of the worst slums. The dramatic scheme of urban renewal carried out by Georges-Eugène Haussmann in Paris from 1853 had shown what could be achieved.

After the First World War, slum clearance gained momentum in Britain, where some 250,000 houses were demolished and replaced with new council houses. The dilapidated four-storey tenements of Glasgow's East End were swept away and, by the 1970s, some 100,000 residents had been rehoused. It now has the highest proportion of public housing in Britain after Tower Hamlets in London. Slum clearances continued in Britain until the beginning of the 1980s. By then some two million houses – home to five million people – had been demolished and three million more improved with government grants.[79]

In the US, the cost of slum clearance was prohibitive. City authorities had to pay 'fair market value' for unsanitary buildings. In the 1920s, a city block on the Lower East Side would have cost the city $1 million. Even in the 1930s, the cost of rehabilitating the Lower East Side was estimated at $½ billion – a vast sum. For this reason slum clearance didn't catch on in America until after the Second World War, when federal aid for the redevelopment of urban areas became available.[80]

The authorities in modern Mumbai have spent many years discussing what to do about Dharavi. The favoured option is a $2 billion project to rehouse the slum dwellers on the outskirts of the city and to redevelop what is now a piece of prime real estate in the city centre, initially creating five million square feet of new office and residential space and a total of forty million square feet within seven years. Just as the authorities in Boston razed the city's West End district in the 1950s, or as Beijing has destroyed its historic hutongs, so Mumbai intends to sweep away Dharavi's hutments and replace them with new

A shanty town in Pasay City, part of the metropolitan region of Manila, Philippines. Behind it rise the towers of the financial district of Makati City.

office and residential towers designed by 'starchitects'. But as Europe and America discovered in the 1960s and 1970s, slum clearance can create as many problems as it solves.

Slums are a human and not just an architectural problem. Bulldozing tenements and shacks that offend the sensibilities of the middle classes destroys communities as well as eliminating poor housing. Families and friends are uprooted and displaced. In Dharavi, long-term residents will be allocated apartments in high-rise blocks on the outskirts of the city. But where will they work? Many fear that the businesses they have built up will not survive the move to the city fringes. As a result it is likely that within a few years the new residential districts will become vertical slums, home to a dispossessed population and a breeding ground for crime and even terrorism. Dharavi's residents are sceptical, not to say cynical, about the proposed redevelopment: 'All the politicians, the local crooks, and social workers are going to earn a good amount of money,' says one. 'Only we will be sufferers.'[81] Although it was slated to begin in 2009, by the end of that year the project was in abeyance.

But there is another way to improve the lives of slum dwellers. In Rio de Janeiro they tried slum clearance in the 1960s, but by the 1990s the authorities were exploring a new approach. They transformed migrant *favelas* – illegal settlements named after the flowering tree that grows

Gentrification

Europe and America have learned from past mistakes and accepted that slum clearance is not the only answer to what used to be termed 'urban blight'. When it comes to urban renewal today, incremental revitalisation is the approach favoured by planners. Gentrification can also play an important, though controversial, role. Gentrification refers to the way a working-class area is gradually colonised by the middle classes. It is said to have begun in Philadelphia in the 1950s, when wealthy people moved back into the riverside area of Society Hill, restoring the once grand eighteenth-century houses. This influx of the moneyed classes is not always welcomed by the locals. One Philadelphia resident observed bitterly that 'urban renewal means Negro removal'.[86] It is, however, a process that has been part of urban life for many years. In 1836, Charles Dickens noted how as an area of London became more middle class, its 'old tottering public-house' was converted into 'spacious and lofty "wine-vaults"', with its name displayed in gold-leaf lettering.[87] One result of gentrification is the displacement of on hillsides around São Paulo and Rio – into legal neighbourhoods and set about improving the infrastructure.[82] In Rocinha, Rio's biggest *favela*, a new covered market has been built, part of a policy of creating public urban spaces in these communities.[83] This ground-up approach – incremental improvement rather than clearance and redevelopment – is now accepted as the best way to transform the lives of slum dwellers without destroying communities. Even the World Bank supports this approach. It has provided some 900,000 people in Brazil's *favelas* with drinking water piped directly into their homes and connected about the same number to the sewerage system. The cost was just $84 per person. The bank is also investing $192 million in Mumbai's slums to build pay-toilets for more than 400,000 people.[84]

Offering slum dwellers the legal title to their properties can be an important step towards transforming shanty towns. Peru has issued 1.2 million property titles to poor urban slum households.[85] Slum dwellers who don't have to fear the bulldozer have the confidence to set up businesses – restaurants, shops, bars – and to improve their own homes. In Turkey, squatter cities are called *gecekondu*, which means 'it happened one night'. This is because if you build a home during the night and are living in it by morning, you cannot be legally evicted. Squatters make up 40 per cent of Istanbul's population. Robert Neuwirth, author of *Shadow Cities*, says that thanks to

poor communities. Local families can no longer afford to live in an area newly popular with affluent buyers. Within a few years the character of an area can change radically. Traditional shops and businesses are replaced with new high street franchises reflecting the change in demographics. Although many regret this, James Howard Kunstler defends gentrification, seeing it as part of a continuing cycle of urban decline and regeneration. Without gentrification, he asks, 'how would any city neighbourhood escape the fate of an ultimate slide into slumdom?'.[88]

The Cans Festival, Leake Street, London, 2008.

this law the 'squatter city' of Sultanbeyli in Istanbul, home to 275,000 people, even has 'an independent seven-storey city hall with lifts, built by the squatters, and a mayor who is also a squatter'.[89]

São Paulo is the most important metropolis in South America. A hundred years ago its population was less than 100,000. Now some ten million live in the city and at least nineteen million in the metropolitan region. Brazilian society is riven by inequality: 20 per cent of the urban population live in *favelas*.[90] São Paulo is a city of gated communities and guarded malls for the rich and sprawling *favelas* for the poor. The largest *favela* is Heliopolis with a population of about 120,000. Next biggest is Paraisópolis (80,000) adjacent to one of São Paulo's richest districts, Morumbi. In Paraisópolis the authorities are now working with the local people to develop renewal plans for their community. The *favela* is being gradually improved with sewers, mains electricity, libraries and public transport (which in some hillside *favelas* includes cable cars) – the kind of services and facilities that city dwellers in the developed world take for granted.[91]

Even in Brasília – described by Joseph Rykwert as the 'most elaborately zoned of all cities' – *favelas* have thrived.[92] One appeared before construction of the new city had begun in 1958. The shrewd settlers called their community 'Villa Sara' after the president's wife, hoping this would protect their shacks from demolition. Their ploy worked and other settlements soon followed, growing on the greenbelt land intended for agriculture. In the end they survived because the city needed them. From the *favelas* came the menial workers – cleaners, porters and security guards – without whom the city could not function. Even today, most of Brasília's population growth is in the *favelas*.[93]

No city is perfect. Urban reality never quite lives up to the dreams of the ideal city planners. There will always be urban slums because cities are magnets, attracting people in their thousands with the promise of better opportunities – education, healthcare – as well as greater freedom. But even the cities of the developed world have much to learn from slums. Charles, Prince of Wales, visited Dharavi in 2003 and praised its 'underlying, intuitive grammar of design' and 'timeless quality and resilience'. Not only are such shanty towns built of materials that might otherwise end up on the scrap heap, but the communities they create are walkable, high-density and successfully integrate commercial and residential uses. In an age of climate change, these are qualities that urban planners are trying to build into today's cities.

From Garden Suburbs to Boomburbs

I grew up on the outskirts of Romford, in Essex. By 1970, when my parents bought a dilapidated house here, this former medieval market town had long since been absorbed into the sprawling conurbation of London, virtually indistinguishable from the rest of the suburban mosaic of brick houses, asphalt roads and neat grass lawns that spread inexorably during the twentieth century.[94] On my way to school each day I passed Gidea Park station, a half-hour commute from London's Liverpool Street Station. It had been built in 1910 as part of a garden suburb designed by architects inspired by Ebenezer Howard's idealistic vision of a decentralised urban future. 'Town and country *must be married*,' Howard had written, 'and out of this joyous union will spring a new hope, a new life, a new civilisation.' Here, on the north-eastern fringe of one of the world's greatest cities, they created a new settlement of architect-designed houses on tree-lined streets, connected to the metropolis by the essential umbilical cord of the railway. Although it was still surrounded by the Essex countryside in 1910, Gidea Park – like all garden suburbs – was a hybrid, neither completely urban nor rural, a liminal place caught between two worlds. But in the course of the twentieth century, such cosy, middle-class suburbs were swamped by wave after wave of new houses, among them the utilitarian but unlovely 1930s semi into which our family moved in 1970.

The suburban dream of owning a home in the countryside within easy reach of the city is almost as old as urban life itself. A letter to the King of Persia, from 539 BC, written in cuneiform on a clay tablet, testifies to its enduring appeal: 'Our property seems to me the most beautiful in the world. It is so close to Babylon that we enjoy all the advantages of the city, and yet when we come home we are away from all the noise and dust.'[95] At its peak 4,200 years ago, there were suburbs around the city of Ur when its population exceeded 100,000 and many had to move out beyond its walls. Nevertheless, as Kenneth Jackson, a historian of suburbia, has said, if you wanted 'to have a place in man's true home', then you had to live in the heart of the city: 'To live outside the walls, away from palaces and cathedrals, was to live in inferior surroundings.'[96]

In England the word 'suburb' was first used by John Wycliffe in 1380, then soon after by Chaucer in *The Canterbury Tales*, where an alchemist's servant tells how his disreputable master practises his dark arts in 'the suburbes of a toun' (Prologue, *The Canon's Yeoman's Tale*, 1387). London's suburbs were infamous places of lawlessness, full of 'base tenements' and noxious industries, such as soap-making and tanning.[97] The author of a sixteenth-century guide to the capital alluded to their sleazy reputation when he asked: 'London, what are thy Suburbes but licensed Stewes?' ('Stewes' were brothels.) Indeed, at the time 'suburb sinner' was a common term for a prostitute.[98] Shakespeare alludes to the rowdiness of the suburbs in *Henry VIII*: 'Theres a trim rabble let in; are all these / Your faithfull friends o' th' suburbs?' (V. iv. 76)

The suburbs were not just a place, but an insult. Lord Byron's crushing assessment of a lady's lack of sartorial judgement shows the contempt in which the suburbs were held. She looked 'vulgar, dowdyish and suburban', said Byron.[99] This view of suburbia was shared in cities around the world, from New York to Tokyo. In Paris, 'le faubourg' (literally 'out-of-town') was distinctly non-U, as Nancy Mitford might have said, the adjective 'faubourien' connoting working-class environs.[100]

But in the eighteenth century, as cities became increasingly successful and overcrowded, attitudes towards the suburbs began to change. At this time in colonial, mercantile cities such as British Madras or Dutch Batavia (modern Jakarta), suburban enclaves were being built. Here 'Ladies and Gentlemen' could escape the noise and bustle of the city centre for a more leisured, rural setting where they lived in detached 'garden-houses'. By the end of the eighteenth century, Madras had become a suburban society, with Indian and European professionals commuting into the city centre to do business. The lifestyle here and at Chowringhee, Kolkata, was admired by visitors from Britain, where the Industrial Revolution was sucking vast numbers of workers from the countryside into the cities.[101]

By 1851, the census revealed that more British people lived in towns than the country. But as cities became more densely populated, those with money – the new middle classes – sought to escape the increasingly congested centre for the more tranquil urban fringes. The economic and technological forces that created William Blake's 'dark Satanic mills' had transformed city skylines. Now they were dominated not by church steeples, but industrial chimneys pumping out soot-laden smoke. The middle classes fled the dirt, noise and congestion for the suburbs where they hoped to keep alive the dream of England's 'green and pleasant land'. William Cowper poured scorn on this exodus of the nouveau riche:

Suburban villas, highway-side retreats,
That dread the encroachment of our growing streets,
Tight boxes neatly sash'd, and in a blaze
With all a July sun's collected rays,
Delight the citizen, who, gasping there,
Breaths clouds of dust, and calls it country air.[102]

For the first time, suburbs were becoming fashionable. They were no longer beyond the social pale, but were being transformed into a bourgeois promised land – a dramatic volte-face in attitudes and a paradigm shift in urban history.

Beginning in Britain, suburbanisation represented a revolution in urban life. St John's Wood in north London is generally regarded as the first English suburb. Plans for its development were first drawn up in 1794. Rather than the conventional terraces, semi-detached houses were included, a radical step as this style of house had previously only been used for artisanal dwellings. By the 1820s, St John's Wood was a thriving suburb of several hundred homes.[103] But it was the railways that made the dream of suburban living – as well as the daily commute to and from work – a reality for millions of people from all classes.[104] Thanks to the rapidly expanding railway network, the population of London's outer suburbs grew by about 50 per cent each decade between 1861 and 1891. At the same time, the population of the City fell. 'Suburbia was a railway state,' one person recalled, 'a state of existence within a few minutes walk of the railway station, a few minutes walk of the shops, a few minutes walk of the fields.'[105]

Due to the cost of railway tickets, the commuter suburbs were initially inhabited by white-collar workers. Le Vésinet, the first commuter suburb of Paris, was developed in 1856 by a railway company for its employees, but was soon colonised by the middle classes.[106] In London, similar suburbs were built around stations such as those at Richmond, Putney and Clapham. Indeed, Clapham had enjoyed a daily coach service to Gracechurch Street in the City since 1690. From the eighteenth century, prosperous merchants began building houses here and commuting by coach.

Bedford Park, in west London, was one of the first purely residential suburbs – a 'dormitory' suburb. Developed in 1875, just after Turnham Green railway station opened, its distinctive Queen Anne-style red-brick houses and oriental blossoming cherry trees quickly made it a place of pilgrimage for architects keen to see the future of urban planning. Even before 1880, publicity material for Bedford Park (designed by architects from the Arts and Crafts Movement, William Godwin and Norman Shaw) described it as a 'garden city', anticipating Howard's idea.[107] In the 1860s, Hippolyte Taine had noted that in Britain 'the townsman does everything in his power to cease being a townsman, and tries to fit a country house and a bit of country into a corner of the town'.[108] He was right. The English never felt quite at home in big cities. In contrast to Parisians, who have always aspired to live in the city centre, Londoners immediately embraced the idea of garden suburbs. After 1872, when the Great Eastern Railway introduced workmen's trains – twopenny return tickets for journeys up to ten miles – out of Liverpool Street Station, working-class suburbs were developed in north-east London, for example in Ilford.

'When we get piled upon one another in large cities, as in Europe, we shall become as corrupt as Europe', wrote Thomas Jefferson in *Pestilence City*.[109] From the eighteenth century to Frank Lloyd Wright's *Disappearing City* in the 1930s, there had always been a profound distrust of city life in American thought and a preference for semi-rural living. Boston, Philadelphia and New York all had suburbs before the Revolutionary War. Brooklyn Heights, across the harbour from Lower Manhattan, emerged as a popular suburb in the early nineteenth century. In 1800 this largely rural area had a population of just 2,378. Within forty years it had risen to over 36,000 and by 1880 what Walt Whitman called 'Brooklyn the Beautiful' was home to more than half a million people.[110]

Frederick Law Olmsted was America's foremost landscape architect and the man who designed Central Park in New York. He saw the suburbs as the 'most attractive, the most refined, the most soundly wholesome' form of residential living.[111] At Riverside, Illinois (1869), nine miles from Chicago, Olmsted created the classic garden suburb out of what had been flat prairie land. Thousands of imported trees were planted in this 'suburban village', as it was called. Its curving street plan, which soon became synonymous with suburbia, contrasted sharply with the gridiron layouts of cities such as New York.

According to Olmsted, curved streets 'suggest and imply leisure, contemplativeness, and happy tranquillity'.[112] Olmsted's romanticised suburbia struck a chord with Americans. Pollution, immigrant slums and labour radicalism filled the American middle classes with fears of an imminent explosion of urban class warfare at the end of the nineteenth century. The suburbs offered a safe haven, a bourgeois utopia whose semi-rural location made possible a relaxed, outdoor lifestyle while affirming values deemed central to American society, such as the sanctity of the family and property ownership.

Brentham Garden Suburb, Ealing (1901).

Suburban living soon became synonymous with the American Dream. A natural symbiosis between city and suburbs was implicitly accepted: 'no great town can long exist without great suburbs', Olmsted had said in the 1860s.[113] As the trolley car system expanded in the 1880s, suburbs mushroomed across America and by the twentieth century suburbanisation had made the United States into one of the world's most decentralised industrial societies. 'Suburbia has become the quintessential physical achievement of the United States,' says historian Kenneth T. Jackson. 'It is perhaps more representative of its culture than big cars, tall buildings, or professional football.'[114] The railways had driven suburbanisation in nineteenth-century Britain. In twentieth-century America it was the invention of the car that brought suburbia within everyone's reach. Los Angeles – where even in the 1920s people were four times more likely to have a car than the average American – pioneered 'a new model of urban growth – dispersed, multicentred, and largely suburbanized'.[115] This city offered a glimpse of things to come around the world. As *Harper's* declared in 1949, Los Angeles was 'the first modern, widely decentralized industrial city in America'.[116] Los Angeles was also where the first regional shopping centre was built: the Crenshaw Center, in 1947. The mall was to become an essential feature of American suburbia. With their atriums and fountains, malls became out-of-town cathedrals, temples to suburbia's religion – consumerism.

By 1940, the United States was mainly suburban, with over half

145

Commuting

Building News commented in 1903 that the expansion of late Victorian suburbs was 'one of the social revolutions of the time'.[117] In 1861, 400,000 people lived in London's suburbs. By 1911 that had increased to 2.7 million. The daily commute to work was now part of many people's lives. The word 'commuter' emerged first in America in the 1840s, referring to those who used a 'commutation ticket', the American term for a season ticket (in the sense that the daily fare is 'commuted', or replaced, with a single payment). In the cities of 1815, only one in fifty people travelled as much as a mile to work. Cities were generally compact with everything within walking distance. Shops, places of work and residential buildings were mixed in together.[118] (Unfortunately, the Modernist planning idea of zoning, whereby areas are restricted to either work or residential use, often means that cities lose this human scale.) By 1906, nearly a quarter of a million people commuted each day into London, a its population — some sixty-seven million people — living in 147 metropolitan areas. In England 40 per cent of the population was suburban.[121] After the war, suburban developments such as Levittown on Long Island, New York (1947), proved hugely popular. It was the first of four Levittowns, named after developer Abram Levitt. Such affordable housing coupled with low-interest loans, cheap cars and even cheaper fuel brought the American Dream within reach of even ordinary working-class people. However, many architects and cultural commentators condemned this flight from the cities, describing suburbia as a 'subtopia' and predicting landscapes consumed by 'slurbs' (slum-suburbs). Lewis Mumford attacked the suburbs as an 'anti-city': 'a multitude of uniform, unidentifiable houses, lined up inflexibly at uniform distances on uniform roads in a treeless communal waste, inhabited by people of the same class, the same income, the same age group, witnessing the same television performances, eating the same tasteless pre-fabricated foods.'[122]

Similarly, Richard Sennett criticised the desire of people to leave 'dense, disorderly, overwhelming cities' for more homogeneous but less stimulating communities in the suburbs. 'Suburbanites are people who are afraid to live in a world they cannot control,' he declared. As people turned their backs on the 'adult city', he predicted they would experience an impoverished social life and create a 'society of fear'.[123] These criticisms — rejected by some as snobbery — inspired

146

figure that would rise to 1.7 million in thirty years. Across the Channel, by 1930 more than 400,000 people commuted into Paris from the suburbs every day.[119] In modern Japan, some two and a half million people commute daily into central Tokyo. Today, people commute into London from across the entire south-east of England, home to nineteen million people. New York City residents spend the longest time commuting in the United States: an average of 38.4 minutes each day. That's about one full week a year.[120]

Traffic at a crossing in Shanghai.

many fictional depictions of suburbia, such as Mike Leigh's *Abigail's Party* (1977), Ira Levin's *The Stepford Wives* (1972) and the movie *American Beauty* (1999, directed by Sam Mendes). Many pop musicians (such as David Bowie, who grew up in the London commuter town of Bromley in Kent) mocked the suburban values of their parents' generation. Like George Orwell, they shared a view of suburbia as terminally conventional and conservative, its houses 'semi-detached torture-chambers where the poor little five-to-ten pounders quake and shiver, every one of them with the boss twisting his tail and the wife riding him like a nightmare and the kids sucking his blood like leeches'.[124]

But although intellectuals and creative people often mock it, suburbia remains popular. According to Joel Kotkin, since 2000 more than four-fifths of metropolitan growth in America has been in suburbs and exurbs.[125] In Britain, too, there has been an 'exodus from the cities'. Since 1981, Greater London and the six former metropolitan counties of Greater Manchester, Merseyside, South Yorkshire, Tyne and Wear, West Midlands and West Yorkshire, have lost some 2.25 million people in net migration exchanges with the rest of the UK. This represents an average of 97,800 people a year. In 2003, 143,500 made the move from urban to suburban and rural areas.[126] This is reflected around the world, with suburbs gaining population while city cores have tended to decline: in Mexico City, São Paulo, Buenos

Aires, Manila, Kolkata and Jakarta population growth has been in the suburbs.[127] China, which in little over two decades has experienced 'the largest scale of urbanization' in human history, has chosen to follow an American suburban model.[128] Shanghai has become the most populous city in China, with at least seventeen million people, a figure that is rising steadily. Twenty-five years ago, Shanghai had a hundred buildings over eight storeys high; today there are more than ten thousand. There are plans to accommodate a further 5.4 million people by building one new city and nine new towns. Each town is built in the style of a different European city, truly postmodern suburbs. Thames Town in Songjiang New City lies forty kilometres southwest of Shanghai, but its cobbled streets, Tudor-style houses and red phone boxes make it look like a garden suburb of London.[129]

In the twenty-first century, suburbs are evolving and increasingly they resemble urban areas. Welcome to the age of 'suburban urbanization', when dormitory suburbs offer more jobs than bedrooms. Now developers inspired by New Urbanist ideas are creating downtown areas in suburbs. And as the architecture changes, so too do the demographics. Suburbs in America are no longer the preserve of the white middle classes: the proportion of ethnic minorities has increased from 19 per cent in 1990 to 25 per cent today. Poverty is also increasing. In 2005, for the first time, more people were below the poverty line in American suburbs than in central cities.[130] Inner-city problems such as crime have migrated to the suburbs, too.

Whereas downtowns were once the engines of the American economy, now 'boomburbs' are the new economic powerhouses. Grouped around freeway intersections, shopping strips and office parks, boomburbs are a product of the suburban 'exit-ramp economy'. They are a new type of city, in which aspects of suburbia and the central city are combined. For example, although boomburbs may have the population density of a suburb, they usually have a downtown. One recent study describes boomburbs as 'the ultimate symbol of the sprawling postwar metropolitan form'.[131] In 2006, there were sixty with a population of more than 100,000 in America. Half are in California. By definition boomburbs are fast-growing areas. Between 2000 and 2006, seventeen of the twenty-five fastest growing places in America with more than 100,000 people were boomburbs, including six out of the top ten. In 2006, five boomburbs had more than 300,000 residents, putting them among the top sixty American cities. The biggest, Mesa,

Arizona (447,000), is larger than Kansas City. In America, yesterday's suburbs are now the fastest growing cities, a phenomenon that is being repeated around the world.[132]

In the last thirty years, cities have grown into megacities and continued expanding to form 'huge urban galaxies' – sprawling, polycentric cities that spread across whole regions, forming continental conurbations, or megaregions.[133] Metropolis has become exopolis. They are evolving faster than our ability to describe them. A recent scholarly article listed fifty terms describing new metropolitan forms and a further fifty describing relations between cities.[134] The old relationship between central cities and suburbs is dead and new ones are being forged. Recent trends also suggest a decline in population of the outer suburbs and a repopulation of the inner cores of some cities ('recentralisation'). Indeed this might be a timely reaction to climate crisis and peak oil. Some have even argued that suburbia is the 'landscape of the dinosaur'.[135] For today, the conditions that gave rise to suburban sprawl – cheap oil, cars, credit and land – are gone. Unless new carbon-zero transport systems can be created, owning a home on the outskirts of a city or a boomburb may become an expensive luxury.

Carlyle Hotel, South Beach, Miami, Florida. Designed by Richard Kiehnel and John Elliot, 1939. (following page)

The Hotel

'Can you do something startling, something that has never been done before?' This was the question American champagne millionaire and financier George A. Kessler put to the manager of London's Savoy Hotel in July 1905. Kessler didn't want an ordinary dinner party. He wanted something extraordinary. And he wanted it ready for the following evening.

Within minutes of the request, the hotel's manager, Henry Pruger, had summoned 120 carpenters, electricians and scene painters from across the city. By the next day the old courtyard of the Savoy had been flooded to create an artificial lagoon in which floated a white, silk-lined gondola. That evening, Kessler's twenty-four guests walked across a wooden bridge into the large, flower-decked gondola and sat down on golden chairs around a long table. Dinner was cooked by fifteen chefs and served by waiters dressed in handmade Venetian costumes. Music specially composed for the occasion was played by musicians in another gondola, floating nearby. The buildings on either side had been draped with painted backdrops of Venice – the Piazza San Marco and the Doge's Palace – while around the dinner guests fluttered a hundred white doves, settling among the 24,000 or so carnations and roses that decorated every surface. The whole magical scene on that balmy evening was illuminated by the flickering light of four hundred Venetian paper lamps.

After dinner a tiny elephant from the Royal Italian Circus, nicknamed 'Baby Jumbo', crossed the bridge to the gondola carrying on its back a candlelit cake no less than five feet high. This 'Idyll of Venice' in central London was brought to a close by Enrico Caruso singing 'O Sole Mio' beneath a paper moon, while Kessler and his guests sipped Moët & Chandon 1898. There had been just one flaw in the whole magical fantasy – the live swans that were supposed to have been swimming in the lagoon were poisoned by the blue dye used to colour the water. Despite this, there is no question that it was, as the Savoy's manager had promised, a quite remarkable dinner. Of course, such extravagances are not cheap. It was rumoured to have cost £3,000.[136]

Grand hotels such as the Savoy are often described as the second homes of the wealthy. Cities today are unimaginable without them but they are in fact a relatively recent type of urban building, made possible by new construction techniques – London's Ritz Hotel (1906) was, for example, the city's first large steel-framed building – but also by a new means of mass transport: the railway. This brought a flood of travellers into cities newly enriched by the Industrial Revolution. Travellers have always needed accommodation in foreign cities. Trading centres, like Venice, often had colonies of different nationalities where merchants could find inns and lodgings among their own language communities. Indeed, the ancient forerunners of today's hotels are the caravanserais, where merchants and their heavily laden camels spent the night. Generally these were large, square enclosures, located along trade routes every twenty or so miles (a day's journey). In cities they were often near the main gate, and the merchants would wait there while the tax on their goods was calculated. The Iranian caravanserai next to the Madrassa Madir-I-Shah, on Isfahan's Naghsh-e Jahan Square, dates from the eighteenth century. Where once dusty camels and merchants stayed is now a wonderful urban space, with trees and flowing water, part of the elegant Shah Abbâssi Hotel.[137] Pilgrimage cities, too, offered accommodation to their pious visitors. In the fourteenth century, Padua's Bull (Hospitium Bovis) was Italy's best inn, with stabling for some two hundred horses. In the following century, Rome had no fewer than 1,022 inns.

The word 'hotel' in English dates from 1765 and is taken from a French contraction of 'hostel'. Originally, it meant 'an inn, especially one of a superior kind'.[138] It was distinct from the short-stay coaching inns and post-houses found along main roads, such as the Angel & Royal, Grantham, on the Great North Road, where King Richard III stayed in the fifteenth century and which claims to be England's oldest inn. Modern-style hotels began to appear in cities during the last decades of the eighteenth century, as the wealthier classes sought an alternative to inns, which were crowded with wayfarers recovering from a hard day's travelling. In a hotel, guests would generally stay longer than one night and could expect private sitting rooms, residents' coffee rooms and possibly a second dining room. A large hotel would typically have an imposing Assembly Room, such as the fine eighteenth-century ballroom at the Lion, Shrewsbury. This helped to make the hotel into a centre of urban society and entertainment. The Royal Hotel, Plymouth (1819), even had a theatre and athenaeum, and has been described as 'a leisure complex of its day'.[139]

From the end of the eighteenth century, America led the world in designing the biggest and best hotels. 'The American Hotel is to an English hotel what an elephant is to a periwinkle,' said one (British) observer, in 1866.[140] The City Hotel (1794–6; burned down 1818) was the first of its kind in New York, with seventy-three rooms on five floors. In Boston, the seven-storey Exchange Coffee House (1806–9, Asher Benjamin), which also housed the city's merchant exchange, had a striking architectural feature which would become common in later hotels, including Mumbai's Taj Mahal: a circular domed rotunda with balconies running around the inside. With its seventy-foot dining room and grand ballroom reached by a splendid curving staircase, the Exchange Coffee House was clearly a hotel and not an inn. Also in Boston, Tremont House (1827–30; demolished 1894), designed by the pioneering hotel architect Isaiah Rogers, was 'a landmark in hotel design'.[141] It offered 170 bedrooms, eight bathrooms and the same number of water closets. In particular, the owners raised the bar as regards standards of service. Their staff were taught that respect for customers was paramount, something that could not be taken for granted in hotels of the day. When Charles Dickens toured a number of American cities, including New York, Philadelphia, Washington and Pittsburgh in 1842, he was astonished by Tremont House. It had, he said, 'more galleries, colonnades, piazzas and passages than I can remember, or the reader would believe'.[142] He was also struck by the number of 'boarders' in the hotel. In America, it was not uncommon for whole families to live all year round in a hotel.

The 1830s was boom time for hotels in America, with cities competing to offer the finest accommodation. Americans wanted comfort and privacy – lockable rooms provided with a jug, bowl and soap – as well as amenities. The six-storey Astor House, in New York (1832–6), also designed by Isaiah Rogers, exceeded even Tremont House's impressive standards. At this time in Britain, a hotel with a hundred beds was considered large.[143] Astor House had 309 rooms, seventeen basement bathrooms, privies on upper floors, twenty parlours, as well as separate dining rooms and drawing rooms for ladies and gentlemen. The staff were attentive to their guests' every need; there was a fine wine cellar and excellent cuisine. The Mayor of New York, Philip Hone, boasted that it was 'the marvel of the age'. The charge of $2 a day for a room was high enough to ensure that only the right class of person could afford to stay at the hotel, namely royalty, politicians, captains of industry, as well as literary and stage personalities.

Frequented by wealthy and fashionable people, hotels soon became centres of the high life. Eagle-eyed newspapermen watched the comings and goings, keen to pick up juicy titbits of society gossip. London's Langham Hotel (1865, John Giles), which cost £300,000 to build and ruined its first owner, soon became *the* place to be seen for the litterati of the day. The guest list included Harrison Ainsworth, William Gladstone, Mark Twain, Arthur Conan Doyle, Oscar Wilde and many others.[144] This reputation for glamour and celebrity has remained a key ingredient of life at the best hotels. Their very names evoke instant images of exclusivity and style – New York's Waldorf Astoria, Raffles in Singapore, Lucerne's Schweizerhof or the Adlon in Berlin.

One of the largest and most glamorous hotels ever built was in France. The Grand Hôtel was a jewel in the crown of 'Nouveau Paris', as it was known after Baron Haussmann's radical programme of urban renewal that began in 1853. Sited in the Place de l'Opéra, in the fashionable 9th *arrondissement*, it was designed by Alfred Armand, who had also worked on the impressive Grand Hôtel du Louvre (1855).[145] The Grand was built in fifteen months (1861–2), with construction work continuing day and night under arc lamps. Napoleon III had commissioned Haussmann to transform Paris into a modern city and the Grand was one of the capital's new glories. It was among the biggest and most luxurious hotels in the world, with eight hundred bedrooms, sixty-five salons and the city's first hydraulic lift. The hotel provided its guests with everything the wealthy visitor could ever want: a telegraph desk, a carriage service, couriers, a letter box, interpreters, a cash desk, a theatre ticket desk, a laundry, an unequalled wine cellar containing a million bottles of wine with a reserve in Bordeaux, and milk from a model dairy in Paris. The Salle des Fêtes on the ground floor was the grandest, most opulent space in any hotel, providing a dramatic backdrop for banquets, balls and receptions. Even the most sophisticated Parisian socialites were awed by its splendour. The Empress Eugénie confessed that it was 'absolutely like home; I feel that I am at Compiègne or Fontainebleau'.[146]

Hotels like the Paris Grand prided themselves on satisfying every whim and desire of their affluent guests. In their range of services and amenities, such hotels became a city within a city. The Taj Mahal Hotel, built in 1903 for a cost of £500,000, is still one of the finest in the world with one employee for every guest. The hotel had its own steam laundry, aerated bottling plant, electroplating plant and a burnishing machine for table silver, a telegraph service, post office, Turkish baths, and for medical emergencies there was a chemist and a doctor always in residence. Here visitors were assured of feeling safe and pampered, like royalty in a palace.[147]

However, the fortunes of the grand hotels began to decline in the wake of the First World War, reflecting changes in society and technology. And just as the railways had helped create demand for hotels, so it was a new mode of transport, the automobile, that produced a new kind of hotel in America in the 1920s – the motel, aka the motor court or roadside inn. By the 1950s, for every four hotels there were three motels.[148] But at the same time, the dawn of the age of mass air travel after the Second World War brought a renaissance for the hotel.

In the era of globalisation, tourism has become a major industry and in the twenty-first century no great city is complete without prestigious hotels to lure wealthy travellers from abroad. Hotels are beacons of urban pride in a global market that pits world cities against each other. They include designer hotels, such as Beijing's intriguingly named Opposite House (2009, Kengo Kuma), which has done away with the traditional check-in desk in favour of staff equipped with tablet computers, and Richard Bofil's twenty-six-storey 'W-Barcelona' (2009), christened by locals 'La Vela' due to its dramatic sail-like shape rising proudly above the harbour entrance. Even the North Korean regime felt the need for a grand hotel to proclaim the putative success of its Stalinist system. In 1987 it began building a vast pyramidal hotel some 105 storeys and 330 metres (1,083 feet) high in its capital, Pyongyang. There were to be three thousand bedrooms and, in the rotating storeys on the top, seven restaurants. But after six years the money ran out, leaving the half-finished Ryugyong Hotel – renamed by critics The Hotel of Doom or The Phantom Hotel – looming above the city, a grotesque urban ruin in a country that can barely feed its own people. (As the hundredth anniversary of the birth of Kim Il Sung approaches on 15 April 2012, construction work has resumed. It's estimated that the cost of completion would amount to 2 per cent of the country's GDP.)[149]

Although pilgrims' thoughts are supposed to be on matters spiritual, it seems luxury hotels are also needed in holy cities. In Mecca, the Fairmont Raffles group of international hoteliers has recently opened two exclusive hotels close to the Sacred Mosque – the Raffles Makkah

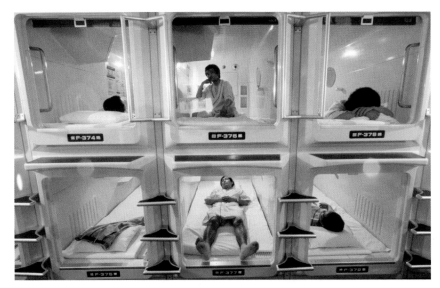

Capsule hotel, Japan.

Palace and the Makkah Royal Clock Tower hotel. The latter has over a thousand rooms and is within one of the tallest towers in the world, some 600 metres, or nearly 2,000 feet high. It is surmounted by a giant clock, with faces more than forty metres across, five times larger than Big Ben. Visible ten miles away, the clock announces daily prayers to the Muslim world.[150]

It's perhaps not surprising, though, that the most extravagant urban hotel of recent years is to be found in the desert city state of Dubai, renowned for its wealth and architectural excesses. The 1,500-room Atlantis hotel is the centrepiece of the Palm Jumeirah, and cost some $1.5 billion to build. Even the opening festivities in November 2008 – with 100,000 fireworks – cost a staggering $20 million. Clearly, no expense has been spared in this hotel where rooms cost from $450 to $35,000 a night. Among its many astonishing features is an aquarium with 65,000 marine animals. 'In Dubai, if you have a fantasy, you don't just fantasize about it, you build it,' says Sultan bin Sulayem, one of the co-owners of the hotel and the man whose company built the Palm.[151] I don't doubt that George Kessler would have felt very much at home in the Dubai Atlantis.

Of course, most visitors to twenty-first century cities will not be able to afford such expensive hotels. The vast majority will stay in more modest accommodation – a stylish boutique hotel, perhaps, a concept first created by New York City nightclub entrepreneur Ian Schrager in 1984, or an 'urban lodge' such as London's Hoxton Hotel,

Resort Cities

The Palm Jumeirah in Dubai is the ultimate seaside resort. Created by land reclamation, this astonishing network of artificial islands is in the shape of an Arabian palm, best viewed from an aeroplane or even space. In this desert city-state the development adds some 1,200 miles (2,000 kilometres) of beachfront to a coastline that was just 37 miles (60 kilometres) long.[152] The seaside resort is an urban form that is barely three centuries old. The Romans popularised the practice of staying at a spa (named after the town of Spa, near Liège, Belgium, whose Roman name was Aquae Spadanae). Examples include Baden-Baden in Germany and Bath in England, which remain popular destinations today.[153]

Cap Ferrat poster by C. Couronneau, 1922.

But it was in Britain at the end of the eighteenth century that people first began visiting the seaside for their health. The Prince of Wales (later Prince Regent and then George IV) first visited Brighton on the south coast of England in 1783 and liked it so much he returned every year. He even had a delightful oriental-style palace built there – the Royal Pavilion. From 1819, visitors to Brighton could stay in hotels such as the Royal Oak. Brighton can also claim to have had the very first British hotel called the Grand, designed by John Whichcord and completed in 1864. It had 260 rooms and five hydraulic lifts, serving seven out of nine storeys. With its monumental design and seafront location, it set the standard for later Grand Hotels.

By the 1890s, there were some four hundred European seaside resorts and numbers continued to rise. Marcel Proust stayed at the Grand Hôtel in Cabourg, Normandy, as a child. He returned as an adult for a fortnight each year from 1907 to 1914. In *À la recherche du temps perdu* (begun 1909) the hotel became the 'Grand Hôtel de la Plage' and Proust evocatively describes sitting in the dining room and gazing out through the hotel's large windows.[154] Thomas Mann described Venice as 'incomparable, fabulous, like nothing else on earth'.[155] The Grand Hôtel des Bains on the Venice Lido is where Gustave Aschenbach spends his last, obsessive days in *Death in Venice*. Mann had stayed here in 1911 and it was in the hotel that he saw the 'perfectly beautiful' Polish boy on whom Tadzio is based, with his 'expression of gracious and godlike seriousness'. Mann was less than impressed with the hotel, which he considered pretentious and overpriced.[156] The Hôtel du Cap (later renamed Eden Roc) in Antibes, was F. Scott Fitzgerald's model for the Hôtel des Étrangers in *Tender Is the Night*, with its 'bright tan prayer rug of a beach'.[157] In real life, the guests included Ernest Hemingway, Marlene Dietrich and Winston Churchill.

opened in 2006 by Sinclair Beecham (co-founder of the Prêt à Manger chain). He described his new hotel as offering 'beautiful little boxes people can stay in'.[158] Indeed, in future cities, where space will be at a premium, such compact hotels will be increasingly common.

Capsule hotels – aptly nicknamed 'coffin hotels' by William Gibson in his novel *Neuromancer* (1984) – are by no means luxurious but offer an efficient way of accommodating the maximum number of people in as small a space as possible. They were invented in Japan by architect Kisho Kurokawa, who designed the Nakagin Capsule Tower, Ginza, Tokyo, in 1972, a novel structure which consists of a concrete core into which accommodation pods are bolted as and when needed.[159] He designed the first capsule hotel seven years later, in Osaka. Typically each pre-moulded, fibre-glass capsule provides only enough room for the occupant to lie down, being about 6.5 feet long by 5 feet wide and containing little more than a light, a small TV with earphones, coat hooks and a blanket. Capsules are stacked two units high with thin plastic shutters across the entrance.

Love hotels are another product of Japan's hi-tech, high-density urban culture. There are some 25,000 love hotels in Japan, generally near railway stations with names like 'Hotel For You' or 'Sunpalace'. Rooms are available to rent by the hour. There are no receptionists and guests check in using a touch screen and a credit card. Your key is dispensed by a machine. Some hotels are themed: you can, for example, stay in a replica of the *Titanic*, complete with statues of Leonardo DiCaprio and Kate Winslet on the prow. Other love hotels cater for clients' sexual fantasies, with rooms designed to look like classrooms or even railway carriages. It's a lucrative business, worth £25 billion annually, with some five hundred million visits to love hotels a year (each room is used on average four times a day).[160] In the future, this may be the answer for couples seeking brief moments of intimacy and privacy in crowded cities. As the planet's population grows ever larger and more people flock to the cities, urban densities will rise and living space will become increasingly scarce and expensive. Capsule hotels and love hotels may soon be coming to a city near you.

Japan's *Shinkansen* railway network, known as the Bullet Train. (following page)

5 GETTING AROUND

Walking

On an autumn afternoon in London during the 1830s, a man sat alone in the large bow window of a coffee house, idly reading a newspaper and smoking a cigar. Bored with the printed news, he glanced first at the other occupants of the room and then out of the window. The coffee house was on one of London's busiest streets. People had been hurrying past all afternoon and now, as the working day drew to a close and dusk began to fall, it seemed as though the crowds were increasing by the minute.

The man soon forgot his newspaper as, through the smoke of his cigar, he began studying a far more compelling spectacle – the passing citizens of London, illuminated by the flickering light of the street's gas lamps. Every player in the ceaseless drama of human life was represented on this urban stage beyond the window: rich and poor, the righteous and the wayward, labourers and men of leisure. He readily identified noblemen, merchants, lawyers, tradesmen, stock-jobbers, junior clerks – 'young gentlemen with tight coats, bright boots, well-oiled hair, and supercilious lips' – and upper clerks: 'they had all slightly bald heads, from which the right ears, long used to pen-holding, had an odd habit of standing off on end'. At the other end of the social scale were pickpockets, beggars, prostitutes and drunkards. Joining this motley procession were various hawkers and street workers, 'pic-men, porters, coal-heavers, sweeps; organ-grinders, monkey-exhibitors, and ballad-mongers, those who vended with those who sang; ragged artizans and exhausted laborers of every description'. It seemed as though all of humanity rubbed shoulders on this London street.

Suddenly the man leaned forward, his face close to the grimy windowpane. There among the crowd was a face unlike any he had seen before. The 'absolute idiosyncrasy of its expression' was quite remarkable. To our observer of the urban street, the face of this old man contained a world of human emotion and experience. It conjured up 'ideas of vast mental power, of caution, of penuriousness, of avarice, of coolness, of malice, of blood-thirstiness, of triumph, of merriment, of excessive terror, of intense – of supreme despair'.

Without a moment's hesitation he leapt from his window seat, grabbed his hat, coat and cane and rushed into the crowded street. As he gave chase he, too, became part of that flood of humanity. By now night had fallen and the city was shrouded in the thick fog common in this damp and smoky city. His quarry passed through elegant squares and crowded bazaars without once realising that he was being followed. There was something mysterious, even dangerous, about the old man. He was an enigma, an anomaly who didn't fit into any of the usual typologies of street life: 'His clothes, generally, were filthy and ragged; but as he came, now and then, within the strong glare of a lamp, I perceived that his linen, although dirty, was of beautiful texture; and my vision deceived me, or, through a rent in a closely buttoned and evidently second-handed *roquelaire* which enveloped him, I caught a glimpse both of a diamond and of a dagger.'

The old man walked for a night and a day through the streets and alleys of the city, restless and insatiable in his footloose yet apparently aimless quest. Eventually, our observer of London's crowds was forced to admit defeat and give up the pursuit. But as he watched the old man disappear into the city, he realised that this strange and inscrutable character was 'the type and the genius of deep crime. He refuses to be alone. He is the man of the crowd.'

This haunting urban encounter is described by Edgar Allan Poe in his story 'The Man of the Crowd', from 1840. By this time London had become the largest city the planet had ever seen, home to one and a half million people, larger even than ancient Rome. It was the urban wonder of the world. Twenty years earlier, Poe himself had lived in the heart of the great metropolis. His foster parents had taken rooms at '47 Southampton Row, Russell Square, Parish o' Bloomsbury', as the young boy was taught to say in case he ever got lost in this vast, teeming city. He lived in London for five years, attending school first in Chelsea and then in Stoke Newington, at that time still a village just north of the city, once home to Daniel Defoe. Poe's memories of crowded London streets – the Strand and High Holborn – undoubtedly informed his descriptions of the city in the story.[1]

Poe had just moved to the neat and orderly city of Philadelphia when he wrote 'The Man of the Crowd'. Before that, he and his wife had been living in New York. This city, with its narrow, muddy streets, was still decidedly provincial in comparison with London, its population about 300,000. But already it had that unmistakable buzz of a big city – an edgy, vibrant feel – and that was what Poe needed. City life was in his veins. When he wasn't writing in his Greenwich Village apartment, he was meeting his literary friends, visiting the magazine offices and bookshops of Lower Broadway, or just strolling through the streets observing the people and the sights of the city.

In New York there was a thriving press and Poe made a habit of reading all the newspapers, delighting in their sensationalist stories of disasters and modern marvels, such as the demonstration of the electric telegraph at the White House in February 1838. Indeed, each edition seemed to carry details of some new technological wonder. The industrial age was transforming the Western world and for many contemporary observers the astonishing growth of cities was dramatic evidence of the social revolution that was unfolding before their eyes. The future was urban.

London led the way, but Paris, Berlin and Vienna were not far behind. As cities grew to unprecedented sizes, people were both awed by their potential but also profoundly unsettled by their scale and energy. Vast crowds thronged the city streets from dawn till dusk, different classes and nationalities rubbing shoulders with each other, 'a mass of strangers who would remain strange', to use Rebecca Solnit's memorable phrase.[2] Were these urban masses going to drive the engine of capitalism to ever greater achievements, people wondered, or would they turn into mobs and unleash the spectre of revolution? Would the streets of these new cities be paved with gold or splashed with blood? The city and its burgeoning population – most of whom lived in slums – had become an alien landscape, an urban jungle.

Into this uncharted territory ventured journalists and writers like Charles Dickens. They became explorers of the urban street. A great walker and lover of London, Dickens turned the beauty and the squalor of the city into universal narratives that struck a chord with readers around the world. *Sketches by Boz* was a collection of articles penned by his journalistic alter ego, Boz, whom he describes as a 'speculative pedestrian'. They were written originally for the *Morning Chronicle*, on such subjects as streets at night and Vauxhall Gardens. On its publication in 1836, it was reviewed in glowing terms by Poe, who was particularly struck by the piece on London's gin shops.[3]

In Paris they had a word to describe an observer of the urban street such as Boz or Poe's narrator in 'The Man of the Crowd': *flâneur*. The French word is wonderfully untranslatable, evoking a sense of leisurely observation conducted while strolling through the city. In nineteenth-century Paris, the *flâneur* made the boulevards and cafés into his drawing room. He was a scientist of the sidewalk, a detached observer, dissecting the metropolitan crowd. The reports of these street semiologists appeared in French newspapers and British journals, like the *London Magazine*. For their genteel, bourgeois readers, who had probably never seen a slum, such articles helped them make sense of the intimidating chaos of the crowd.

A woman walking by the River Seine, Paris, past the Pont de l'Archevêché.

Not everyone welcomed the exuberant growth of the cities. For some the city was a threat. William Wordsworth, writing as early as 1800, warned that 'the encreasing [*sic*] accumulation of men in cities' had a negative effect on people's sensibilities, producing 'a craving for extraordinary incident' and a 'savage torpor'.[4] The old man in Poe's story seems to personify Wordsworth's fear that urban environments would induce both a passivity and a desire for sensationalism. Unable to be alone, Poe's character seeks out the excitement of the crowd. He draws his inexhaustible energy from the *perpetuum mobile* of the metropolis itself. And yet he remains a voyeur, a consumer of impressions rather than a participant – as is Poe's people-watching narrator. In the metropolis, Poe's story suggests, everyone is both a stranger and a connoisseur of crowds.

The Parisian poet Charles Baudelaire grasped the creative tension at the heart of city life. For him the metropolis was the very epitome of modernity and the *flâneur* was the ideal aesthetic citizen of this new urban age: 'The crowd is his element, as the air is that of birds and water of fishes. His passion and his profession are to become one flesh with the crowd.'[5] Baudelaire was inspired by Poe's story of the chase through London's streets. He celebrated the paradoxical idea of the *flâneur* as both a 'passionate spectator' and a participant in urban life. 'The spectator is a prince who everywhere rejoices in his incognito,' he wrote.[6] The *flâneur* is the idealised spirit of the city, experiencing the ebb and flow of urban life, yet never quite being swept away by its flood of impressions. He is part of events but also apart, a watchful stranger in the street.

After the 1848 Revolution, Baudelaire realised that traditional art was no longer able to describe the dynamic complexity of modern city life. Social and economic changes brought about by industrialisation demanded a new form of creativity. The *flâneur*, the urban walker, was for Baudelaire the embodiment of this new era. He personified 'the ephemeral, the fugitive, the contingent', urban qualities he rightly believed would transform modern life and art.[7]

In the 1920s and 1930s, the cultural historian Walter Benjamin, whose unfinished 'Arcades Project' (*Das Passagen-Werk*) revisited the subject of nineteenth-century Parisian street life, memorably described the *flâneur* as 'a botanist on asphalt'.[8] The *flâneur* – as the urban spectator, explorer or even sightseer – remains an immensely evocative figure in our increasingly urbanised world. In twentieth-century literature he is Leopold Bloom walking through 'dear dirty Dublin'. He is Robert Musil's 'man without qualities', precisely observing a traffic accident from his window in Vienna. She is Virginia Woolf's Mrs Dalloway: 'I love walking in London. Really, it's better than walking in the country.'[9] The great street photographers – such as John Thomson (1837–1921), E. O. Hoppé (1878–1972), Brassaï (1899–1984) and Robert Frank (1924–) – are also descendants of the *flâneur*. Indeed, we are all *flâneurs* now. After all, who hasn't indulged in the intoxicating pleasures of people-watching from an urban café or bar?

In 1930, the Weimar cultural critic Siegfried Kracauer wrote a beautiful essay about the 'intoxication of the streets' in Paris.[10] There is indeed something deeply evocative about the contrast between Haussmann's straight and rather inhuman boulevards and the older, more intimate side streets with their hidden arcades. Perhaps unsurprisingly, it was here in the 1950s and 1960s that the *flâneur* re-emerged, this time in radical garb. Led by Guy Debord, the Situationists set out to map the 'psychogeography' of Paris. Their exercises in urban drifting (what they termed *dérive*) charted the shifting, noumenal ambiances of Parisian streets. The *dérive* was an act of urban (and self-) exploration, best conducted under the influence of alcohol. With their maps, the psychogeographers aspired to depict an augmented urban reality. For urban drifting was, they believed, the key to unlocking the city's secrets and revealing the imaginary, and even the ideal, city that lay beneath the mundane surface. This was the city as harbinger of utopia.

The spirit of the *flâneur* can also be seen in the Street Observation Science Society, founded in 1986, whose objective was to document what remained of old Tokyo before it disappeared under a tide of anonymous concrete and steel. Their symbol was the sole of a shoe on which was drawn an all-seeing eye.[11] The Renaissance alchemist Paracelsus would have recognised this instantly. Unlike most of his scientific contemporaries, he was convinced that you could not

Mumbai's Skywalks

About 55 per cent of Mumbaikars walk or cycle to work, a very high proportion. In the United States, only 2.5 per cent of people walk to work.[14] But for commuters in Mumbai, the walk from the railway station to the office has become increasingly difficult. As this vast megacity of some nineteen million people has grown ever larger and more successful, its roads have become choked with a motley assortment of three-wheeled auto-rickshaws, trucks, cars and buses. The footpaths, too – which are often little more than strips of dirt – are crammed with pedestrians, street sellers and squatters. Sixty per cent of trips in Mumbai are made on foot, one of the highest rates for any city. Blocked pavements threaten the efficiency of the city. But now Mumbaikars have an alternative that will lift them (literally) out of the congested streets – an elevated skywalk, or, as the locals call it, the 'Yellow Caterpillar'. It is twenty feet above street level and takes pedestrians about a mile, snaking over the city to one of the many understand nature and the universe merely by reading books. You had to see the world with your own eyes. 'He who wishes to explore Nature must tread her books with his feet' was his motto. Paracelsus practised what he preached. He was a great walker and spent his life wandering from land to land, reading the pages of the *Codex of Nature* through the soles of his feet.

Anyone who really wants to get to know a city should follow in Paracelsus's footsteps. The city needs to be explored at a walking pace and discovered step by step. For understanding a city is, indeed, a cumulative process not unlike turning the pages of a book. Like a book, a city is both a technological triumph and a product of human creativity. It also exists in time and space: imagination (as Calvino showed in *Invisible Cities*) is required to read the text of a city.

In the seventeenth century, London was described as a labyrinth waiting to trap the unwary. The city was a 'country-mans Laborinth, he can find many things in it, but many times looseth himselfe'.[12] This is a wonderfully ambiguous passage. It suggests that in the urban maze you might lose more than just your sense of direction. You might lose your very self and emerge from the labyrinth a new person, an idea that would have delighted the Situationists. Indeed, Paul Auster describes New York as a 'labyrinth of endless steps' in which, by wandering aimlessly, one can leave oneself behind.[13]

A city can be overwhelming, even bewildering. As you wander

new business parks. It has proved popular with office workers (if not with the street vendors). 'Our city is so crowded we don't have a place to walk or exercise,' says commuter Shubhangi Ambardekar. 'My friend and I come up to the skywalk for our evening walks.'[15] The breeze on the skywalk also offers a welcome respite from the stifling streets below. The city plans to build fifty more at an estimated cost of $300 million.

Mumbai's Yellow Caterpillar skywalk.

its labyrinthine streets and alleys, the city can seem like a riddle in search of a solution. Each twist and turn reveals a different layer of the answer. Sometimes, like Kracauer, you seem to be on a Proustian quest for lost memories. Streets can be neural pathways; turn a corner and you step back in time: *déjà vu* – I have been here before. For Freud, a walk through an unfamiliar city became an uncanny journey into his subconscious. The Situationists were alive to the power of such resonances. But they also wanted to reveal the hidden histories of the city. Even the bricks have a story to tell, providing you can read their hieroglyphs. Like San Clemente in Rome, a city has layers of experience, all of which contribute to its *genius loci*, its unique sense of place and history.

There is a rich literary tradition of urban walkers, from Iain Sinclair and Will Self in today's London, through Walt Whitman in New York and stretching back to well before Poe and the *flâneurs* of Paris. All have sought to understand the city through what Michel de Certeau beautifully termed 'the long poem of walking'.[16] John Donne's *Satyre I* (1593) evokes 'the sinewes of a cities mistique bodie'. It is rich with scenes of London's street life in the early 1590s, especially the city's many temptations – from a 'plumpe muddy whore' and a 'prostitute boy', to exotic animals (an elephant and 'the wise politique horse', a bay gelding that could apparently count).[17] At the same time as Donne was writing, the 'survey' emerged as a new genre in the wake of John Stow's seminal city guidebook, the *Survey of London* (1598). Stow's book was organised as a walk tracing his route across London from east to west: 'I will beginne at the East, and so proceede thorough the high and most principall streete of the cittie to the west … by the conduite to the West corner against the Stockes … then by the said Stockes (a market place both of fish and flesh standing in the midst of the cittie) through the Poultrie (a streete so called) to the great conduite in west Cheape, and so through Cheape to the Standarde … Then by the Standard to the great crosse … And then to the little Conduit by Paules gate.'[18] Similarly, John Gay's jaunty poem 'Trivia: Or, the Art of Walking the Streets of London' (1716) leads the reader through 'long perplexing Lanes untrod before', past 'jostling Crouds' and even to 'the slimy Shore' of the Thames. In a more sombre key, William Blake wandered the streets of London at the beginning of the nineteenth century and observed 'Marks of weakness, marks of woe' in every face he passed.[19]

Street life is fleeting and fragmentary. 'An intoxication comes over the man who walks long and aimlessly through the streets. With each step, the walk takes on greater momentum; ever weaker grow the temptations of bistros, of shops, of smiling women, ever more irresistible the magnetism of the next street corner, of a distant square in the fog, of the back of a woman walking before him.'[20] This is Walter Benjamin describing the peripatetic philosophy of the *flâneur*. But in the consumer economy, as Benjamin warned, the *flâneur* can all too easily degenerate into a mere window shopper. Indeed, for many today that is the only time they will stroll through a city's streets. Of course, buying and selling has always been an essential part of urban life. There is nothing wrong with window shopping (although for the Situationists urban drifting was a subversive activity because of its apparent aimlessness and lack of economic purpose). But if you want to feel something of the unique identity of a city you have to learn to see beyond the glittering veneer of glass and neon that has brought an homogenous look to streets around the world.

Look above the shopfronts and you begin to sense the history of the original buildings: exposed beams, time-roughened brickwork as red-raw as abraded skin, a plaque recording a creative life spent in a building, faded lettering advertising a long-defunct product. As you stand in the high street, to the ubiquitous CCTV cameras you are just one more figure among the crowds of shoppers, someone with time to kill and money to spend. But as you begin to notice these traces of the past and read the urban text, the city starts to come alive. You become part of its history, more than a mere consumer of products. You are ready to begin a journey that can take you back to the roots of civilisation itself. It is time to start walking.

Traffic

In the ancient world, no one built better roads than the Romans. And as all roads led to Rome, it's not surprising that this archetypal megacity experienced some of the first urban traffic jams. Indeed, Julius Caesar was so frustrated by the city's congested roads that he banned carts during daytime. It seemed like a great idea at the time, indeed the decree remained in force for many years after Caesar's death. Unfortunately, all it did was increase traffic and noise during the night. The citizens of Rome were not pleased. 'What sleep is possible in a lodging?' complained the satirist Juvenal. 'The crossing of the wagons in the narrow, winding streets, the swearing of drovers brought to a standstill would snatch sleep from a sea-calf or the Emperor Claudius himself.'[21] The price cities have always paid for success is congested streets. And as Rome's citizens found, the apparent solutions have sometimes turned out to be as bad as the problem itself.

The horse-drawn carriage, or coach, was a new mode of transport in the middle of the sixteenth century. Cardinal Charles Borromeo advised that two things were essential in order to get on in sixteenth-century Rome: to love God and to own a carriage. At the time, there were more carriages in the Eternal City than in any other city – no fewer than 888 by 1594. As well as carriages, Rome's streets were thronged with many thousands of pilgrims and to help both them and the cardinals move freely around Rome, Pope Sixtus V put forward a bold plan for the city's redevelopment at the end of the sixteenth century. A network of broad, straight avenues, with monuments at intersections, would replace the narrow medieval streets. As Sigfried Giedion has said, 'it was in Rome that the lines of the traffic web of a modern city were first formulated and were carried out with absolute assurance'.[22] The Pope's plan transformed Rome into an imposing world capital, providing a model for later imperial and national capitals from Haussmann's Paris to L'Enfant's Washington, DC.

Of course, carriages were only for the wealthy – even in the nineteenth century people still referred to the upper classes as 'carriage folk'. John Stow notes that the first coach was brought to England in 1564 for the use of Queen Elizabeth. By 1636 there were some six thousand coaches in London.[23] Traffic jams were the inevitable result. In Paris they even had a name for it: 'l'embarras de Paris'. A seventeenth-century guidebook claimed that 'filth in the streets and traffic have made it impossible to go about in Paris except in coach'. The streets of Paris were, indeed, famously filthy and the mud that coated every street was notorious. Known as 'la boue de Paris', one visitor described it as 'a black unctuous Oil'.[24] The truth was that Parisian streets were effectively open sewers and if you wanted to keep your fine gown or shoes clean, you needed to be physically carried from door to door. As a result, for aristocrats and the wealthy a coach became *de rigueur*. In the seventeenth century, sedan chairs were also popular with the upper classes, only adding to the congestion in the streets. One effect of this increasing popularity of coaches and sedans was to distance the wealthy from the squalor of city life as experienced by the ordinary citizen. But no matter how posh you were, having your own transport was no guarantee of arriving on time.

During the Industrial Revolution levels of congestion for both pedestrians and vehicles increased dramatically as people flocked to the cities in unprecedented numbers. In American cities, both sidewalks and streets became virtually impassable during the daily rush in and out of downtown. Some hoped that the arrival of the automobile would solve the city's transport problems. In 1908, the inventor Thomas Edison confidently predicted that if New York's horse-drawn vehicles 'could be transformed into motor cars overnight' it would 'so relieve traffic [congestion] as to make Manhattan Island resemble "The Deserted Village"'.[25] Of course, nothing could have been further from the truth. By 1923, driving a car was no faster than walking in many American downtowns. Within a decade, 50,000 to 100,000 cars were entering the centres of Boston, Philadelphia and Detroit each weekday. More than 100,000 came into downtown Chicago, and more than 250,000 into Los Angeles, where there was one car for every two people (nationally the figure was one for every five people).[26]

To cure urban congestion in the twentieth century and to get the traffic moving again, highway engineers hacked their way through cites 'with a meat ax', to use the colourful phrase of New York urban planner Robert Moses. Just as railway lines had scythed their way through cities in the nineteenth century, so whole neighbourhoods were destroyed to make way for the motor car. In New York, there was even a proposal in the early years of the twentieth century to sell off Central Park so that land could be bought between Sixth and Seventh Avenues, from Lower Manhattan to the Harlem River, in order to build a parkway (a road buffered from residential areas by green belt) that would have cut a swathe through the heart of the city.[27]

To get the constipated urban traffic system flowing freely again, multi-lane freeways, bypasses, traffic lights and one-way streets were all introduced. In London the first one-way street dated back to 1801, when Humphry Davy's chemistry lectures at London's Royal Institution drew such large audiences to 21 Albemarle Street in 1801, that the street was blocked with carriages. One-way traffic was the solution. The first American one-way street appeared in Philadelphia in 1908, with one in Boston the year after. Multi-level streets were also seriously considered in the United States. Not just 'Double-Deck Streets', as one magazine termed them, but streets with up to six levels stacked one on top of another, as was proposed in New York in 1927.[28] Local traffic would have travelled on the bottom, trucks on the next level, then two levels for buses, with passenger cars on the fifth and high-speed cars on top. Unsurprisingly, the cost of such schemes proved prohibitive, although elevated highways were built in Europe and America.

As fast as they were constructed, the new freeways filled up with cars and the traffic jams grew longer and longer. In James D. Houston's 1964 story 'Gas Mask' there is gridlock in an American city for more than seven days: 'The jam now included not only the freeways, but all main streets and key intersections, where buses, streetcars and trucks were still entangled. It even extended beyond the city.'[29]

In 1961, British architect and urban planner Sir Geoffrey Jellicoe imagined a transport utopia – *Motopia*. He predicted a city of raised roads where people use cars and helicopters to commute. Unfortunately, the reality of transport in the modern city has been far from utopian. One billion cars were manufactured in the twentieth century and by 2030 it's thought that there will be at least that number on roads around the world.[30] The twenty-first-century American city contains almost as many cars as people and traffic jams remain very much a feature of urban life. The average American commuter spends about a working week each year just sitting in traffic.[31] In São Paulo, where there are nearly seven million registered cars, traffic jams can stretch for 100 miles (160 kilometres) at rush hour.[32] In China – the country that holds the record for road deaths (110,000 a year) – a traffic jam in Beijing took police three days and two nights to unblock.[33]

Perhaps more than any other human technology, the car has shaped our everyday lives. For thousands of years, cities were designed principally for the pedestrian, with networks of narrow, winding streets and alleys linking public spaces. A mere 10 per cent of the city's surface was used for movement.[34] Vehicles changed that – first carts, then carriages, coaches and sedans, followed by streetcars – all had an impact on the urban streetscape. People's freedom to walk in the city has been increasingly restricted to pavements and sidewalks. But in the twentieth century, cities began to be designed with the car, not pedestrians, in mind. 'Instead of planning motor cars and motorways

A traffic jam in Athens due to a strike by public transport workers.

to fit our life,' complained Lewis Mumford in 1957, 'we are rapidly planning our life to fit the motor car.'[35] Traffic flows became the urban planner's priority, resulting in cities dominated by monotonous linear structures. In the ideal cities of the Modernists, streets were replaced by multi-lane expressways and pedestrians were herded on to sky-walks or down into underpasses. The result was car-centric cities such as Brasília and Milton Keynes.

The quality of urban life took a back seat, as French philosopher Henri Lefebvre has said: 'City life is subtly but profoundly changed, sacrificed to that abstract space where cars circulate like so many atomic particles.'[36] Roads grew wider to accommodate ever more vehicles and they became barriers to social interaction in the city, dead zones that were dangerous for the vulnerable. In 2004, there were 1.2 million deaths and fifty million injuries each year on the world's roads. In the ten to twenty-four age group, accidents involving cars are the leading cause of death worldwide.[37]

The car as technology was perfected in the city of Detroit, aka Motor City or Town. But it was in Los Angeles that the car really came into its own as an integral part of urban life.[38] The city's mild climate and affluence made it the perfect place to sell cars. Whereas cities such as New York or Chicago became major centres during the streetcar era, Los Angeles became a world city only after the car became a feature of everyday life. It is one of the first cities whose

175

form was moulded by the automobile. From 1920 Los Angeles developed a new idea of public transport: 'the public provides the road, and, to use it, you must bring the car.'[39]

As Jean Baudrillard has said, Los Angeles 'is in love with its limitless horizontality, as New York may be with its verticality'.[40] This sprawling, multi-centred city made up of low-density, single-family housing offers people a lifestyle that is only possible thanks to the car. Angelinos use the car for virtually everything: from commuting and visiting the mall or the cinema, to buying a hamburger. But even in autopia there are traffic jams. Los Angeles has 'evolved from a car owner's paradise to an increasingly congested and compromised megalopolis'.[41] Today it is the most congested urban area in the United States, with the average commuter being stuck in traffic for seventy hours a year.[42]

What Guy Debord called 'the parasitical existence of personal cars' has transformed the modern city and encouraged the flight to the suburbs.[43] It has also fundamentally changed people's relationship to the city. Carriages distanced the affluent from the dirt of the street. But cars have removed people of all classes from the public life of the

Parking Meter

The parking meter – a timepiece on a pole – was invented by a former Oklahoma newspaperman, Carl Magee, in North Dakota. The world's first parking meter – the 'Park-O-Meter' – was installed in Oklahoma City on 16 July 1935, charging a nickel for an hour or less. Soon they appeared on every downtown street, one every twenty feet, spreading like wildfire throughout the Southwest. By 1937, some 20,000 meters were in use in 35 cities. Three years later there were 70,000 in 160 American cities.[45] In the 1967 film *Cool Hand Luke*, Paul Newman plays a character who does something many drivers have longed to do: he

systematically cuts the heads off an entire row of parking meters.

In Britain parking meters were first installed in Grosvenor Square, in London's Mayfair, in 1958. They were designed by Kenneth Grange.[46] The so-called 'meter maids', who serviced the meters, achieved lasting fame in the song 'Lovely Rita' (1967) by The Beatles. New York City introduced parking meters in 1951 to help ease congestion on the roads. The clockwork mechanisms had to be wound up every week. The city retired its last mechanical parking meter on 20 December 2006. It was located at the south-west corner of West 10th Street and Surf Avenue in Coney Island, Brooklyn. The new battery-powered digital meters, first used street, cocooning them in an air-conditioned bubble, insulated from the outside environment. You don't meet strangers in a car: instead of other people's voices, you hear music or the radio; instead of people's faces, you see the rear of the car ahead of you. The transformative encounters and experiences of the city are lost to the car passenger. In addition, the structure of the city has changed. Urban space itself is increasingly fragmented by fast roads and car parks. Most Americans have no choice but to use cars because they don't live in a walkable environment: their streets have narrow sidewalks and are poorly lit; their roads have infrequent pedestrian crossings and are often so wide (six lanes) that crossing them is impossible.[44] Indeed, in many American states, jaywalking – a term that emerged at the beginning of the twentieth century to describe careless crossing of a road – is an offence. Urban thoroughfares have become no-go zones for pedestrians, who have been reduced to second-class citizens.

But change is in the air. Transport generates nearly a quarter of the UK's carbon dioxide emissions and over half of that comes from cars and vans. To maintain the health of the planet, we need to get out of our cars. In the age of climate change and peak oil, 'walkability'

in 1995 and which now account for all of the city's 62,000 single-space parking meters, are more accurate and more difficult to break into.

Carl C. Magee, inventor of the parking meter.

'The world changes. Just as the subway token went, now the manual meter has gone,' said New York's transportation commissioner, Iris Weinshall. She admitted feeling nostalgic for its passing. As a child in Midwood, Brooklyn, she recalled running errands with her father: 'Whenever my father would park, it was really a thrill to put the coin in the meter and turn that little handle.'[47] Even in the age of multi-storey car parks, parking remains a major problem in cities. For example, there are 6.8 million cars licensed in São Paulo's metropolitan area. If each car needs ten square metres for parking, then that means sixty-eight square kilometres of space is provided for car parking: an area larger than Manhattan.[48]

is the new buzzword in urban planning. And public transport is also experiencing a renaissance – even in America.

In 2010, United States Transportation Secretary Ray LaHood stated on his official blog: 'This is the *end* of favoring motorized transportation at the expense of non-motorized.' This could represent a watershed in how Americans move around their cities. For the first time in modern America, the official policy is now to treat walking and bicycling equally with cars.[49] This shift is part of a change occurring throughout the developed world as cities try to cut car use and increase environmentally friendly means of transport – cycling, walking and mass transit. Unfortunately, in much of the developing world the reverse is often still true. In Mumbai, 150,000 more cars are added to the city's roads each year.[50] Until the 1980s, Shanghai invested in cycling infrastructure and bicycles were on every street. Then central government policy was reversed in favour of motor cars. 'Let's build roads to get rich' runs a current Communist Party slogan.[51] Now cycling has dropped from 40 to 25 per cent of all journeys and bicycles have even been banned on certain city streets.[52] The result? Traffic jams and choking levels of air pollution.

Today Shanghai is considering introducing a congestion charge for road users. Singapore was the first city to introduce congestion charging in 1975. In the northern hemisphere, road pricing has become a popular way of managing car use. London began charging car users in the city centre from 2003. Bus use and cycling have now increased significantly, the latter by 83 per cent since 2000. There are currently an estimated 480,000 cycle journeys and an estimated 5.7 million walking journeys each day in the United Kingdom's capital.[53] London also charges more for those vehicles that produce higher levels of pollutants. The revenues generated are reinvested in public transport. A reduction of eighty thousand cars per day in London has been achieved, although it still has a relatively high rate of car use (36 per cent) compared to New York City (30 per cent) or Istanbul (13 per cent).[54] Congestion charging has been adopted in Stockholm, Milan and Rome, but Mayor Bloomberg's 2008 proposal for congestion pricing in New York was not implemented. Currently, weekday traffic in Manhattan's business district moves at an average of 9.5mph, which, as the *New York Times* says, is 'about the speed of a farmyard chicken at full gallop'.[55] And this is in the city that has the lowest automobile-to-resident ratio of any city in the United States:

over three-quarters of Manhattan's households don't own a car.

Pedestrians are increasingly reclaiming their city streets from cars. In 1962, Copenhagen was the first city to pedestrianise a main thoroughfare. The two-kilometre-long Strøget remains Europe's longest pedestrian street. Jan Gehl, an influential Danish urbanist and architect who has played a key role in transforming Copenhagen, argues that shopping should not be the main reason people come into the city centre. Rather, people should be attracted to the city by its atmosphere – the vibrancy of its street life and urban culture. Pedestrianised areas play a significant role in creating this. Today Copenhagen's pedestrian network has expanded to about 100,000 square metres, making it one of the most extensive in the world, a model of urbanism copied from Melbourne to Montreal.[56] Europe's largest car-free urban zone is Vauban in south-west Germany. The rate of car ownership in this pioneering development is 220 per 1,000 residents, compared to 520 per 1,000 in the nearby city of Freiburg im Breisgau. Seventy per cent of Vauban's families do not own a car. Those that do have to leave it in the multi-storey car park on the outskirts for an annual charge of £12,500 per parking space. But in Vauban the need for a car has been drastically reduced by fast buses, an efficient tram service and a network of cycle paths.[57]

In the 1960s, the Netherlands was a trail blazer in developing urban areas that minimised the impact of the car. In areas known as a 'woonerf', or home zone, traffic-calming measures were used to make drivers more aware of pedestrians. The Dutch engineer Hans Monderman (who died in 2008) went much further while working as a traffic safety officer in the 1980s. He was tasked with reducing the accident rate in the village of Oudehaske, where two children had been killed in road accidents. As he had little money for traffic calming measures, he removed traffic signs and lights, as well as kerbs and street furniture that created boundaries between driving and walking areas. The result was that car drivers slowed down by 40 per cent. In 2004 at Drachten, Holland, all traffic lights and road markings were removed from one junction used by twenty thousand cars a day. Instead of the chaos that some predicted, people drove more carefully and accidents have fallen on average from nine a year to just one. The town has since removed almost all of its traffic lights and signs. For Monderman the explanation was obvious. Creating a 'naked street' by removing the barriers and signs made drivers interact with their environment. It forced people 'to look each other in the eye, to judge body language and learn to take responsibility – to function as normal human beings'. To demonstrate his faith in the theory he even walked backwards with his arms folded into oncoming traffic. He was not knocked down. Indeed, Monderman claimed there had never been a fatality in any of his schemes. Monderman's revolution in street design is based on the urbanist ideal that 'eye contact and the consultation between civilians in public space is the highest quality you can get in a free country'.[58]

Today this idea of 'shared space' is being introduced in cities across Europe. Kensington High Street in London was redesigned in 2003 without barriers. The number of accidents subsequently fell by 44 per cent.[59] Similarly, in 2009 barriers were removed at Oxford Circus and an X-shaped crossing introduced.[60] Returning streets to pedestrians is also becoming popular. Even in Manhattan cars were temporarily excluded on Broadway from 47th to 42nd Streets and from 35th to 33rd Streets. Tourists and New Yorkers alike loved the pedestrianised area so much that it was made permanent in 2010.[61] In Paris each summer since 2002 a section of the two-lane urban expressway (the Voie Georges Pompidou) on the Right Bank of the Seine has been turned into an urban beach – the 'Paris Plage' – complete with sand and deckchairs. In 2010, the city's mayor, Bertrand Delanoe, proposed permanently changing stretches of the road on the Left Bank and part of the Right Bank from a 'motorway' into a 'human, lived-in boulevard', with parks, foot and cycle paths.[62] Despite its love affair with the car, Shanghai has also embraced car-free urban zones, as in the recent redevelopment of Xintiandi in the Shikumen neighbourhood.[63]

In the twenty-first century, the threat of climate change and concerns about pollution have turned the car from saviour to villain. As well as walking and cycling, public transport is enjoying a renaissance in many cities. In the southern hemisphere, Bogotá, the capital of Colombia, has pioneered bus rapid transit (BRT) schemes that have revolutionised transport in the city in a way comparable to the railways in nineteenth-century British cities. Bogotá is a city of seven million people. Since 1997 it has vigorously pursued a campaign to improve safety on its streets, investing in public transport and redesigning streets rather than in new urban motorways. It is now held up as a model to the rest of the world. Thanks to the policies of

mayors Antanas Mockus and Enrique Peñalosa, who ran the city from

1995 to 2003, the number of deaths from traffic accidents in Bogotá has been almost halved, falling from 914 fatalities in 1998 to 553 in 2006. Mayor Mockus even employed mime artists to draw attention to bad driving. The sight of mime artists pretending to pull vehicles that were dangerously parked became common on Bogotá's streets. Most importantly, Mayor Peñalosa brought in a new bus rapid transit system (called TransMilenio), with dedicated lanes, modelled on the successful one at Curitiba, Brazil. It now carries 1.3 million passengers a day, 18 per cent of transit trips in the city.[64] (In the United States, 4.7 per cent of commuters used public transport to travel to work in 2005, while 77 per cent drove alone.)[65]

Bogotá also actively encourages its citizens to walk and cycle. 'Cycling is only a more efficient way of walking,' says Peñalosa. 'People should not feel inferior if they are on a cycle. The public good must always prevail over the private.'[66] The city has now pedestrianised a twenty-four-kilometre-long street and Peñalosa says he would like to see more such streets, as well as improved pavements and cycle lanes. The city hopes to eliminate private vehicles from the city centre by 2015.[67]

Going Underground

'A subterranean railway under London was awfully suggestive of dark, noisome tunnels, buried many fathoms deep beyond the reach of light or life; passages inhabited by rats, soaked with sewer drippings, and poisoned by the escape of gas mains. It seemed an insult to common sense to suppose that people who could travel as cheaply to the city on the outside of a Paddington 'bus would ever prefer, as a merely quicker medium, to be driven amid palpable darkness through the foul subsoil of London.'[68]

Two years after this article appeared in *The Times*, tens of thousands of Londoners were choosing to travel each day 'through the foul subsoil' of the capital. The world's first underground railway line opened in 1863 and ran from opposite Paddington railway station in the west, to Farringdon Street on the edge of the historic City of London. The line was built by the Metropolitan Railway Company and was known as the Metropolitan, the origin of the word now used around the world to refer to subways – 'Metro'.

London was the first city to use railways for its public transport system. Two techniques of building underground railways were pioneered here: sub-surface lines (using the cut and cover method) such as the Metropolitan, and deep level, or 'tube', lines. The first true tube line was opened in 1890, running between King William Street in the City (now defunct, but near Monument station) and Stockwell in south London. Today, the London Underground forms an extensive subterranean labyrinth of tunnels, the deepest lying 220 feet beneath the city streets. Building the network was 'a truly miraculous undertaking', says the historian of the Underground, Christian Wolmar.[69] Indeed, the idea of running a railway system under a city was so original that it took nearly forty years before another city tried to follow London's example. And nowhere else attempted to use steam locomotives underground, an idea which would rightly appal today's health and safety officials.

This 'magnificent organism' hidden beneath Londoners' feet has played a vital role in the city's success and in the development of its institutions.[70] It helped London expand at a time when the number of office workers was rising steadily in the City and in Whitehall, where 160,000 civil servants were employed by the first decade of the twentieth century. The Underground also helped create the consumer society, providing cheap and efficient mass transport to the new department stores – such as Harrods, in Knightsbridge – which were often built on the outskirts where land was cheaper. Whiteleys opened its first store just a few weeks after the Metropolitan line, in Westbourne Grove, about a mile from Paddington.

Like the citadel at the heart of the first cities, London's Underground became a place of safety in times of conflict. During both world wars, the Underground protected London's citizens from the new technology of urban mass destruction: aerial bombing. By September 1917, 100,000 people were sheltering in Tube stations each night and during the whole of the First World War more than four million took refuge beneath ground. In the Second World War, sleeping on station platforms became a familiar experience for Londoners. 'Last night, not six inches from me, lay the most beautiful girl,' wrote one young man. 'Then she began to snore and her loveliness faded.'[71] At Aldwych station a library was provided and Shakespeare's plays were performed, while above ground Nazi bombers blitzed the Elizabethan bard's city. Those priceless treasures of another great city, the Elgin Marbles, were moved from the British Museum and stored in the tunnels at Aldwych for safety.

But the Underground has also been a place of fear and even terror. On 7 July 2005 three suicide bombers blew themselves up on Underground trains, killing fifty-two people and injuring more than seven hundred. It was the worst loss of life on the Underground, but it was not the first time terrorists had struck at the city's heart. In the 1880s, Irish nationalists planted bombs on Tube trains and in 1897 a bomb killed two men at Aldersgate (now Barbican). 'The four inside compartments were smashed … Almost the whole of the roof of the carriage had been blown off,' reported *The Times*.[72]

London's public transport system began with omnibuses in 1829. George Shillibeer ran twenty-seater horse-drawn carriages from Paddington to the Bank of England for the relatively high sum of a shilling. (Thirty years later the Metropolitan's early morning workmen's trains would offer a whole week's travel for a shilling.) Within a decade there were 620 omnibuses in London. Streetcars or horse-drawn trams, which ran through the street on iron rails, were introduced to Britain by an American, George Francis Train, who some say was the inspiration for Jules Verne's character Phileas Fogg. They appeared in London in 1870 and became the main form of mass transport here until the end of the century.

London was the centre of the British Empire and, like imperial Rome, its streets were chaotic. By the middle of the century, London's veins were clogged with traffic. Nearly 250,000 people came into the City each day to work. As well as omnibuses, hansom cabs and hackney carriages (uncomfortable and expensive, at eightpence per mile), there were horse-drawn wagons, advertising vans pulled by horses, costermongers with carts, and animals being driven to market through the streets. By the end of the century, London's fifty thousand horses used for public transport were depositing one thousand tonnes of dung a day on the capital's streets, creating an unpleasant hazard for pedestrians and a boon for gardeners.[73]

The construction of railways in central London had been banned by Parliament. As a result, terminals were built on what were then the edges of the city and transport into the centre was a problem. Railway lines elevated on viaducts, such as those later built in New York, were regarded as unacceptable in the historic City. But London did have the perfect geology for tunnelling – a thick layer of clay, 450 feet deep. As early as 1825, the father and son team of Marc and Isambard Brunel had begun building a tunnel under the River Thames. When it was eventually completed in 1843 it was the world's first tunnel built under water. If London had been built on rock (as is New York) or on gravel (as is much of southern London), the Underground's deep tube tunnels would never have been constructed and the history of public transport would have been very different.

Approval for the first underground line was given in 1854. But in order to realise this revolutionary project, major engineering problems had to be overcome: a subterranean spaghetti of sewers, pipes and drains had to be diverted, and the engineers had to ensure that tunnels were not flooded by rivers or that the foundations of buildings were not undermined. Wherever possible they followed the line of the roads, thus avoiding the need to demolish buildings. Nevertheless, some 12,000 people were displaced during the construction of the first section. Later, when the Metropolitan line expanded westwards, part of an elegant terrace had to be demolished. As a result a fake façade was built between numbers 23 to 24 Leinster Gardens, near Bayswater.

Underground Arts

London's Underground has had a pervasive impact on the city's culture, from popular music to poetry. The French poet Arthur Rimbaud, who lived for fourteen months in London, wrote an evocative prose poem about a journey on the 'Métropolitain' in 1874. When the Metropolitan railway was extended northwest into the Buckinghamshire countryside in 1887, the new developments and 'garden villages' that were built here became known as Metro-Land from 1915. The suburban dream made possible by the Underground was immortalised in many of John Betjeman's poems, such as 'Harrow-on-the-Hill' (1954) and 'Metroland' (1971).

Walter Sickert's *Queen's Road (Bayswater) Station* (1916) is one of the first paintings whose theme is the Underground. It depicts a seated figure waiting for a train beneath a sign for Whiteleys. In the 1930s, London Transport commissioned leading artists such as Paul Nash and László Moholy-Nagy to design a series of posters for the Underground which became works of art in their own right. The colour-coded map of the Underground is itself now a design classic. Based on an electrical circuit diagram, the genius of Harry Beck's 1932 map is that it did not try to represent the real distances between stations. Instead this 'geo-schematic' map offers a simplified plan of the network that has since been copied by subway systems around the world, from Sydney to St Petersburg.

Despite the scepticism of some journalists, Londoners loved their new subterranean railway. At least thirty thousand people travelled on the line when it opened on Saturday, 10 January 1863. In its first year, 11.8 million people used the Metropolitan line – four times the population of the capital, and a daily average (including Sundays) of 32,300 travellers. Most used it not for travel between railway termini, as had been expected, but for short trips – the essence of urban transport.[74] The fares were affordable. Bankers were as likely to travel underground as were workers and artisans. There were three classes of fare, costing threepence, fourpence and sixpence for a single journey. Some 70 per cent of the Metropolitan's passengers travelled third class.

From 1864 an early morning workmen's service was provided, with a return fare of just threepence. Journalist and social campaigner Henry Mayhew travelled on it (departing at 5.15 a.m.), and found the carriages to be 'extremely handsome and roomy vehicles'. He found that the Underground was already changing Londoners' lives. A labourer told him that he could now live further out of town, where rents were more affordable and conditions better. Even his family life

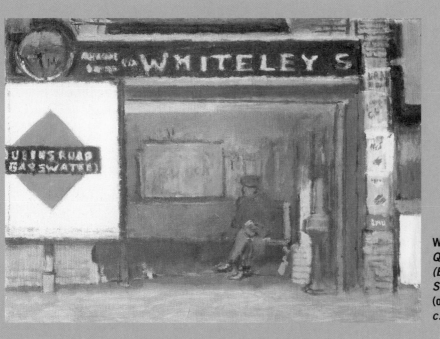

Walter Sickert, *Queen's Road (Bayswater) Station* (oil on canvas, *c.* 1916).

had improved, as he no longer had a long walk home each night.[75]

The Metropolitan was undoubtedly popular. But operating steam locomotives in tunnels was far from ideal. The air in the stations and carriages was filled with a suffocating mix of steam, sulphurous smoke and coal dust. Members of staff who worked long hours underground experienced appalling conditions and some undoubtedly died as a result of the toxic fumes. For this reason, engine drivers didn't wait the full minute at stations, often pausing for just twenty seconds, much to the annoyance of customers who missed their stop. One journalist reported his experience riding in the driver's cab: 'By the time we reached Gower Street I was coughing and spluttering like a boy with his first cigar. "It is a little unpleasant when you ain't used to it," said the driver, with the composure born of long usage, "but you ought to come on a hot summer day to get the real thing!"'[76] A chemist near Gower Street station (now Euston Square) sold bottles of 'Underground Mixture' to resuscitate those who were regularly overcome by sulphurous fumes.

Following the success of the Metropolitan, new lines began rapidly spreading out across London. At the same time as Baron Haussmann was changing the face of Paris above ground, London was being transformed beneath its streets. The Hammersmith & City line opened in June 1864, running from Green Lane (now Westbourne Park) to Hammersmith, a village previously only known for 'its spinach and strawberries'.[77] With the arrival of the Underground station (a District line station was also built in 1874), Hammersmith soon became a commuter suburb. Today it's easy to forget that many of these stations – such as Latimer Road or Goldhawk Road – were built in open fields. Property developers were quick to buy up the land in order to exploit the housing needs of that new urban species: the commuter.

In 1864, Parliament approved plans for companies to build a circular underground train line beneath central London. The Metropolitan was to be extended from Paddington to South Kensington in the west and through Moorgate to Tower Hill in the east. A new company would build a line – known later as the District – from Tower Hill to South Kensington along the Thames. This was the first of many circle lines carved out beneath cities around the world.

By the middle of 1866, *The Times* reported that two thousand navvies were digging tunnels for the District line, while kilns at Earls Court were producing 140 million bricks for tunnels and embankments. The Metropolitan was running a service to South Kensington by 1868. Construction of the District line through densely populated areas such as Westminster and Victoria took longer, reaching Mansion House by 1871. It was not until 1884 that trains could run round the entire Circle. Initially, people were rather bemused by the idea of a railway line that went nowhere. But it soon became vital to London's economy, both for commuting and leisure. The District line also expanded west to Richmond in 1877, via Barons Court and Bedford Park, and then on to Ealing Broadway in 1879 and Wimbledon in 1889.

These lines were all sub-surface, built by the cut and cover method, effectively digging a deep trench to lay the tracks and then roofing it to form a tunnel. In 1886, work began on the first deep-level 'tube' line, the City & South London. It was built using similar techniques to those employed by the Brunels in their tunnel under the Thames. The tunnels were dug using a huge circular wooden shield containing several men, each in a separate compartment and armed with a pickaxe. As the earth was hacked out and removed, the shield was edged forwards and the tunnel roof secured with cast-iron segments bolted together. The circular tunnel was just 10 feet 6 inches in diameter, and between 45 and 105 feet deep. The first tube line was opened in November 1890 by the Prince of Wales (later Edward VII). He expressed the hope that 'this first electric railway … will … do much to alleviate the congestion of the traffic which now exists'.[78]

Ten thousand people flocked to use the Tube on its first day. Afterwards the figure rose to 15,000 a day. *The Times* memorably described the new tube line as being like a 'gigantic iron drainpipe, thrust by main force through the solid London clay, much in the fashion in which the cheesemonger thrusts a scoop into his Cheddar or Gloucester'.[79] The trains were small, just three carriages with thirty-two seats in each. They were lit by electric bulbs and had no windows, just glass strips above head height. For the first time on Britain's railways there was just one class and a flat fare, twopence. Stockwell to the City took just eighteen minutes, at an average speed (including stops) of about 11.5 mph, twice as fast as the quickest surface transport.

The second deep tube line was the Central London Railway (now known as the Central line), which opened in 1900. A truly modern tube line, each train could carry some four hundred people. (Today 1,300 people can be crammed into peak-time trains.) Straps hanging

from the ceiling of the carriages made life easier for standing passengers during the bumpy journeys and a new word was born that became familiar to commuters across the world: strap-hanging.

Soon 100,000 people were using the Central line daily. During the early 1900s, the annual total of passengers was 45 million, or 125,000 daily. By 1904 the District line carried 51 million passengers a year and ran on average twenty trains an hour between South Kensington and Mansion House. Today more than a billion passenger journeys a year are made on the London Underground, a figure equalled by the subway systems of New York (built 1904) and the Paris Métro (1900).

Shanghai opened its first line in 1995, but its rapidly expanding Metro has now become the longest subway network in the world. Moscow's underground is one of the busiest in the world, carrying nine million people a day or some three billion people a year, a figure only matched by Tokyo. Moscow's first subway line opened in 1935 and the system became the pride of Stalin's USSR. Designed as people's palaces, the stations are fabulously decorated, with murals celebrating Russian prowess in sport, war and industry. During the Cold War, very deep sections of subway were built (for example, part of the Arbatsko–Pokrovskaya line from Pl. Revolyutsii to Kievskaya) to serve the dual purpose of transport and as a nuclear shelter. [80]

Stockholm's modern subway, the Tunnelbana, is small by international standards – about a quarter the size of the London Underground. But its stations are quite unlike those anywhere else. Cut out of solid rock, the designers have chosen to leave the rock bare, emphasising the sense of being beneath ground and creating a memorable cave-like atmosphere.[81]

Today, going underground is a familiar experience for city dwellers around the world. Building subways and trams is also seen as a way of revitalising cities. Mass transit systems are more environmentally friendly than cars (a very inefficient form of urban transport) and make affordable travel available to all sections of society. As Paul Bedford, former City of Toronto chief planner, has rightly said: 'It should be possible to build a city and a region where you can go your whole life without owning a car and not feel deprived.'[82]

Workmen take a cigarette break on the eagle gargoyles on the sixty-first floor of the Chrysler Building, New York, in the 1940s. (following page)

The Skyscraper

When the Sleeper in H. G. Wells's 1910 novel awakes after 203 years and sees London in 2100, he is overwhelmed by the scale of the city. The man from the nineteenth century has never seen skyscrapers before. To his mind the soaring architecture of the metropolis can only be compared to geological structures – to mountains, canyons and 'cliffs'. Later, as he looks down on the metropolis from an aeroplane, he realises that London has lost its sleepy suburbs. Now there is a sharp vertical boundary dividing city from countryside, 'like a wall, like a cliff, a steep fall of three or four hundred feet, a frontage broken only by terraces here and there, a complex decorative façade'. Future London rises from the landscape like a vast tower, a 'great machine' filled 'with a thousand classes of accommodation, thousands of dining halls, chapels, theatres, markets and places of assembly'.[83]

Although buildings within cities have not yet fused to form a single structure as Wells imagined, the scale of architecture in today's cities is unprecedented in urban history. In nineteenth-century London and other European cities, the tallest structures were generally church steeples. At 111 metres (365 feet), St Paul's Cathedral dominated London's skyline for well over two hundred years after it was built in 1710. (Today, London's tallest building is One Canada Square at Canary Wharf (236 metres/771 feet,) but this will soon be surpassed by Renzo Piano's seventy-two-storey glass tower, Shard London Bridge, at 310 metres/1,017 feet). Even in the industrial nineteenth century, few buildings rose above five storeys. After all, not many people were prepared to climb more than five flights of stairs. But in the second half of the century, advances in technology and the rapid growth and wealth of American cities brought about a revolution in architecture that would eventually transform urban skylines around the world.

In 1853, at the Crystal Palace Exhibition in New York, Elisha Graves Otis chose a dramatic way to demonstrate the safety of his new hydraulic elevator. He stood on top of it and cut the hoisting rope. Instead of falling, the platform came to a stop. 'All safe, gentlemen!' he declared triumphantly.[84] The age of vertical people movers, or 'perpendicular railways' as they were termed, had begun.[85] Within a few years, large stores and hotels in American cities were installing elevators, or lifts. The first office building to have steam elevators was New York's seven-storey Equitable Life Assurance Building in 1870. Elevators were an essential stage in the evolution of skyscrapers. By the end of the century, Manhattan had three thousand elevators transporting 1.5 million passengers a day into the skies.

Although New York was the city that would become synonymous with the skyscraper, the revolution in construction that made the vertical city possible happened in Chicago. The fire of October 1871 had devastated the city. It also created 'one of the biggest urban building booms in history'.[86] Some of America's most talented architects began working here, men like Daniel H. Burnham, John Wellborn Root, Louis Sullivan and William Le Baron Jenney (who had collaborated with Olmsted on the planning of Riverside). These architects pioneered the use of steel-framed buildings. Traditionally, structures had been supported by masonry walls and the higher the building the more massive these had to be. The highest masonry structure ever built was Chicago's sixteen-storey Monadnock Building (1889–92, Burnham and Root). It was so heavy that it began sinking into Chicago's boggy ground.

With steel-framed buildings, the walls no longer support the building but hang from the girders like curtains. Their function is simply to keep the weather out. The idea of using a steel skeleton or cage was inspired by Britain's iron bridges and iron-framed buildings, such as Joseph Paxton's Crystal Palace exhibition hall (London, 1851). New York's Tower Building (1889) was described by its designer as a 'steel bridge stood on end' and, like bridges, skyscrapers were supported on reinforced concrete piers dug deep into the ground by gangs of men working in caissons, or pressurised chambers.[87] Like the roots of some giant tree, the cylindrical piers of New York's skyscrapers descended as much as 178 feet (in the case of the Municipal Building in 1913) to reach the ancient and compacted bedrock, Manhattan schist.

Chicago's ten-storey Home Insurance Building (1883–5), designed by Jenney, was one of the first buildings constructed using structural steel. Others soon followed in the city, such as Burnham and Root's Rand McNally Building (1888–90). It was at this time that the word 'skyscraper' came into common usage. In 1891, Maitland's *American Slang Dictionary* included the word for the first time, defining it as 'a very tall building such as are now being built in Chicago'.[88] But the city's building boom resulted in an oversupply of office space. Financiers and property developers soon realised that Chicago could only support a limited number of skyscrapers. However, New York was both bigger and richer. As the price of land on Manhattan Island rose, so too did the city's skyline. By 1903, the price of prime real estate in New York City was four times what it was in Chicago. There were fortunes to be made from sky-high buildings.

New York skyscraper architect Harvey Corbett described the use of steel frames as 'the most momentous step in the history of architecture since the days of Rome. In a single bound architecture was freed from the shackles of stone-weight and made flexible beyond belief. Suddenly architecture gained a new dimension.'[89] New York's more conservative architects took a decade to catch up with their colleagues in Chicago. But during the 1890s, Manhattan's skyline assumed its now familiar vertiginous aspect. Indeed, the word 'skyline' began to be used at this time to describe its horizon.[90] Until 1890, the 280-foot-high Trinity Church spire in New York had been the tallest structure in the city. But in that year George B. Post's New York World Building, built for the paper's owner Joseph Pulitzer, exceeded it by some twenty-five feet. In the future, church spires would be replaced by cathedrals of commerce on the urban skyline.

As well as elevators and new construction techniques, the electrification of cities helped drive the skyscraper boom. It was in 1882 that the first electricity-generating station was built in Lower Manhattan at Pearl Street. In 1902, *Harper's Weekly* enthused about how such technological advances were part of a new dynamism that was animating the modern metropolis: 'The city is simply bursting its bonds. It is as if some mighty force were astir beneath the ground, hour by hour pushing up structures that a dozen years ago would have been inconceivable … The distribution of electrical energy through the streets and the invention of the steam-drill, together with the use of skeleton frames for immense buildings, have transformed the outward appearance of the town.'[91] Electricity was the life blood of the vertical city – it illuminated the new streets in the sky and drove the fans and machines that made high-rise life possible. It also powered the elevators and the subways that brought workers to and from their offices. Electricity is still playing a role in the evolution of skyscrapers. In the future, the concrete structure of skyscrapers may contain steel or carbon fibres so that it conducts electricity, creating a building that can monitor itself.

194   The major corporations in America – particularly newspapers and

insurance companies – competed with each other to build the most dramatic and the tallest skyscraper. These were far more than functional office buildings. They were corporate advertisements, brand names written into the city's skyline. Frank Woolworth boasted that his record-breaking building was 'a giant signboard'.[92] The silhouettes of skyscrapers such as the forty-seven-storey Singer (1906) and the Chrysler buildings (1930) became instantly recognisable to people – consumers – around the world.

Other cities had also built up into the sky, albeit not on the scale seen in America. In the deserts of Yemen, a country proud to have the oldest cultural tradition in Arabia, the walled city of Shibam is also known as the Manhattan of the Desert because of its remarkable architecture. Located on the ancient incense road, it was an important centre for the caravan trade. Rather than expand beyond its fortified wall (vital to protect residents from Bedouin attacks), houses in this largely sixteenth-century city have been built as high as eleven storeys. They are made of sun-baked mud bricks, painted with limewash to protect them during the rainy season. From a distance, the city is strikingly beautiful, its houses rising vertically against the perennially blue sky, a dense island of habitation in an arid landscape.

But skyscrapers were a uniquely American style of architecture. When H. G. Wells visited New York in 1906 he was awestruck by the Flatiron Building (originally known as the Fuller Building) on Fifth Avenue, which had been completed just four years earlier and was the tallest building in the city. Wells stood at the base of this elegant, wedge-like building and gazed up at its twenty-two storeys: 'I found myself agape, admiring a skyscraper – the prow of the Flat-iron building, to be particular, ploughing up through the traffic of Broadway and Fifth Avenue in the afternoon light.'[93]

Not every visitor to New York was impressed by the city's attempt to reach for the skies. Henry James had visited a couple of years before Wells and was appalled to find the spire of Trinity Church lost among the new towers. For James and other critics, who preferred the more human scale of European urban skylines, the vertical city seemed to express the brash materialism of the New World.

As the *New York Standard Guide* rightly asserted in 1917, the view of Manhattan Island from the water had 'no parallel in the cities of the world'. The skyscrapers were like 'tremendous cliffs' and to walk the streets of downtown Manhattan was to pass 'from one shadowy *cañon* into another'. In 1919, when A. G. Gardiner, the former editor of the *London Daily News*, arrived in New York harbour he mistook the city for 'the serrated mass of a distant range of mountains'. Only gradually did he realise his mistake: 'the sky-line is broken with a precision that suggests the work of man rather than the careless architecture of nature'. Even on the water it was obvious where downtown was located – that was where the tallest skyscrapers were. Such descriptions recall the first impressions of Wells's Sleeper. The architecture of the vertical city inspired the kind of sublime awe previously only experienced in mountains or canyons.

One skyscraper in particular symbolised New York's architectural ambition: the Woolworth Building. It was, said A. G. Gardiner, like 'a great street, Piccadilly or the Strand, that has been miraculously turned skyward by some violent geological "fault"'.[94] From the start, Frank Woolworth had wanted to build 'a spectacular urban landmark', the tallest building in the world.[95] In particular, he wanted to exceed the Metropolitan Life Insurance Tower in midtown Manhattan. Rumour had it that they had once turned him down for a loan and he was determined to beat them. With its fanciful Gothic features (gables and gargoyles) as well as cutting-edge technology and engineering, the Woolworth Building has been described as 'New York's paradigmatic skyscraper of the early twentieth century'.[96] For New Yorkers, it was a triumphant statement of America's new-found economic and technological prowess. Like a pointing finger, it seemed to say that the sky was the only limit recognised in this city.

The opening of the Woolworth Building was a theatrical event, watched by thousands. Overnight, it transformed the skyscraper into 'the most widely known office building in the world'.[97] At 7.30 on the evening of 24 April 1913, President Woodrow Wilson pushed a button on his desk in Washington, DC, sending a telegraphic signal to New York where it set off an alarm bell in the engine room of the skyscraper. Four mighty Corliss-type engines and dynamos were immediately set in motion. In an instant, some eighty thousand incandescent bulbs flashed on, illuminating for the first time the world's tallest skyscraper. Crowds had gathered in City Hall Park and along Lower Broadway to witness the dazzling electrical spectacle that marked the opening of this fifty-five-storey addition to New York's soaring skyline. On the New Jersey shore people caught their breath as the tower appeared, shimmering against the night sky, a gleaming beacon of modernity visible from ships a hundred miles away. As the 792-foot-tall skyscraper was bathed in electric light, the news was transmitted from its pinnacle by Marconi wireless to a receiver on the Eiffel Tower. From there it was beamed around the world. This modern media extravaganza was, as one commentator said, 'the premier publicity stunt of this or any other day'.[98]

Three-quarters of New York's population was foreign-born by 1900. Because of the confusion caused by the different languages (some two thousand workers were on site), the construction of the Woolworth Building was compared to the Tower of Babel. Indeed, there is no doubt that this was a triumph of organisation and logistics, as well as of engineering and technology. Architecture was pushed to its very limits in this building. Construction took twenty-nine months, beginning in April 1910. The foundations alone took ten months. It was one of the largest architectural caisson jobs ever undertaken. In stifling heat inside pressurised cylinders, two hundred men worked around the clock in three eight-hour shifts, digging down by hand more than a hundred feet to reach bedrock. Each of the sixty-nine concrete piers took about two weeks to excavate and fill.

In total, 200,000 tons of materials were moved to and from the site by horse-drawn cart. Some 24,000 tons of structural steel were used in the building. One of the main load-bearing girders was among the heaviest ever used: a forty-two-horse team was needed to drag it to the site. The steelwork began rising in October 1911. It went up at the remarkable rate of a storey and a half each week. The highest piece of steel (792 feet) was erected on 1 July 1912, nine months later. Riveting the girders was dangerous work. On rainy days the upper levels of the structure disappeared in mist and cloud. There was at least one injury a week on the site.

The Apartment

In the high-rise, high-density cities of the future, most people will live in apartments. The first apartment block was the Roman 'insula' (meaning 'island'). At the time of Caesar, the middle classes – officials and merchants – paid relatively high rents, as much as four times more than in other Italian towns. But most ordinary Romans endured dire conditions. Insulae reached unprecedented heights, as Juvenal described, in the second century AD: 'Behold the mansion's towering size / Where the floors on floors to the tenth storey rise'.[100] The least desirable apartments were on the top floors. As Lewis Mumford has said, 'the main population of the city that boasted its world conquests lived in cramped, noisy, airless, foul-smelling, infected quarters, paying extortionate rents to merciless landlords'.[101]

From the seventeenth century, purpose-built apartment blocks were common in Paris and Vienna, while remaining virtually unknown in cities such as London and Amsterdam. In eighteenth-century Paris, even the wealthy owners of houses on the Place Vendôme would live on the main floor and let out the rest of the building, something that would have been unthinkable in London. Baron Haussmann transformed Paris in the following century, and the new boulevards were lined with middle-class apartment blocks. They have provided a rich vein of urban social life for novelists to explore, from Émile Zola's *Pot-Bouille* (1883) to Georges Perec's *Life: A User's Manual* (1978), a meticulously detailed account of apartment life at 11 rue Simon-Crubellier. Other novels set in apartment buildings include Alaa Al Aswany's *The Yacoubian Building* (2002), *The Death of Vishnu* (2001) by Manil Suri, set in a Mumbai apartment block, and J. G. Ballard's *High-Rise* (1975) in which he speculated that 'living in high-rises required a special type of behaviour, one that was acquiescent, restrained, even perhaps slightly mad'.[102]

The idea of two unrelated families living in the same building, as happened in Paris, appalled middle-class, nineteenth-century Americans. In 1869, respectable New Yorkers lived in private houses. But

Woolworth promoted his new building as a 'city within a city'.[99] Like a citadel or royal palace in an ancient city, it was a self-contained community, virtually self-sufficient. It had its own transport system of twenty-eight Tiffany-decorated elevators. The three express elevators travelled at a record-breaking 700 feet per minute. The system could carry six thousand passengers an hour. The building's vertical sewer system was as complex as that of a small town. Its six coal-fired boilers drove four engines and dynamos to provide energy for the elevators, thousands of lights, fans, and 850 synchronised clocks. The building had its own medical facilities and fire-fighting system. There had even been plans to give the building its own artesian water supply. The idea

as cities grew and accommodation became more expensive, the idea of apartment living began to gain in popularity. The first New York apartment building was the Stuyvesant on East 18th Street, designed in 1869 by an architect trained in Paris. Others soon followed, all built in reassuringly opulent style. The Dakota, built in 1884, had sixty-five luxury apartments described at the time as 'French flats', each offering between four and twenty rooms with fifteen-foot-high ceilings and carved marble fireplaces. It was 'a cross between a millionaire's mansion and a Parisian hotel'.[103] Soon vertical living became acceptable to wealthy families. In 1893, Moses King wrote that 'apartment-life is popular and to a certain extent fashionable. Even society countenances it, and a brownstone front is no longer indispensable to at least moderate social standing.'[104] By 1929, 98 per cent of New Yorkers lived in multiple dwellings.

Apartment block in the new town of Tung Chung on Lantau Island, Hong Kong, China.

of the skyscraper as a city in itself was popular at this time, used, for instance, to describe Chicago's famous Rookery (1885–8), among others. What architect Rem Koolhaas has called 'one of Manhattanism's most insistent themes' transformed the modern metropolis into 'a collection of architectural city-states, all potentially at war with each other'.[105]

For nearly a century, New York City could boast that it had the world's tallest buildings. Throughout the twentieth century, it was the city people associated with the skyscraper. Even in 1974, there were as many sixty-storey buildings here as there were in the rest of the world combined. From the Woolworth and the Empire State Buildings, to the ill-fated twin towers of the World Trade Center – all for a time the tallest in the world – New York's skyscrapers have declared to the world the economic dominance of this city. But in the twenty-first century, as the locus of world power shifts from West to East, the cities that are breaking records in their attempts to touch the sky are Dubai and Shanghai.

The accolade of tallest building in the world is only ever temporary. Chicago's 108-storey Willis Tower (originally the Sears Tower) became the tallest building in the world in 1974, at 1,451 feet (442 metres), higher even than New York's World Trade Center towers. In 1998, the eighty-eight-storey Petronas Towers in Kuala Lumpur, Malaysia, claimed the title after exceeding it by just thirty feet, or ten metres. Six years later, Taipei 101, in Taiwan, went up another 165 feet, or 50 metres (509.2 metres/ 1,676 feet). But Dubai's Burj Khalifa is in a different league entirely. Unveiled at the end of 2009, it is more than a thousand feet higher than Taipei 101.

At 2,717 feet (828 metres) tall, the 160-storey Burj (which means 'tower') is roughly twice the size of the Empire State Building. It was designed by architect Adrian Smith and engineer William Baker, both of the Chicago firm Skidmore, Owings & Merrill. The Y-shaped floor plan of the tower grows more slender as it rises into the sky, a design inspired by desert flowers and Islamic architecture. Although there are forty-nine floors of offices and a 160-room hotel run by Armani, it is mostly luxury apartments – 1,044 in all.

Some 30,000 tons of steel were used in the Burj. The building was constructed at a rate of one storey every three days using a steel frame into which concrete was poured, having been pumped under pressure more than 460 metres (1,509 feet) up the building, setting a new world record for vertical concrete pumping. The tower's exterior glass and steel would cover seventeen football pitches and take some eight weeks to clean from top to bottom. Its 28,000 glass panels are coated with silver to deflect UV and infrared rays. In Dubai, where it is often 40° C in the shade, air conditioning is essential in a glass and steel tower. The condensation from the cooling system fills twenty Olympic-sized swimming pools a year and is used to water the grounds of the building. Its elevators are among the fastest in the world: it takes about two minutes to get to the summit at speeds approaching 40mph (or eighteen metres a second). From the observation deck on the 124th floor of the tower visitors can see as far as eighty kilometres on a clear day.[106]

In the 1930s, New York was the biggest city in the world, with a population of some seven million (eleven million in the metropolitan region as a whole) and two hundred skyscrapers. This was more than the total in the rest of the world's cities. Manhattan changed the way people thought about cities. But today it is in Shanghai that the blueprint of the urban future is being created, particularly as regards other Asian cities. The pace of growth and construction in the city has been unprecedented. Its economy has grown faster than any other megacity since 1990, at about 15 per cent a year. The changes that happened in New York from 1880 to 1930 took place in Shanghai in less than twenty years. In 1980, there were 121 buildings over eight storeys but by 2005 that had risen to more than ten thousand. There are now some four thousand high-rise buildings of twenty storeys or more. In the historic core of the city, Puxi, traditional dense but low-rise *lilong* (or *lòngtang*) neighbourhoods with their two- or three-storey *shikumen* town houses have been demolished. The municipal government has built satellite cities, such as Thames Town in Songjiang New City, and densely populated high-rise complexes on the periphery to accommodate a population that has grown eightfold since the 1920s. Shanghai is now China's most populous city. There are some 26,000 people per square kilometre living in the centre of Shanghai, compared to 7,800 in London and 12,400 in Mexico City.[107]

To the east of Puxi, across the Huangpu River, lies Pudong, which until 1990 was rice fields and countryside. Now it is the location of the Lujiazui financial district. About the same size as Lower Manhattan, it contains more than forty skyscrapers in excess of forty storeys, creating a dramatic skyline when viewed from the historic Bund on the opposite bank of the river. Three skyscrapers are among the world's

When skyscrapers rise, do markets fall?

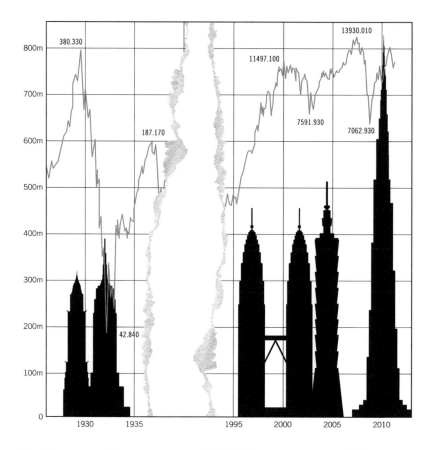

The Skyscraper Index was proposed in 1999 by property analyst Andrew Lawrence, who argued that skyscrapers embody the 'irrational exuberance' of financial markets. According to his theory, the highest towers are often planned when stock markets are soaring. But by the time construction workers leave, boom has turned to bust. The Empire State Building was completed just after the Wall Street Crash of 1929 and was known as the 'Empty State' for many years. The Petronas Towers were finished the year after the Malaysian stock market crashed in 1997. Following the recent global banking crisis, Dubai had to borrow billions of dollars from its neighbour, Abu Dhabi. The Burj Dubai was then hastily renamed the Burj Khalifa, in honour of Sheikh Khalifa bin Zayed al-Nahyan, ruler of Abu Dhabi. The graph plots the heights of super-tall buildings against the rise and fall of the Dow Jones Index, and shows how the construction of ambitious and costly buildings can be used as a key indicator within the business cycle. The lesson, suggests Lawence, is that when skyscrapers rise, we should prepare for a stock market crash.

top supertall towers: the pagoda-like Jin Mao (1999), which is eighty-eight storeys and 1,380 feet (421 metres) high; the Shanghai World Financial Center (2008), which is taller than any US skyscraper, at 1,614 feet (492 metres); and the 128-storey Shanghai Tower, which at 2,073 feet (632 metres) will be the tallest building in China and the second tallest in the world when it is completed in 2014. The latter is also claimed to be the most environmentally friendly skyscraper in Shanghai, featuring a double skin and wind turbines.[108]

Within a generation, Shanghai has become a vast, sprawling metropolis of high-rises and highways, an astonishingly rapid transformation. About twenty million people now live and work in this city, a figure set to rise still further in the coming years. Indeed, half of China's population is expected to move to the cities by mid-century and it is expected that some fifty thousand skyscrapers will be built over the next twenty years. By then Shanghai may even become the city with the most high-rise buildings, a record currently held by Hong Kong, which has about 7,600. These cities reveal the shape of things to come for much of the urban world. As global population rises steadily, growing urban populations will need to be accommodated with the minimum impact on the environment and the planet's scarce resources. Architect Norman Foster, whose Commerzbank Tower (1997) in Frankfurt, Germany, was the first skyscraper designed according to ecological principles, believes that high-density, high-rise living is essential: 'We need skyscrapers.'[109]

6 MONEY

Markets

At the heart of the town where I grew up was a field of cobblestones, worn smooth by generations of feet. There had been a marketplace in Romford since King Henry III decreed that a sheep market be established there in 1247. It became one of the largest in the county of Essex and, by the end of the seventeenth century, Romford was renowned as 'a great market town for corn and cattle'.[1] When I was a boy, the livestock had long gone, but I do remember the marketplace echoing to the shouts of Cockney barrow boys, their stalls piled high with muddy potatoes and downy peaches. Held three days a week, the market's best bargains were always to be had at the end of the day, as traders dismantled their stalls. By then a sickly sweet smell of over-ripe fruit hung over the stalls and a bag of mottled bananas could be yours for a few pence.

The marketplace and its oriental iterations, the bazaar and the Arab *souk*, have been the bustling centre of urban life for millennia. (*Souk*, or *souq*, is the Arabic equivalent of the Persian word 'bazaar', meaning commercial street or marketplace.) For Paul Bowles, Tangier's 'true center' was its open-air market, the Zoco de Fuera, where vociferous peddlers sold 'everything from parakeets to buttermilk, from Berber blankets to hot roasted chestnuts, from sofa cushions to Japanese dolls'.[2] The marketplace is where the city really comes alive – in the cries of sellers trying to attract your attention, the haggling over dubious bargains, the push and shove of the crowd milling round the stalls, the colourful chaos of wares shipped from across

A Japanese businessman walks past the falling arrows on the Nikkei stock
exchange index board in downtown Tokyo in 2008.

207

the world, chance meetings with acquaintances glimpsed among the throng, and the mouth-watering aroma of just-cooked street food.

The most perfect displays of fruit and vegetables I have seen in a market were not in Romford but in Munich's Viktualienmarkt, just around the corner from the central Marienplatz. I've never actually witnessed them polishing the fruit, but it wouldn't surprise me at all if they did just that. A more workaday market, with no less delicious produce, is held each morning in Rome's Campo dei Fiori, presided over by the brooding statue of Giordano Bruno, burned to death here for heresy in 1600 by the Inquisition – a *memento mori* amidst the blood-red oranges and watermelons. France prides itself on the quality and variety of its fresh food and its cities have wonderful markets, and not just for food. In Paris there is also a bird market – the Marché aux Oiseaux – held on Sundays on the Île de la Cité, and the famous second-hand book market with its stalls all along the banks of the Seine. The same city boasts what Edmund White has called 'the world's most luxurious flea market', at Porte de Clignancourt, known as Les Puces (the Fleas), an astonishing mélange of antiques, bric-à-brac and clothing.[3]

The largest fish market in the world is to be found at Tokyo's Central Wholesale Market, known locally as Tsukiji, built on fifty-six acres of reclaimed land south of Ginza. Here, every day, over 1,500 wholesale stalls sell 2,888 tons of seafood – more than four hundred different types in all, from glistening silver tuna to sea urchins and seaweed.[4] If you want the freshest sashimi and sushi, this is the place to come. Amsterdam's Singel Canal has a floating flower market and in the city of Can Tho, in Vietnam's Mekong Delta, there are also markets (such as Cai Rang) where everything is offered for sale from gently bobbing boats.

The Egyptian hieroglyph for a town was a circle with a cross in it – the circle representing defensive walls and the cross the meeting of routes at a marketplace.[5] Similarly, the Sumerian ideogram for a market was a 'Y', symbolising the market as a juncture of traffic routes.[6] In the earliest Mesopotamian cities, shrines and temples were centres of economic power, as goods were brought here for taxation and redistribution in what was a controlled rather than a free economy. Temples provided space for craft workshops, as well as for storage of goods such as grain, vegetables, sesame seeds, dates, preserved fish, fat, beer, wine, skins, reeds and rushes, and mats. As urban populations increased, temple precincts began to be used as markets where people could barter goods. By 2000 BC at the latest, 'the two classic forms of the market, the open place or covered bazaar, and the booth or shop-lined street', had become familiar urban forms.[7]

It was not the palace or temple that was the focal point of daily life in Greek city-states from about 700 BC, but the agora: the place of assembly. The Agora of Athens was the antecedent of the market-place as we know it today – a noisy, chaotic, smelly yet vital concourse where citizens met to exchange both goods and news. Socrates came here to challenge his fellow citizens to turn their thoughts from food to matters of the mind. He was in his element in the city, declaring: 'The country places and the trees don't teach me anything, and the people in the city do.'[8] The agora was where sacred dances were performed, as well as drama (on improvised wooden stages), athletic games and equestrian events. Eventually, specialised buildings – such as theatres and stadia – were built to house these activities, but the agora retained its place at the heart of urban life.

By the sixth century BC, the use of coins had become widespread in Greek cities and the agora was primarily a marketplace. It was where you would go to have your hair trimmed, to buy a pair of shoes or to choose a costly perfume. The poet Euboulos described the impressive range of goods and services that were on offer there: 'you will find everything sold together in the same place at Athens: figs, witnesses to summonses, bunches of grapes, turnips, pears, apples, givers of evidence, roses, medlars, porridge, honeycombs, chickpeas, lawsuits, beestings-pudding, myrtle berries, allotment machines, irises, lamps, water-clocks, laws, and indictments'.[9] But the Agora at Athens was not just a jumble of stalls and products, like some modern car-boot sale. Rather, it was more like a department store, with different parts of the market specialising in certain types of goods. To the west was the metal market, and to the south-east the peddlers' market. There was the famous *ichthyopolis*, or fish city, which was itself subdivided into sections for smoked and non-smoked fish. Fruit, olive oil, wine, flowers, drugs and spices, craftwork (pottery, wool, clothing etc.), slaves, and book scrolls – all were traded in their own sections, or circles (*cycloi*). There was even the 'Agora of the Kerkopes', a black market where stolen goods were traded. Similarly, the traditional Arab *souk* is arranged so that similar merchandise and tradesmen are available in one alley, as is the case in Damascus.

Other Greek cities had their own agora, each with its own unique character. Some were spacious open squares, and others – as at Thera – were little more than a widened main street, a 'Broad Way'. Essentially, the agora was an open space used for civic purposes. Law courts and government buildings were located here. Although it has been described as an 'informal club', it was an exclusive one, for the agora was mainly the preserve of men, with just one part set aside for housewives. Indeed, Athens was a hierarchical and profoundly unequal city: out of a total population of about three hundred thousand – of whom a third were slaves – forty thousand were full citizens, most them aristocrats and all of them men. Those who created the wealth of the city were excluded from being citizens. Foreigners ran the market and, along with anyone who was concerned with business, trade or skilled crafts, they were looked down on by the elite of the 'polis': 'the foreign trader in the fifth-century Greek economy played a part not dissimilar to that which the Jew played in the Christian economy of the medieval town: he was needed but not wanted.'[10] Despite this, the agora became the most distinctive element of the Greek city. Today, its spirit lives on in the *campo* and the *piazza*, the square and the plaza – bustling, lively public spaces, full of chatter and incident, where people meet to gossip and to take the pulse of the city.

The Forum in Rome was originally a place of assembly for local tribes. Located between the Capitoline Hill and what later became the Colosseum, it was the centre of life in this great city and defined the shape of Roman towns across the empire. A precinct rather than a square, it combined the functions of the Greek agora and the acropolis. Its temples, law courts and colonnades attracted people to shop and to socialise. Successive emperors added architecturally to the *Forum Romanum*, creating a space of monumental scale, the symbolic heart of the empire. It was here, too, that Romans watched military leaders march proudly through the triumphal arches, parading their latest royal captives. In medieval Rome, the Forum fell into ruins as the market was moved to the more defensible Capitoline Hill. Today, this ruined but deeply evocative space still throngs with crowds, but now they are tourists recreating the public heart of imperial Rome in their imaginations.

In the thirteenth century, when just 4 per cent of Europe's population was urban,[11] English kings began granting exclusive market rights to urban communities to enable them to generate income from taxes. This happened across the continent as trade increased and cities expanded. The market often became a town's main source of revenue and the most successful medieval cities were those sited at the centre of a national or international trade network. The fair at Saint-Denis, near Paris, which drew traders from across Europe, dated back to AD 629 and became one of the biggest on the continent.

In England, Salisbury – a new town laid out in the thirteenth century – had an open marketplace where country peasants and town craftsmen bought and sold from each other. Among the products typically offered for sale were meat, poultry, eggs, kitchen pots and pans, grain, wool, yarn and cloth. Stallholders who became prosperous eventually built shops around the market. At Salisbury, streets such as Butcher Row, Fish Row and Pot Row have encroached on to the marketplace and their names reveal what was once

A floating market in Bangkok, Thailand.

sold here. Civic buildings and covered markets were also built in the marketplace as towns grew wealthy from trade, including the original Bishop's Guildhall at Salisbury and Lübeck's Rathaus (completed 1308). Such buildings often had an open arcade on the ground floor for marketing and civic rooms on the second floor. The finest of these market halls was Ypres' Cloth Hall (1200–1304). Although it was used all year, it was built to house the annual cloth fair. Destroyed in the First World War but subsequently rebuilt, this impressive 433-foot-long building is larger than most cathedrals, and a monument to the wealth generated by the Flemish cloth trade.

In Europe during the Middle Ages and the Renaissance, urban life revolved around the market: economic exchange was 'the most basic function of almost every English town'.[12] The officials whose task it was to administer trading were located in the marketplace: the toll gatherers, sweepers, ale conners, leather searchers and wool aulnagers (inspectors). A market watcher was also generally employed to ensure by-laws were observed. The town hall was usually in the marketplace and would maintain equipment used in the regulation of marketing, such as scales, weighing beams and standard weights and measures – the latter being essential to ensure fairness in transactions. But as well as being tightly regulated places, paradoxically, medieval marketplaces were also sites of disorder. It was here that folk festivals, carnivals and rituals of social inversion (or misrule) also took place. 'The marketplace was the center of all that is unofficial,' said Mikhail Bakhtin.[13]

Markets were essential to the livelihoods of urban craftsmen, allowing them to sell their goods to people from the surrounding

Moneyville

Some five thousand years ago, in the earliest Mesopotamian cities, clay tokens began to be used to record that the bearer was owed a certain quantity of, say, barley at harvest time. Mesopotamians were also familiar with charging compound interest on long-term loans, as mathematical exercises dating from the reign of Hammurabi (1792–1750 BC) show. The Code of Hammurabi reveals that every three years debtors had their debts wiped clean. Most loans at this time were advances from royal or religious storehouses, but from this emerged the idea of credit – a fundamental principle in the history of banking and wealth creation.[14]

In the Temple of Artemis at Ephesus, near Izmir in present-day Turkey, archaeologists have found some of the earliest coins. They are Lydian coins made of electrum (a natural alloy of gold and silver), dating from 600 BC and were first used in the late seventh century BC in Lydia, a kingdom in west Anatolia.

From the early sixth century BC, Greek cities began issuing coins, sometimes bearing the name of the city. In Athens, the standard silver coin was the *tetradrachm*, with the head of Athena on one side and an owl (associated with Athena for its wisdom) on the other. The Romans introduced coins of different value: the gold *aureus*, silver *denarius* and the bronze *sestertius*. On one side was the head of the reigning emperor and on the other Romulus

Greek coins: Athenian silver *tetradrachm* with Athena and owl, fifth century BC; Gold *stater* from Panticapaeum with Pan and a griffin, mid fourth century BC.

countryside and further afield. In medieval Oslo and Uppsala, common urban traders included bakers, leather workers, crossbow-makers, joiners, masons, shoemakers, metalworkers and tailors. In high medieval London there were craftsmen practising at least 175 different specialist trades. London's market street was Cheapside, its name derived from the Saxon word for market – *céap*. There were once as many as four hundred stalls or kiosks along Cheapside. Other famous London markets include the fish market at Billingsgate (a name that became a byword for foul language, thanks to the profanities of its workers), which was formally established in the seventeenth century, and the meat market at Smithfield (originally 'smothe field'),

and Remus, the legendary founders of Rome. Metal coins began to be used in China from 221 BC when a bronze coin was introduced by the first emperor, Qin Shihuangdi. Much later, in the seventh century AD, China became the first country to issue paper bank notes.

From the thirteenth century banking became a vital part of the economic life of European cities. Credit transactions became common, as did international banking, with many monarchs – and even entire cities, such as Venice – borrowing money. At the same time, domestic banking grew as people began depositing money, first in Genoa and then in Florence, Barcelona and Bruges. By the early fourteenth century, Florence had eighty banks. The Italians pioneered the bill of exchange, shipping insurance and double-entry book-keeping. According to Niall Ferguson, 'banks and the bond market provided the material basis for the splendours of the Italian Renaissance'.[15]

By the seventeenth century, the dynamic commercial city of Amsterdam was the capital of banking and finance in Europe. London and Paris took over this role in the industrial age,

with the City of London becoming increasingly dominant. By the second half of the nineteenth century, London's stock market capitalisation was worth more than that of Paris and New York combined.

In the twentieth century, banks became a major urban employer, with some 100,000 Berliners working in banking (5 per cent of the workforce) by 1925. New York rose to prominence after the First World War, but London remained an important financial centre. London had over 100 foreign banks in 1961, but by 1987 that figure had risen to 450. In comparison, Stockholm had only twenty-six foreign banks in 2006. By 2004, 311,000 people were employed in London's financial sector compared to just 90,000 in Frankfurt.[16] Today, in both London and New York City, financial and business services comprise nearly a third of total employment, with only a small number employed in manufacturing. By contrast, Shanghai – which aspires to global city status – still has a significant manufacturing base, with 32 per cent working in industry but only 12 per cent in the financial sector.

which dates from the eleventh century. Daniel Defoe described this as the greatest market in the world and by the beginning of the nineteenth century a million sheep and a quarter of a million cattle were sold here annually. Today 120,000 tons of produce pass through the market each year.[17]

Vast amounts of food are needed to keep any major city supplied and, if nothing else, cities are a triumph of logistics and human organisation. The Spanish were awestruck when they arrived in the Aztec capital of Tenochtitlán in 1519 and were particularly impressed by the market with its astonishing display of goods rivalling anything in Europe: an agora of the New World. They calculated that the city needed fifty-five tons of grain, beans and other produce a day, most of which had to be transported in dugout canoes. Tenochtitlán was at the centre of a network of trade routes spread out across what is now Mexico. Tributes and levies of food, raw materials, tropical bird feathers and craft goods were sent to the city, which was the focus of imperial power.

By the 1850s, London was the largest city the planet had yet seen, a teeming metropolis of more than one and a half million people. A contemporary observer estimated that half a million people were employed directly and indirectly feeding London. Each year 200,000 pineapples were brought from the Bahamas to the capital. In the winter months, 240 clippers (fast sailing ships) transported sixty million oranges from Portugal and the Azores. To provide meat for the Sunday lunches of Londoners, each Friday night 1,200 cattle and 12,000 sheep were slaughtered near Smithfield market. Every day, fresh fish arrived at Billingsgate market by the ton. Londoners ate two hundred million kippers, a million lobsters and five hundred million oysters annually.[18] From the 1870s, the thousands of barrels of beer that arrived daily by train from Burton-on-Trent were kept in vaulted storerooms beneath St Pancras Station. It was estimated that the amount of bread eaten in a year would form a pyramid 200 feet square and nearly three times the height of St Paul's Cathedral.

Each morning, trains took fresh fruit and vegetables to Covent Garden market from market gardens at Greenwich, Chelsea, Battersea, Putney and Worthing on the south coast, which became known as 'the tomato capital of Britain'.[19] In the nineteenth century, strawberry growers went to remarkable lengths to ensure the freshness of their produce arriving at market in London. Pickers began work at 3 a.m. in the strawberry fields between Swanley and St Mary

Cray in Kent, which had direct rail links to the capital. By dawn, the punnets were being packed on to specially designed railway carriages, destined for the early morning market at Covent Garden.

In the 1840s, New York was home to just 400,000 people. But within forty years this figure had risen to nearly two million, an astonishing rate of growth. Local farmers could no longer keep the city supplied and so food had to be imported by rail and sea. On some days as many as three hundred carloads of produce would arrive in the city, creating a surplus which was often sold off quickly on the streets by pushcart peddlers. Legally, pushcarts were not allowed to remain stationary on the streets for longer than thirty minutes, but enforcement of the laws was lax and pushcart markets soon became a common sight around New York. The first was at Hester Street, from 1886. By 1900 there were some 25,000 immigrant pushcart traders. Many of them were women and children.

Open-air pushcart markets became an integral part of New York City life, particularly in Jewish and Italian neighbourhoods, where they offered employment and a place where people could shop while speaking their own language. By 1925 there were 53 pushcart markets: 34 in Manhattan, 17 in Brooklyn and 2 in the Bronx. At some markets there were nearly five hundred pushcarts. By 1930, pushcarts provided the main source of income for 47,000 people, generating about $40–$50 million a year. But the era of the pushcart markets came to an end in 1934 when Fiorello LaGuardia was elected mayor. He forced them off the streets and into permanent indoor markets. By the end of the decade most peddlers had gone, and many people regretted their passing.[20]

The first market in New York, when it was still known as New Amsterdam, had been held on a small piece of vacant land between the warehouse of the Dutch West India Company and Fort Amsterdam. Settlers called it Market Street, or Market-field. Here Native Americans and people from the country (nicknamed 'strangers' by the first Dutch colonists) offered corn, fish and pelts to the residents of the settlement. After 1641 a regular market day was established: Monday. In the nineteenth century, the Fulton Market opened in 1822, followed six years later by what became the city's biggest, Washington Market. Today the Hunt's Point Market, South Bronx (which took over from the Washington Wholesale Market in 1967), is the largest produce market in the world, handling more than $2 billion of produce a year. Sited on 329 acres beside the East River, up to 60 per cent of the nearly four billion pounds of fruit and vegetables eaten each year in New York passes through this market. In 1976, a farmers' market returned to Manhattan, at Union Square. Today some twenty thousand New Yorkers shop regularly here each year and there are more than forty such markets across the five boroughs of the city. Farmers' markets are experiencing a renaissance across America and Europe, as the popularity of locally produced food gains momentum. There's now a farmers' market at Romford, twice a month, and the cathedral city of Winchester in Hampshire hosts the largest farmers' market in the United Kingdom, with nearly a hundred stalls. The Roman name for the town, Venta Belgarum, means 'the market of the Belgae', a southern British tribe. It's reassuring in the age of hypermarkets and internet shopping that the traditional marketplace still retains its vital place in urban life.

The Jewel Box of the World

From the very beginning, cities have grown rich from trade. The important Assyrian city-state of Ashur (or Assur) on the River Tigris in northern Iraq is typical of urban communities in the Near East some four thousand years ago. Despite intense rivalries, the cities of the region were linked by close trading ties. For instance, Susa in southwestern Iran was part of a network that stretched from Afghanistan in the east to the cities of southern Iraq in the west. Ashur – named after the Assyrian god and home to some 15,000 people – was an important node on a trade network that spread across Iran, southern Mesopotamia and central Anatolia.

From 2000 to 1750 BC, Ashur's kings were not all-powerful. Rather, the city appears to have been governed by businessmen and merchant families meeting in a specially designated building – known as 'the house of the city', 'bīt ālim' in Akkadian – to decide commercial, legal and diplomatic issues.[21] Trade was a family matter. Male relatives were sent from Ashur to live in Anatolian colonies to coordinate business. Donkey caravans would deliver consignments of goods such as textiles and tin (for making bronze), which the traders would sell, sending the profit – 100 per cent on tin and 200 per cent on textiles – back to Ashur. It was a lucrative business, with many merchants becoming millionaires. But earning such great riches came at a personal cost. A poignant letter has been discovered, written to one of these merchants by his wife, pleading with him to devote less of his time to earning money and to return to his family: 'Here we ask the women who interpret oracles, the women who interpret omens from entrails, and the ancestral spirits and the god Ashur sends you a serious warning: "You love money! You hate life!" Can't you satisfy Ashur here in the city? Please when you have heard the letter then come, see Ashur's eye and save your life!'[22]

The city of Ashur also conducted trade with the Phoenicians, whose sea cities lined the Levant coast like a string of costly pearls. In the golden age of the Phoenicians (1150–850 BC), cities such as Tyre, Sidon and Byblos grew fabulously wealthy through trade. One historian has described the island city of Tyre as a 'miniature Manhattan' due to its tall buildings and its economic power. The Hebrew prophet Ezekiel spoke of the city's 'perfect beauty': 'every precious stone was thy covering, the sardius, the topaz, and the diamond, the beryl, the onyx, and the jasper, the sapphire, the emerald, and the carbuncle, and gold'.[23] The fifth-century Greek poet Nonnus imagined the city, with its jetty walls stretching out into the sea, as being like a young girl bathing: 'O city, well esteemed by the world, a picture on earth, the image of heaven. Never have I seen such beauty. What god built this town? What godly hand designed it?'[24] Every day, ships arrived in Tyre from a trading empire that stretched from the Lebanese coast to Gibraltar and beyond. The Phoenicians even traded with England and Ireland. Cities such as Tyre were the forerunners of more recent ports such as Venice, Amsterdam and Osaka. What is remarkable about these Phoenician cities is that their power came not from military strength, but from their skill at conducting business and from the desire of people in other lands to trade with them.

Trade played a vital role in the growth of cities in medieval Europe. Fairs helped kick-start trade on the continent. Fairs were sprawling wood and canvas temporary cities, which had been held outside the walls of cities since the Dark Ages. They resembled today's Black Rock City, created for a few weeks each year in the Nevada desert for the Burning Man festival. Fairs were great occasions in the life of the city – 'vast and elaborate pageants', which usually took place during religious holidays and attracted droves of traders, entertainers and visitors.[25] As Richard Sennett has said, fairs helped to develop 'the first tissues between cities, connecting market to market'. Fairs taught Europeans the power of trade and, as cities became more wealthy, trade began to be conducted not just during the fair but throughout the year.[26]

The revival of trade brought luxury goods flooding into European cities – fine wool from England, mellow Rhenish wines, spices and silks from the East, gleaming armour from Lombardy, saffron and quicksilver from Spain, as well as exquisite textiles from Flanders. Cities prospered as never before in Europe, thanks also to technological advances in the twelfth century that produced agricultural surpluses. Cities became freer and more equal places. Traders and craftsmen began organising themselves into guilds that became powerful urban institutions. As individuals gained more control over their lives, so, too, did cities, gradually winning rights for themselves: to

World's Fairs

Inspired by the tradition of medieval fairs, the first international exhibition took place in 1851. More than six million people visited the 'Great Exhibition of the Works of Industry of All Nations', which was held in the Crystal Palace, in London's Hyde Park. Joseph Paxton's revolutionary wrought-iron and glass structure was 1,851 feet long (to correspond with the date), contained 300,000 plates of glass and yet took only six months to build. Its 800,000 square feet of space was sufficient for more than 14,000 industrial exhibitors to display their products. Among the novel items revealed to the public were the first public conveniences, known as Retiring Rooms. They housed sanitary engineer George Jennings's Monkey Closets. During the exhibition over 800,000 visitors paid one penny each to use them – the origin of the expression 'to spend a penny'. As well as a polished seat, for a penny they received a towel, a comb and a shoe shine.[28]

The Exposition Universelle of 1889 in Paris commemorated the centennial of the French Revolution and was visited by thirty million people. Without doubt its most famous attraction was the Eiffel Tower, which served as the entrance to the 'Expo'. At the time this 300-metre cast-iron structure (held together with over a million rivets) was the tallest building in the world. The critics savaged it, describing the structure as 'useless and monstrous'. Its designer, Gustave Eiffel, begged to differ. He said it had been shaped by the wind and was 'beautiful'. Today, seen at night and illuminated from within, few would disagree with him.[29]

World's fairs attracted many millions of visitors, drawn by the desire to see the latest technology of the day, from elevators and steam engines to televisions. For host cities they were an opportunity to raise their profile in an increasingly global marketplace. As a result many cities invested heavily in infrastructure. Barcelona improved its drainage system for the hold markets, to coin money and to establish weights and measures. The Hanseatic League, a medieval trade network which originated in northern Europe in the thirteenth century, consisted of about fifty towns including Hamburg, Bremen, Danzig and Lübeck. The League had its own parliament (the 'Hansetag') and currency (the 'pfund') and transformed northern Europe into a powerful economic region: 'The cities and the organization that they had together created became for a time the single most dynamic force in northern Europe, and the city-state showed all the signs of becoming the next type of state in Europe.'[27] Above the gates of some of these cities were inscribed the words 'Stadtluft macht frei' – city air sets you free. In a rural landscape that had not changed for centuries, cities became bastions of hope, offering freedom from generations of feudal bondage. Many

Universal Exhibition of 1888. There had been more than three thousand deaths from cholera in 1885 and it was unthinkable for this to be repeated during the Expo. For three cities – Chicago in 1893, Paris in 1900 and Montreal in 1967 – the decision to build a metro system was prompted by the chance to host the international exhibition.

Originally intended to showcase newly

Environmental sustainability will be at the heart of the Milan Expo in 2015. The original plan includes a botanical garden inspired by the design of Roman cities, with a central forum.

manufactured products, today Expos are less about trade than entertainment. The 1939 New York World's Fair and the 1949 Stockholm World's Fair started a fashion for utopian speculation about the 'World of Tomorrow' (the theme at New York). The most popular exhibit at New York was Democracity, a diorama of the 'city of the future', designed by Henry Dreyfuss and housed in the strikingly spherical Perisphere building. In the General Motors pavilion, Norman Bel Geddes's Futurama anticipated what the city would look like in 1960, focusing in particular on the impact of the automobile on future life. Some twenty-five million awestruck people visited. Shanghai's 2010 Expo had an urban theme: 'Better City – Better Life'. It is thought that staging the event cost the Chinese government as much as $58 billion (£38 billion), more than the 2008 Beijing Olympics. The next scheduled Expo is to be held in Milan in 2015 and will focus on sustainable development, with its theme of 'Feeding the Planet, Energy for Life'.[30]

Hamburg harbour, Germany, in the 1890s.

of them remained free cities up to the time of Bismarck.

This period of urban growth in Europe was led by the cities of northern Italy and foremost among these was Venice. A unique and evocative city, Venice rises almost miraculously from the swamps and sand-banks (*lidi*) at the head of the Adriatic Sea. It was a far from ideal site for a city: no fresh water and farming was almost impossible. All they had here was fish and salt. And yet Venice became the 'jewel box of the world', to use Jacob Burckhardt's phrase. Venice was the world's wealthiest city, not because of its military might but, like the cities of the Phoenicians, because of its commercial prowess. This water-borne city shaped like a fish grew rich on goods shipped around the world: 'From the outset its life blood was trade and the city remained above all a community of merchants.'[31] Emerging in the fifth century out of the ruins of the Roman empire, by AD 1000 Venice was the dominant power in the Adriatic and the second most prosperous city in Europe after Byzantium (now known as Istanbul). Venetians began trading in salt from the local coastal marshes. But from this humble beginning the city became the 'hinge of Europe', bringing silk and spices from the East to the West: saffron, cumin, nutmeg and juniper from India and other Asian lands; pepper from India and the east coast of Africa (via the Egyptian port of Alexandria); and cinnamon from Ceylon.[32] In Shakespeare's *The Merchant of Venice* (1596–8), Antonio refers to how 'the trade and profit of the city / Consisteth of all nations'.[33]

The Arsenal quarter in Venice is one of earliest planned ports. The city owned a fleet of merchant galley ships which travelled in convoys, called *muda*. They were hired by merchant families, like the Grimani family, who would then rent out space to smaller spice merchants. Eventually, the republic – which was run largely as a business concern – controlled Europe's trade with the Middle East, India, South Asia and China. Martino da Canale said in the thirteenth century: 'merchandise passes through this noble city as water flows through fountains'.[34] In 1423, Venice's income was between 7.5 and 15 million ducats, equal to that of Spain. The Grand Canal was lined with the most elegant and expensive palaces. In the fifteenth century the city's population was some 100,000, rising to 150,000 in the following century. Most worked with their hands for a living. As well as being a merchant city, Venice became Europe's workshop, with the city divided into industrial districts long before the idea of functional zones became a principle of urban planning. There was also no shortage of unskilled work for porters and gondoliers, of whom even in 1880 there were still some ten thousand; today there are only four hundred. By the sixteenth century it was the wealthiest city in Europe and the forerunner of the modern world city. Not only did Venice demonstrate the power of trade but also the importance of the city-state, introducing the ideal of the ancient Greek 'polis' into the new Europe.

Venice's success lasted well into the seventeenth century, by which time Amsterdam assumed the role of Europe's main entrepôt and banking centre. The Netherlands had become 'the most urbanized society in Europe', with half its population living in cities. A vast Dutch fleet sailed the oceans of the world, hunting for profitable trade, and Amsterdam's harbour was always full of ships. In 1616, the English ambassador to the city marvelled at 'the numbers of all nations, of all professions and all religions there assembled, but for one business only, of merchandise'.[35] The frieze on the western pediment of Amsterdam's imposing seventeenth-century royal palace (originally the town hall) shows all the continents of the world bringing their goods – including the tulip – to the city. This efficiently designed city of alleys, wharves and canals attracted people from around the world, creating a diverse and vibrant culture in which philosophy and the arts flourished. With their global connections, merchant cities from Ashur four thousand years ago to modern Dubai have always been cosmopolitan centres, which is a key factor in their success.

But Amsterdam's dominance did not last long. In 1664, Britain seized the colony of New Amsterdam, then a settlement of just a thousand people, and renamed it New York. It signalled the emergence of

London as the new commercial capital of the world. Founded by the Romans on a major river, the city of London became a great port and the centre of an empire, in the late nineteenth century, stretching from China and India to North America. In the sixteenth century, London's population grew from 60,000 to 225,000. When it was rebuilt after the devastating fire of 1666, it became Europe's largest city. By 1790, it was home to some 900,000 people, four times the size of Amsterdam. London was booming, but not everyone was pleased. King James I complained: 'With time, England will only be London, and the whole country be laide waste.'[36]

In the era of containerisation and globalisation, many port cities – from Hong Kong and Singapore, to Hamburg and Los Angeles – continue to grow rich from international trade. Dubai is one of these. In little more than forty years, it has gone from being a regional port and trading centre to a global city. Up to the 1950s, the pearl trade was central to Dubai's success. By the 1970s, Dubai was the third largest buyer of gold in the open market, with illegal gold smuggling an important part of the economy. Import and re-export has always been Dubai's core business and Jebel Ali is now one of the largest deepwater ports in the world. Today, Dubai is an economic and social boomtown with many transnational corporations attracted to its various free-trade zones, such as Media City, Internet City, Knowledge Village and Academic City. As much as 90 per cent of its population is made up of foreign workers. In the twenty-first century, cities market themselves like brands and 'Dubai Inc.' has successfully promoted itself as a shopping destination. Eighty-four per cent of UAE residents go shopping as 'something to do'. Today 30 per cent of Dubai's GDP comes from tourism. Its malls are as vast as any in the world. In a nod to its trading forerunner there is a Venetian-themed mall, as well as one designed in the style of an Arab *souk*.[37]

But boomtowns are not just created by trade and commerce. On 5 July 1851, a Melbourne publican announced that he had found gold in the Yarra River, sixteen miles from Melbourne. People immediately rushed to the area to make their fortune. Ships were marooned in port as their crews deserted and, of Melbourne's forty policemen, thirty-eight resigned to go and dig for gold. Soon gold-diggers were arriving in Melbourne and the state of Victoria from around the world, the fastest ships sailing from England in about eighty days. By the end of 1854, more than 140,000 had travelled from the UK, 20,000 from

China and other foreign ports, and 110,000 from Australian cities. In 1853, the people of Victoria spent more on English beer and cider than they had spent on all imports before the gold rush. Thousands of prefab homes were imported from Britain and for a time Victoria became 'one of the most important customers of the greatest trading nation in the world'.[38] In 1851 there had been 77,000 people living in Victoria. Just seven years later there were half a million there. Thanks to the gold rush, Melbourne became the biggest city in Australia.

Got to Pick a Pocket or Two

In New York City during the 1870s, a real-life Artful Dodger called George Appo could earn more than $600 a night picking pockets, an amount equivalent to the annual salary of a skilled manual labourer. When Appo's Chinese father was sent to prison for murder, his Irish mother, an alcoholic, deserted the boy and he grew up with an impoverished family in the alleys of the notorious Five Points area of the city. Appo never went to school. Instead he became one of the city's estimated 15,000 street children. Known as 'gutter-snipes', 'street rats' or 'Arabs', street kids were a common sight in nineteenth-century cities, as they are today in many Asian and Latin American megacities. Most of them lived, slept and ate in the alleys and hallways of the slum tenements, scraping a very meagre existence by blacking boots, sweeping sidewalks, selling newspapers and picking pockets.[39] Their harsh life was immortalised in Charles Dickens's novel *Oliver Twist* (1837–8).

Nimble-fingered youngsters like Appo could find rich pickings on New York's most crowded streets. Lower Broadway was described at the time as a 'pickpockets' paradise'.[40] By 1876, some 242 pickpockets were being brought to trial in New York each year, mostly boys aged between fourteen and seventeen. Nearly two decades later the situation had not improved. Jacob Riis quoted a New York judge in 1894: 'In all my career on the bench I have never seen so many cases of boy thieves and burglars. Hardly a day passes but that there are from two to six or seven boys arraigned, charged with some kind of crime, all of them under fifteen years old.'[41]

Depressingly, the profile of offenders remains similar today, even in the affluent cities of the developed world. Half of those convicted each year in the United Kingdom are males aged between fifteen and twenty-one. 'There is a strong association,' writes one researcher, 'between crime and being male, young, and from the inner city.'[42] The causes of crime – whether in the city or the suburbs – are complex. Research in the early part of the twentieth century seemed to suggest that there was a link between urbanism and high levels of crime. Now, however, crime is viewed as a product of community-wide social issues, such as inequality, poverty, drug abuse, racism, unemployment, poor education and lack of social mobility. When combined with dilapidated housing, inadequate infrastructure and policing, these pervasive problems create high-crime areas within cities and suburban areas alike.

Crime is by no means a recent feature of life in cities. Medieval Italian cities could be extremely violent places, so much so that a new form of architecture emerged in them – the tower house, fortified buildings with a tower rising seventy-five metres or more, affording protection to a clan or family. The skylines of northern Italian towns such as Florence and Bologna, which had as many as two hundred, resembled mini-Manhattans. Most have long since disappeared, although two remain in the centre of Bologna and there are fourteen still standing in the medieval Tuscan town of San Gimignano. In fifteenth-century Paris, most offences were described as 'passionate crimes', that is violence against individuals rather than theft.[43] This was in part because of a lack of opportunity: merchants hired private guards to accompany them everywhere and very wealthy people employed small private armies to protect their property. There were municipal policemen in Paris from 1160, but their duties were restricted largely to protecting public officials.

In England, every town had a cell (or 'lock-up') for drunken brawlers and other miscreants, often in the cellar or attic of the town hall. Even by medieval standards, conditions in them were bad, and they were infested with vermin and diseases such as typhus, plague and gaol fever. After 1500, as cities became wealthier, town halls were judged unsuitable for such unsavoury institutions and lock-ups were moved, often to gatehouses in the city wall.

In seventeenth-century Paris, the violence on the streets shocked the aristocracy and bourgeoisie. At this time, the centre of the Parisian underworld was purported to lie in the so-called 'Cour des Miracles', described by one contemporary as a 'stinking, muddy, irregular and unpaved' square next to the Filles-Dieu convent in the area now lying between the rues Réaumur, Damiette and des Forges.[44] It was a criminal city within the city, a sinister heart of darkness where, supposedly, all of Paris's criminals, beggars, con men, cutpurses, pickpockets, murderers and whores lived according to their own laws and customs. They even had their own king, the Grand Coesre. But according to historian Colin Jones, the popular story of the Cour des Miracles was merely 'a myth which played into wider bourgeois anxieties about public order'.[45]

Such fears intensified in the nineteenth century as cities expanded at unprecedented rates, forcing many to live at ever higher densities in squalid slums. The growth and extent of the booming industrial cities fostered widespread concerns about their effect on people's physical and moral wellbeing, anxieties that were eagerly exploited by unscrupulous newspaper editors. Criminality troubled the middle-class readers of journals and novels, especially in America, where, says Robert Zecker, 'the city was regarded as a violence-soaked threat to the nation a hundred years before the dawn of gangsta rap'.[46] As early as 1844, popular novelists were depicting the American city as 'an open sewer', reflecting a deep ambivalence about urbanism in American culture.[47] A reduction in the cost of mass printing brought a flood of cheap urban newspapers on to the streets. In America, the penny newspapers – beginning with New York's *Morning Post* and *Sun* in 1833 – sensationalised urban crimes and scandals. Trial pamphlets, which were sold on the streets, and criminal biographies also became popular at this time. By 1841, cases such as that of the unsolved murder of Mary Rogers – a beautiful young cigar salesgirl found floating in the Hudson River – made front-page headlines in all the newspapers.

In April 1841, two months before the killing of Mary Rogers, Edgar Allan Poe's story 'The Murders in the Rue Morgue' was published. It is the first detective story. Crime fiction emerges at the same time as the rise of the great industrial cities of Europe and America. In popular journalism and fiction of the time, the teeming, restless city often appears as a threatening and new phenomenon. 'The Murders in the Rue Morgue' reveals Paris to be a community of strangers, where – apart from commercial relationships – the victims were largely unknown to their neighbours. As well as highlighting the anonymity of urban life, Poe presents Paris as Babel, a biblical trope often used as a warning against urbanist hubris. At the time of the murders of Mme L'Espanaye and her daughter, the 'shrill voice … of a foreigner' is heard. But the neighbours cannot agree what language was being spoken – was it Spanish, German or Russian? Everyone imagines a different foreign assailant. Those who rush to the assist-ance of the two women also reflect the cosmopolitan nature of this great city. Among them is an Englishman, a Spaniard, an Italian and a Dutchman. Newspapers play a key role in the story, too, for it is through crime reports (headlined 'Extraordinary Murders') that Poe's archetypal urban sleuth, C. Auguste Dupin, learns of the case and the many different explanations of what might have happened. In many respects, this is a mystery that is uniquely urban.

When 'The Murders in the Rue Morgue' was first published, the word 'detective' did not even exist in the English language. The first detective department appeared the year after, in 1842. Even in 1840, New York – a city smaller than Paris, with a population of some 300,000 – had no full-time, professional police force. Indeed, there was little serious crime. But over the coming decades the situ-ation changed as the city grew rapidly. In 1859, the *New York Herald* complained: 'Our record of crime to-day is truly appalling. Scarcely is the excitement attending one murder allayed when a fresh tragedy equally horrible takes place'.[48] By the end of that year, murders had

Gangsta

Gangs have been part of the urban fabric of America since at least the middle of the nine-teenth century. In New York, the 'Bowery B'hoys', with their gaudy suits, walking sticks and tall beaver hats were the most noticeable of many gangs on the streets of the working-class districts from the 1840s. Other gangs included the Dead Rabbits (the subject of Scorsese's film), the Roach Guards, the Hudson Dusters, the Chichesters, the Bottle Alley Gang and the Shanty Gang. But the most organised and the most brutal of them all were the Whyos. Herbert Asbury described them as 'the most ferocious criminals who ever stalked the streets of an American city'.[49] During their heyday at the end of the nineteenth century, they controlled Manhattan's pickpockets, pimps, prostitutes and even counterfeiting, as well as extorting protection money from businesses – the traditional revenue stream of the gang. As one New Yorker said in 1892, the city was 'ter-rorized by gangs'.[50]

Today in the United States it is estimated that there are some 788,000 gang members in more than 27,000 gangs. Los Angeles is the gang capital of the United States with some 120,000 gang members. Gang problems are most wide-spread in the largest cities (where 55 per cent of gang members are found), although gangs are a growing problem in suburban areas.[51] 'Gangsta' culture is a global phenomenon, with traditions of criminal urbanism found in Russia, Vietnam, Nigeria, Mexico and else-where. Some gangs are now transnational, increased by nearly 50 per cent from the previous year, up from 40 to 59. Within thirty years, policing became New York City's single largest expenditure and there was a growing fear of organised crime.

At the same time, the 'city mysteries' or dime novels titillated readers with their lurid tales of urban vice and corruption in America. Periodicals like *Century* and *McClure's* featured stories about slum characters – waterfront toughs and Italian gangsters wielding stilettos – stereotypes that reappeared in the gangster films of the twentieth century, movies such as *The Public Enemy* (1931), *Scarface* (1932) and *Little Caesar* (1931). Similarly, the post-war genre of *film noir* initiated the suburban movie-goer into the mysteries of the urban jungle, offering glimpses of dingy boarding houses, seedy gambling dens and smoke-filled bars. Jules Dassin's edgy, realistic crime films, such as *The Naked City* (1947) – whose title was taken from Weegee's famous book of crime photographs – as well as *Night and the City* (1950), were shot on the streets of New York and London respectively. They set the stage for the documentary-style urban police dramas that now run almost nightly on our TV screens, including the acclaimed series *The Wire*

such as the people-smuggling gangs of Fuzhou in China.

Gangster films and novels have proved to be a popular genre of crime fiction. From Benjamin Baker's play *A Glance at New York* (1848), about a Bowery Boy called Mose, to Edward G. Robinson's portrayal of the quintessential

Gang members in Ciudad Juarez, Mexico.

urban hood in *Little Caesar* and Francis Ford Coppola's *Godfather* series (1972–90), audiences with no personal experience of organised crime can glimpse the shadowy figures controlling their city's underworld. Bollywood's popular gangster films, such as *Satya* (1998), portray Mumbai as an urban jungle, where violence occurs against a cityscape of slums, dark alleys and crumbling tenements. It is in stark contrast to the glamorous tourist images used to promote the city. From the slums of Asia to the public housing projects and council estates of the developed world, zones of poverty and social exclusion are fertile ground in which gangs can grow, their outlaw capitalism providing an alternative, black economy for communities without hope.

(2002–8), filmed in the rundown section of Baltimore known as Oliver.

From the 1960s, cities in the United States experienced a surge in crime and violence. Crime statistics worsened until, by the 1980s, New York routinely had some two thousand murders a year. In Martin Scorsese's *Taxi Driver* (1976), Travis Bickle's tirade against the whores, skunks, junkies and other 'scum' on New York's mean streets expressed what many Americans felt about crime and the city. Hollywood offered solutions, too. Films like *Death Wish* (1974) suggested that vigilante violence was the way to solve the problem of urban crime; either that or the brutal police methods of Harry Callahan (*Dirty Harry*, 1971). The fear of crime has become a major political issue around the world and, particularly in the United States and the United Kingdom, it is often presented as an urban issue.

The most influential (and controversial) recent attempt to solve crime in urban areas was the so-called 'broken windows' theory. It was proposed by social scientists George L. Kelling and James Q. Wilson in 1982. They argued that relatively minor offences reinforce the impression of neglect in an area and represent the beginning of a slippery slope leading to serious criminality: 'one unrepaired broken window is a signal that no one cares, and so breaking more windows costs nothing'. Their warning that a stable neighbourhood could soon turn into a 'frightening jungle' struck fear into the heart of middle-class America.[52]

When Rudolph Giuliani was elected Mayor of New York in 1993, he and his police chief William J. Bratton put this theory into practice, clamping down on minor incivilities, such as begging, graffiti and fare-dodging on the subway. But although during his eight years in office there were dramatic falls in crime (in fact, crime was already falling under the previous mayor), there is no evidence that this was due to 'zero tolerance' policing. Indeed, crime fell in cities throughout the United States in the early 1990s. In San Diego, where there was no broken windows policy, it actually fell more rapidly. Many studies have since concluded that the fall in crime was due largely to a reduction in the crack epidemic that was sweeping America. James Q. Wilson has himself admitted, 'I still to this day do not know if improving order will or will not reduce crime.'[53]

The 'zero tolerance' approach has proved influential around the world, not least in the United Kingdom where, in order to combat the fear of crime in urban areas, British cities have pioneered a revolution in surveillance technologies. The urbanist Jane Jacobs famously advocated 'eyes on the street' as the best way of providing 'natural surveillance' and thus safe cities.[54] But modern Britain prefers camera lenses to human eyes. Today, the land of George Orwell's Big Brother has more surveillance cameras than the rest of Europe combined. Nearly all town centres in the United Kingdom have CCTV systems. There are some 500,000 security cameras in London alone. In Liverpool, one of the UK's most deprived cities, UAVs (unmanned aerial vehicles, or drones) are now used for police surveillance. More familiar in the skies of Afghanistan, these high-tech eyes in the sky will also be used during the London 2012 Olympics and will probably become a permanent feature in the capital's skies thereafter.[55]

The fear of crime and terrorism is reshaping urban architecture and the design of our streets. The buildings we live in can indeed influence crime levels. Research suggests the residents of high-rise blocks are more likely to be victims of crime: 'each additional floor in your building increases your risk of being robbed in the street or having your car stolen by 2.5 per cent – if your building has 12 storeys rather than two, your chance of being mugged rises by a quarter,' writes economic journalist Tim Harford.[56] The lesson seems to be that houses rather than high-rises are needed to create a safe urban environment, not something Le Corbusier would have been pleased to learn.

Few would object to designing housing developments on a more human scale. But the fear of crime has become an obsession for politicians, urban planners and architects alike. Cities are now protected by CCTV systems equipped with automatic number-plate recognition and facial recognition software, UAVs with night vision, and even real-time iris scanners monitoring citizens (recently installed in the city of León, Mexico). Planners talk about 'defensible space' – a term coined in 1973 to describe how public areas can be monitored and controlled – and 'hardened architecture', designing buildings with features to discourage thieves and vagrants. A recently completed luxury London apartment block, One Hyde Park, offers bullet-proof windows, a purified air supply and secure panic rooms. (Apartments cost between £20 million and £140 million.) The use of such advanced technologies is part of the new military urbanism that is changing the face of our cities. However, some believe that these changes herald the dawn of a more fearful age.

In his 1990 book *City of Quartz*, Mike Davis was one of the first to

The
Paraisópolis
(Paradise City)
favela borders
the affluent
district of
Morumbi in
São Paulo,
Brazil.

draw attention to the way 'the neo-military syntax of contemporary architecture insinuates violence and conjures imaginary disasters' in cities. He also described the retreat of wealthy Angelinos into gated developments and foresaw the emergence of 'Fortress LA'.[57] These walled private citadels are the modern equivalent of medieval tower houses. In nineteenth-century London, private security guards used to man gates separating the wealthy Georgian squares from the rest of the city. Such sights are increasingly common today as gated developments are built in cities across the United States, Argentina, Brazil, Saudi Arabia and elsewhere. In cities such as São Paulo, distrust of the police and the lack of a welfare state has created an environment in which the rich feel they have no option but to retreat into private gated enclaves protected by razor wire, while all around the poor live in *favelas* run by drugs gangs.

Gated developments are the result of fragmented, divided and unequal societies. Those who live in them hope to insulate themselves against crime and to create what Richard Sennett has termed 'purified communities', ones that exclude strangers and reduce the exposure to difference and otherness that is fundamental to the big city experience.[58] Yet research suggests that, despite their security measures, the fear of crime is often greater for those inside such communities. Gated developments represent the balkanisation of the city, and are a sign of a society divided against itself.

Drugs are one of the major causes of crime in today's cities. Thanks to its proximity to the United States – the world's largest illegal drugs market – Mexico has become the drug-trafficking centre of the Americas. Violent crime and murder are now a daily fact of life. In 2008, 5,300 people were killed there in drug-related violence. Once Mexico City had some of the lowest crime figures on the continent. But after the economy crashed in 1995, crime levels rose together with unemployment. Now there are 17.6 murders per 100,000 people in the capital. (In New York there are 6.7 murders, in London 2.1 and in Shanghai 1.5.) There is a widespread 'culture of fear' in the city.[59] Some 95 per cent of crimes go unsolved and, in August 2008, 150,000 people gathered at Zócalo square in Mexico City to protest about the lack of police action. 'It's a really dangerous city,' says Mexican novelist Guillermo Fadanelli. 'Its bright side is beyond compare, but its dark side is horrible – practically hellish … It's a city that can't be governed.'[60]

The creation of private walled citadels for the wealthy in cities is a desperate measure, a sign of a community at war with itself. But the war could become much, much worse. Around the world, a spectre haunts politicians, police chiefs and urban planners alike. It is the spectre of 'feral cities', of cities that have gone wild, where law and order has broken down, and where the AK-47 has become an essential piece of urban survival equipment.[61] In cities that have been torn apart by war it is already a reality: in Mogadishu, for instance. After Hurricane Katrina devastated New Orleans, America was horrified by news of the tide of lawlessness that swept the city. It was as if all America's nightmares about the city as a 'violence-soaked threat to the nation' had come true. The film *Escape from New York* depicts one dramatic solution. When a crime wave forces law-abiding citizens to flee Manhattan Island, a wall is built around it to keep the criminals inside. The city is turned into a prison, isolating the contagion of criminality. The city wall, which had once been a symbol of safety that attracted people to an urban life, was now used by a suburban nation to permanently quarantine the city of crime.

Galeries Lafayette, Paris, with its 33-metre-high glass dome, was opened in 1912. (following page)

The Department Store

In February 2001, shoppers on London's Oxford Street noticed that something rather unusual was happening in the building that had once housed C&A's flagship department store. Behind the plate-glass window, an industrial conveyor belt had been set up and yellow trays containing bags were slowly circulating. People in identical blue overalls were standing by the conveyor belt and periodically one of them would remove a tray and take an item out of the bag. The person then began to take the object apart. For this was a disassembly line and here, in this disused department store on London's premiere shopping street, someone's possessions – all they had ever bought or been given – were being methodically broken down and destroyed. At the end of two weeks, everything had been either shredded or granulated.

The owner of the 7,006 items – from socks and family photographs to David Bowie CDs and a Saab 900 car – was artist Michael Landy. As part of the project, which was called 'Break Down', each of his possessions had been systematically categorised, entered on to a database, labelled and bagged before being destroyed. Landy described what he was doing as an examination of society's romance with consumerism: 'I see this as the ultimate consumer choice. Once Break Down has finished, a more personal break down, will commence – life without my self-defining belongings.'[62]

Our love affair with shopping began in ancient Rome, the city that became 'the centre of the world's commerce'.[63] More than one million people lived in Rome by the third century AD. In order to feed this unprecedented population, vast warehouses and markets were needed, such as the fruit and vegetable market at the *Forum Holitorium* and the cattle market at *Forum Boarium*. But the Romans were not satisfied with food alone. The specialist shops whose window displays catch our eye on Main Street or in the mall made their first appearance in Rome, where there were shops for books, for precious stones and furniture. Rome even had the first supermarkets (known as *horrea*). Many Romans lived in *tabernae*, consisting of one or two rooms which opened directly on to the street and which, as well as homes, doubled as shops or workrooms. Indeed, look around the alleys and squares of old Rome today and you will see that there are still many shops that open on to the street, often without glazing or doors, and which are sealed at night using shutters. This style of shop became common in cities throughout Europe during the Middle Ages.

Rome also had the world's first recorded shopping centre or mall – Trajan's Market, built AD 107–10. This impressive tiered complex, some five floors high, lies just north of the Roman Forum and is reached today from Via IV Novembre. The brick-faced concrete structure is one of the finest examples of Roman urban architecture in the heyday of the Middle Empire. Built on a hillside, it comprises three separate street levels connected by staircases. It contained more than 170 rooms used as shops and (on the fourth floor) government offices, such as the offices of public assistance (*stationes arcariorum Caesarianorum*). On the ground floor were cool, vaulted storerooms for oil and wine. Fruit and flowers were also sold on this level. More expensive products, such as spices and pepper brought by merchants from the distant East, were sold on the second and third floors. Fish could be bought on the fifth floor, where they were kept alive in tanks of either fresh water (filled by an aqueduct) or salt water. Today, the high, vaulted entrance hall, with its two storeys of shops, remains a strikingly beautiful urban space, one of the most evocative buildings in this historic city. As you walk along the streets lined with empty shops, you can almost smell the pungent spices from two thousand years ago and hear the voices of traders still haggling over prices.

In Arabian cities the bazaar was traditionally the only place where trade could be conducted. Generally subdivided according to merchandise, bazaars took many forms, from irregular streets lined on each side with booths for traders, to domed colonnades and whole districts of covered bazaar streets. The ancient Long Bazaar in Damascus was originally a Roman colonnaded street known as the Via Recta, or 'the street which is called Straight', as it is translated in the Acts of the Apostles (9: 11). This famous shopping street crosses the city from east to west, where part of it is covered and known as the Souk Medhat Pasha. Damascus also has a covered spice market, the Bzouriyya Souk, a place of constant movement and colour where, as Rafik Schami and Marie Fadel say, 'the scent of a peculiar mixture of perfume, sweat and spices fills the nose'.[64] But it is in the Iranian city of Isfahan that the most beautiful bazaars in the Middle East are to be found. A European traveller described these 'great covered streets which are filled with shops' in 1811: 'The majority consist of brick buildings covered by vaults, though some have domes. Light enters through large air-holes in the ceiling and through the entrances for the intersecting streets. Hence, one can walk through all of Isfahan in any weather and remain dry under the covered ways.'[65]

Permanent shops selling luxury goods existed in the larger European cities from at least the twelfth century. Some three hundred years later, London's Cheapside had no fewer than fifty-two goldsmiths and Florence more than eighty shops between the Via di Maggio and Via San Martino, selling what was described as 'splendid and precious silks'.[66] In London, indoor stores with shop windows were common from 1600 and it was the first European city to develop 'a large-scale, full-time, cosmopolitan shopping centre'.[67] In London's Strand, the New Exchange opened in 1609, combining a stock exchange with two floors of independent shops selling a wide range of fine items including silks, feathers, ceramics and medicines.

By 1700, markets and fairs were declining across Europe in the face of competition from specialist retailers. Retailing grew steadily in importance as incomes rose, urban populations increased and people paid less heed to religious disapproval of luxury. In the 1750s, London had one shop for every thirty inhabitants. But after 1800, the number of shops increased dramatically, rising across the country by more than 300 per cent in the first half of the nineteenth century, a pattern that was later repeated in other European cities. In Vienna, for example, the number of shops trebled between 1870 and 1902, and the Parisian suburbs saw an eightfold increase over the same period. By the 1820s, London's Regent Street was 'a fashionable shopping parade with its glass shop fronts, shop blinds, pedestrian pavements and street lighting'.[68] There were also as many as 45,000 street traders in London by mid-century, serving the less affluent end of the market. Baedeker's 1898 guide *London and its Environs* noted that 'shops abound everywhere. In the business-quarters usually visited by strangers it is rare to see a house without shops on the ground floor.'[69]

London's New Exchange – itself a throwback to Trajan's Market – proved to be an influential prototype for a form of urban retailing that became popular at the start of the nineteenth century: the arcade, known elsewhere in Europe as the *passage* or *galleria*. It emerged first in Paris, where in the 1780s the Duc d'Orléans had turned the gardens and arcades of the neo-classical Palais Royal into a public space full of shops, restaurants and coffee houses. It became popular both for shopping and as a promenade, a dynamic and fashionable space, one of those essentially urban focal points that emerge almost spontaneously to meet the needs and desires of city dwellers. In 1786, the Marquis de Bombelles observed: 'With money in one's pocket, in a single day and without leaving its precincts one can buy as prodigiously much in the way of luxury goods as one would manage in a year in any other locality.'[70]

From 1800 to 1830, at least seventeen arcades opened in Paris and this form of retailing quickly spread to other European and American cities. In the industrial age, these modern versions of Trajan's Market were transformed into graceful iron and glass structures, such as Burlington Arcade in London (1819), and the grandest of all, Milan's Galleria Vittorio Emanuele II (1864–7). Filled with daylight and protected from the weather, they were ideal spaces for displaying goods and for leisurely shopping. 'They radiated through the Paris of the Empire like grottoes,' wrote Walter Benjamin in the 1920s. 'For someone entering the Passage des Panoramas in 1817, the sirens of gaslight would be singing to him on one side, while oil-lamp odalisques offered enticements from the other … they were the hollow mould from which the image of "modernity" was cast.'[71] For Benjamin they symbolised the innocent beginnings of the consumerism that became a dominant force in society from the late nineteenth century. At the forefront of that revolution was the department store.

Harrods, in Knightsbridge, London. In a recent opinion poll, Londoners placed the capital's shops top of the list of what they liked most about their city.

The origins of the department store can be traced back to the late eighteenth century and the 'Europe shops' found in colonial cities, such as Kolkata. They offered a cornucopia of enticing wares for Europeans, from pianofortes, wines and pickles to feathered hats, doeskin breeches, guns and speaking trumpets. According to one writer in 1789, British women could easily spend thirty or forty thousand rupees in one morning in a Europe shop, 'for the decoration of their persons'. As a result, he added, 'many husbands are observed to turn pale as ashes, on the bare mention of their wives being seen to enter them'.[72] The best known of the European shops in Kolkata was

Dring's Long Rooms, in the Lall Bazaar. This 200-foot-long shop was a veritable Aladdin's Cave of tempting products.

Until the 1830s, shops had specialised in one area of merchandise. But in Paris, the 'magasins des nouveautés' (such as Pygmalion, which opened as early as 1793 in rue Saint-Denis) proved that there was a demand for general stores selling a variety of goods, from silks to lingerie and gloves. The arcades had demonstrated that bringing together many different shops under one roof was also popular with customers. The department store was the next step in retailing, emerging on both sides of the Atlantic from the mid nineteenth century. It

Arcades, Bazaars and Malls

Arcades emerged to meet the need for a public space protected from both the weather and traffic. They were principally inspired by the idea of the oriental bazaar, but other influences included medieval 'rows' (such as the two-storey covered shopping street in Chester, in the north of England) and colonnaded streets, as in the ancient city of Antioch, in Turkey, which was nearly four kilometres long. The arcade consisted of an association of rented shops. One of the earliest was the Passage du Caire, Paris, which dates from 1799, although it is uncertain whether the glass roof was a later addition. The Passage Delorme (1808) is probably the first arcade with a continuous glazed roof. The Philadelphia Arcade (John Haviland, 1826–7), on Chestnut Street in Philadelphia, was the first one built in America. It was an impressive structure, its façade dominated by four tall arches as high as a three-storey building. The most monumental arcade is Milan's Galleria Vittorio Emanuele II (1864–7). Built to celebrate the unification of Italy, it has been described as 'a pantheon of bourgeois society' and its influence can be seen in later arcades from Manchester to Berlin.[74]

Bazaars were a type of arcade formed from a series of courtyards with skylights and galleries, and were particularly popular in Britain. The first was the Soho Bazaar, designed by John Trotter in 1816, which was founded as a charitable institution to provide employment for relatives of those who had fallen in the French wars. There were more than two hundred traders.

The Pantheon on Oxford Street was originally built for the 'nocturnal adventures of the British aristocracy' (namely balls and masquerades), by James Wyatt in 1772.[75] After it was redeveloped in 1834 it became the city's most famous bazaar. The Bazar de l'Industrie Française (1827–9) between Boulevard Montmartre and rue Montmartre was the first to use a cast-iron structure with two storeys of galleries, which became the subsequent style for bazaars. Unfortunately few of these buildings have survived. The Upper Trading Rows (now the 'GUM', or Main Department Store) in Moscow is one notable exception. Built in 1888–1893 by A. N. Pomerantzev, its striking façade is nearly 800 feet long and its three floors contain some three hundred shops.

offered customers an unprecedented range of goods, which for the first time were displayed in an eye-catching and even theatrical way to entice them to part with their hard-earned cash. One of the earliest department stores was Alexander T. Stewart's 'Marble Palace' in New York (1846), which has been described as 'the first multi-story building expressly designed to handle a large volume of trade'.[73]

In an age of mass production and rising personal wealth, department stores were more than mere shops: they became temples of consumption and good taste. The aspirational lower classes flocked to them to learn how to become bourgeois. In the weeks after it opened

A mall is an enclosed shopping centre. It extends the idea of the arcade and the bazaar on a vast scale. Today's megamalls exceed a million square feet and contain not just stores and restaurants but multiplex cinemas, post offices, ice-skating rinks, even theme parks. Malls were pioneered by Victor Gruen, a Los Angeles architect inspired by Lewis Mumford's criticism of the car's impact on urban communities. He believed malls could

Elements Mall (2007) and The Arch residential skyscraper (2006) in West Kowloon, China.

become the new agoras or medieval market places. His design for the Southdale Shopping Center in Edina, Minnesota, was inspired by European arcades. Opened in 1956, it was the first enclosed shopping mall.

During the golden age of mall development, at least 28,000 malls were built in North America and more than half of all retail sales were made in them. The Mall of America, in Bloomington, Minnesota, opened in 1992, covering some forty-five acres. From the outside it is as tall as an eight-storey building, a vast, windowless structure like an aircraft hangar. Inside it offers more than five hundred stores, as well as restaurants, cinemas and even a wedding chapel (over five thousand weddings have been performed in the mall). Eight acres of skylights allow some 400 trees and 30,000 plants to grow in the mall. The mall receives an astonishing forty million visitors each year. Today nine of the world's ten largest malls are in Asia. (The largest in Europe is Cevahir, Istanbul, Turkey.) The South China Mall in Dongguan, China, is the biggest in the world, though this monument to retail hubris has struggled to attract customers, perhaps because it is located in the suburbs and accessible only by car.

in 1855, Wylie and Lockhead's new department store in Buchanan Street, Glasgow, was flooded with so many people that they decided to open on Saturday afternoons just to allow customers to view, but not buy, the merchandise. In that same year in Paris, the Grands Magasins du Louvre opened as part of the preparations for the Exposition Universelle. By the end of the 1860s, it had become the first Paris store to reach a turnover of one hundred million francs a year.[76]

Le Bon Marché (literally, 'the good market') had opened for business in the French capital as early as the 1830s. Although not so opulent as the Grands Magasins du Louvre, under its new dynamic owner, Aristide Boucicaut, Le Bon Marché would become the leading department store in Paris and, indeed, the world. In 1869, Boucicaut laid the foundation stone for what was to be Europe's first and most extravagant purpose-built department store. When it was complete, Le Bon Marché covered the entire block bordered by the rues Babylone, Sèvres, Bac and Velpeau – some 52,800 square metres of floor space, making it the largest store in the world. For many, Le Bon Marché became the epitome of the nineteenth-century *grand magasin*, the quintessential big store. Émile Zola described it as 'the cathedral of modern commerce, solid and light, made for a people of customers'.[77] Zola closely observed the workings of Le Bon Marché and other Parisian department stores while writing his novel *Au Bonheur des Dames* (1883). The novel reflects the sheer excitement and modernity of this new kind of shopping. Watching the crush of the crowds in Le Bon Marché, he was constantly aware of 'the vastness of Paris – a city so vast that it would always be able to supply customers'.

Department stores revolutionised the process of buying and selling. They pioneered new technology, such as pneumatic tubes to send orders around the store, cash registers for instant transactions (Le Bon Marché had no fewer than seventy-three in Zola's day), as well as lifts and escalators (the first department store to have an elevator was in New York City at the corner of Broome Street and Broadway in 1857). People were encouraged to regard the shop as an exhibition hall. There was no obligation to buy and staff were not pushy or intrusive: the idea was to let the display sell the goods. Victor Horta, the art nouveau architect of the Brussels department store L'Innovation (1901), described the guiding principle as 'remarkably simple. It was to grab the attention of those passing by the store and to turn them into purchasers and, once inside the "cage", to compel them to pass and to pause before the articles on display, no matter how insignificant.'[78]

All prices were fixed and clearly ticketed. There was no haggling. Goods could even be returned if customers changed their mind. Home delivery and mail order were also available. The Samaritaine store in Paris (Frantz Jourdain, 1905–10) featured motor-driven conveyor belts to take packages from the shop floor to the delivery bays. Le Bon Marché offered free delivery of most goods, even abroad. Zola noted that there were several hundred men employed in the mail-order department in the basement of the store. France's colony Algeria was at the top of Le Bon Marché's foreign mail order league in 1902–3, with goods dispatched there worth 1,208,371 francs. England was in second place, ordering goods worth 1,084,899 francs.

Like the new market halls and railway stations being built in cities throughout the industrialised world, department stores were designed for large numbers of people. Haussmann's broad boulevards had made it easier to move efficiently around Paris. By 1860, the carriages of the newly unified Compagnie Générale des Omnibuses were carrying seventy million passengers around Paris each year. The architecture of the stores was dramatic, with striking façades, large plate-glass windows and expansive, light-filled interiors in which galleries and balconies offered views on to both the displays of goods and crowds of shoppers. The new stores soon became must-see features of cities, listed in guidebooks alongside famous monuments. Baedeker's 1912 guide to Berlin told tourists to go to Wertheim's store simply to admire the interior: 'visitors need not make any purchase'.[79] These were new and exciting urban spaces. Just to walk through them was to be part of the modern age, an age of mass production and mass consumption, or, as Marx dismissed it, 'commodity fetishism'.[80]

Stores brought a new dimension to urban life, transforming society beyond the city as bourgeois culture embraced the consumer age. For women in particular, department stores offered a space in which they were free to socialise without men and where, eventually, they would find employment. When Zola visited Le Bon Marché in 1882, there were 152 women sales assistants out of a total staff of some three thousand. Traditionalists were appalled, accusing Le Bon Marché and other department stores of being 'towers of Babel', immoral places where women were seduced by products into neglecting their families and tempted into becoming shoplifters.[81]

Zola was immensely impressed by the theatricality and spectacle of department stores, which hosted regular concerts, fashion shows, pageants and extravaganzas. One of the most important events in Le Bon Marché's calendar was the annual white sale, the 'exposition du blanc', held in late January or early February, in which white merchandise from every department was displayed. On the first day alone, sales would be boosted by 300 per cent compared to an average day. Meticulous planning went into the 'blanc', with one million catalogues sent out to the provinces alone for the 1910 sale. As ever, the aim was to create 'a kind of spectacle out of the store', to imbue the goods and the experience with an aura of glamour.[82] The intention was to overwhelm the consumer by transforming the store into 'a great fair and fantasy land of colors, sensations and dreams'.[83] This was, after all, the era of world's fairs, the expositions, at which Paris in particular excelled.

When Zola was researching his novel, Le Bon Marché had thirty-six departments. Boucicaut famously boasted that 'everything useful, convenient, and comfortable that experience has been able to produce' could be found in his store.[84] From the 1880s, department stores did, indeed, contain everything the consumer could desire, from animals to carpets, toys and sweets. By the turn of the century, Le Bon Marché even sold its own toilet paper (with, of course, the Bon Marché trademark clearly displayed). People were astounded by the range of goods on offer at department stores. Whiteleys, which opened in London in 1863 and employed some six thousand people by 1914, boasted that it was the 'Universal Provider'. At the beginning of the twentieth century, a journalist enumerated some of the seemingly infinite possibilities on offer at London's stores: 'When you have bought your medicines, your literature, your pictures, your saddlery, the latest bicycle and electric plant, flowers for the epergnes, bacon, eggs, and vegetables, fish, poultry, boots and butter, you may, if you have time, step aside and sit for your photograph, having first made a special toilet, beginning with the bath and ending with the hairdresser and manicurist. Even then the "stores" have not been fully explored!'[85]

The heyday of the department store in Paris was from about 1870 to 1914. By the interwar period, the United States led the world in retailing. Gordon Selfridge's store on London's Oxford Street (opened 1909) was modelled on American retail techniques. A steel-framed building – one of the first of its type in Europe – it had eight floors, a hundred departments and 1,400 employees. In America, the great department stores were on Market Street in Philadelphia, State Street in Chicago, and on New York's Broadway, part of which was known as the 'Ladies' Mile', the city's elite shopping district, described in 1890 as 'a stage for the fashion conscious'.[86] This was where you would find Alexander Stewart's 'Cast Iron Palace' at 10th Street (opened in 1863 with no fewer than six elevators), designed for fifty thousand customers a day. Its great rival was Rowland H. Macy's department store which, until 1902, could be found on Sixth Avenue. By 1879 there were some twenty major department stores on this street, including Lord and Taylor, Brooks Brothers and Tiffany.

When the department store was at the peak of its popularity, H. G. Wells predicted that the city would be transformed from an economic powerhouse into a 'bazaar, a great gallery of shops and places of concourse and rendezvous'.[87] But after the Second World War, the same forces that were sapping the vitality of downtown – the automobile and suburbanisation – favoured the rise of out-of-town shopping centres. The Crenshaw Center (1947), now known as Baldwin Hills Crenshaw Plaza, was one of the first, about eight miles from downtown Los Angeles. Such centres could hold up to a hundred stores, although usually they were anchored by just one or two large department stores, such as Le Bon Marché, J. L. Hudson or Jordan Marsh.

In Britain, these regional centres, such as the Whitgift Centre in Croydon, south of London, began to appear in the 1960s. By this time American shopping centres were entirely enclosed and air-conditioned. Journalists waxed lyrical about their benefits: 'Look at the beautiful malls – with fountains and green trees – and soft, sweet music where women can shop in a relaxed and pleasant atmosphere.'[88] Today, vast malls continue to be built around the world, particularly in Asia and the Middle East. But in an age of rising petrol prices and internet shopping, the popularity of malls has peaked. In response to this, developers have begun building malls in city centres, such as Horton Plaza in San Diego (1985) and Westfield London (2008), Europe's biggest inner-city shopping complex, boasting more than 1.6 million square feet of space and costing more than £1.5 billion to build. The developers hope that some twenty-one million people will visit this centre each year, lured by a type of urban shopping that the Romans first invented nearly two thousand years ago.

Sydney Opera House (1973) and Sydney Harbour Bridge. (following page) 243

7 TIME OUT

The City and the Stage

Cities are places of spectacle, arenas for the human drama of everyday life. After all, to spend some time as a *flâneur*, sitting in a city centre café, watching people pass by, is to experience theatre in its purest form. Studying faces you do not know and are never likely to see again, faces from every continent, is endlessly fascinating.

There is something intrinsically theatrical about urban life, one of the themes explored by Jonathan Raban in his classic study *Soft City*. A city can be defined as a community in which you are likely to meet strangers. You are repeatedly thrown together with unfamiliar people and you have to make snap judgements based on superficial evidence, such as how they dress or speak, or whether their smile is trustworthy or suspicious. These random encounters are at the heart of the urban drama, a performance in which we are all players.

In a community of strangers you remain anonymous. You are free to play whatever role you like, donning a different mask and costume for each. Who shall I be today? Mr Angry or Mr Couldn't Care Less? But which one is really you? And does anyone know the difference? We're all strangers here, anyway. Perhaps some people are even strangers to themselves, spending their entire lives dazzled by the bright lights of the big city.

But the anonymity of city life has always offered an escape from the straitjacket of convention, freedom from the feudal bondage of village life and the expectations of clan or family. For many, the big city becomes a crucible in which the self can be forged anew. This, as well as the promise of jobs, is what draws people to the glittering metropolis. And this gift of self-discovery is reflected in the institutions of the city, in its museums, libraries, galleries and theatres.

For two and a half thousand years, theatre has provided a forum in which city dwellers have come together to share the tragedies and comedies of their daily lives. Its prehistoric roots may lie hidden in the seasonal rituals of the village, but theatre as we know it today first appeared in ancient Greece and is particularly associated with Athens. Here plays were performed as part of festivals held to honour the god Dionysus, such as the five-day City Dionysia in late February. Sacred dances and drama were probably first seen in the agora, but eventually special buildings were constructed to house these festivals. On the slopes of the Acropolis in Athens there are still two ancient theatres, the Odeion of Herodes Atticus and the older Theatre of Dionysus. The latter dates from the fourth century BC, but it was on this site many years before that Athenian drama began.

Tragedy was at the heart of the City Dionysia from the sixth century BC. The first recorded performance is from about 533 BC, by the actor Thespis (hence our word 'thespian'). By the middle of the next century, tragedy also formed part of the Lenaea festival, held in the autumn at the time of the grape harvest. The more subversive and edgy genre of comedy (from *kômos*, meaning a riotous company) featured later, appearing at the City Dionysia from 486 BC and at the Lenaea from 445 BC. These religious and civic festivals were immensely popular events in the life of the city and its people. Plays were performed to rapt audiences of 14,000 or more, although women and slaves were excluded. For each festival three authors were selected to compete for the prize of best playwright and, from 449 BC, the best actor – the Oscars of the ancient world. There were five judges and the reaction of the audience was central to their decision. Each author offered three tragedies and a light-hearted 'satyr-play', all highly stylised, as might be expected in a religious festival.

Actors performed in long robes and masks on the flat piece of ground known as the 'orchestra', in front of the sloping 'theatron' (Greek for 'watching place'). Between scenes there were interludes of singing and dancing by a chorus, although none of the music has survived. Tragedies drew on a rich history of mythological traditions to depict symbolic conflicts between men and gods, or between people, touching on themes that affected Athenians both as individuals and as members of the 'polis'. To watch such plays with your fellow citizens would have been a powerful, emotionally charged experience for these urban audiences. In comedies, such as those by Aristophanes, the emotions provoked were of a different order, with playwrights subverting virtually every aspect of Athenian culture and society, from politicians to the gods. From the first official appearance of comedies at the Lenaea to the last plays of Aristophanes a century later, some six to seven hundred comedies were performed. We know the names of about fifty comic dramatists from the period and the titles of half the plays, but today only eleven survive, all by Aristophanes. Indeed, we know only a fraction of the dramatic heritage of classical Greece. Sophocles is said to have written up to 130 tragedies, of which only seven remain. Most were lost in subsequent disasters, such as the burning of the Library at Alexandria, leaving a terrible lacuna in the history of the human mind.

During the golden age of Greek drama when the great Athenian tragedians such as Aeschylus, Sophocles and Euripides were writing, Athens also produced the philosophy of Socrates and Plato and architecture of such enduring beauty as the Parthenon. It was one of the most creative cities the world has ever known, a towering example of how cities can change the course of human history and civilisation.

Aristotle once said that 'men came together in the city to live; they remain there in order to live the good life'.[1] The truth of this statement can be felt even today in these first theatres. I have felt it in the Teatro Greco (the Greek Theatre) in Taormina, on Sicily. Sitting in the bowl-shaped 'theatron' is an unforgettable experience. You look down on the 'orchestra' where actors have performed for millennia and out across a breathtakingly beautiful panorama of the Sicilian coastline, with the smouldering shadow of Etna in the distance.

Although the Teatro Greco was built originally by the Greeks in the second century BC, it was rebuilt by the Romans at the end of the first century AD. Major Roman towns generally had a theatre or amphitheatre, or even both, as at Cirencester and St Albans in England. Despite being one of largest cities in the west of the Roman Empire, with a population of about sixty thousand, Londinium (London) appears only to have had an amphitheatre. It was rediscovered in 1987 under the Yard of the Guildhall (part of it is preserved beneath the new Guildhall Art Gallery). Built in AD 70–1, initially from earth and timber but later brick, London's amphitheatre had room for some six thousand spectators. Theatrical performances consisted of shows mounted during festivals to honour gods and political figures. They were organised by city magistrates and would have included blood sports involving troupes of gladiators as well as animals, such as bulls and bears. There would also have been acrobatics, wrestling, boxing, and even racing, although this was generally held in a circus. At this time, tragedy and comedy had gone out of fashion among Romans, who now preferred mime and pantomime (or dance-drama).

Once the Romans left Britain in AD 410, London's amphitheatre fell into ruin. For over a thousand years, London had no public open-air theatrical building. However, folk plays and street theatre (such as the *commedia dell'arte* in Italy) undoubtedly persisted and by the end of the twelfth century London emerged again as an important performance centre. Indeed, its reputation was such that, in the late twelfth century, it earned a place in a chronicle by the Winchester monk Richard of Devizes. His narrative took the form of a warning to a young man about the many pitfalls of London life, including the city's theatrical attractions. Like taverns and gambling dens, the 'theatrum' (meaning a place where secular and possibly lewd plays were performed) was to be avoided, while 'histriones' (actors) were listed as urban 'evildoers', along with 'jesters, smooth-skinned lads, Moors, flatterers, pretty boys, effeminates, pederasts, singing and dancing girls, quacks, belly-dancers, sorceresses, extortioners, night-wanderers, magicians, mimes, beggars, buffoons' and other supposed miscreants.[2]

It was not until the end of the sixteenth century that London once again had its own permanent public theatre. Until then, troupes of actors performed in the yards of inns, like the Bull, in Bishopsgate Street. But in 1576, James Burbage, who was a member of the theatrical company known as Leicester's Men and (conveniently) a trained carpenter, built a theatre in Shoreditch, half a mile from Bishopsgate, just beyond the City limits, to avoid taxes and censorship. London's first purpose-built playhouse, the Theatre, lasted for more than two decades. Indeed, such was its popularity that in the following year a second theatre, the Curtain, opened nearby. It was at Burbage's Theatre in 1594 that the work of a then unknown playwright was first performed. His name was William Shakespeare. Both *Romeo and Juliet* and *A Midsummer Night's Dream* opened there.[3]

The building of Burbage's Theatre was part of an extraordinary explosion of creativity in London at the time, particularly in drama.

Between 1590 and 1642, some 2,500 plays were written by named

The Red-Light District

Organised prostitution is largely an urban phenomenon. Prostitution thrived in ports, garrison towns and boomtowns. Red-light districts often emerged in cities where there were many economic migrants, usually single men. For migrant women, too, prostitution has traditionally offered a way of earning money when there are no other means of support.

In ancient Rome, the Subura was a well-known red-light district and there were at least forty-five brothels in the city.[4] In Pompeii, too, there were many brothels and commercial sex was widely available.

By contrast, in medieval European cities prostitutes were often forbidden from operating within the city walls. However, many French towns at this time had a 'maison de ville' or bath house in which prostitution was permitted and controlled. In medieval English cities, what we might now call a red-light district was known by the rather more earthy name of 'Gropecunt Lane'. They could be found in the cities of York, Norwich, Oxford, Bristol, Newcastle, Southampton, Hereford, Wells, Banbury, Reading, Worcester and Shrewsbury. Today, these streets have often been renamed.

In the seventeenth century, Japan created legalised red-light areas. One of these was the Yoshiwara district in Tokyo which existed from 1618 to the 1950s. The sophistication of its courtesans inspired many plays, haiku and exquisite *ukiyoe* woodblock prints. During the nineteenth century, there were as many as nine thousand prostitutes here. But in March 1945 Yoshiwara was razed to the ground in the American fire-bombing of Tokyo, killing at least four hundred of the prostitutes.[5]

In cities around the world, red-light districts have become popular tourist destinations. Among the best known are Soho in London, De Wallen (Walletjes) in Amsterdam, King's Cross in Sydney, the Reeperbahn in Hamburg, Tokyo's Kabukicho, the Tenderloin in San Francisco and Patpong in Bangkok.

A 1775 woodcut of the Yoshiwara district in Tokyo.

authors (of which some two thousand survive). Most were professional playwrights such as Thomas Dekker, Thomas Middleton, Shakespeare, Christopher Marlowe, Ben Jonson, John Webster and Thomas Heywood, who claimed to have written no fewer than 220 plays.

At the end of the sixteenth century, it was not just the theatre that was booming in London. England's main export at the time was woollen cloth and most of this was exported through London. Prosperous merchants here could earn £2–3,000 a year, equivalent to the income of a wealthy aristocrat. The discovery of gold and silver in the New World had also inflated the money supply. By 1579, one contemporary observed that 'the realm aboundeth in riches, as may be seen by the general excess of the people in purchasing, in buildings, in meat, drink and feastings, and most notably in apparel'.[6] The population of the city expanded rapidly, rising from 120,000 in 1550 to 200,000 by the start of the new century. London was England's wealthiest city and, more so than any other European capital, it played a dominant role in the cultural life of the country.

In 1598, the year after James Burbage died, George Allen, who disapproved of playhouses, refused to renegotiate the lease. Burbage's sons and other members of the company, including William Shakespeare, taking advantage of a clause in the lease, dismantled the Theatre and moved it to Bankside, where they used the timber to build the Globe Theatre. This circular, thatched building, with its centre open to the sky – a 'wooden O', as Shakespeare describes it – was of a similar size to the nearby Swan, able to accommodate an audience of three thousand. Soon the watermen on the Thames were transporting some three to four thousand people every afternoon to the playhouses. The cheapest ticket cost a penny (1d.) at the Globe, a price pitched low enough to be affordable to ordinary Londoners.

This was popular rather than elite entertainment. The comedies of the time (1590–1630), such as Middleton's *A Chaste Maid in Cheapside* (1613) or Jonson's *Bartholomew Fair* (1614), depicted familiar London locations and urban characters – shopkeepers, priests and prostitutes – people whom the audience would have come across every day on the city's streets. Audiences consisted of people of all classes. There were servants and apprentices, as well as students from the Inns of Court and wealthy gentlemen, who would go to the theatre in the afternoon to meet friends, hear gossip, pick up a woman or simply to sleep off a big lunch. Theatre became a vital part of London's vibrant social life.

James Burbage had borrowed £666 from his brother-in-law to build the Theatre. The larger Globe cost £1,400, a small fortune at the time. But the theatre was a lucrative business. Authors were paid £6 or £7 for a play (rising to £20 by 1615). Each theatre employed about thirty people, including musicians, actors and prompters. Elizabethan theatre became 'the world's first entertainment business'.[7] By the time Shakespeare died in 1616, nearly a dozen theatres had been built and at least eight hundred new plays performed in London.

In his remarkable study *Cities in Civilization*, Peter Hall has argued that 'creative cities are almost certainly uncomfortable, unstable cities, cities in some kind of basic collective self-examination, cities in the course of kicking over the traces'.[8] Creative cities are edgy places, where conservative, traditional forces collide with new, radical ideas in a shower of brilliant sparks. Great cities are complex, even disorderly, cosmopolitan communities. They are certainly not the easiest or safest places in which to live (housing conditions in Athens were far from ideal). Such cities are often overwhelming and intense environments. But this is often why they are such creative places. After all, it's the irritant of sand in an oyster that produces the pearl. But there is no fail-safe recipe for making a creative city.

Berlin at the beginning of the twentieth century was such a city. The critic Herbert Jhering arrived there in 1907. The city had three opera houses and fifty theatres, as well as music halls. In Berlin, he wrote, 'the stage was a respiratory organ for the city, a part of its very body, as necessary as the River Spree, Lake Wannsee or the Grunewald, as necessary as work, factories and Potsdam'. For Jhering, the theatre was part of 'everyday life' and, like life in Berlin and other great cities, it was 'excited, charged, alert, clever, rousing'.[9] Berlin between the wars was a deeply troubled city — its population had doubled to nearly four million, it had endured the hyperinflation of 1922–3 when newspaper presses were used to print banknotes, and the Nazis and the Communists were regularly fighting pitched battles for dominance on the city's streets. But paradoxically it was also an incredibly dynamic city, attracting artists, writers and scientists. Albert Einstein had arrived in the city in 1914 and it was here in November 1915 that he completed his general theory of relativity. It was a 'great work of art,' said the physicist Max Born, 'the greatest feat of human thinking about nature, the most amazing combination of philosophical penetration, physical intuition, and mathematic skill'.[10]

Thea Alba, 'The Woman Who Writes with Her Feet and Her Hands', Berlin, Germany, 1931.

Berlin became the intellectual capital of Europe, a cultural magnet drawing to it the English writer Christopher Isherwood and later the poets Stephen Spender and W. H. Auden, among many others. Isherwood's *Berlin Stories*, which became the film *Cabaret* (1972), immortalised the myth of the Golden Twenties in Berlin. With its smoke-filled jazz clubs and seedy cabarets, the city became, as Stefan Zweig put it, the orgiastic 'Babylon of the world'.[11] Bertolt Brecht, whose epic theatre would revolutionise modern drama, arrived here in 1924. Four years later, the opening of his and Kurt Weill's *The Threepenny Opera* became a night people remembered all their lives. Alfred Döblin's novel *Berlin Alexanderplatz* (1929) captures the incredible dynamism of the metropolis at this time. The novel echoes with the lost sights and sounds of Berlin: faces glimpsed among the crowds, snatches of conversation, phrases from songs and advertising hoardings, newspaper headlines, the rattle of trams in Berlin's streets, the rhythmic thud of the steam pile-driver in front of Aschinger's bar on Rosenthaler Strasse ('rumm, rumm'), and the squeals of dying animals in Berlin's new slaughterhouse.[12] Living in Berlin was undoubtedly a hard-scrabble existence for many people, but the city had an undeniable energy and, like an illicit drug, once it was in your veins you couldn't survive without it.

City of the Mind

Museums, libraries and art galleries have become ubiquitous in cities around the world. But their origins are buried in the sandy ruins of the earliest cities. The Royal Library of Assurbanipal was the forerunner of today's great collections, such as the Library of Congress in Washington, DC, the largest research institution in the world with more than twenty-one million catalogued books. Assurbanipal was an Assyrian king who ruled from 668 to 627 BC and built his library in the city of Nineveh, near present-day Mosul in Iraq, by the River Tigris. It was the first attempt to bring together the sum of human knowledge in one building – an idea that would resonate throughout the following centuries, long after Assurbanipal had been forgotten.

The vast store of clay tablets and wax-covered writing boards in Assurbanipal's library contained all of Mesopotamian literature, texts such as the Gilgamesh epic, inscribed in cuneiform script, as well as works of astrology and astronomy, omen texts and rituals. Sadly, this great repository of knowledge did not outlive Assurbanipal. The library burned down after the king's death and its remains were only rediscovered in the nineteenth century. However, today some thirty thousand clay fragments have been recovered and are currently being catalogued and translated, appropriately enough, by a modern-day descendant of Assurbanipal's library – the British Museum in London.

The most famous museum and library of antiquity was in the city of Alexandria, on the Mediterranean coast of Egypt, just west of the mouth of the River Nile. Alexandria was the first great cosmopolis, a true melting pot of cultures and peoples. It was founded by Alexander the Great in 331 BC. There was nothing apart from a small fishing village here when Alexander first saw this stretch of coast. Unfortunately, he did not live to see his urban vision realised in stone. The city that emerged from the sand was built by King Ptolemy I, who became ruler of Egypt after Alexander's death in 323 BC. Designed by Dinocrates of Rhodes, Alexandria was constructed around a gridiron plan, based on the principles of Hippodamus of Miletus. By the middle of the first century BC it had become a thriving, wealthy port city of some 300,000 people and it served as the capital of Ptolemy's empire for nearly a thousand years.

Alexandria's fleets traded with cities as far afield as India and Africa. For centuries, Jews, Greeks, Babylonians and Egyptians lived peacefully side by side in this cosmopolitan city. Unlike in Greece, women gained property rights here and were free to become politicians, poets and architects. But what set this city apart from all others and made it into the cultural and intellectual centre of the Hellenistic world was its great Museum and Library. Advised by the Athenian statesman and philosopher Demetrius of Phalerum, Ptolemy transformed the heart of his city from just a palace – a focus of imperial power – into a museum, a 'place of the Muses', and a centre of intellectual authority. Here the world learned the true power of knowledge – the power to change minds and, with them, the world.

As Ptolemy filled his palace to overflowing with texts from all cultures – Alexandria was where the Hebrew Bible was translated into Greek (the Septuagint) – he was forced to expand the palace complex, adding space for scholars to live and work. Laboratories, observatories and zoological gardens were built, creating 'a city of the mind'.[13] Some of the greatest intellects of the age were drawn here, men like the mathematician Euclid (325–265 BC) and the pioneering anatomist Herophilos of Chalcedon (335–280 BC). Although the Greeks didn't permit human dissection, it was allowed in Alexandria and, indeed, Herophilos conducted them in public. As a result of these studies, Herophilos relocated the centre of thought from the heart to the brain and also showed that blood rather than air flowed through veins and arteries. He grasped, too, the link between the heart and the pulse, even using it to diagnose illness. These were major advances in the understanding of the human body, at a time when the gods were commonly viewed as the cause of illness.

In the reign of Ptolemy II (283–46 BC), the Museum was rebuilt alongside the palace on the waterfront, its façade gleaming with white marble. As well as the Library, it contained lecture theatres, assembly halls, observatories and collections of plants and animals. Above the entrance to the great Library was a plaque proclaiming it to be 'A Sanatorium for the Mind'. Inside the Library were ten connected rooms or halls, each devoted to a specific field of learning, such as rhetoric, mathematics or poetry, with the papyrus scrolls stored in alcoves around the walls. Smaller rooms were provided for scholars to read the scrolls and to discuss them. Ptolemy's vision of a city of the mind had been triumphantly realised, creating 'the first integrated scientific research complex in the world'.[14]

However, Alexandria's great Library would eventually suffer the same fate as that at Nineveh. The only difference was that Assurbanipal's clay tablets were more fire-resistant than papyrus scrolls. When Julius Caesar burned Cleopatra's fleet in Alexandria's harbour in 48 BC, the flames were so intense that fire spread to the Museum. At the time, the Roman historian Livy said that there were as many as 400,000 texts in the building (although that is thought to

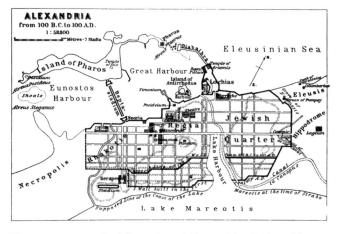

The reconstructed gridiron plan of Alexandria, designed in about 331 BC by Dinocrates of Rhodes.

be an exaggeration). It's not known how many scrolls survived, but of those that did many were probably later destroyed by Christian rulers who despised pre-Christian knowledge, viewing it as pagan.

By placing a great library at the heart of his city, Ptolemy set an important precedent. The city had always been a centre of power, religion and wealth. Now it became a place of self-discovery. Socrates never put his ideas down on paper, preferring to pass on his thoughts orally to his followers. But in the future, libraries, museums and other institutions, such as galleries and universities, would become storehouses of history and ideas, intellectual resources not found in traditional rural communities outside of monasteries. One day, in a more democratic age, the city would be the place from where anyone could set out on a journey of self-discovery.

In September 1746, the *London Evening Post* carried an advertisement for an educational course: 'Gentlemen', it said, could learn 'the Art of Dissecting ... in the same manner as at Paris.'[15] This was William and John Hunter's new anatomy school in Covent Garden. For the first time in Britain, students who wanted to understand the human body were given their own corpse to dissect. The school was an instant success with students, who rushed to enrol. Courses had to be held during the winter to slow the decomposition of the corpses and reduce the resulting stench. During twelve years in Covent Garden, John Hunter estimated that over two thousand bodies were dissected. Among the many students attracted to Covent Garden were the economist Adam Smith and historian Edward Gibbon.

257

In 1788, John Hunter – then the most famous surgeon in Britain – opened a museum to the public. It was unlike anything seen before in Europe. Located in his home at 28 Leicester Square in London, it was the culmination of his life's work to discover the secrets of the human body. There were 14,000 exhibits: more than 1,400 pickled body parts, bones, skeletons, stuffed animals (including a giraffe), and many thousands of pathological preparations revealing the effects of diseases. But this was far more than a museum: it was a research tool that allowed Hunter to demonstrate to the world his theory of the fundamental interrelatedness of life, including his radical idea that (as he told visitors) 'our first parents, Adam and Eve, were indisputably black'.[16] Thanks to Hunter's work and his museum, by the end of the eighteenth century London had become the capital of anatomical studies.

Urban scientific institutions, such as Hunter's school and museum, were part of a tradition that stretches back to the great museum and library at Alexandria, a tradition in which cities played a vital role in the propagation of knowledge. After the scientific revolution in the seventeenth century, cities became centres of debate and discovery for

The Bilbao Effect

Today, museums and galleries are often built as part of urban regeneration schemes. The most famous example of this was at Bilbao, where, in 1997, Frank Gehry's soaring titanium-clad Guggenheim Museum of modern art transformed a town previously known for its heavy industry and port into an international tourist destination. In an age of increasing globalisation, such high-profile architectural developments are vital to cities competing on an international stage. Iconic, or 'signature', buildings capture headlines around the world, at least when they are opened. After two decades of decline, the Basque city's fortunes have indeed improved in recent years. But while some claim this is due to the remarkable publicity generated by the Museum, others point out that so far the substantial foreign investment that was anticipated has not materialised. Nevertheless, in an attempt to reproduce the 'Bilbao effect' by attracting the creative classes and investment to post-industrial cities, 'starchitects' have been drafted into other urban centres and tasked with creating dramatic new museums and cultural centres. The results, both economic and aesthetic, have been mixed.

The motivation behind the planned Guggenheim Abu Dhabi, in the United Arab Emirates, is less urban regeneration than an attempt to brand a city as a high-end cultural destination. It is to be designed by Frank Gehry and built on the empty Saadiyat Island off the coast of Abu Dhabi. It will form a the new sciences. Public lectures and salons became hugely popular. The Royal Institution of Great Britain was founded in 1799. From 1801, Humphry Davy's chemistry lectures were drawing large audiences to the Institution's home at 21 Albemarle Street in London. Indeed, so many people arrived in their carriages that Albemarle Street was declared London's first one-way street. Davy's successor at the Institution was Michael Faraday, who initiated the famous Christmas Lectures for young people, a tradition that continues to this day.

Today's public museums that attract millions of visitors each year grew out of private collections (often known as a 'cabinet of curiosities' or 'Wunderkammer' in German), such as John Hunter's. The first was the British Museum, which was initially housed in the late seventeenth-century Montagu House in London's Bloomsbury. Founded in 1753, the Museum was based on Sir Hans Sloane's private collection. But until 1805, access was only by written application and guided tour. The Louvre in Paris, which opened in 1793, more closely resembled what we think of today as a public museum. It was free and open

cultural hub, part of a leisure and residential district which will include luxury hotels, golf

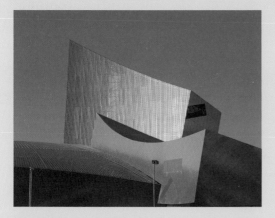

The Imperial War Museum North, Trafford, Manchester. Designed by Daniel Libeskind and opened in 2002.

courses, museums, a theatre and a park, that is expected to cost $27 billion (£14.5 billion) and attract 1.5 million visitors a year once it is finished in 2018. There will also be a franchise of the Louvre (an 8,000-square-metre museum designed by Jean Nouvel), the Sheikh Zayed National Museum (by Norman Foster), a performing arts centre (by Zaha Hadid) and a maritime museum (by Tadao Ando). The Guggenheim Abu Dhabi (scheduled to open in 2013) will be the largest Guggenheim in the world with 13,000 square metres of exhibition space. The acquisitions budget for the museum has been described as 'potentially unlimited'.[17] In such ambitious plans one can, perhaps, hear a distant echo of Ptolemy's grand vision for Alexandria, 2,300 years ago.

regularly to the public, who visited in large numbers. The Louvre provided a model for art galleries everywhere. Among the first of these were Munich's sculpture gallery, the Glyptothek (1830), and art galleries, the Alte Pinakothek (1836) and the Neue Pinakothek (1853). Art lovers from around the world flocked to the city and its galleries opened people's eyes to the delights of art exhibitions. One held in Munich in 1869 drew 100,000 visitors.

The French Enlightenment popularised the idea of erecting great public buildings in cities. British industrial cities, such as Birmingham, municipalised institutions, such as libraries, museums and art galleries, housing them in fine buildings. They consciously modelled themselves on great historic cities, hoping to educate and inspire the burgeoning populations of their smoky new metropolises with the art and artefacts of earlier urban civilisations. But such ideals were soon overtaken by less noble motives, as cities began building art galleries, museums and libraries not just to educate their citizens but as a way of proclaiming civic pride and urban status. By 1887, England had fifty municipal museums and there was a fierce international rivalry between cities to build the finest public institutions.

'Libraries have improved the general Conversation of Americans, made the common Tradesmen and Farmers as intelligent as most Gentlemen from other Countries, and perhaps have contributed in some Degree to the Stand so generally made throughout the Colonies in Defence of their Privileges.' These were the words of Benjamin Franklin. In 1731 he had organised what he termed 'the Mother of all American Subscription Libraries', the Library Company of Philadelphia, an idealistic institution in which the money of stockholders was used to buy books that all could borrow.[18] It is America's oldest cultural institution and this independent research library is still free and open to the public.

Circulating libraries had begun in the eighteenth century, charging a small fee for the right to borrow books. By 1818, London had thirteen such libraries stocked with new titles from the six to eight hundred books published in the capital each year. Paris had twenty-three reading rooms by around this time, rising to 118 in 1893. In British towns from the middle of the century, Working Men's Institutes began offering 'facilities to the working men of the city, and others for social intercourse, for reading the periodical literature of the day, for obtaining such information as is to be derived from books and from lectures of interest and importance'.[19] In 1852, Charles Mudie, founder of Mudie's Lending Library, opened his latest and most impressive library on London's New Oxford Street and boasted that he was buying 180,000 books a year to supply his branches. But legislation brought in at this time made provision for free public libraries and as a result the days of fee-charging libraries were numbered in Britain.

Today, there is once again a great library in the city of Alexandria. The modern Bibliotheca Alexandrina would even have impressed Ptolemy, with shelf space for over eight million volumes. Sadly, lack of funds means that currently it only has 500,000 books. At the current rate of purchases it will take a century to fill the shelves.

Street Food

The people of southern China are very broadminded about what they eat. It's said that in the city of Guangzhou they will eat 'anything with four legs but a chair, anything that flies but a plane'.[20] At the animal markets of Guangzhou, until quite recently you could buy practically any wild animal on the planet (apart from pandas), most of them still alive. Sacks of writhing cobras and other snakes were sold by the kilo and turtles, wild boar, raccoons, badgers, squirrels, deer, ferrets, ponies, bats, monkeys, rats, as well as a wide range of birds and reptiles were also sold, many to be killed and cooked in front of you. But the Chinese government, sensitive to foreign media stories about cruelty to dogs and cats, and fearful of a repeat of the SARS outbreak, when a virus leapt the species divide from civet cats (sold in the markets) to humans, has now closed many of them.

The Chinese are certainly passionate about food. Kai Strittmatter, who for many years was a foreign correspondent in the country, says that 'eating is to the Chinese what sex is to the Europeans – only it is celebrated and practised even more obsessively'.[21] As a result, they have one of the world's finest cuisines. In the thirteenth century, the Venetian traveller Marco Polo marvelled at the number of fine restaurants he saw in Hangzhou, which at the time was the world's most populous city. Some specialised in a specific type of food, such as shellfish, salted fish or dog meat, while others offered cooking from different regions of China, such as spicy Sichuan food. In this city there was always something to tempt even the most jaded of urban palates.

Although restaurants are an important part of city life, street food is a uniquely urban phenomenon. I love Chinese food and I'm particularly keen on their dumplings, or *bao*, of which there are countless varieties. If you've ever eaten dim sum, you'll be familiar with these delicious bite-sized parcels of food. When I stayed in Shanghai you could buy them throughout the city from street stalls or hole-in-the-wall restaurants. *Bao* come in all shapes and sizes, steamed or fried, and with different fillings of meat, seafood or vegetables. In Shanghai the bigger ones sometimes contain a meat broth, which you drink through a straw in the top (these are known as *Tang bao*).

But dumplings are by no means the only kind of street food on offer in Chinese cities. At night markets, such as the ones on Yunnan Lu in Shanghai (east of Renmin Park), Temple Street in Kowloon's Yau Ma Tei (especially good for seafood), or the Donghuamen Yeshi on Wangfujing Dajie, Beijing, you will find scores of stalls offering *xiaochi* (literally, small food). On a brief stroll through one of these markets you can take a culinary tour around the entire country, sampling specialities from all over China, including such delicacies as skewered scorpions or grasshoppers.

Every day, more than 2.5 billion people eat street food around the world. On the global street food menu today there might be a *vadai* (a deep-fried savoury dal or lentil fritter) or *pav bhaji* (curry and bread) in Mumbai, a *falafel* (deep-fried chickpea ball) in Damascus, Cairo or in Tel Aviv, a *döner kebap* (lamb in a flatbread) in Istanbul, *takoyaki* (octopus dumplings) in Tokyo, *nasi lemak* (steamed rice in a banana leaf) in Kuala Lumpur, or *pho* (noodle soup) in Hanoi. Street food's timeless appeal is that it is cheap and convenient: for many low-income workers and students, the first meal of the day is bought from a street stall and eaten while travelling to work or school. The most vibrant street food cultures are found in the vast, sprawling megacities of the developing world. The street food of such cities, which are full of rural migrants, reflects local cultures and is a vital part of urban life.

Setting up a street food stall requires minimal capital outlay and low (or even no) rent. For this reason it provides employment for large numbers of city dwellers. In the 1980s, it was estimated that the Indonesian city of Bogor had one street food business for every fourteen people. Often whole families depend on it for their income. Bangkok has twenty thousand street food vendors who provide the city's inhabitants with 40 per cent of their energy intake, according to the UN's

Food and Agriculture Organization (FAO). In Latin American cities, as much as a third of household budgets is spent on street food. But as stalls are outdoors and have only the most rudimentary facilities with which to prepare and cook food, there are often problems with hygiene, as well as a potential risk of contamination from heavy metals or pesticides. In 1996, when the FAO conducted tests on food from some of the 130,000 street-vending stalls in Kolkata, India, they found the bacteria *E. coli* (often a sign of faecal contamination) in 55 per cent of the samples.[22] For this reason, savvy locals often stick to trusted stalls or buy fried rather than cold food.

Today, traditional street food vendors are facing fierce competition from global fast food chains. Kentucky Fried Chicken opened a store in Beijing in 1987, its first in mainland China. Twenty years later, KFC had proved so popular with Chinese people that it was opening a new store in China nearly every day. In 2008, there were more than 2,300 KFCs and Pizza Huts in the country and a thousand McDonald's. These global fast food chains now dominate high streets across Europe and America, often driving out traditional local food vendors, such as fish and chip shops in Britain, which have been common since about 1900. As with other aspects of modern life, globalisation is creating a more homogenised urban experience as increasingly cities are dominated by 'non-places', to use Marc Augé's term. However, in those districts where there are strong immigrant communities, regional street food businesses can survive. KFC may be popular in China, but in Chinatowns around the world I'm happy to say that you can still find all sorts of tasty *bao* for sale.

City dwellers have been buying snacks and meals on the street for thousands of years. In ancient Rome, there were vendors selling everything from wine by the glass, to hot chickpeas by the plateful for as little as an ass (the smallest Roman denomination). There was such fierce competition between vendors that food in Rome was cheap. In Pompeii, archaeologists have discovered some two hundred bars, taverns and shops where you could buy fast food, quite a number for a town of 12,000 people. A common sight on the streets of Renaissance Florence and other Italian cities were the *treccole* or *trecche*, women selling fresh fruit, vegetables and cooked food from baskets which they carried, somewhat precariously, on their heads. The streets of early modern cities, such as Paris and London, were filled with a motley crew of hawkers, criers and tradesmen. Street food had been a feature of the British urban landscape since at least medieval times. At that time, lower-class households may not have had a kitchen and so buying hot foods from cook shops and street vendors was common.

In British cities, oysters were a popular and inexpensive snack, widely available from stalls on street corners or from oyster taverns. From the sixteenth century, 'they were the food of street life and the food of intimate conversation'.[23] In the nineteenth century, the railways provided a nation-wide distribution network and cheap oysters, known as 'scuttle-mouths', could be bought two for a penny (about twelve pence each in today's money). They became a subsistence food for the working classes in industrial cities across the country. 'It is a very remarkable circumstance, sir, that poverty and oysters always seems to go together,' says Sam Weller in Charles Dickens's *The Pickwick Papers* (1837).

Office workers eating their lunch at a street food stall in Mumbai.

When he visited New York in 1842, Dickens had a great time 'roistering and oystering' in the city, eating oysters from stalls with a friend and gossiping with the vendors.[24] Another British visitor at this time observed that 'there is scarcely a square without several oyster-saloons; they are aboveground and underground, in shanties and palaces. They are served in every imaginable style: escalloped, steamed, stewed, roasted, "on the half shell", eaten raw with pepper and salt, devilled, baked in crumbs, cooked in patés, put in delicious sauces on fish and boiled mutton.'[25]

In the middle of the nineteenth century, it was estimated that nearly five hundred million oysters passed through Billingsgate fish market each year in London. The first metropolis of the industrial age had a street food culture that was unparalleled in its variety. While writing his remarkable study *London Labour and the London Poor* (1852), Henry Mayhew talked to the city's street vendors and observed their business in detail: 'Men and women, and most especially boys, purchase their meals day after day in the streets. The coffee-stall supplies a warm breakfast; shell-fish of many kinds tempt to a luncheon; hot-eels or pea-soup, flanked by a potato "all hot", serve for a dinner; and cakes and tarts, or nuts and oranges, with many varieties of pastry, confectionary, and fruit, woo to indulgence in a dessert; while for supper there is a sandwich, a meat pudding, or a "trotter".'[26]

Mayhew lists some of the food and drink that would have tempted London pedestrians in the nineteenth century: pickled whelks, oysters, sheep's trotters, fried fish, ham sandwiches, kidney puddings and boiled meat puddings. Hot peas (known as 'scaldings of peas') were available in season. They were boiled in the pod and dipped in melted butter, salt and pepper, then drawn through the teeth to extract the peas, just as edamame beans are still eaten in the Far East.[27] According to Mayhew, street pie-sellers were 'the most ancient of the street callings of London'.[28] The street menu included beef, mutton, kidney and eel pies, as well as sweet ones, such as rhubarb, gooseberry, cherry, apple, damson, cranberry, or traditional English 'mince' pies. For those with a sweet tooth there were also cakes and biscuits: you could choose from plum cake, currant, almond and lardy cakes, as well as tarts, gingerbread, Chelsea buns, sweets and ice cream – a new delicacy in Mayhew's day. Drinks available on the city's streets included tea, coffee, cocoa, ginger beer, lemonade, Persian sherbet, hot elder cordial or wine, peppermint water, curds and whey, as well as rice milk. In some of London's parks there were cows and you could buy milk fresh from the udder.

There were about five hundred sellers of muffins and crumpets on London's streets during the winter. They were sold hot, 'swatched in flannel, to retain the heat'.[29] One vendor, a 'sharp lad of fourteen', tells Mayhew: 'My best customers is genteel houses, 'cause I sells a genteel thing. I likes wet days best, 'cause there's werry respectable ladies what don't keep a servant, and they buys to save themselves going out.'[30]

A fried-fish seller (known as 'Fishy') told Mayhew he could make thirty shillings a week, which was 'a good mechanic's earnings'.[31] The trade in ham sandwiches on London's streets was still relatively recent and business was brisk. Mayhew estimated they sold 436,800 sandwiches a year. But it was a hard life. A young ham sandwichman, 'his dress old and worn', told Mayhew: 'I am *so* sick of this life, sir. I *do* dread the winter so. I've stood up to the ankles in snow till after midnight and till I've wished I was snow myself, and could melt like it and have an end. I'd do anything to get away from this, but I can't.'[32]

From fast food to fine dining, today eating out is big business in modern cities. New York has more than twenty thousand restaurants. Businessmen think nothing of paying $400 for a restaurant meal in Manhattan, but you can still buy a Yemeni hummus sandwich on Brooklyn's Atlantic Avenue for about $2. A city's true wealth is its people and the rich cultural diversity they represent. There are more than 170 immigrant groups in New York and such a multicultural city has a very diverse palate. The waves of immigrants who have swept into this city for centuries have all contributed their own specialities to the

Coffee Houses

The coffee house has been part of city life in Western Europe for some 350 years. Coffee originated in Ethiopia, and it was first tasted by Europeans in the late sixteenth century in Constantinople, then the largest city in the world. The English gentleman George Sandys noted in his pocketbook in 1610: 'Although they are destitute of Taverns, yet have they Coffa-houses, which something resemble them. There sit they chatting most of the day; and sippe of a drinke called Coffa (of the berry that it is made of) in little *China* dishes, as hot as they can suffer it: blacke as soote, and tasting not much unlike it.'[34] Constantinople's first coffee house dated from 1554 and along with others quickly became a central part of Turkish Ottoman society, places where men gathered to talk, to listen to music and to play chess.

Christendom's first coffee house opened in London in about 1652. Located in St Michael's Alley, just off Cornhill, near the Royal Exchange, it was little more than a stall, run by Pasqua Rosee, from the city of Smyrna in the Ottoman Empire. It proved such a success with the merchants and traders of the area that other coffee houses soon opened. By the 1670s, Paris had its first café, as did Venice by 1683, and Vienna a couple of years later. At the beginning of the eighteenth century, London had at least five hundred coffee houses. As in Constantinople, coffee houses became important spaces for socialising. Class distinctions were left in the street, as in a coffee house you took the first free seat (there were no reservations). Coffee houses were like today's Facebook or Twitter: they were places to meet people, to chat and to pick up the latest gossip or news, places for networking and debate.

Located as many of them were in the commercial heart of London, coffee houses played metropolitan menu. The first Dutch settlers brought delicious sweet foods, including 'olykoeks' (oil cakes), sweet, deep-fried dough balls – the original doughnuts. They also loved biscuits and their 'koekjes' (little cakes) later became better known as 'cookies'.[33]

From the earliest days, there were street vendors in Manhattan. By the nineteenth century, peddlers (or 'hucksters') were selling such items as buns, clams, fish, gingerbread, oysters, soda, milk, knishes (a Yiddish baked or fried dumpling), sausages, peanuts, popcorn, pretzels, chestnuts, halvah, and *arbis* (hot chickpeas). Ice cream was advertised in New York as early as 1777 and became very popular during the nineteenth century. By the end of the century, New York's streets were full of vendors competing with each other for customers.

In 1873, a German immigrant named Auguste Ermisch included a 'Hamburger Steak' made from minced beef on the menu of his New York restaurant at Nassau and John Streets. This is the first known

an important role as places where financial information was exchanged. Edward Lloyd's coffee house in Lombard Street became the centre of the London shipping world after its owner began collecting and publishing details of ship movements from 1696. His publication became *Lloyd's List*, which is still published to this day, and out of this informal gathering of shipowners and insurers Lloyd's of London insurance market was born.

By 1900, continental cities such as Budapest had several hundred cafés. Cafés were at the heart of the creative culture of cities. In Berlin between the wars, the artist George Grosz, who used to walk the streets with a sign reading 'Dada über Alles', often frequented the neo-Gothic Romanisches Café dressed as an American cowboy, with boots and spurs. In Paris, many cafés are now forever associated with the writers and intellectuals who were regulars – the Closerie des Lilas (Boulevard du Montparnasse) with Ernest Hemingway, Les Deux Magots and Café de Flore (both on the Boulevard Saint-Germain) with Jean-Paul Sartre and Simone de Beauvoir.

Café Dobner, a Viennese coffee house popular with writers and artists, *c*. 1900.

reference to the dish in America. By the 1890s it was being sold in buns by street vendors in cities up and down the land. There were also other convenient American sandwiches, including the po'boy and the hot dog. The Frankfurter was invented in Frankfurt am Main, Germany, in the seventeenth century, but it was Nathan Handwerker who put them in a bun and sold them from his 'Nathan's Hot Dogs' stand on Coney Island in 1916. However, no fast food is more closely associated with America than the hamburger. It's an urban classic – a cheap and nourishing meal you could eat easily while hurrying along the sidewalk. It has spawned a multimillion-dollar global food industry. Today's chains of fast food restaurants date from the 1920s. McDonald's began in the 1940s, and by 1952 they were selling one million burgers and 145 tonnes of fries a year. Even France – the home of *haute cuisine* – has succumbed to the fast food trend. More than a million people a day now eat at McDonald's in France. By 2007, it had a thousand branches and had become the second most profitable market for the US company in the world.

Fast food businesses are now ubiquitous on city streets throughout the developed world: takeaway burger or pizza bars, ice-cream vans, hot-dog stalls, and – in New Orleans – sno-ball stands. In 1986 there were more than 140,000 different kinds of fast food restaurant in the United States alone, with McDonald's taking 17 per cent of the eating-out market. Today's fast food chains may not be dogged by the hygiene issues that plague street food vendors, particularly in the developing world, but fast food – which fits so well with our hectic urban lifestyles – is now partly blamed for twenty-first-century medical conditions such as obesity and heart disease. The result of eating so much high-fat food can be seen both in our clogged arteries and our blocked urban infrastructure. In urban areas where there are large numbers of fast food businesses and restaurants, the sewers regularly become choked with congealed fat. Underneath London's Leicester Square, a team of 'flushers' kitted out with breathing apparatus recently used shovels and high-pressure water hoses to clear an estimated 1,000 tonnes of putrid fat from the nineteenth-century sewer tunnels. One flusher said: 'We couldn't even access the sewer as it was blocked by a four-foot wall of solid fat.'[35]

Gladiators and Marathon Runners

Sport, like play, is universal and is found in every culture. The first evidence for it comes from the early third millennium BC in Egypt and Mesopotamia, where texts reveal that wrestling and boxing were popular. An ancient Assyrian text from Ashur mentions that 'in the Month of Gilgamesh for nine days men contest in wrestling and athletics in their city quarters'.[36] At this time, rulers also took part in ritualistic displays of their strength and prowess in order to demonstrate their right to govern. But it was in the city-states of ancient Greece that sport became an integral part of urban life. 'Greeks saw sport as an essential part of a good education,' says historian Donald Kyle, 'a way to establish social status and individual pre-eminence, an index of manliness, a therapeutic outlet for aggression, a preparation for warfare, and an appropriate way to honour gods and heroes in festivals.'[37]

Today, there is no more important sporting festival than the Olympic Games, hosted by a different city every four years. The tradition began in Greece where, from the eighth century BC to about AD 400, games were held during late summer in Olympia every four years, with the competition lasting three to five days. It became one of the most significant celebrations of Greek identity and culture. From across Greece and its colonies, men travelled to watch the games. (Married women were excluded, perhaps due to the origin of the games in fertility rituals.) In the stadium they came together with some forty thousand fellow Greeks for what must have been a powerful and unifying cultural experience. Events included foot races, wrestling, boxing, the pentathlon (discus and javelin throwing, long jump, running and wrestling), as well as chariot racing. Athletes competed here solely for honour, the winners of each event being awarded not prizes but a wreath at the end of the games.

Although the sporting festival at Olympia was the most important, there were three other Panhellenic events – the Pythian Games at Delphi, the Isthmian Games near Corinth and the Nemean Games at Nemea. By around 500 BC there were also a number of local, civic athletics contests across the region: 'Greek city-states prided themselves as homes of athletes and athletic competitions, and any Greek city-state (polis) worthy of the name had to have a gymnasium as well as a theatre.'[38] Among the local games, the one held in July at Athens was the most prestigious. It was known as the Panathenaia. In Athens, athletics were a vital part of urban life. In the city there were three gymnasia (from 'gymnos', meaning naked, after their practice of exercising without clothing) – the Academy, Lyceum and Kynosarges. Like today's gyms and fitness studios, they were popular with affluent citizens who attended in order to demonstrate their physical superiority as well as to enhance their social status.

We know that athletic games were part of the Panathenaia festival from at least 566 BC (and probably far earlier), for this is the date when prizes were first awarded. Victors could expect to receive beautiful, ornate amphoras filled with sacred olive oil. The winner of the 200-yard *stadion*, or *stade*, race could receive as many as a hundred vases of oil, worth today more than $135,000. The winner of the *tethrippon* chariot race would take home 140 vases. But still the honour of winning a wreath at Olympia was worth far more in terms of glory than even these valuable prizes.

Initially, athletics contests in Athens probably took place in the Archaic Agora, north-east of the Acropolis. But in the late fourth century BC events moved to the new Panathenaic Stadium, whose embankments could hold fifty thousand spectators. The opening three days of the nine-day Panathenaia were reserved for music and drama, but athletics took up the remainder of the festival. There were more than twenty events, divided into three age ranges (for boys, youths and men), with both team and individual competitions. They included gymnastics, equestrian events (such as javelin throwing from horseback), chariot races, running, wrestling and boxing. The whole city (including women) came together to watch these events: 'whether athletes, officials, vase-painters, or spectators, Athenians appreciated the thriving athletic life of their city'.[39]

The Roman people, said the orator Marcus Cornelius Fronto, were obsessed with two things above all else – their food supplies and shows. The rulers of ancient Rome realised that to keep their subjects happy they needed to ensure that people were neither hungry nor bored. Ordinary Romans certainly had plenty of leisure time. According to historian Jérôme Carcopino, they had one day of holidays for every working day. Furthermore, there were 150,000 people who were supported by public assistance and a similar number who had finished work by midday. With a sure but cynical grasp of mass psychology, Rome's rulers understood instinctively that to maintain control of the world's most populous city it was vital to keep their subjects entertained. And so mass entertainment – from thrilling chariot races to bloody gladiatorial combats – was invented in Rome.

Rome's Circus Maximus was the place to go to see dramatic chariot racing, with teams of up to ten horses. Created from a natural valley between the Palatine and Aventine Hills, it was Rome's oldest public space, dating back to the sixth century BC. Among the many events held here were the Roman Games (*Ludi Romani*), a fifteen-day festival in September. It was often filled to overflowing. Caesar carved tiers out of the hillside to provide seating for 150,000 spectators in 46 BC, but by the first century AD it could accommodate an astounding 250,000 people. Being part of such a vast crowd must have been an exhilarating experience. Under Emperor Augustus (27 BC–AD 14), there were twelve races a day on the 540-metre track. Under Caligula (AD 37–41), this rose to twenty-four a day. There was also horse racing here and champion jockeys became celebrities in the city. Juvenal complained that 'all Rome today is in the Circus. Such sights are for the young, whom it befits to shout and make bold wagers with a beautiful girl by their side.'[40]

There is no doubt, however, that the most famous arena in Rome was the Flavian amphitheatre, better known since the Middle Ages as the Colosseum. Completed in AD 80, this imposing structure – the largest amphitheatre in the Roman world – is oval in shape. It measures some 545 metres around its elegantly arcaded outer walls, which rise like a sheer cliff face nearly fifty metres above the street.

The Colosseum could hold 45,000 seated spectators as well as 5,000 standing. Walking round it today among the throngs of modern tourists, it is easy to imagine this immense space echoing to the roars of the Roman crowd nearly two millennia ago. Special boxes on the lower levels were reserved for the emperor and the Vestal Virgins. Above them sat the senators, then the knights, followed by the plebeians above them, with the poorest spectators, as well as women and slaves, standing in the upper galleries, nearly fifty metres above the arena. The arena was eighty-three metres long by forty-eight metres wide and the largest in the Roman world. But few buildings of such inspiring design can have served a more gruesome and inhumane purpose. For this was a theatre of death.

The arena was originally wooden and covered with sand. Around its perimeter ran a metal grating. The purpose of this was to protect the audience from being attacked by wild animals. These were kept below the arena in underground chambers, ready to be hoisted up and then released through trapdoors. Some events staged in the Colosseum would not seem out of place in a modern circus: panthers drawing chariots, or elephants kneeling before the imperial box. But most were violent spectacles: duels between animals – a bear pitted against a buffalo, or an elephant fighting with a rhinoceros. There were hunts in which men with lances and spears pursued and slaughtered animals as the crowd bayed and cheered. Sometimes the hunters would toy with the animals, just as Spanish matadors flaunt a red cape in front of a bull before running it through the neck with a sword. But the scale of the slaughter that took place here is truly chilling. As many as five thousand animals were killed in a single day in AD 80. In fact, the Colosseum consumed so many wild animals that entire species were eradicated from nearby regions, including lions from Mesopotamia and elephants from North Africa.

But as well as animals, humans, too, provided spectacles of bravery, savage violence and death. Gladiatorial shows were also staged in the Colosseum. They were known as *munera* ('dutiful gifts'), murderous displays in which armed men fought to the death. The combat was brutal and relentless. The audience was utterly gripped by the scenes of violence that took place before their eyes in the arena and there was feverish betting and speculation on who would win each fight. Again, the scale of the carnage is shocking. In AD 107, the Emperor Trajan celebrated a military victory with a 123-day show involving 11,000 animals and 10,000 gladiators – a true festival of death for the amusement of Rome. For all its impressive architecture, the Colosseum was indeed 'a torture-chamber and a human-slaughter house'.[41]

The night before the *munus* took place, the gladiators were treated to a lavish meal which they ate together. Some gorged themselves, while others ate sparingly, mindful of the next day's combat. This strange rite was a last supper for the condemned. In the morning there was a parade during which the gladiators solemnly greeted the ruler who had ordained their brutal fate: 'Hail, Emperor, those who are about to die salute thee!' (*Ave, Imperator, morituri te salutant!*)

Who were these fighters prepared to forfeit their lives to entertain the emperor and the citizens of Rome? They were prisoners of war, criminals, slaves, as well as professional fighters – volunteers working on fixed (and usually very short-term) contracts. Some were women. Each gladiator specialised in a different technique of fighting. The *retiarius*, for example, was armed with a trident and a net, whereas the Thracian had a scimitar and a round shield.

With its chariot races, bloody combats and even dramas (there was room for fifty thousand in Rome's three main theatres), the Eternal City offered sports and entertainment on a scale not matched until the heyday of the great Hollywood studios. Sport and spectacle, it seems, were the true opium of the masses in Rome.

The Colosseum, Rome, completed AD 80.

Ancient Romans were, of course, not unique in enjoying barbaric sports. Animals were also tortured for entertainment in medieval cities such as London. 'Throwing at Cocks', or throwing objects at tethered birds, was popular in Chaucer's day. The baiting of animals with dogs, such as mastiffs, was also widespread. There were bear pits in many cities and in 1539 Henry VIII watched bear-baiting at Paris Garden, on the Southwark bank of the River Thames, London. In the age of Shakespeare, baiting animals was highly profitable and theatres were often used as venues. The Elizabethan impresario Philip Henslowe, who owned the Paris Garden from the beginning of the seventeenth century, made twice as much from animal shows as from plays. At Christmas 1608, the takings for three days at his Fortune Theatre (just north of the City) were £5. 14s. 9d. During the same three days, he made £13. 13s. 0d. from the Bankside bear pit, near Shakespeare's Globe theatre.

When baiting was eventually banned in 1835, ratting became popular in London and other cities. Events often took place in the back room of an inn. An enclosure was built in which terriers were set on rats to see how many they could kill in a set period of time. It was hugely popular and betting was as fast and furious as the action. According to Richard Tames, 'one prize ratter, stuffed and exhibited in the Seven Bells pub in St Giles, was claimed to have killed a hundred rats in five minutes'.[42] In an overcrowded and unsanitary city such as London, there was certainly no shortage of rats.

Today, there are still plenty of urban rats but fortunately in our more enlightened age such cruel sports have all but disappeared. Instead, organised and team sports, such as football, fulfil people's need for both exercise and sporting spectacle. Indeed, football has now become far more than a mere sport; it's a tribal affinity. For many city dwellers, which football team someone supports defines their urban identity. Football began as a village sport, in which the streets served as the pitch. Matches between villages could be violent affairs, providing the opportunity to settle old rivalries and scores. In cities, too, football was played in the lanes and squares, often resulting in rowdy scenes, as a visitor to London in the 1720s witnessed. It was, he said, 'very inconvenient to passers-by – you sometimes see a score of rascals in the streets kicking at a ball and they will break panes of glass and smash the windows of coaches and also knock you down without the slightest compunction; on the contrary they will roar with laughter'.[43]

Affluent property owners and the new urban middle classes – ever fearful of the mob and disorder among the working classes of the new industrial cities – began to prevent such events during the nineteenth century. Instead, national sporting bodies were set up and the working classes were encouraged to take part in organised competitive

Surfing the Streets

Like parkour (see page 277), skateboarding challenges conventional ideas about how cities and urban spaces should be used. In cities around the world, from the Annenberg Center for Performing Arts, in Philadelphia, to the concrete walkways of London's Southbank Centre or Prague's National Theatre, skaters have invented new uses for parts of their urban environment. Iain Borden, a skateboarder as well as an architectural historian, argues that, like graffiti, this is a subversive act. For Borden, skateboarding is a physical expression of the evocative Situationist slogan of 1968: *au dessous les paves, la plage*: 'beneath the pavement lies the beach'. Skaters turn the utilitarian structures of the city into 'a cement playground', showing that it is not just a place for work and consumption, but for play.[44] According to one skater: 'the corporate types see their structures as powerful and strong. I see them as something I can enjoy, something I can manipulate to my advantage.[45]

Skateboarding emerged first in the suburbs of Californian beach cities in the late 1950s. By the mid-1980s, skaters were surfing the city streets of Venice Beach, Los Angeles, San sports. The Football Association was established during a meeting at the Freemasons' Tavern, Great Queen Street, Lincoln's Inn Fields, London, in 1863 and the Football League kicked off in 1888. New sports, such as hockey and golf, also gained popularity among the working classes in Britain and abroad. By the 1880s, there were athletics clubs in Paris as well as football clubs by the following decade. At the same time, St Petersburg in Russia could boast clubs for rowing, hockey, tennis and skating.

By the twentieth century, competitive sport was a popular pastime for city dwellers of all social classes and, increasingly, young people and women. In 1904–05, Battersea Park in south London attracted 70,000 people to play tennis, 22,000 for cricket and 16,000 to kick a football around. Reduced working hours meant that people had more time to enjoy sport. By 1960, more than one in ten London men were playing cricket, football and other sport in the city's parks. In the following decade, nearly half the residents of Helsinki took part in outdoor sports and jogging began appearing in European cities, a practice imported from North America. By the 1990s, event running – such as marathons – was a new urban sporting craze. According to the legend, Phidippides ran from Marathon to Athens bringing news of the Greek victory over the Persians in 490 BC. On reaching Athens, he was

Francisco and Santa Barbara. Today, there are skateboarders in cities on every continent, 'taking over public squares and plazas, scratching benches and planters, gouging out the tops of stone and brick walls, leaving traces of paint on handrails and steps, creating noise and visual surprise and speeding past pedestrians'.[46] To the consternation of the municipal authorities, skaters see railings, steps, fire hydrants, bus benches, kerbs, handrails, bollards, fences and embankments as challenges and opportunities to test their gravity-defying skills. The mundane street and its furniture becomes a new and exciting terrain beneath their decks:

'These are my streets. I know every crack of every sidewalk there is down here.'[47]

Skateboarders, Chicago, 1965.

just able to gasp 'Be joyful, we win!' before dying from exhaustion. Marathon running was included in the first modern Olympiad, held at Athens in 1896, with competitors retracing Phidippides' historic route to Athens. At the 1908 London Olympics, the marathon became twenty-six (rather than twenty-five) miles, when it was decided the race should begin at Windsor Castle, in Berkshire, partly so that the young princes could see the race start from their nursery window.

Today, marathons are one of the most high-profile urban sporting events. The London Marathon was first run on 29 March 1981 and televised by the BBC. There were 20,000 entries, of which 7,747 were accepted and 6,255 completed. By 2009, 746,635 runners had completed the London Marathon, and a record 35,694 people finished in 2007. It is the world's largest single annual fund-raising event, generating a world-record breaking £46.7 million in 2008 and more than £500 million since it began. Not everyone is a fan, however. Jean Baudrillard has described the New York Marathon – the inspiration for London's race – as 'the end-of-the-world show', a post-modern symbol 'of the mania for an empty victory'. Like taggers and spray-can artists, marathon runners are saying: 'I'm so-and-so and I exist!'[48]

Stadiums, like cultural institutions, have been used in recent years to revitalise post-industrial areas. Since 1990, city and state authorities in the United States have spent over $10 billion subsidising stadiums. As in ancient Greece, where local athletics festivals were expressions of civic pride, today the building of sports arenas, such as the 2008 stadium for the Washington Nationals baseball team, is a way of boosting a city's image and prestige. Today, sport is big business and cities compete on an international stage to host multimillion-dollar events such as the Olympics. Just as Greek athletes brought honour and glory to their cities by triumphing at Olympia, so cities become famous around the world thanks to the achievements of their sports teams, such as the Boston Red Sox or Liverpool FC. Similarly, the fields of glory in which historic sporting moments have taken place become hallowed ground. London, for example, is the home of Wimbledon, Lord's, Wembley and Twickenham – sacred names for fans of tennis, cricket, football and rugby respectively.

But for many ordinary city dwellers around the world, the streets remain their only pitch or playing field. Today street basketball (aka the 'city game') is not only played in cities across America, but is also hugely popular with young people in Chinese cities – a sign of the globalisation of sport. Some four hundred million Chinese now play or watch basketball, more than the entire population of the United States, and there are public courts in cities throughout China. But the street games of the future may well be played using GPS-enabled mobile phones. In 2009, 'Great Street Games' was trialled in British cities. In this 'huge, participatory, high-tech athletics tournament' (to quote the game's designers, KMA), participants in Gateshead, Sunderland and Middlesbrough competed against each other in inter-active 'courts' on to which lights were projected. Thermal-imaging technology was used to track players as they moved around the court during the ten-minute games and leagues were created showing the performance of each city with results posted on a website and on Twitter. As Augmented Reality apps become increasingly common for mobile phones, real-time MMORPGs – massively multiplayer online role-playing games – that mash up the virtual world with actual urban geography will be the city sports craze of the coming years.[49]

In the real rather than the virtual world, the most extreme and spectacular urban sport is one which does not just use the street but the walls and roofs of the buildings. Parkour, or 'l'art du déplacement' as it was first called, began in the southern Paris suburb of Lisses, in 1988. The first 'traceur' was David Belle, the son of a fireman who had developed a rigorous series of training exercises to help colleagues deal with dangerous situations.[50] A mix of athletics, gymnastics and martial arts, parkour is about discovering new and creative ways of moving rapidly around the urban environment. Belle has appeared leaping effortlessly across rooftops in *Rush Hour* (BBC, 2002) and these techniques were used in the opening sequence of the James Bond movie *Casino Royale* (2006). According to Belle: 'Parkour turns the city into nature for me by transforming a building into a mountain and a wall into a tree.'[51]

Central Park, New York City. (following page)   277

The Park

When I'm staying in an unfamiliar city, one of the first things I do is to scan the map looking for areas of green. I love city parks and it's always a special moment when you step out of a busy city street and into a public garden, with a canopy of leaves above you and people all around relaxing or eating their lunch.

One of my favourite green spaces in London is Russell Square Garden. It was designed some two hundred years ago by Humphry Repton for the then landowner, Sir Francis Russell, fifth Duke of Bedford. The garden has recently been restored to its original design. The shrubbery and flower beds now reflect Regency period horticultural principles and the tunnel of lime trees that once covered the original horseshoe-shaped path that runs around the garden is being replanted. When it is complete it will form a wonderful walkway with a roof of golden leaves in autumn. One concession has been made to modernity. In the centre of the garden, Repton's 'reposoir', a trellis-lined shed which once contained the gardeners' tools, has been replaced with a tumbling fountain, now much loved by children as well as the city's pigeons.

Today, Russell Square Garden is surrounded by busy roads, but it remains an island of tranquillity amidst the clamour of the modern city. It lies in the heart of Bloomsbury, one of the most beautiful parts of London. Architectural historian Sigfried Giedion has described this area of Georgian brick terraces and garden squares as an architectural composition the equal of St Peter's Square in Rome or the Place de la Concorde in Paris. It is, he wrote, 'a district that for its human treatment remains unsurpassed to this day'.[52]

Russell Square is just a few minutes walk from University College London where I used to teach. Now I pass through here regularly on my way to the area's research libraries and I'm always tempted to take a short detour through the garden. Overlooking the square is the University of London Library, housed in what in the 1930s was the city's tallest skyscraper, Senate House. Bloomsbury has always been popular with leading cultural and scientific figures. It was, of course, the centre of the Bloomsbury Group, and Virginia Woolf, Vanessa Bell and Lytton Strachey all lived nearby. In the nineteenth century, Charles Darwin lived in Gower Street and Charles Dickens in

Tavistock Square, both a short walk from Russell Square, albeit in different directions. In the 1920s, T. S. Eliot worked at 24 Russell Square in what were then the offices of the publisher Faber & Faber. The scientist Leó Szilárd lived in a hotel overlooking the square's garden after fleeing Nazi Germany in the 1930s. It was while walking down one of the streets alongside the square that Szilard had the eureka moment that led to the invention of the atomic bomb. Whenever I sit in Russell Square Garden watching the grey squirrels, I often think of the many creative people in the last two centuries who have wandered beneath its trees, their thoughts lost in poetry or equations, before once again heading off into the busy city streets.

Although Russell Square is one of London's largest squares, the garden is small in comparison to most city parks. You can walk across it in a couple of minutes. In winter, when the trees have lost their leaves, you can see the traffic rushing past on the surrounding streets. Even in summer, the sound of cars and buses is always there in the background, like urban white noise. But I like that: despite the forest trees and green lawns, you can never quite forget that you are in the heart of one of the world's most vibrant and historic cities, one of the great creations of human civilisation. It is this meeting of the natural and the man-made that makes city parks so special.

Even in the earliest cities, greenery was used to soften the rectilinear forms of major structures. The ziggurat at Ur had trees on its upper terraces and King Nebuchadnezzar's palace was greened by the famous Hanging Gardens of Babylon. Beijing has been an urban centre for far longer than London – some four thousand years. Chinese imperial cities were designed according to strict cosmological principles. From the first millennium BC, royal parks in Chinese cities were located to the north of the palace. The summer palace of Yuanmingyuan in the north-west of the city was begun in 1709 by Kangxi and expanded by subsequent emperors. It formed the largest royal garden in the world, with two hundred pavilions and temples set in an artificial landscape of lakes and gentle hills. Some of the formal gardens were designed by Jesuit monks living at the Chinese court and the buildings were a unique fusion of Rococo and Chinese architectural styles. Sadly, in an act of retribution and cultural barbarism, it was destroyed by the British in 1860, on the orders of the High Commissioner of China, Lord Elgin (it was his father who removed the Elgin Marbles from Athens). Today, one of the most beautiful places in Beijing – which can be an austere city – is Yiheyuan, the new Summer Palace, which is now a public park with a large lake fringed by rolling hills. Built by Emperor Qianlong in the eighteenth century, its most breathtaking sight is the elegant Seventeen-Arch Bridge.

One of the Jesuit monks at the Chinese imperial court, Jean-Denis Attiret, described Yuanmingyuan in a letter of 1743. 'There reigns almost everywhere a graceful disorder, an anti-symmetry,' he wrote. 'It is a natural, rustic countryside they wish represented.' Another letter from a Jesuit describes the Daoist inspiration of Chinese gardening: 'Everything that is ruled and symmetrical is alien to free Nature. There one never finds trees growing in lines to form avenues, flowers brought together in beds, water enclosed in ponds or in regular canals.'53 The symbolic geometry of Chinese cities contrasted with the freedom and organic forms of their gardens, epitomised by the exquisite private gardens of Suzhou, near Shanghai, some of which are eight hundred years old. The Chinese approach to gardens found an appreciative audience back in Europe.

During the eighteenth century, there was a heated debate in Europe between the proponents of the Baroque French style of gardening and the Romantic English approach. French formal gardens, typified by Le Nôtre's designs at Versailles in the seventeenth century, were dominated by geometrical patterns, which extended the architectural lines of the palace out into the landscape. By contrast, the more natural English style of landscape gardening, pioneered by William Kent (1684–1748), was inspired by idealised paintings of Italian landscape, such as those by Claude Lorrain. As in Chinese gardens, there were no straight lines, just gently winding paths and curving contours. In Germany, Munich's Englischer Garten (opened in 1791) is, as the name suggests, an early and very fine example of a public park designed in the Romantic, English style. Today, it's a wonderful place for a quiet walk or for sunbathing; there is even a nudist section.

In their time, the layouts of formal gardens at palaces such as Versailles, with their long, straight avenues, were highly influential on the design of cities, inspiring Christopher Wren in his plan for rebuilding the City of London after the Great Fire of 1666, as well as L'Enfant's design for Washington, DC. 'Whoever knows how to lay out a park will have no trouble in drawing up the plan according to which a town is to be built,' said the eighteenth-century architectural theorist

Abbé Laugier. 'It will need regularity and fantasy, associations and oppositions, random incidents to introduce variety, great regularity in the detail, and confusion, clash and ferment in the whole.'[54] Laugier scorned the medieval layout of Paris, describing it as 'an immense forest', an untamed primeval landscape that the city authorities should be able 'to cut and prune at will'. Referring to Versailles, he said 'let the design of our parks serve as the plan for our towns'.[55] Ironically, when large swathes of medieval Paris were swept away in the following century to make way for a new city of long, straight boulevards and parks, it was not formal gardens but picturesque, English ones that were built. Jean-Charles Adolphe Alphand (1817–91) designed them, creating some of the most famous Parisian parks, including the Bois de Boulogne, the Parc des Buttes Chaumont, Parc Monceau, the Bois de Vincennes and the Parc Montsouris.

Many European cities have fine parks that were once the preserve solely of royalty and the aristocracy. They include the Retiro Park in Madrid, Phoenix Park in Dublin, Warsaw's Lazienki Park, the Tiergarten in Berlin, Vienna's Prater and Gorky Park in Moscow. Most were open to the public by the late eighteenth century. By then, promenading in parks had become a fashionable activity for the upper classes. Promenades were known as Malls, Walks or Parades and were generally fenced and lined with trees. In Paris there were promenades in the gardens of the Palais Royal, the Cours la Reine and the Tuileries. The place to be seen promenading in 1720s London was the Mall in St James's Park: 'Society comes to walk here on fine, warm days, from seven to ten in the evening, and in winter from one to three o'clock. Some people come to see, some to be seen . . .'[56] Soon every European city had its own Mall. In Dublin there was Beaux' Walk on St Stephen's Green and Gardiner's Mall on today's O'Connell Street. In Berlin, Unter den Linden had a promenading enclosure running down the middle. In St Petersburg, Nevsky Prospect was the place to be seen promenading in the late afternoon sunshine. Residents of Mexico City did the same in the sixteenth-century Alameda Central park. By the middle of the eighteenth century, Bordeaux even had a promenade that was not just restricted to the upper classes, but was open to all.

Pleasure gardens were a London invention. The first was Vauxhall Gardens – or the New Spring Gardens, as they were originally known – which opened in 1661. For the price of a small admission fee, people

could stroll along gravel walks laid out in a grid, between fruit trees. On his first visit, Samuel Pepys was rowed across the river by watermen. He was impressed by the 'abundance of roses' and feasted on 'cakes and powdered beef and ale', before being carried home by boat. Vauxhall was a place to meet old acquaintances and new friends: 'the people who came were a mixture of fine ladies, clergymen, apprentices, prostitutes, dukes, officers of the guards, city merchants, pick-pockets and adventurers'.[57] In the eighteenth century, under the management of Jonathan Tyers, a bandstand (the Orchestra) was built, as well as private supper boxes in which people could listen to the music in the open air. At dusk the grounds were illuminated with some 20,000 oil lamps (by 1822) and there was music and singing until midnight, often accompanied by displays of fireworks, creating a magical experience. Each summer season, some 100,000 people would visit, often arriving at the gardens by way of the Thames. An encounter at Vauxhall Gardens inspired the Romantic London poet John Keats to write his sonnet 'To a Lady seen for a few Moments at Vauxhall', with its wistful lines: 'And yet I never look on midnight sky, / But I behold thine eyes' well memory'd light'. Another, less romantically inclined, visitor noted that he would have preferred the gardens if there had been 'more nightingales and fewer strumpets'.[58] But the Vauxhall pleasure garden proved immensely popular with Londoners and by the middle of the eighteenth century there were several others, including

Ranelagh and Cremorne Gardens. French cities also copied the idea, opening a number of what they called 'Wauxhalls'. Cafés and restaurants began opening in public gardens, too. Other famous pleasure gardens included the Augarten in Vienna, New York's Elysian Fields, Castle Gardens and Harlem Gardens, as well as Copenhagen's Tivoli Gardens (opened 1843).

Britain also pioneered publicly funded urban parks. It was the first country in which more than half the population lived in cities. The effects of rapid industrialisation and urbanisation created appalling overcrowding. By the beginning of the nineteenth century, parks were seen as a way of improving the conditions of urban life for ordinary people, providing places for recreation and exercise. 'The parks are the lungs of London,' said William Windham in the House of Commons, on 30 June 1808.[59] In 1883, the Select Committee on Public Walks also described urban green spaces as the 'lungs of the city', a sound bite that was to be repeated often in subsequent debates about urban planning around the world.[60] Indeed, in the current era of climate change, the phrase has gained a new relevance.

The British landscape architect J. C. Loudon (1783–1843) was one of the first to call for public parks at public expense. He laid out the Derby Arboretum for public use and it has been claimed that this was 'the first truly public park'.[61] It was given to the city in 1839 by a benefactor and subsequently maintained by the local council. Victoria Park, London, opened in 1845 on land bought by the Crown Estate. But Birkenhead Park near Liverpool was the first publicly funded park, opening in 1847. It was designed by Joseph Paxton, the architect some four years later of the Crystal Palace that housed the Great Exhibition. In 1853, he also created Kelvingrove Park in Glasgow. Other early public parks included Philips Park, Manchester (1846), and Stanley Park, Liverpool (1870). Often containing sports fields, water features and flower beds, they were conceived as 'ideal landscapes that would benefit urban society'.[62] But ordinary people were not much interested in ideal landscapes or in using them to improve themselves in the way the middle classes intended. Young people, women and workers used the new green spaces for everything from drinking and casual sex, to cleaning carpets and hanging out laundry.

One early visitor to Birkenhead Park was Frederick Law Olmsted, destined to become America's foremost landscape architect. In a book describing his travels in England, Olmsted wrote: 'five minutes of

The Hanging Gardens of Babylon

The Hanging Gardens of Babylon were one of the Seven Wonders of the World. Tradition has it that they were built by a king – probably Nebuchadnezzar – for one of his wives who longed to see the wooded mountain scenery of her homeland. Constructed on the stone terraces of the royal palace, they were described by the Greek historian Strabo as being 'quadrangular in shape' and built using arched vaults on 'checkered, cube-like foundations': 'The checkered foundations, which are hollowed out, are covered so deep with earth that they admit of the largest trees, having been constructed of baked brick and asphalt – the foundations themselves and the vaults and the arches. The ascent to the uppermost terrace-roofs is made by a stairway; and alongside these stairs there were screws, through which the water was continually conducted up into the garden from the Euphrates.'[63]

Descriptions of the methods used in its construction vary. Some say the terraces were built using palm beams, others refer to baked brick, bitumen and lead. But ancient accounts agree

admiration, and a few more spent studying the manner in which art had been employed to obtain from nature so much beauty, and I was ready to admit that in democratic America there was nothing to be thought of as comparable with this People's Garden. Indeed, gardening, had here reached a perfection that I had never before dreamed of.' He was particularly impressed by the fact that 'the privileges of the garden were enjoyed about equally by all classes'.[66] This People's Garden was, he decided, ideally suited to America.

At the time, New York was a city of violent race tensions and prone to riots and epidemics. In 1835, a great fire had destroyed much of the city. In 1848, America's first major landscape architect, Andrew Jackson Downing, suggested the rapidly expanding city needed a vast 'lung' to improve living conditions for its inhabitants.[66] The result was Central Park. It was designed by Olmsted, together with Calvert Vaux, and constructed between 1857 and 1873. Olmsted was no fan of New York's gridiron layout. For him the city's rigid plan symbolised its obsession with money and commerce. His park would bring nature into the city and give it back its soul, he believed, creating a verdant foil to what became the first vertical city of the modern age.

Central Park was built in Upper Manhattan, on what was a swampy area studded with outcrops of Manhattan schist rock left by glaciation. The land was not uninhabited. Seneca Village, New York's first community of African American property holders, had to be cleared that the depth of soil in this extraordinary roof garden was sufficient to allow large trees to be grown. According to a Roman historian, they formed a 'huge forest' consisting of many fruit trees, planted among green lawns and flowers of all kinds. The gardens contained 'everything that is most agreeable to the eye and conducive to the enjoyment of pleasure'.[64] The sight of this forest in the sky, growing on the roof of the royal palace, must have astonished visitors arriving in the city more than two and a half thousand years ago. Sadly, no trace remains today of this remarkable urban garden.

The Hanging Gardens of Babylon.

from the site before the park could be built. It took twenty thousand workers sixteen years to create the ponds, lakes, streams, some thirty bridges and fifty-eight miles of footpaths, as well as planting millions of trees and flowers. Olmsted planted the high trees around the park to 'completely shut out the city'.[67] But by the 1880s, buildings such as the eight-storey Dakota on the west side of the park soared above the trees and it is now ringed by a dramatic wall of architecture.[68] It was hugely popular with New Yorkers from the very beginning. Some forty thousand ice skaters took to Central Park's lake one winter's day in 1858. Today the park is visited by twenty-eight million people a year. It is also popular with birdwatchers. Some 275 bird species have been identified in this park at the heart of one of the world's great metropolises.

Olmsted described Central Park as 'a democratic development of the highest significance'.[69] In reality the park was mostly used by those who could afford a private carriage: 'Manhattanites were free to walk to Central Park but it was quite a hike for most – the park was, we should remember, fairly uptown in this era, and there was no subway until the first decades of the twentieth century.'[70] Most poor New Yorkers didn't go to Central Park, but to pleasure gardens where, although entry was not free, there was a plentiful supply of beer and dancing. In fact, much of Central Park was not even designed to be experienced on foot, with many of the drives being reserved exclusively for private carriages: 'The entire park appears to have been constructed with the end of providing a view from the carriage drives.'[71] But this feature proved popular with wealthy Americans and, by 1890, all the largest cities offered at least twenty miles of park drives.

Other North American cities soon followed New York's lead and built their own urban parks, many designed by Olmsted, including the Boston parks known as the Emerald Necklace and parks in Chicago and Detroit, as well as Mount Royal Park in Montreal. America's urban parks are far larger than those in Europe, mostly because it was easier to acquire land in such new cities. Chicago's eight parks cover some 1,800 acres. Philadelphia's Fairmount Park is the largest in the United States at about 3,800 acres. With their lakes, sports fields, bandstands, canals, conservatories, zoos, footpaths and carriage roads, many were large enough for a full day's excursion: 'this was a conscious effort to provide a civilizing public setting for an urban population with a growing amount of leisure time.'[72]

Today, as well as providing somewhere to spend your lunch break, practise T'ai Chi, play football or throw a Frisbee, there is a growing realisation that urban green spaces can help mitigate the environmental impact of cities. For example, every 5 per cent of tree cover added to urban areas reduces water run-off by 2 per cent. In hot summers, treeless streets are 5.5°C (10°F) warmer than tree-lined ones. For these as well as for aesthetic reasons, cities around the world are planting more trees and rediscovering the value of their green spaces.

The creation of new parks is also seen as an opportunity to revitalise run-down or neglected areas. New York City's High Line is a widely acclaimed linear park built on an elevated railway line that dates from the 1930s and had not been used since 1980. Opened as a park in 2009, it runs thirty feet above street level for about a mile through Manhattan's West Side, from midtown to Greenwich Village. Part of the beguiling beauty of urban gardens, such as Russell Square, is the illusion that you are entering a rural idyll. You know you are in the city centre and yet by a willing suspension of disbelief you convince yourself that you are in the countryside. The High Line cleverly exploits this sense of being simultaneously in the city and in nature. Although visitors appear to be walking on a country path, surrounded by wild flowers and grasses, they are in fact three storeys

above the busy urban traffic. Their route takes them through canyons of tall buildings, before eventually arriving in the heart of the city. The High Line has been so successful that new buildings have been commissioned beside it and other cities, such as Rotterdam, are considering similar schemes.

Recent scientific evidence also suggests that parks are good for people's health. Research based on the health records of people in the Netherlands found that those living near parks had lower rates of more than a dozen diseases, including cardiovascular, respiratory, neurological, digestive and mental disorders.[73] Scientists at the University of Illinois have also found that urban parks relieve mental fatigue and reduce feelings of irritability and aggression. They claim that the experience of sitting in a park helps restore people's 'directed attention capacity' (a measure of a person's ability to concentrate on a task).[74] So if one afternoon you find that you're unable to work and your thoughts keep straying, don't just buy another coffee. Slip out of the office and walk round your local park. Afterwards, I promise you'll feel like a new person.

8 BEYOND THE CITY

The Wired City

During the 1870s, time was pumped beneath the streets of Paris. Spread out under the city was a network of pipes filled with compressed air from industrial steam plants. The pipes emerged into homes and commercial premises, where they were connected to clocks. From a control room in the rue du Télégraphe, a pressure pulse periodically rippled through the system of pipes beneath the streets, pneumatically synchronising the clocks of the French capital to the standard time of the Paris Observatory.

Paris's pneumatic system was a particularly ingenious way of keeping its citizens on time. But there are many such technological networks hidden just beneath the skin of cities everywhere. They are part of the complex tracery of subterranean veins and arteries that sustain life in the urban body. Our modern cities and exurbs could not exist without their urban infrastructure, from subways and sewers to fibre-optic cables. Yet most city dwellers spend their lives in blissful ignorance of the complex networks that lie beneath their feet. Each day, millions of gallons of water gush unheard and unseen into the city, while drains and sewers channel a similar quantity of waste away. Power grids are electrified by gigawatts of energy and cables seethe with petabytes of digitised information – videos, telephone messages, music, e-books, photographs – carried beneath the city in a ceaseless torrent of data. As well as the engineered infrastructure that honeycombs the urban underworld, city dwellers are also surrounded by less tangible but equally vital systems, such as those controlling the traffic or maintaining security. Whether you are stepping on to a bus

Yan'an elevated road interchange (1996), Shanghai, China.

or dropping a piece of litter in the street, you are interacting with city-wide services that are not only essential to the running of the city, but which shape the lives of those who live there.

Like so many aspects of urban life, infrastructure is not new. In the third millennium BC, the city of Mohenjo-daro, north-east of modern Karachi, provided its inhabitants with fresh water through a sophisticated system of clay pipes. There was also a network of covered drains. In ancient Rome, eight aqueducts brought more than 220 million gallons of water into the city each day, supplying public baths and nearly six hundred fountains, as well as topping up the fish tanks in Trajan's Market. Rome's sewer system was without compare in the urban world. It was constructed over a long period of time, beginning in the sixth century BC and improved continually until it was completed around 33 BC. Some of the *cloacae* (sewers) were so large that a cart full of hay could pass through them. The oldest and largest is the vaulted *Cloaca Maxima*, the central sewer, whose five-metre arch is still visible today, opening on to the River Tiber below the Ponte Rotto.

Until relatively recently, many cities were unhealthy places. Dense centres of population, in which people lived in often unsanitary conditions, provided ideal conditions for diseases to spread. In an outbreak of bubonic plague in 1654 up to 80 per cent of Moscow's population died. After the seventeenth century, smallpox became one of the main urban killers, along with measles, typhoid and water-borne diseases, such as dysentery. Babies and children were particularly vulnerable. The infant mortality rate in London exceeded 350 per 1,000 births in the early eighteenth century. (In 2008, the infant mortality rate in the United Kingdom was 8 per 1,000 births. The rate for the same year in Angola, one of the world's poorest countries, was 130.) In fact, burials exceeded births in most large cities. And yet people continued to stream into the cities from the countryside. Indeed, immigration has always been essential to the economic growth of cities (although new arrivals did not have immunity to urban diseases and so were more likely to fall victim to epidemics). Along with improved medical services and treatments such as vaccination, creating adequate infrastructure to provide clean water and to dispose of waste and sewage was an essential stage in the development of healthy cities.

By the 1850s, London's population had risen to two and a half million, in a city thirty miles in circumference. Even a modern planned city would struggle to cope with a situation in which its population more than doubled in fifty years. And yet this was a city whose infrastructure had changed little in centuries. London's ancient sewers had been built to deal with rainwater and until 1815 it was in fact illegal to use them for human waste. Instead, this was deposited in the city's 200,000 cesspools. Houses were often built over cesspools. It was not unheard of for people to fall through rotten floorboards and drown in the sewage below. Cesspools were supposed to be emptied regularly by 'night-soil men', but many were left to overflow because Londoners could not afford the shilling they charged to dig one out by hand.

As the city grew ever larger, London was drowning in its own effluent. Not even Buckingham Palace was immune to the problem. Its drains were so bad that its elegant rooms stank of human excrement. One effect of such conditions was that rats, our unwelcome urban companions since the earliest settlements, infested the Victorian city. The Queen was even forced to employ her own royal rat catcher, Jack Black.

After 1830, the increasing popularity of the water closet – a British invention – only made the problem worse in London. The city's sewers drained straight into the River Thames and, as more and more people began flushing sewage into them, the river became increasingly polluted. 'The Thames is now made a great cesspool instead of each person having one of his own,' observed the builder Thomas Cubbitt.[1]

Networks of privately owned water pipes had been installed in British cities from the middle of the eighteenth century. Being able to fill up a cup with water in your own home was a wonderful experience for city dwellers, at least for those who could afford it: even in 1821, less than two-thirds of London's houses had access to piped water. Nevertheless, continental Europe looked to British cities as a model of how to supply water to urban populations. Some of London's water companies took supplies directly from the Thames. When the river had been clean this was not a problem, but after 1848, when new laws required buildings to be connected to the sewers, there was a cholera outbreak which claimed 14,789 lives.

At this time, it was widely believed that diseases such as cholera were spread by 'miasmas', or foul odours. In American cities at the end of the eighteenth century, men, women and children walked around with cigars in their mouths in the belief that the smoke helped ward

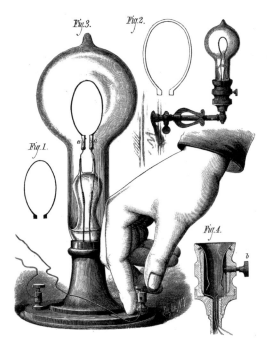

Thomas Alva Edison's carbon filament lamp, 1880.

off infection. However, the London physician John Snow was convinced that cholera was water-borne. In the early 1850s, he was able to show that one in a hundred customers supplied by the Southwark and Vauxhall Water Company (which took water from the Thames at Battersea) died of cholera, whereas not a single person died among the 14,632 people supplied by the Lambeth Water Company, which used a new waterworks at Long Ditton. It was an important piece of evidence in support of his hypothesis and a powerful argument for modern urban plumbing.

Despite thousands of deaths from cholera, it was not until what became known as 'the Great Stink' of 1858 – when the stench rising from the river during an exceptionally hot summer was so appalling even Parliament had to close – that Her Majesty's Government was forced to accept that London urgently needed a new sewer system. Finally, the city embarked on what was to be one of the great engineering projects of the nineteenth century.

Today's Londoners have reason to be immensely grateful to the project's engineer, Joseph Bazalgette, whose tireless dedication has created a safe environment for them to live in. The eighty-two miles of new sewers were built using three hundred million bricks and nearly a million cubic yards of concrete. The sewers were beautifully designed: ovoid in profile, with the pointed end of the egg directed down. This provided the tunnels with great strength (to prevent them collapsing under the weight of the buildings above) as well as guaranteeing maximum flow and ensuring they were self-cleansing. Although the complete system was not fully operational until 1875, sewage from the northern and southern suburbs was being discharged east of London just six years after building began. Opening the Crossness pumping station in 1865, the Prince of Wales – no doubt mindful of the foul odour pervading Buckingham Palace – looked forward to a future 'when London will have become one of the healthiest cities in Europe'.[2] London's sewer system became a shining example of how public works can transform life in a city, not just for its current inhabitants, but for future generations.

Each day, more than a billion gallons of water flow into Manhattan along two tunnels from upstate New York. A third tunnel has been under construction for forty years and is due to be completed in 2020. In the developed world, 98 per cent of city dwellers now have access to clean water. In the developing world, however, nearly a third of urban households do not have clean water, a figure that rises to 60 per cent in informal settlements. But urban plumbing is just one, albeit vital, aspect of the city's infrastructure. The remarkable technological systems on which modern urban life depends are a reminder that the city is a uniquely human achievement: an artificial environment forged by our ingenuity and skill. The city is a machine, brought to life by our needs and desires.

Modern city dwellers take street lighting for granted – until they walk down an unlit and unfamiliar street. Then they realise why it is so important. In sixteenth-century Paris, householders were told to place candles in their windows at night in order to make the city's streets safer. In the early eighteenth century, London was probably the best-lit city in the world, with some five thousand flickering lamps burning whale oil. A visitor reported that the view of the city and its street lamps created 'a most striking effect, particularly at a distance'.[3] New York followed London's example, introducing oil lamps on its sidewalks from 1762. But by the early nineteenth century, oil began to be replaced by gas as a fuel for street lamps. Usually produced from the coking of coal, gas gave rise to the first urban energy network.

In 1812, Frederick Albert Winsor's Light and Coke Company began installing gas lighting in London and by the 1820s it was a common sight in the city's streets. Baltimore was the first American city to use gas lighting in its streets, from 1816. By 1822, Paris had begun to install gas lighting and, in the following year, New York City built its first commercial gas plant. Within thirty years, London – the capital of the industrial world – had as many as 30,000 gas-lit street lamps, a figure that rose to 91,000 by 1900. By this date, practically all large European cities were served by extensive gas systems providing illumination for streets, shops, restaurants, public buildings and the homes of the wealthy.[4] As the cities of the industrial age grew ever larger and their streets more labyrinthine, street lighting represented a huge advance, encouraging sociability and night life. Cities

– the ultimate man-made environment – no longer had to follow the natural rhythms of the sun.

The first experiments with electric lights in London began in 1858. Twenty years later electric arc lights were used – at great expense – to illuminate the front of the Gaiety Theatre in the Strand and in 1879 the new Victoria Embankment was also lit by electricity. The incandescent light bulb was born that same year, invented independently by Thomas Edison in America and Joseph Swan in England. Everyone was convinced that electricity would be the energy of the new century: the city of the future would be wired.

Already in the heyday of gas, the bright lights of the big city had become a powerful signifier of modernity. New York's Pearl Street generating station, owned by the Edison Electric Illuminating Company, had started operating on 4 September 1882. Its power grid consisted of fifteen miles of wire connected to little more than four hundred street lights which illuminated one square mile of the surrounding area. The next morning the *New York Herald* reported that 'in the stores and business places throughout the lower quarter of the city there was a strange glow last night. The dim flicker of gas … was supplanted by a steady glare, bright and mellow, which illuminated interiors and shone through windows, fixed and unwavering.'[5] It was clear that the age of the gas lamp was drawing to a close.

At the dawn of a new millennium, electricity captured people's imagination. The current flowing through the city's wires would power a dynamic, idealistic age and the capital city of this new era would be New York, a city of skyscrapers shining with artificial light. Just as visitors to London in the eighteenth century marvelled at its lamps twinkling in the darkness, so the illuminated skyline of today's cities from New York to Hong Kong has become one of the iconic images of our urban age.

New York City's power grid is the largest underground electric cable system in the world – some 86,000 miles long, enough wire to encircle the globe more than three and a half times. Without electricity to power its lights and elevators, the vertical city could not exist. New York consumes as much electricity as an entire country – about the same energy each year as Greece. The summer peak load in New York City is about 11,000 megawatts.[6] But city living represents an efficient use of energy – New Yorkers consume 2,000 kilowatt hours per year, about half the national average. Nevertheless, energy usage

Air Mail

As well as in Paris, there were also pneumatic networks beneath the streets of American cities. In 1893, Philadelphia had a system for delivering not time, but mail. Compressed air was used to propel a two-foot-long cylinder containing letters through a six-inch cast-iron pipe, linking two post offices some half a mile apart. In 1897, a larger network of cast-iron pipes was constructed some four to six feet below the streets of New York. This 27-mile-long loop under Manhattan connected twenty-three post offices across the city. The system was pressurised by compressors in eleven power stations. Travelling at between 30 to 40 mph, the canisters were blasted around the city at the rate of five a minute. Each held some five hundred letters and every day about 100,000 letters were moved in this way. A journey that could last forty minutes by road took a cylinder sent through the pneumatic tube network just seven minutes. But it was a costly way of shifting mail and Philadelphia mothballed its network in 1918, switching instead to a new transport technology – automobiles. New York, too, suspended its subterranean mail service for a while, only to reinstate it by popular demand in 1922. It remained operational until 1953.

Berlin's *Rohrpost* network (1865–1963) was one of the largest pneumatic mail systems, extending for some 400 kilometres. In Paris, pneumatic mail systems (or 'tubes pneumatiques') continued to be used until 1983, when telexes and fax machines made the service redundant. Prague's system was still in use in 2002 and is currently being restored.[7]

Placing a mail canister into a pneumatic tube, 1930.

here and elsewhere continues to grow, which is a problem at a time when every city is working to reduce its carbon footprint.

New York's first telephone exchange opened at 82 Nassau Street in 1879 and the city's first telephone directory contained a mere 252 names. Today, there is enough telephone cabling beneath the city to reach the sun. But the world's most wired and connected city is the South Korean capital of Seoul. Nearly every household in this modern high-rise city of twelve million people is linked to the cable network and can access the internet at a speedy 100 megabits per second. (Currently, in the United Kingdom the average speed for home broadband is 4 mbps.) But by 2012, Seoul intends to upgrade its network to reach lightning speeds of up to one gigabit per second. The whole city has also been transformed into a wifi hotspot, thanks to an innovative wireless network which allows commuters on the subway to watch TV on their mobile phones. Those same commuters pay for their bus and taxi journeys with a radio frequency identification (RFID) card containing a smart chip which is able to calculate the distance travelled and the fare due.

Seoul is also upgrading itself into an 'open data city' in the belief that an informed city is a more efficient city. Thanks to the 'Ubiquitous Seoul,' or 'U-city', project, Seoul's online citizens will be able to access real-time urban data from sensors around the city, such as air-quality information and traffic updates. Ozone alerts will be sent out to those with respiratory problems, and commuters will be instantly warned about the shifting pattern of traffic jams. New homes in Seoul are being designed with 'Ubiquitous life' ('U-life') features, allowing them to be centrally controlled by a keypad or remotely with a smart phone. Forget to turn off a light? No problem. You can switch it off from the train using your phone. More controversially, perhaps, they are even planning 'U-safety zones' for children, who will be given a 'U-tag' which can be monitored by CCTV systems. Parents will be alerted automatically if their child leaves a designated zone, such as a school, and the child can then be located using their mobile phone signal.

Seoul made the decision to invest in this high-tech urban infrastructure over a decade ago after entering a severe recession. Just as the Industrial Revolution transformed cities and the lives of their inhabitants, so, too, the information revolution will undoubtedly change urban environments and require existing infrastructure to be radically updated. For the old cities of Europe, retrofitting these new technologies will take time and the cost may well force planners to reconsider how infrastructure is designed so that cities can quickly adapt to change in the future.[8]

Increasingly, the infrastructure of tomorrow's smart cities will be controlled by computers. Already some of the largest technology and computing companies, such as Cisco and IBM, are designing software that will integrate all the vital systems that ensure cities run smoothly. By bringing these disparate systems together, IBM claims it will allow cities to 'operate like living organisms, sensing and responding quickly to potential problems before they occur to protect citizens, save resources and reduce energy consumption and carbon emissions'.[9]

Cities are already being built around the requirements of the new information technologies. In the city of New Songdo in South Korea, Cisco is implementing its vision for the smart cities of the future. Under construction since 2001, New Songdo is being built on a man-made island in the Yellow Sea, forty miles south-west of Seoul. Its ambitious plan involves creating an electronic central nervous system for the city. The city will 'run on information'.[10] A pervasive network of sensors and smart chips, spread throughout the city, will transform what is usually a collection of separate machines, buildings and networks into a single urban organism, a sentient city.

Just as the parts of the city will talk to each other electronically so, too, will the inhabitants. Every home will be equipped with TelePresence screens, which will be the citizen's interface with the urban operating system and a communications system for everything from booking a restaurant table to talking to your doctor. The city's data and services will be instantly available without the need to step outside your apartment. New Songdo City is due for completion in 2015. It is viewed by its developers, the New York-based Gale International, as the first of many such smart cities across the region. And who knows – as the technology improves, maybe eventually you will have an app for your city. One day the city itself may even talk to its citizens.

Eco-Cities

We are living through a unique period in the history of our planet. No other species has ever disrupted the delicate balance of the earth's climate before. As the Nobel prize-winning chemist Paul Crutzen has said, we have entered a geological epoch of our own making – the Anthropocene. But it remains to be seen whether we can control the forces we have unleashed.

The current level of carbon dioxide in the atmosphere – about 390 parts per million – is higher than at any time in the last half a million years. And it is set to rise still further. As the developing world rapidly industrialises, the International Energy Authority predicts that, from 2000 to 2030, humankind will pump more carbon dioxide into the air than was produced between 1750 and 2000. Some people may still dispute the evidence that suggests we are responsible for climate change. But what is beyond doubt is that the planet is warming.

In the twelve years between 1995 and 2006, every year except one was among the warmest, with 2010 equaling 2005 as the hottest year since records began in 1880.[11] In its 2007 report, the Intergovernmental Panel on Climate Change (IPCC) predicts that by 2100 temperatures will rise by anything from a modest 1.1°C to a catastrophic 6.4°C. During the twentieth century, Arctic temperatures were increasing twice as fast as the global average. The Greenland ice sheet is already beginning to melt and the sea level is rising at an accelerating rate. It had already risen 0.17 metres in the last century.[12] 'It's hard to see west Antarctica's ice sheets surviving the century, meaning a sea-level rise of at least one or two metres,' says climatologist James Hansen, head of NASA's Goddard Institute for Space Studies.[13]

There has already been a dramatic increase in the number of weather-related disasters, such as floods and droughts. Red Cross figures show a rise from about two hundred each year before 1996, to over seven hundred at the start of the new century. And, as both global temperatures and the sea level climb inexorably higher, the situation is set to deteriorate. Coastal flooding caused by storms already kills more people 'than any other natural hazard'.[14] In the future, low-lying coastal regions will be increasingly prone to flooding. Wave heights around the southern and western coasts of the United Kingdom are rising steadily. Opened in 1984, London's Thames Barrier was built to protect the capital from floods that threaten the city when storms coincide with a high tide. It was designed to withstand a one in two thousand years flood. Between 1986 and 1996, the barrier was raised twenty-seven times, but in the following decade it had to be raised no fewer than sixty-six times. In the future, it will be used ever more frequently and it may be overwhelmed in as little as twenty years.

The same danger faces many cities that lie on or near the coast, including fifteen of the world's twenty megacities and two-fifths of cities with populations of between one and ten million. The number of extreme weather events has increased more than fivefold since the 1950s. In the future, storms and flooding will threaten such major cities as Tokyo, Osaka, New York, Kolkata, Mumbai, Dhaka, Karachi, Manila, Shanghai, Tianjin, Bangkok and Seoul. Coastal populations have doubled in the United States in the last fifteen years. As the sea level rises and the temperature of the oceans increases, these people will face more frequent and more powerful storms. As well as killing some 1,500 people, the bill for the devastation wrought by Hurricane Katrina on New Orleans in 2005 was $200 billion, making it the most costly disaster in American history. New York City had a lucky escape in 2011 when Hurricane Irene swept through without causing serious damage. But New York – the largest city in the United States and home to some eighteen million people – is now 'the American city at second highest risk for potential total economic loss from a major hurricane'.[15]

As well as the rising sea level, cities will have to contend with hotter summers. In the 2003 heat wave, 35,000 people died in Europe. But the continent needs to get used to such sweltering temperatures, for by 2050 these will be the average during summer in the region. By then, 2,800 deaths are predicted annually for the United Kingdom, a 250 per cent increase. Heat stress will be particularly acute in cities and even Londoners will have to consider installing air conditioning. The higher temperatures will also mean that city dwellers are likely to face greater concentrations of ground-level ozone. As a result, it is predicted that New York may experience a 4.5 per cent increase in deaths caused by ozone.[16]

As summers become hotter, water shortages will pose serious problems for many cities, not least in China, which recently announced a major $62 billion engineering project, known as the South-North Water Diversion, to siphon water from a tributary of the Yangtze River, 570 miles south-west of Beijing, to keep the capital's taps supplied. As temperatures soar, cities will also be threatened by wild-fires, the choking effects of which were experienced by the residents of Moscow in 2010. Vast tracts of Africa and Asia will suffer regular drought and famine. A warming of just 1–3°C may even cause a decline in the productivity of cereal crops, increasing the likelihood of serious food shortages in the future and making radical solutions, such as vertical farms in cities, more likely to be adopted. Insects and animals will colonise new habitats, spreading diseases such as malaria and dengue fever to areas that have no evolutionary protection against them. By 2085, for instance, models suggest that five to seven billion people will be at risk from dengue, compared to 3.5 billion in a world without climate change.

In the coming years, as cities become ever larger, the effects of natural disasters such as earthquakes are likely to be magnified. It is estimated that some three and a half million people were killed in natural disasters in the previous century. In the century of the megacity and global warming we may begin to see the first mega-disasters, catastrophes that claim the lives of more than a million people. The San Francisco earthquake struck at 5.12 on the morning of Wednesday, 18 April 1906. The quake and resulting fire killed three thousand people and left hundreds of thousands homeless. But how many will die in the next major earthquake to strike this city, whose current population is nearly 800,000, double what it was in 1906? The fate of New Orleans showed that even the world's most advanced superpower struggled to cope with the devastation caused by nature's wrath. Cities around the world need to look into the future and prepare for the worst.

It has even been suggested that the rising sea level may lead to increased geological activity in coastal regions. Large changes in the sea level will increase the weight of water on the continental margins, potentially causing 'volcanoes to erupt, active faults to move, and huge landslides to collapse from continental shelf regions'.[17] The earthquake that struck Japan's north-east coast in 2011 was the most powerful ever recorded in the country. As well as being at risk from storms and a nearby volcano, a major earthquake is expected to hit Tokyo in the near future. It will cause an estimated $33 trillion of damage. Such a devastating catastrophe striking the world's biggest city will send shockwaves through the global economy and may well trigger a wider financial collapse. The twentieth century is remembered by historians for its bloody wars, in which humankind annihilated whole cities with weapons of mass destruction. In the twenty-first century, the greatest threat to our cities may come from nature and its arsenal of storms, earthquakes and volcanoes.

This is not the first time that *Homo urbanus* has had to face catastrophic climate change. Anthropologist Brain Fagan argues persuasively that the invention of urban society in Mesopotamia was 'an adaptation to much drier climatic conditions'.[18] From 3800 BC, Mesopotamia's climate changed rapidly, becoming more arid. The effect of this was to increase the rate of urbanisation in the region. In order to cope with a newly erratic climate, in which rain would arrive at the wrong time and floods would inundate whole villages, intensive irrigation of farmland was essential. Cities provided both the manpower and the organisational skills necessary to keep fields watered, crops growing and people fed: 'In its earliest iterations, the Mesopotamian city was a unique way of responding to environmental crisis.'[19] Although by 2000 BC the proportion of people living in cities had fallen from 80 to 50 per cent, Mesopotamian civilisation managed to survive the change in the climate, which finally returned to normal in about 1900 BC. But the measures its people were forced to take ultimately proved fatal to the first cities: intensive irrigation led to the salinisation of the soil. Eventually, all that would grow in the fields beyond the walls of the first cities were date palms.

In a world that is now predominantly urban, most people on the planet are experiencing city climates. Today's megacities are the largest artificial structures ever built. They are awe-inspiring examples of humankind's ability to control and transform its habitat. As well as changing the face of the landscape, these soaring environments of concrete, glass and steel affect the weather around them just like natural geological features, such as volcanoes or deserts. Cities create their own unique zones of windflow, humidity, rainfall, air pollution and temperature. Cities form a distinct urban heat island in the landscape. The average temperature in large cities is 0.6 to 1.8°C above that found in rural areas. High walls, dark roofs and concrete absorb the sun's energy, radiating it at night. Industry, transport infrastructure and the dense concentration of population in cities all contribute to the urban heat island. As a result there is less snowfall in cities, plants bud or bloom earlier than normal and birds unfamiliar to the region flock to urban areas. The higher temperatures lead to more deaths in summer due to heat stress and increase the need for air conditioning, but in winter urban buildings need less heating than their rural equivalents. Cities also experience increased rainfall and more intense storms than the surrounding countryside. A study of south-east England found that there were more thunderstorms over built-up areas. In North American cities, there is 9–27 per cent more summer rain than in rural areas. There is also a 10–42 per cent greater incidence of thunderstorms and the frequency of hailstorms is increased by 67–430 per cent.[20] As cities grow ever larger and the climate warms, the effect of the urban heat island will become more pronounced.

If cities influence their own weather, does this mean they are also changing the earth's climate? Until recently it had been thought that cities were the worst carbon sinners on the planet, responsible for up to 80 per cent of greenhouse gas emissions. However, as David Satterthwaite of the International Institute for Environment and Development has shown, the real figure is likely to be nearer 30–40 per cent.[21] Indeed, rural areas generally have higher carbon dioxide emissions per person than urban ones, due to the fact that people outside cities live in larger, detached or semi-detached houses, drive multiple cars and commute longer distances (cars are responsible for 12 per cent of greenhouse gas emissions in Europe and as much as 50 per cent in some parts of the United States). The regions with the biggest carbon footprints in the United Kingdom are not the large cities of Glasgow or London, but the mainly rural north-east of England, as well as Yorkshire and the Humber.

Surprisingly, the per capita emissions of London are the lowest of any part of the United Kingdom. In 2006, each Londoner produced greenhouse gas emissions equivalent to 6.18 tonnes of CO_2, just over half the national average (which was 11.19 tonnes per capita in 2004). Similarly, if you are a city dweller in the United States your carbon footprint is likely to be smaller than the average American citizen's. However, there is considerable variation between cities, with the most energy-efficient places generally being the larger metropolitan areas.[22] 'Blaming cities for greenhouse gas emissions,' argues Satterthwaite, 'misses the point that well planned and governed cities are central to delinking high living standards from high consumption levels and high greenhouse gas emissions.'[23] Tokyo, for instance, actually has lower per capita emissions than Beijing, suggesting that there is not an automatic link between prosperity and carbon footprint.

Vertical Farms

Cities of the future will certainly be more green. In an oil-poor future when fertile land is increasingly scarce, fruit and vegetables as well as some animals and fish may be produced within cities, in 'vertical farms'. Ultra-efficient greenhouses can already grow crops on 10 per cent of the water used in conventional farms. They are also more productive and require less land. Using hydroponics, where plants are grown in solutions of nutrients, vegetables and fruit could be cultivated in greenhouses on top of skyscrapers. In 2007, a floating greenhouse in the Hudson River, called the Science Barge, used solar power and recycled water to grow fruit and vegetables, demonstrating that self-sufficient greenhouses were viable.

New Yorkers eat, on average, about a hundred kilograms of fresh vegetables a year. The city's rooftops offer twice the amount of space needed to keep New Yorkers supplied with produce grown in greenhouses.

There are even plans for skyscraper farms. Dickson Despommier, a parasitologist at Columbia University, claims that a thirty-storey farm could feed ten thousand people, supplying vegetables, fruit, eggs and even meat to cities. Upper floors would grow hydroponic crops and lower ones would house chickens and fish that consume the plant waste. Heat and lighting could be generated by solar or geothermal sources. Despommier's goal is to allow the 'city to behave like an ecosystem' and to produce its own food.[24]

An artist's impression of a 132-storey vertical farm designed in the shape of a dragonfly's wing and built in New York's East River.

We need to start seeing cities not as the problem, but as part of the solution to climate change. During the last decade we crossed a major threshold – for the first time in our history we became a truly urban species, with more than half the world's population living in cities. Currently 3.3 billion people live in cities – more than the total population of the world in 1960. By 2030 that figure will reach five billion, with 95 per cent of the growth in the developing world. In the next thirty years, Africa's city dwellers will more than double, from 294 to 742 million, and Asia's urban population will double, rising to 2.6 billion. Half of China's population is expected to leave the countryside for the cities by mid-century and it was recently estimated that some fifty thousand skyscrapers will be built there in the next twenty years.

According to the United Nations, 'the battle for sustainable development, for delivering a more environmentally stable, just, and healthier world, is going to be largely won or lost in our cities'.[25] With temperatures and population levels increasing, concentrating people in cities is a highly efficient way of bringing clean water, sanitation, healthcare and energy to large numbers of people, while minimising the per capita emissions of greenhouse gases. Public transport systems, the creation of walkable cities, as well as bicycle schemes such as those now operating in Paris, Montreal and London, can all help to reduce the reliance on individual cars in cities. By reducing our carbon footprint, urbanisation might just save the planet.

One pioneering project that offers a glimpse of the sustainable cities of the future is Masdar City. This carbon-neutral eco-city is being built some twenty miles from Abu Dhabi, in the United Arab Emirates, which, ironically, is the world's fifth largest exporter of oil. Designed by Norman Foster, this walled city on a square plan is inspired by the mud-brick tower houses of Shibam in Yemen. Foster has said that 'a zero-waste, zero-carbon city is like putting a man on the moon' and undoubtedly this is an ambitious project, driven by high ideals.[26] But it remains to be seen to what extent the vision of a fully sustainable city will be realised here.

With a projected resident population of about 45,000, Masdar City will be powered entirely by renewable energy. Initially, the designers hoped that its energy could be generated from within the city limits, but that has proved too ambitious. Instead, a 100-megawatt concentrated solar power plant, with 768 parabolic mirrors, is being constructed nearby. Known as Shams 1, it is the largest of its kind in the world. Energy is also generated from photovoltaic fields, wind turbines and a geothermal plant. Air conditioning is supplied by an innovative solar thermal cooling system. The water of this desert city will be supplied by a solar-powered desalination plant, with waste water being recycled for irrigation. Residents and visitors must park their cars outside Masdar City and most of the transport in the city will be provided by a futuristic fleet of driverless, pod-shaped electric cars – the personal rapid transport system.

Home to hi-tech industries and scientific research institutes, Masdar City is planned as an 'open-data city', with free wireless networks providing ubiquitous access to the internet. The Masdar Institute for Science and Technology has already opened, with buildings that have halved the typical energy and water consumption for the UAE. Solar panels on the roof will generate a third of the Institute's energy and a microclimate has been created in the outside spaces to allow people to walk around the campus, despite scorching temperatures, rather than using air-conditioned vehicles. This has been achieved by minimising the urban heat effect – the outside spaces are smaller, wind corridors have been created, and pavements are light in colour. Buildings are also designed to reduce the absorption of the sun's energy and to provide shade. In a warmer urban future, such ideas may prove useful in other cities. The first phase of Masdar City is due for completion in 2015, with the entire six-square-kilometre city being finished five or ten years later.

Masdar City is a new, planned city. For older cities, the route to sustainability will be costly and complex. But the price of doing nothing will be immeasurably greater. As urban ecologist Herbert

Masdar City, designed by Norman Foster, is an eco-city currently being built near Abu Dhabi, in the United Arab Emirates.

Girardet has said, 'there will be no sustainable world without sustainable cities'.[27] Cities everywhere are indeed taking steps to reduce their carbon footprint. The European Union recently announced that it will pioneer innovative energy-saving technologies in twenty-five to thirty 'smart cities'. Existing houses will be highly insulated and as far as possible energy will be generated from waste, sun and wind, which will then be used to power an integrated transport system of electric cars, trams and buses. There are energy savings to be made simply by changing a city's light bulbs. LEDs (light-emitting diodes) can reduce energy usage by 40 per cent compared with sodium lighting. Although they cost more to install, they have a longer lifespan. Integrated urban energy systems offer a very efficient way of supplying entire cities with both energy and heat. Helsinki's system currently heats more than 91 per cent of the city's buildings, using hot water produced from the generation of electricity.

The ultimate goal is for cities to produce as much as possible of what they need to sustain themselves, for example by generating their own power from renewable sources of energy. In Berlin, there are eight thousand roofs fitted with photovoltaic or solar thermal systems. If all suitable roofs in the capital were utilised (some 500,000) this could supply 77 per cent of the power needed for private use. In Santa Coloma de Gramenet, near Barcelona, 462 solar panels have recently been erected over mausoleums in a cemetery containing the remains of 57,000 people. As an open space in a crowded city, the cemetery is an ideal site for solar generation. Currently it generates power for just sixty homes, but there are plans to extend the scheme and triple the amount of power being generated.

Urban rivers also offer power-generating potential. The Roosevelt Island Tidal Energy project has been testing six turbines in New York's East River since 2006 and the company that runs it, Verdant Power, hopes to install more turbines in the waters around the city. Electricity can also be generated from organic and human waste using anaerobic digesters. In the future, each home might be provided with its own unit to generate power. A smart electricity grid, which communicates with each house and allows users to generate their own power and sell it back to the grid, will be essential in the urban energy economy of the future. A central computer system will control the city's power generation, using sensors in every building to adjust the supply and drawing on a city-wide network of micro-generators, as well as a range of renewable energy sources.

As the designers of Masdar City have shown, measures can be taken to reduce the effect of the urban heat island. In October 2010, New York's mayor, Michael Bloomberg, climbed on to the roof of the Betances Development in the South Bronx to coat the one millionth square foot of rooftop with whitewash. In the previous six months, volunteers had painted some 105 roofs white. This simple measure keeps the roof cool and reduces air-conditioning costs by 50 per cent in a one-storey building, or 10 per cent for a five-storey one. Similarly, green roofs planted with grass or vegetation have the same effect, as well as reducing run-off and allowing rainwater to be captured and reused. In the eco-city of the future, green roofs could be used to grow food in hydroponic greenhouses. At street level, planting trees creates shade which prevents the absorption of solar energy by concrete or asphalt areas, such as car parks. Materials used for pavements can also be modified to increase porosity and to help them reflect more energy.

More than 40 per cent of New York's office space was built before 1945 in an age that knew nothing of the need to conserve energy and reduce greenhouse gas emissions. Many of America's older skyscrapers are now being retrofitted to reduce their carbon footprints. The Empire State Building's 6,514 windows are being insulated at a cost of $500 million. Similarly, at the Willis Tower in Chicago, 16,000 single-pane windows are being replaced with double-pane ones. Energy savings of up to 38 per cent are expected from these and other measures. New skyscrapers, such as London's tallest residential building, Strata (opened in 2010), are now incorporating power generation into their architecture. The 147-metre-tall Strata (486 feet) is crowned by three giant wind turbines, each with nine-metre blades. They will generate enough power to light, heat and ventilate the building's public areas, as well as running its three lifts and automated window-cleaning rigs. Fitting the turbines was extremely expensive. Indeed, it has been estimated that creating a 'green' building adds about 30 per cent to the cost, and developers are often reluctant to spend this kind of money. But if climate change is to be halted such measures are vital. As the UN Secretary-General Ban Ki-Moon has said, 'investing in the greener, more resilient city of tomorrow is an essential insurance policy for a more disaster-prone world. It is one of the smartest, most cost-effective investments we can make in our common future.'[28]

Futuropolis

Unless there is some unforeseen global catastrophe, the twenty-first century looks set to experience the greatest flowering of urban civilisation in human history. By 2050, it is expected that nearly three-quarters of the world's inhabitants will be urbanites, some 6.4 billion people. Many cities are growing at an astonishing rate. It has been estimated that the land area covered by the world's cities is set to treble by 2030 to some 600,000 square kilometres. The growth of all cities with 100,000 or more people in the developing world would cover an area larger than Japan or Germany.[29] Such cities are growing ten times as fast as those in the global north. Indeed, in the developed world four out of ten cities actually experienced a decline in population during the 1990s. In Europe and North America, where more than 70 per cent of people already live in cities, the growth in urban population is expected to be modest in the coming years and almost entirely due to migration from poorer countries.

Europe is the only region without a megacity. There are now some twenty-two megacities – those with populations of more than ten million people. These unprecedented concentrations of humanity are home to 5 per cent of the world's population. Considerably more people live in metropolitan Mumbai than in Norway and Sweden combined. With a population of some twenty million people, greater São Paulo has just one million people less than the whole of Australia. In the last two decades, three million people a week have been flocking to the cities of the developing world. By 2030, the urban population of Africa will exceed the population of Europe. By then it is also predicted that megacities such as Shanghai will have to manage fourteen square miles of new growth each and every year. As they grow, some megacities are joining together to form 'super-urban regions', areas such as the Chengdu-Chongqing corridor city in China. This 'urban goliath' has been created in the last thirty years and Chongqing alone is growing at a staggering rate of 10 per cent a year (the global average is 1.83 per cent). More than twenty-six million people now live in the two metropolitan areas, linked by a 221-mile highway.

In our urban future, medium-sized cities will also play an important role. In Asia, cities such as Singapore – with a population of about five million – have shown that it is possible to be more successful economically than bigger cities, such as Bangkok (eleven million), whilst avoiding many of the problems associated with megacities. Similarly, Near Eastern cities such as Cairo and Tehran have been outstripped by younger, much smaller cities, like Abu Dhabi and Dubai. In India, government policy has been to encourage the growth of intermediate cities in order to stimulate rural economies. Now 39 per cent of India's population live in such cities, compared to just 12 per cent in China. Jon Turney, author of *The Rough Guide to the Future*, says that by 2050 more than half of the world's urbanites will be living in cities of about half a million people: 'That means well over 5,000 cities that size, far more than there have ever been before, each one able to experiment with viable ways of twenty-first-century living.'[30]

Predicting the future is not an exact science. In 1950, one urban scholar claimed, somewhat prematurely, that 'the age of the city seems to be at an end'.[31] This may have seemed a likely scenario at a time when decentralisation and suburbanisation were sapping the life blood of cities in North America, but events have confounded the experts. Today, despite revolutions in information and communication technology that make out-of-town homeworking easier than ever, cities around the world have enjoyed a renaissance. Indeed, the new communication technologies will play a key role in the smart cities of the future, as they strive to become more sustainable.

But no matter how technologically advanced they are, one thing is certain about the cities of tomorrow: to be successful they will need to satisfy many of the same demands and desires that city dwellers have had for millennia. The urbanites of the future will still want to walk through parks, grab a bite to eat from a street food vendor, marvel at the displays in a museum, try on the latest fashions in a store, or simply sit in a café and watch people walking by on the street. For cities are far more than the sum of their infrastructure or architecture: they are human communities, the natural habitat of a very social species, and this is why, as I have tried to show throughout this book, there are so many similarities between cities from all ages and cultures.

Since at least the time of the Industrial Revolution, when science and technology began transforming urban infrastructure with such wonders as gas street lighting and underground railways, people have been eager to learn what the cities of the future might look like. Writers, filmmakers, architects and other futurists have been happy to oblige, conjuring up fantastic cities equipped with moving pavements, travelators, airships and aerial taxis landing on the tops of skyscrapers, personal jet-packs, computer-controlled vehicles, vertiginous glass skyscrapers, and even bioluminescent trees to replace street lights.

Among the wondrous catalogue of imaginary cities that people have described are ones that float in the air, such as Cloud City in *Star Wars*, underground cities like Zion in *The Matrix* trilogy, cities built on far planets (as in Robert Heinlein's *The Moon Is a Harsh Mistress*), cities that can blast off from earth like spaceships, as described in James Blish's *Cities in Flight*, and urban spaceships (the subject of Heinlein's *Universe*). We live today in an age of rapidly expanding megacities, and it is therefore not difficult to imagine a future in which the world itself has become a continuous city, such as Trantor in Isaac Asimov's Foundation and Empire series of novels, a phenomenon known as 'Ecumenopolis', a word first used in 1967.

In a future world with ever more people and fewer resources, it no longer seems fanciful to imagine the creation of 'megastructures' (a word coined by Rayner Banham in the 1970s), in which a whole city is contained within a single building. The Situationist architect Constant Nieuwenhuys proposed a utopian megastructure called New Babylon as early as 1956. If, as scientists predict, the glaciers melt and sea levels rise dramatically, then ship-cities such as Armada in China Miéville's *The Scar*, or cities built out across water, as in architect Kenzo Tange's elegant 'Plan for Tokyo' (1960) which extended the Japanese capital out into the bay, might become reality. Transparent domes protecting cities are another idea popular with science fiction authors. In 1968, American futurist Buckminster Fuller actually proposed covering part of New York City in a vast air-conditioned geodesic dome. And who knows – in an age of climate change, such a scheme might indeed be necessary to protect downtowns from violent storms or stifling heat. Other urban futures include walking cities and plug-in cities, such as those proposed in the 1960s by the wonderfully inventive British architectural group Archigram, mobile or nomadic cities as described in Christopher Priest's novel *Inverted World*, underwater cities, inflatable cities, cities on stilts (for example, architect Arata Isozaki's 'City in the Air', from 1960), and temporary cities such as Black Rock City.

In 1939, the science fiction magazine *Amazing* imagined 'the city of tomorrow', conjuring up fantastic visions of 'gigantic buildings connected by wide, suspended roadways on which traffic will speed at unheard of rates'. Every building would be 'a city in itself, completely self-sustaining, receiving its supplies from great merchandise ways

EACH WALKING UNIT HOUSES NOT ONLY A KEY
ELEMENT OF THE CAPITAL , BUT ALSO A LARGE
POPULATION OF WORLD TRAVELLER-WORKERS.

A WALKING CITY

far below the ground'. The magazine predicted that an urban utopia awaited us in which pollution would be eliminated and people would 'live in the healthy atmosphere of the building tops'.[32]

In the same year as this was published, Dorothy and her fellow travellers in *The Wizard of Oz* caught their first glimpse of the sky-high crystalline towers and domes of the Emerald City glittering on the horizon. 'It's beautiful isn't it? Just like I knew it would be,' says Dorothy. In this fairy-tale film, Dorothy expresses the heartfelt feelings of millions of people who had flocked to cities, such as New York, in the previous century: all of them hoped and prayed this was the city in which their dreams would be realised. In the twentieth century, architects and engineers were convinced that they could build such cities. But for writers and filmmakers, the urban future promised to be a place not just where dreams came true, but nightmares, too.

The Italian Futurists detested the traditional cities of Europe, describing them as 'festering sores'. The movement's founder, Filippo Marinetti, once threw eighty thousand leaflets from the tower of St Mark's in Venice, demanding that the city's palaces be ripped down and the canals replaced with motorways.[33] The Futurists revelled in the energy and speed of the technological and industrial age. They wanted all cities to be filled with vast machine-like structures made of 'concrete, glass and steel'. Marinetti collaborated with the gifted young architect Antonio Sant'Elia on the *Manifesto of Futurist Architecture* (1914), creating a dramatic vision of the *città nuova*: 'We must invent and rebuild the Futurist city like an immense and tumultuous ship-yard, agile, mobile and dynamic in every detail; and the Futurist

A Walking City, a robotic megastructure designed by Ron Herron of Archigram in 1964.

315

house must be like a gigantic machine. The lifts must no longer be hidden away like tapeworms in the niches of stairwells; the stairwells themselves, rendered useless, must be abolished, and the lifts must scale the lengths of the façades like serpents of steel and glass.'[34]

Sant'Elia was killed at the age of twenty-eight in the First World War. Before he died, friends recalled seeing him building Futurist structures in the snow at the front. Across Europe such idealism about the cities of tomorrow was widespread. These cities would not just be agglomerations of homes and offices, but revolutionary environments that would nurture a new kind of person. Glass-fronted skyscrapers are now ubiquitous in cities across the world. But at the beginning of the twentieth century, large glass windows were a futuristic element and one that planners believed could transform city dwellers. 'A person who daily sets eyes on the splendours of glass *cannot* do wicked deeds,' wrote the Expressionist author and artist Paul Scheerbart. His crystalline designs inspired the German architect Bruno Taut in the years immediately following the First World War.[35] A friend of Bauhaus founder Walter Gropius, Taut was enthusiastic about the potential of glass, both architecturally and as a means of creating morally advanced citizens in an urban utopia.

But one futurist's utopia was another's dystopia. A glass city also provides the setting for Yevgeny Zamyatin's powerful novel *We*, which he began writing in 1919. Created some nine hundred years hence, Zamyatin's Modernist city has 'irrevocably straight streets'. Its buildings, pavements, and the Green Wall which separates the city's inhabitants from the world outside, are made entirely of 'immovable, eternal glass'.[36] 'We constantly live in full sight of all,' says the narrator, 'constantly bathed in light and surrounded by our glass walls that seem to be woven of coruscating air.'[37]

Every thought and deed of the dutiful inhabitants of this glass city is dedicated to the service of the One State and its leader, the Benefactor. Their city is a perfectly constructed rationalist utopia. But it is also a vision of hell on earth – a city designed as the ultimate authoritarian surveillance society. Born in Russia in 1884, Zamyatin became a Bolshevik and took part in the 1905 revolution while studying to be a naval engineer in St Petersburg. But his critique of this fictional totalitarian society was so devastating that his novel could not be published in Russia until 1988.

We brilliantly subverted the idealistic zeitgeist of the age, both politically and architecturally. But just as futurists such as Taut could celebrate the utopian potential of glass cities while others saw it leading to urban prison camps, so the 'great, divine, exact, wise straight line'[38] that Zamyatin saw leading to dystopia became the key to the ideal city of the machine age for a Swiss architect working in Paris: 'Man, by reason of his very nature, practises order … his actions and thoughts are dictated by the straight line and the right angle … the straight line is instinctive to him and his mind apprehends it as a lofty objective … he walks in a straight line because he has a goal and knows where he is going … the modern city lives by the straight line, inevitably; for the construction of buildings, sewers and tunnels, highways and pavements. The circulation of traffic demands the straight line: it is the proper thing for the heart of the city. The curve is ruinous, difficult and dangerous; it is a paralysing thing. The straight line enters into all human history, into all human aims, into every human act … geometry is the foundation … the material basis on which we build those symbols which represent to us perfection and the divine.'[39]

There is a remarkable similarity between this passage by Le Corbusier and the rectilinear principles underpinning Zamyatin's nightmarish city. Indeed, it is striking that throughout the twentieth century the idealism of architects and planners about the urban future has been – and, indeed, continues to be – opposed by the deep pessimism of most writers and filmmakers. Time and again, architects offer seductive glimpses of glittering skyscrapers full of hothouse vegetation or sentient cities that satisfy every whim of their inhabitants, while novels and films conjure up visions of alienating cities in which people are reduced to cogs in a dehumanising urban machine.

One of the most powerful of these depictions of the urban future was a movie inspired by the director's first sight of New York City from its harbour. Fritz Lang arrived at Manhattan on the liner *Deutschland* in October 1924, en route to Hollywood. He was kept on board by immigration officials overnight. As he waited, Lang spent hours just staring at New York's dramatic skyline, mesmerised by its soaring illuminated architecture. Later, he recalled seeing 'a street lit as if in full daylight by neon lights and topping them oversized luminous advertisements moving, turning, flashing on and off, spiralling'. For Lang, who was used to the cities of Europe where cathedral spires still dominated the skyline, Manhattan offered a glimpse of tomorrow's cities. It was, he said, 'something which was completely new and nearly fairy-tale-like for a European in those days, and this impression gave me the first thought for a town of the future.'[40]

The film *Metropolis* (1926) was born that night. Lang began working on the movie as soon as he got back to Berlin. At UFA's studio they created detailed scale models out of wood, plaster and canvas of an imaginary city, clearly based on Manhattan. One of these miniatures of a street was at least twenty feet long. Stop-motion animation was used to bring this futuristic city alive, with automobiles driving along packed multi-lane motorways, pedestrians on sky-bridges, trains racing over viaducts far above the roads, and aircraft darting between the towering skyscrapers, the tallest of which was symbolically named the 'new Tower of Babel'. They spent an astonishing 310 days and 60 nights building the sets and filming. Special effects expert Eugen Shüfftan pioneered a new technique of combining glass paintings and live action to create the startlingly realistic urban scenes. Indeed, the images of Metropolis teeming with activity by day while at night it shines with electric lights and illuminated signs were unlike anything that had been seen before. It was a cityscape that defined people's views of the urban future for generations to come.

There are, in fact, two cities in Fritz Lang's Metropolis. While the elite enjoy the luxury of the 'Eternal Gardens' and apartments high up in the clouds, the working classes (who are known by a number, as in Zamyatin's novel) are condemned to live far below in a dark subterranean city. Despite its advanced technology, Metropolis is no utopia, but a deeply unequal and divided society. In this, Lang's film harks back to Wells's novel *The Sleeper Awakes*, based on a story written as early as 1899, which describes a future London that has become a megacity of 'Titanic buildings' and thirty-three million inhabitants.[41] For all its awesome architecture and technology, London was now a 'gigantic glass hive' whose existence depended on the labour of workers condemned to spend their lives in the bowels of the city.[42]

This theme of an unequal society whose divisions are built into the urban structure, creating a layered city, resonates throughout modern film and fiction. In *The World Inside* (1971), Robert Silverberg describes thousand-storey 'urban monads' that are rigidly hierarchical in structure, with higher status people living in the top levels. Similarly, in J. G. Ballard's chilling novel *High-Rise,* a new residential block which is socially stratified, with the rich living on the upper floors, descends inexorably into chaos and extreme violence.

The idea of a layered city also appears in one of the most famous films depicting the urban future – Ridley Scott's *Blade Runner* (1982). Set in the Los Angeles of 2019, the opening sequence shows the city from the air, stretching as far as the eye can see. This influential scene has become 'a paradigm for the future of cities', influencing many architects and designers.[43] The sequence was filmed in the pre-CGI era, using a motion-control camera and a forced perspective miniature of the city, some fifteen feet wide at the back and just eight feet at the front. This haunting panorama – known as the Hades Landscape – reveals a cityscape of soaring skyscrapers shrouded in smog and bathed in a fiery half-light. Golden flames explode from chimneys, flaring against the polluted night sky. The scene evokes Blake's 'dark Satanic mills' and is inspired by Scott's memories of the industrial landscape of Tyneside and Teeside where he grew up. Fritz Lang's film was also clearly a great influence. Metropolis was dominated by a skyscraper, a new Tower of Babel, the headquarters of the city's ruler. Similarly, Scott's future Los Angeles is overshadowed by the vast, seven hundred-storey pyramid of the Tyrell Corporation, its form reminiscent of that most famous ziggurat – the Tower of Babel.

Jean Baudrillard, who visited the city not long after the film was released, noted that 'there is nothing to match flying over Los Angeles by night'. But like the makers of *Blade Runner*, he, too, saw the dark side of this immense, sprawling metropolis: 'only Hieronymus Bosch's hell can match this inferno effect'.[44] Inspired by the real Los Angeles, Ridley Scott's future noir set new standards for depicting the cities of tomorrow. Unlike many science fiction films, the streets and buildings have a convincing, lived-in appearance. Existing architecture in the city, such as the Bradbury Building – which was itself inspired by a work of urban utopianism: Edward Bellamy's *Looking Backward* – stand alongside futuristic structures. Much of the look of the film, including the police spinners (flying cars) and the advertising blimps, was the work of Syd Mead, the film's 'visual futurist'. It was he who suggested the idea of a city where 'decent people' never venture below level 60. In the Los Angeles of *Blade Runner*, ground level is 'a social basement, inhabited by low-lifes and criminals'.[45] The gated communities of today's Los Angeles have been lifted into the clouds. It is a measure of the film's influence that real-life Angelinos now refer to 'Blade Runner' enclaves, by which they mean run-down areas, with street traders and decaying buildings.[46]

Burning Man

Burning Man is a unique arts event, as well as an exercise in city building. It began with a small evening bonfire on a San Francisco beach in 1986. This gathering of twenty friends evolved into today's temporary city of some 47,000 people known as Black Rock City. The event now takes place in the savage 40°C heat and blinding dust storms of the Black Rock Desert, 120 miles north of Reno, Nevada, for one week each year. It is held during the week prior to and including Labor Day weekend in late summer. The forty-foot effigy of 'the Man' is burned the night before Labor Day. The next day everyone packs up their things, removes all traces of the city and drives off across the flat, white desert.

Unlike other festivals, Burning Man is created entirely by its participants. Black Rock City is viewed by the organisers as an experimental community, which encourages its members to express themselves by creating artworks and challenges them to be self-reliant to a degree not normally encountered in everyday life. Selling things or attempting to make money out of the event is forbidden, otherwise there are no rules about how to behave, save those that serve to protect the wellbeing of the rest of the community. Participants have to make up their own minds about how they will contribute to Black Rock City.

The pedestrianised city is built each year in the form of a horseshoe, surrounded by an external perimeter in the shape of a pentagram. The design alludes to ancient megalithic sites and city-states, as well as to Renaissance and mythic ideal cities. But Black Rock City has its own unique culture and history: 'It is at once a very real and yet extremely ephemeral phenomenon, as it must annually arise from nothing, flourish for a few days, and then vanish completely.'[47] In 2008, the site spread across five square miles, about the size of downtown San Francisco.

Aerial view of Black Rock City, a temporary community created for the Burning Man event in the Nevada desert.

Scott's vision of a future city in which scientists have the god-like power to create genetically engineered robots ('replicants') while the streets remain filled with rubbish, the air is polluted and society is still riven by inequality, seems to many people more convincing than most utopias. Perhaps this is a failure of imagination. Or perhaps it is because, as Margaret Mead has said, Hell is always more convincing than Heaven.[48] But in the future, cities will almost certainly develop at an uneven rate, just as they do today, with poverty and outmoded infrastructure existing alongside wealth and cutting-edge technology. As William Gibson – whose *Neuromancer* (1984) echoes *Blade Runner*'s future noir atmosphere – has said: 'The future is already here. It is just not evenly distributed.'[49]

With its polluted, smoggy air and permanently rain-swept streets, *Blade Runner* also reminds us that whatever cities we build in the future we will have to live with the reality of climate change. Nobody yet knows how serious that will be and how our cities will have to change. But it is possible that in the far distant future, when humankind – like the first city builders – is confronted by a hostile climate and a now barren landscape, the city will come to our rescue, serving as a life-support system for the species. Arthur C. Clarke's *The City and the Stars* (1956) describes just such a future city. Diaspar is the last city on earth at a time when the oceans have dried up and the land has turned to desert. Diaspar is an 'artificial womb', nurturing some ten million people and shielding them from the harsh world beyond its walls: 'the city knew neither heat nor cold. It had no contact with the outer world; it was a universe itself.'[50] At the centre of the circular city is a 'green heart', the Park, an Eden of forest and rivers, 'a memory of what Earth had been in the days before the desert swallowed all but Diaspar'.[51] Of course, this is a bleak vision of the distant future, but it is one that reveals the profound trust we have placed in the city as a bulwark against the vagaries of a hostile universe, a trust that has served our species well for millennia. For this reason, it is certain that whatever shape they take, cities are where the future of humanity lies.

Fortuna Street, Pompeii, Italy, photographed between 1890 and 1900. (following page)

The Ruins

'All that is solid melts into air.'[52] In time, even the greatest cities return to the dust from which they emerged. Uruk, Memphis, Mohenjo-daro, Athens, Rome and Tenochtitlán – all cities that shone brightly for centuries before eventually they flickered and died, their walls breached and their palaces reduced to rubble. Some of these cities never recovered, their buildings crumbling into artificial hills. The tell of Çatalhöyük was over sixty feet high when archaeologists began excavating it, and that of Megiddo in Palestine was more than seventy feet high. Dust to dust, ashes to ashes. Beneath your feet lie yesterday's cities. In the seventeenth century, Nicolas Poussin was sketching in the Roman Forum, which by then had become a field of ruins full of grazing cattle, when someone approached him and asked in what part of the city the spirit of ancient Rome was best preserved. Kneeling down, the French painter dug his hand into the soil and held it out to the person. 'Here,' he said.[53]

On the morning of 24 August AD 79, the Roman administrator and poet Pliny the Younger noticed a column of smoke rising 'like an umbrella pine' above the volcano of Vesuvius on the other side of the Bay of Naples. The cloud climbed some thirty kilometres into the sky, eventually turning day into night. People were terrified, believing it was the end of the world. For those unfortunate enough to be living in the Roman towns of Herculaneum and Pompeii it was indeed the end. The following day, an avalanche of hot ash, rock fragments and super-heated volcanic gases engulfed both towns and their inhabitants, burying them under more than thirty feet of mineral deposits. There they remained until a surveyor rediscovered Pompeii in 1748. It was a perfectly preserved time capsule – Roman streets and houses, many with wall paintings still intact, bakeries, shops, bath houses and brothels (complete with obscene graffiti). To walk through the city was like stepping back two thousand years.

Ruined buildings and buried cities are reminders that, for all their splendour, human achievements are only temporary: even the greatest civilisations will one day fall. The broken walls of Troy, the Parthenon, the Templo Mayor in today's Mexico City – all are eloquent fragments of former glories. But in any city street you might come across a ruined house, its windows blinded with boards; or a church where congregations once prayed being pummelled by the wrecker's ball: these urban *memento mori* are all reminders that, despite their flawless plate-glass walls and the seemingly eternal roar of the traffic, even the greatest cities can become ruins.

Tomorrow, as you pass that derelict office building on your way to work, remember that before too long all the other structures in the street will share its fate. Dynamite and demolition gangs will do their worst and then only photographs and memories will remain to record what the street once looked like. Indeed, modern architecture does not seem to age well. New skyscrapers in cities such as New York have a lifespan of just forty years or so. Each urban generation will grow up with a new skyline. But fast forward a few centuries and the city you now see around you, with its traffic-clogged roads and bustling sidewalks, may have vanished and been replaced by trees and undergrowth. Here and there the empty shells of buildings will be shrouded in ivy and cliff-nesting birds will peer down from the shattered remains of skyscrapers. To watch archaeologists excavate a medieval street, as I have done recently in Winchester, or to walk through a ruined city such as Pompeii, is to be reminded of the continuity of urban life throughout history. Paradoxically, it also makes you think about the future, about the day when archaeologists will excavate your street and ask: what was it like to live in this city?

'What a ruin it will make!' said H. G. Wells when he first saw the skyline of Manhattan.[54] Not content to let time do its worst, Wells himself brought ruin to the city he referred to as 'the modern Babylon' in his futuristic novel *The War in the Air*. It was a fate this 'apocalyptic' city was destined to experience repeatedly in fiction and film.[55] Many cities have been labelled the new Babylon, either as a curse or in recognition of greatness. But even ancient Babylon, once the most famous city of its day, ended in ruins.

In 1819, the British painter John Martin exhibited his epic depiction of *The Fall of Babylon*. Thousands of people flocked to see it, buying tickets to the value of £1,000 in just four days. The large canvas, measuring seven by eleven feet, offered a breathtaking panorama of Babylon at the moment when the city was seized by the Persian king Cyrus II in 538 BC. The sky is suitably apocalyptic, slashed by lightning and swirling with clouds. The invading galleys can be seen arriving in the harbour, while on the waterfront foot soldiers, cavalry and battle elephants are locked in bloody combat. In the foreground, terrified Babylonians rush to the promenades to watch the battle that will decide the fate of their city. Martin researched his paintings carefully. The Hanging Gardens can be seen on the right while in the background looms the city's most iconic structure – the Tower of Babel. There is an overwhelming sense of space in the painting and a doom-laden atmosphere that recalls the start of *Blade Runner*. However, Martin's painting moved its viewers not just because of its evocation of ancient history, but because they believed it offered a frightening glimpse of the future. There is little doubt that both Martin and the thousands who came to view his dramatic painting saw clear parallels between the fate of the ancient city and the one often condemned as a modern Babylon – London.

Apocalyptic novels, such as Mary Shelley's *The Last Man* (written from 1823 to 1824) about a twenty-first-century pandemic that kills everyone except one man, added to a growing sense of anxiety during the nineteenth century that, despite the unprecedented scale of urbanisation in Britain and elsewhere, the new cities would not survive. Rather, like the Tower of Babel, they would implode as a result of revolution, warfare or natural disasters. Classical history suggested that even the greatest civilisations ended in ruins and one of the lessons educated Victorians were bringing back from their Grand Tours

John Martin, *The Fall of Babylon* (mezzotint with etching, 1831).

of Europe was that, one day, even London's banks, churches and fine squares would be reduced to a ruinscape of ivy-covered brick and Portland stone.

It was a fear given eloquent form by Gustave Doré's 1873 engraving *The New Zealander*. This shows a man seated on the ruined arches of London Bridge while sketching the shattered dome of St Paul's Cathedral. The historic skyline of London has become a jagged series of broken buildings and the once fast-flowing River Thames is choked with reeds. Doré's apocalyptic image was inspired by a famous comment by the historian Thomas Macaulay in 1840, about a New Zealander visiting a future London that is in ruins. Just as Victorians travelled to ancient sites such as Babylon and Pompeii, so they feared the tourists of the future would pay homage to Britain's faded glory in the ruins of its once great city.[56]

Doré's image shows how depopulated cities could soon become overgrown with plants and trees. Readers of *After London; Or, Wild England*, an 1886 novel by the British naturalist Richard Jefferies, discovered that even the largest city in the world was not too big to be swallowed up by nature. Jefferies describes how, after an unexplained disaster, London is reduced within a couple of decades to a few 'crumbling ruins' in a landscape of marshes and woodland.[57]

It seems scarcely believable that after a few years without people, a city the size of London could be completely taken over by wild plants and animals. Just over a century after Jefferies' novel appeared, the *New Scientist* journal asked modern scientists to consider whether it could actually happen. They confirmed much of what he described. Without the protection of the Thames Barrier, the city would soon be inundated and the Thames flood plain would revert to marshland. Some 30,000 cubic metres of water have to be pumped out of the London Underground system every day and, without electricity, it would quickly fill with water. Other cities also face this problem. To keep New York's subway system dry requires 753 pumps, without which it, too, would flood within thirty-six hours.

In London, fast-growing shrubs such as buddleia, brought to Britain from the Himalayas to adorn Victorian gardens, would indeed spread rapidly throughout the depopulated city. Unchecked, their powerful roots can rapidly destroy walls and foundations. After an initial spread of plants and shrubs, trees would begin growing in open spaces – first alder (which fixes nitrogen in the soil, important for improving the fertility of impoverished urban ground), then birch and sycamore. Pripyat, in Ukraine, was once a modern Soviet city of about fifty thousand people. But after the Chernobyl nuclear disaster in 1986, it was evacuated and abandoned. Within a decade, the concrete paving stones in the city squares had been broken and lifted up almost a metre by tree roots, 'as if a giant earthquake had struck'.[58] Today, wild animals such as deer and boar move freely around the overgrown city, which has become a modern ghost town.

In just twenty years, London's beautiful Georgian squares would become densely wooded thickets, wild Edens enclosed by what were once grand terraces and are now home to insects and animals. Within one or two centuries, skyscrapers would begin to collapse due to subsidence and corrosion of their steel structures: 'In the mid-twenty-fourth century, the Great Leaning Tower of Canary Wharf is a major tourist attraction. The great great grandchildren, many times removed, of those who abandoned London now take ecocruises along the river, its banks lined with elder and willow and the flood plain beyond with poplar and ash. In the distance, a huge oak forest spreads over the low hills towards Hampstead Heath.'[59]

After a thousand years, few of the city's buildings would be left standing. Two millennia of urban history would have been expunged, the land restored to what it would have looked like to Roman colonists. All that would remain is marshland and a large, wooded hill – the tell of London. Nature would have finally reclaimed the land on which the once great city had been built.

But under the ground there will still be traces of the city. Eventually, after millions of years, coastal cities will be buried beneath hundreds of metres of sediments and such cities will become part of an 'Urban Stratum'. Go forward a hundred million years and a future archaeologist might unearth the remains of cities such as London or New York, compressed into a layer many metres thick of rubble, rusting iron artefacts, fragments of plastic and glass, burnt or rotting wood, and the outlines of subway tunnels, sewers, wires and crumpled pipes that were once the essential arteries of a living city. 'It is certain that a good deal of such things can, after burial, survive in some fashion almost forever,' notes geologist Jan Zalasiewicz.[60]

At the end of the movie *Planet of the Apes* (1968), astronaut George Taylor (Charlton Heston) stumbles across the half-buried Statue of Liberty as he is walking along a beach. It is a powerful conclusion to the film and the moment at which he realises that he has not travelled to another world, but forward in time. In 1925, a *New York Times* article speculated about what would remain of the vertical city for a future archaeologist to excavate. As they worked down through the 'traces of city over city, as man of today has found in ancient Troy', how would the archaeologists make sense of the strange urban artefacts they discovered? Among them might be a nightclub painting 'miraculously preserved like murals at Pompeii', a tile from a fireplace in a Harlem apartment, artefacts from the Metropolitan Museum, or a cowboy movie on a 'strange strip of film'. Would they think the flooded subways were the legendary labyrinth of the Minotaur, or mistake the Woolworth Building for the 'temple of a forgotten god'?[61]

In *Beneath the Planet of the Apes* (1970), astronaut John Brent (James Franciscus) discovers the ruins of New York preserved underground – the façade of the Stock Exchange, the Public Library, Radio City and St Patrick's Cathedral. He also finds a cult worshipping a deadly piece of twentieth-century technology – a cobalt doomsday bomb. It is a reminder that if there were a third world war, future archaeologists might find very little indeed of our cities, just ashes and carbonised remains. For the technologies of mass destruction perfected during the twentieth century mean that whole cities could be annihilated – literally wiped off the map – at the touch of a button.

The firestorms unleashed by the bombing of cities such as Hamburg and Tokyo during the Second World War created unprecedented scenes of urban devastation. The inferno caused by the fire bombs forced hot air upwards, sucking in air from the surrounding districts and creating hurricane-force winds. In the city centres, trees tumbled like matchsticks, civilians were blown screaming into the flames and windowpanes melted in the intense heat. People attempting to flee became stuck fast in the molten asphalt of the roads, unable to escape the raging fires. Tens of thousands died in each city. Kurt Vonnegut was a prisoner of war in Dresden when it was firebombed. 'They burnt the whole damn town down,' he recalled.[62] It had been, he said, 'the most beautiful city in the world.'[63] Afterwards, in Vonnegut's novel *Slaughterhouse-Five* (1969), Billy Pilgrim describes the city as being 'like the moon'.[64]

But the atomic bomb represented a revolution in the bloody history of urban warfare. When the first atomic bomb exploded at 8.16 on the morning of 6 August 1945 above the city of Hiroshima it was

The American Acropolis

Detroit – Motor City, the home of America's automobile industry – was once called 'the Capital of the Twentieth Century'.[65] This city was going places. It doubled in size between 1910 and 1920, becoming America's fourth largest city. Even as late as 1950, Detroit was a powerhouse of the American economy. But, sadly, its fortunes went into reverse. Today, Detroit's name is synonymous with urban decline. As one architect has put it: 'Unbuilding has surpassed building as the city's major architectural activity.'[66]

In the twenty years up to 1998, nine thousand building permits were issued in Detroit compared to 108,000 demolition permits. The city has lost half its population – nearly a million people – since it peaked in 1950. As people left to find work in other, more successful cities, their empty homes fell into ruin. By the 1980s, the city was knocking down two thousand buildings a year, but still more needed to be demolished. The remaining residents, fed up with living next door to ruins, lost patience with the authorities and took the law into their own hands. They demolished houses and left the rubble in the street, forcing the authorities to remove it. Others simply torched the empty houses. In Detroit, the night before Halloween became known as Devil's Night, when people set fire to abandoned houses. In 1984, 810 houses were burned in a single night.

Today, large swathes of the city are reverting to open prairie land, just as it was when the first French settlers arrived. About 100,000 of the 386,000 land parcels in Detroit are now empty. Feral dogs roam the city streets. Houses that are still lived in stand next to burnt-out shells, overgrown ruins and empty lots: 'it's like Berlin or Warsaw in 1945'.[67] Detroit is a city in crisis: a third of the downtown population of just under a million lives in poverty. Infant mortality is 50 per cent higher than the national average and the homicide rate here is triple what it is in the state as a whole. The mayor has twenty-seven bodyguards.[68]

In 1995, photographer Camilo José Vergara published *The New American Ghetto*, a documentary study of de-urbanisation, or the process of urban abandonment and recolonisation by nature. He described Detroit's skyscrapers as 'our most sublime ruins' and made a controversial suggestion: 'I propose that as a tonic for our imagination, as a call for renewal, as a place within our national memory, a dozen city blocks of pre-Depression skyscrapers be stabilized and left standing as ruins: an American Acropolis.' He called for the creation of a national park of ruins in the city centre, 'an urban Monument Valley'. He wanted the city to celebrate its ruins rather than be ashamed of them, and to welcome nature into the heart of its city: 'Midwestern prairie would be allowed as though for a few brief but terrible moments the sun had touched the earth. More than four square miles of Hiroshima were scorched reddish-brown by its intense heat. Metal and marble melted. Bodies were instantly vaporised. Nine-tenths of the city's buildings were destroyed. The infrastructure and essential services were wiped out to invade from the north. Trees, vines, and wildflowers would grow on roofs and out of windows; goats and wild animals – squirrels, possum, bats, owls, ravens, snakes, and insects – would live in the empty behemoths, adding their calls, hoots, and screeches to the smell of rotten leaves and animal droppings.[69] Perhaps unsurprisingly, the city authorities chose not to adopt this bold and original proposal, a sign of our uneasy relationship with urban ruins.

Ballroom, Lee Plaza Hotel, Detroit.

at a single blow. Of the 350,000 people in the city that day, more than 100,000 were killed immediately. Five years later people were still dying. The final death toll is thought to be in excess of 200,000.

A single atomic bomb could burn the heart out of a city. In 1946, mathematician and science fiction writer Chan Davis imagined one exploding in the centre of New York: 'A pillar of multicolored smoke rising from the city, erasing the Bronx and Manhattan down to Central Park, shattering windows in Nyack, lighting up the Albany sky.'[70] This was the nightmare of many people during the Cold War. But in the 1950s, scientists developed a new and still more fearsome city killer: the hydrogen bomb, or Hell Bomb as it was dubbed by the press. More than a thousand times more powerful than the Hiroshima bomb, this weapon meant that no city was safe. America's top secret *Emergency Plans Book* from 1958 estimated that almost one in five Americans would die in an H-bomb war. That's twenty-five million people. The same number would be injured, some seriously. The scale of such a disaster is unimaginable and one no country could survive.

The author Stephen Vincent Benét died in 1943 and so never saw what an atomic bomb could do to a real city. And yet his haunting short story 'By the Waters of Babylon' (1937) offers a powerful glimpse of the world after a nuclear holocaust. It is set in the time after 'the Great Burning when the fire fell out of the sky'. People now live in isolated villages. Science and technology have been replaced by super-stition and magic: America has been bombed back to the Stone Age. The cities are 'Dead Places' where no one dares to go. But one young man breaks the tribal taboo and returns to the biggest ruined city, known as 'the Place of the Gods'. He wanders the 'cracked and bro-ken' roads of the once great city whose only inhabitants now are feral dogs. He is awestruck by the few remaining skyscrapers: 'here and there one still stands, like a great tree in a forest, and the birds nest high'. They are, he believes, 'the ruins of the high towers of the gods'. But while exploring one of the apartment buildings, he finds the des-iccated corpse of its former occupant. Only then does he realise that the city dwellers were not gods but men like him: 'he had sat at his window, watching his city die – then he himself had died'. And the name of this city? 'New-york'.[71] The post-apocalyptic urban ruinscape became one of the most powerful motifs of the doomsday years of the Cold War. But the ruined city has now been resurrected as a symbol for the era of climate change, in films such as *The Day after Tomorrow* (2004) or Alexis Rockman's painting *Manifest Destiny* (2004), displayed in the lobby of the Brooklyn Museum of Art.

Ironically, in the end it was not nuclear war but economics that turned swathes of America's cities into ruinscapes. Following the riots of the late 1960s, city centres in the United States entered a spiral of decline. Global recession in the 1970s, exacerbated by lack of government and landlord investment, led to an 'age of rubble' in urban areas such as the South Bronx, Newark and Detroit.[72] From 1973, the night sky in America's ghettos blazed red as countless houses burned. Many of the fires were started by landlords who wanted to claim insurance on their properties, 'a criminal form of urban redevelopment'.[73]

Marshall Berman grew up in the Bronx in better times. When he returned in 1980, he was appalled to see 'an immense panorama of ruins unfolded before me.'[74] South Bronx had lost over 300,000 people in the 1970s. 'I spent many afternoons wandering through the ruins. They went on and on, block after block, mile after mile. For years, the ruins were the most impressive spectacle in New York, a city of spectacles.'[75] It was, he said in 1984, a form of 'urbicide', comparable to the devastation of bombed-out cities during the Second World War. To see one's city, the streets you played in as a child, reduced to ruins is a profoundly traumatic experience. The Old Testament Book of Lamentations powerfully expresses the anguish of the Jews at the destruction of Jerusalem by King Nebuchadnezzar's army in 587 BC:

How lonely sits the city that was full of people!
How like a widow she has become,
She that was a princess among the cities . . .
She weeps in the night, tears on her cheeks,
Among all her lovers, she has none to comfort her . . .[76]

And yet people and cities are immensely resilient. After Babylon was seized by King Cyrus II, the Jewish exiles returned to Jerusalem and rebuilt their city. Similarly, Hamburg, Tokyo, Dresden and Hiroshima have all risen from the ashes. Even the Bronx has a new lease of life. As Berman says, such urban ruins hold an important lesson for us all: they 'can show us what our lives are made of, and how in the midst of death we can make life anew'.[77]

AFTERWORD

In the middle of the twentieth century, New York became the world's first megacity, a metropolitan area with ten million or more inhabitants. By 2007, according to the UN, there were nineteen megacities, a figure that is expected to rise to at least twenty-six by 2025.

Today's cities and megacities are spreading out to form even larger urban systems. The term 'Megalopolis' was first used in 1961 to describe the sprawling city region that comprises Boston, New York, Philadelphia and Washington–Baltimore. Some fifty million people, or one in six of the US population, now live there. The Tokyo–Nagoya–Osaka corridor is an urban agglomeration of up to eighty million people – a megalopolis that offers a glimpse of what the urban future may look like.[1] These vast, amorphous city regions are themselves linked to others around the world by communications networks and by the globalised economy. The effect of decisions made in cities ripple around the world, changing lives in other cities and impacting communities in regions that as yet have no cities. The power and influence of cities is now truly global.

People are moving to cities in unprecedented numbers, particularly in the developing world. Half of China's population is expected to leave the countryside for the cities by mid-century. By then 70 per cent of its population will be urban, and about half of the populations of Africa and India will be city dwellers.[2] But as the number of people living in cities increases so, too, do the problems they face. The climate of the earth is changing and as a result cities are bracing themselves to cope with threats from a more hostile environment, including flooding and extreme storms, as well as rising temperatures and water shortages. They must also deal with profound social problems. For thousands of years, cities have proved highly effective at lifting people out of poverty. But today there is a growing divide between rich and poor. While globalisation and the opening-up of markets around the world has generated great wealth, it is unevenly distributed. The gated communities of the affluent stand next to shanty towns in which households have no clean running water. A third of all city dwellers now live in slums. In many cities of the developed world there is also rising income inequality, resulting in increasingly polarised societies. Inner London is far more divided than any other area in England. In terms of income, it has the highest proportion of households in both the richest tenth (19 per cent) and the poorest tenth (17 per cent) nationwide, measured after housing costs. London also has the highest poverty rate in England, with about two-fifths of children living in low-income households compared to a national average of one-third.[3]

For some, such as Richard Sennett, these trends reflect deep underlying issues concerning the governance and design of our cities: 'Something has gone wrong, radically wrong, in our conception of what a city itself should be.'[4] Today more than ever before we need successful cities – cities that are sustainable, that allow their inhabitants to live fulfilling and prosperous lives in inspiring yet liveable environments, and that bring people together rather than dividing them. For the environmental and social challenges of the twenty-first century will be won or lost in the city.

As the population of the world rises and resources become more scarce, the need to reduce the ecological footprint of cities is urgent. It has been said that the city is 'a fossil fuel construct in search of rapid restructuring'.[5] On average, each resident of Los Angeles spends a hundred hours per year waiting in traffic. Efficient, cheap, public transport systems and high-density living are undoubtedly among the keys to creating tomorrow's sustainable cities. New Yorkers are responsible for the emission of many times more greenhouse gasses than the inhabitants of Mumbai, but those same New Yorkers produce only about a third of the carbon dioxide of the typical American. City living can be green, but there is much work that remains to be done.

In their quest for sustainability, cities will become increasingly involved in generating their own energy from renewable sources. In the green cities of the future, new buildings will harvest their own energy from the sun and the wind, electric – and, one day, hydrogen – cars will render the internal combustion engine obsolete, and solar panels on parking lots and rooftops will power homes. City-wide computer systems will also monitor data from sensors spread throughout the physical fabric of the city so that energy resources are used more efficiently. As these systems are increasingly integrated and centrally controlled, we will see the emergence of sentient cities. In some regions, as the climate becomes more extreme, the urban environment may begin to take on the form of a life-support system, nurturing and protecting its human inhabitants from the elements. With the right policies and technology, urbanisation offers us the best opportunity of preserving our ways of living while minimising our environmental impact on the planet.

Many thousands of years ago, a revolution began when people in Mesopotamia left the villages where their kin had lived for generations and instead began sharing their lives with strangers in large communities. It was a revolution in how people lived and how they saw themselves. These first communities were the crucibles of our now global urban culture. From them emerged the building blocks of civilisation, including essential skills such as writing and mathematics. Wherever cities were built they became centres of worship, of trade, and of power, drawing people irresistibly from the surrounding landscape. These busy, diverse communities were schools of the human mind, stretching and shaping our intellects.

The city is our most remarkable invention. In this dynamic, cosmopolitan space lies the wellspring of our creativity as a species. The greatest cities nurture and stimulate the ideas in science and the arts that are at the very heart of human civilisation. For this reason, sustainable, humane and well-governed cities are our best hope for the future.

Notes

Introduction

1. Fernand Braudel, *The Structures of Everyday Life: The Limits of the Possible*, tr. Siân Reynolds (New York: Harper & Row, 1981), 481.
2. F. Scott Fitzgerald, *The Great Gatsby* (1926; repr. Harmondsworth: Penguin, 1967), 74–5.
3. Gilles Ivain [Ivan Chtcheglov], 'Formulary for a New Urbanism', *Internationale Situationniste*, No. 1 (June 1958), 15–20 (written 1953), cited from Tom McDonough, ed., *The Situationists and the City* (London: Verso, 2009), 33.
4. Heinrich Heine, *English Fragments*, 'London' (1828), in Havelock Ellis, ed., *The Prose Writings of Heinrich Heine*, tr. C. G. Leland (1887), cited from Heine, 'A German Poet's View of London', *New England Review*, 21, No. 2 (Spring 2000), 169.
5. Victor Shklovsky, 'Art as Technique' (1917). Originally published as 'Iskusstvo kak priëm'. In Lee T. Lemon and Marion J. Reis, trs., *Russian Formalist Criticism: Four Essays* (Lincoln: University of Nebraska Press, 1965). 12.
6. Iain Sinclair, *Lights Out for the Territory* (1st 1997; repr. London: Penguin, 2003), 4.

1 Arrival

1. It was the German nineteenth-century explorer Alexander von Humboldt who rather misleadingly named them the Aztecs. The Triple Alliance is a more precise description, as they consisted of people from three cultures of which the Mexica were the largest. It was the Mexica who founded Tenochtitlán, according to legend, in 1325. The god of the Mexica appeared to one of their priests and told him to look in the swamp for an eagle feeding on a fruit-bearing cactus known as a *tenochtli*. When they found the cactus on an island in Lake Texcoco (so the account of the grandson of the Mexica's last ruler goes), the god called out to them: 'Oh Mexica, it shall be there!' At which point the people rejoiced: 'Oh happy, oh blessed are we!/We have beheld the city that shall be ours!' (Charles C. Mann, *1491: New Revelations of the Americas before Columbus* (New York: Knopf, 2005), 115–17.
2. Bernal Díaz, *The Conquest of New Spain*, tr. J. M. Cohen (Harmondsworth: Penguin, 1973), 214.
3. Hernán Cortés, *Letters from Mexico*, tr. and ed. A. R. Pagden (London: OUP, 1972), 102.
4. Díaz (1973), 214.
5. Díaz (1973), 216.
6. Díaz (1973), 218.
7. Díaz (1973), 224.
8. Díaz (1973), 234.
9. Díaz (1973), 234–5.
10. Cortés (1972), 102.
11. Díaz (1973), 235.
12. John Reader, *Cities* (London: Heinemann, 2004), 137.
13. Díaz (1973), 233.
14. Díaz (1973), 229.
15. Stuart B. Schwartz, ed., *Victors and Vanquished: Spanish and Nahua Views of the Conquest of Mexico* (Boston, Mass.: Bedford; Basingstoke: Macmillan, 2000), 6.
16. Schwartz (2000), 11; cf. Mann (2005), 120–21.
17. Edward E. Calnek, 'The Internal Structure of Tenochtitlán', in Eric Robert Wolf, ed., *The Valley of Mexico: Studies in Pre-Hispanic Ecology and Sociology* (Albuquerque: University of New Mexico Press, 1976), 300.
18. Schwartz (2000), 6.
19. Cortés (1972), 108.
20. Mann (2005), 129. The effects of disease were devastating on the entire region. It has been estimated that the population of the region was 25.2 million in 1518. By 1623 that had fallen an astonishing 97 per cent to just 700,000. See Mann (2005), 129–30.
21. Cited in Schwartz (2000), 8.
22. From *Cantares mexicanos*, cited in Schwartz (2000), 213.
23. Jeremy A. Sabloff, *The Cities of Ancient Mexico: Reconstructing a Lost World* (London: Thames & Hudson, 1997), 57ff; Mann (2005), 115–16; Schwartz (2000), 3.
24. Ric Burns and James Sanders, *New York: An Illustrated History* (New York: Knopf, 1999), 226.

25. Lazarus wrote 'The New Colossus' in 1883 in support of the fund-raising campaign for the pedestal of Liberty. She never saw the finished statue, dying of Hodgkin's disease in 1897. A plaque with her poem was placed on the base of the statue in 1903.

26. Henry Roth, *Call It Sleep* (1934; repr. London: Penguin, 2006), 9.

27. 'The rush for our open door', *Leslie's Weekly* (5 January 1901), 10–11.

28. Burns and Sanders (1999), 223.

29. Thomas M. Pitkin, *Keepers of the Gate: A History of Ellis Island* (New York: New York University Press, 1975), 22.

30. See Pitkin (1975), 67; the peak day was on 17 April 1907: <http://www.ellisisland.org/genealogy/ellis_island_timeline.asp>

31. Henry James, *The American Scene* (London: Chapman & Hall, 1907), 84.

32. Pitkin (1975), 68.

33. Pitkin (1975), 68; Stephen Graham, *With Poor Immigrants to America* (1914).

34. Burns and Sanders (1999), 226.

35. *New York Tribune* (April 1896); Pitkin (1975), 24.

36. H. G. Wells, *The Future in America: A Search after Realities* (1906; repr. London: Granville, 1987), 34-5.

37. Louis Adamic, *Laughing in the Jungle: The Autobiography of an Immigrant in America* (New York: Harper & Brothers, 1932), 41–2.

38. *New York Times* (29 January 1911); cited in Pitkin (1975), 108.

39. Pitkin (1975), 71; in 1903, out of 631,885 aliens brought to Ellis Island, 6,839 were deported; Pitkin (1975), 94. The maximum rate of exclusion was reached in 1911, when 13,000 were excluded while 637,000 admitted, a rate of 2 per cent; Pitkin (1975), 73.

40. I. L. Finkel and M. J. Seymour, eds, *Babylon: Myth and Reality* (London: British Museum Press, 2008), 124–6.

41. *Herodotus*, tr. A.D. Godley (London: Heinemann, 1920), 4 vols, I, 225-7. One furlong is equivalent to about 201 metres. Clearly Herodotus exaggerated the size significantly. Belus, or Bel, means 'lord' and is Herodotus's term for Marduk, the greatest Babylonian god, the equivalent of the Greek Zeus.

42. Cited in Spiro Kostof, *The City Shaped: Urban Patterns and Meanings Through History* (London: Thames & Hudson, 1991), 282.

43. Kostof (1991), 279.

44. Giles Edgerton [Mary Fanton Roberts], 'How New York Has Redeemed Herself from Ugliness: An Artist's Revelation of the Beauty of the Skyscraper', *Craftsman*, 11 (January 1907), 458; cited in Gail Fenske, *The Skyscraper and the City: The Woolworth Building and the Making of Modern New York* (Chicago: University of Chicago Press, 2008), 55.

45. 'Towered Cities', *Living Age*, 42 (2 January 1909): 47; in Fenske (2008), 57.

46. See James Sanders, *Celluloid Skyline: New York and the Movies* (London: Bloomsbury, 2002).

47. Jan Morris, 'Manhattan, my isle of joy', *Financial Times* (15 June 2007) <http://us.ft.com/ftgateway/superpage.ft?news_id=ft006152007164821o382>

48. Vikras Swarup, *Slumdog Millionaire* (originally published as *Q & A*, 2005; repr. London: Black Swan, 2009), 178.

49. James Scott, *Railway Romance and Other Essays* (London, 1913), 89–90; cited in Jeffrey Richards and John M. MacKenzie, *The Railway Station: A Social History* (Oxford: OUP, 1986), 7.

50. Anon., *Round London* (London, 1896), 278; cited in Carroll L. V. Meeks, *The Railroad Station: An Architectural History* (New Haven: Yale University Press, 1956), 40–41.

51. Joseph Rykwert, *The Seduction of Place: The History and Future of the City* (Oxford: OUP, 2000; repr. 2004), 110.

52. Respectively: Peter Lecount (cited in Christian Wolmar, *Fire and Steam: A New History of the Railways in Britain* (London: Atlantic Books, 2007), 64), and Henry Noel Humphrys (in Meeks (1956), 40).

53. Wolmar (2007), 64-5.

54. <http://www.discoverychannel.co.uk/machines_and_engineering/building_the_biggest/busiest_railway/index.shtml> Accessed 7 January 2009.

55. Richards and MacKenzie (1986), 4.

56. Meeks (1956), 66.

57. Cited in Meeks (1956), iii.

58. G. K. Chesterton, *Tremendous Trifles* (London, 1909), 219–24; in Richards and MacKenzie (1986), 11–12.

59. Jean Dethier, ed., *All Stations* (London: Science Museum, 1981), 6.

60. Meeks (1956), 124.

61. Paul Theroux describes it as 'just fakery, India mimicking England, a hodgepodge of disappointed Gothic' (*The Elephant Suite* (London: Penguin, 2008), 191). However, in his 1973 travelogue *The Great Railway Bazaar*, he was rather more flattering, describing it as 'the most distinguished architecture the British Empire produced (cover your good eye, squint at Victoria Station in Bombay, and you see the grey majesty of St Paul's Cathedral)'. Paul Theroux, *The Great Railway Bazaar* (repr. London: Penguin, 2008), 140.

62. Mark Twain, *Following the Equator: A Journey Around the World* (1897; repr. New York: Dover, 1989), 345.

63. Twain (1989), 400–404.

64. He was describing Mumbai's commuter station, Churchgate. V. S. Naipaul, *An Area of Darkness* (1964; repr. New York: Vintage, 2002), 39.

65. Paul Theroux, *The Elephant Suite* (London: Penguin, 2008), 191–2.

66. Émile Zola responding to Paul Bourget's assertion that stations were ugly. Richards and MacKenzie (1986), 327.

67. Le Corbusier, *Une Ville Contemporaine pour 3 Millions d'Habitants* (1922), cited from Alastair Gordon, *Naked Airport: A Cultural History of the World's Most Revolutionary Structure* (Chicago: University of Chicago Press, 2004), 69.

68. Meeks (1956), 155; Richards and Mackenzie (1986), 35.

69. 'Circular station is centre of attraction', *People's Daily*, 11 Jul 2006. See also AREP's website: <http://www.arep.fr/en/projects/new-railway-stations/shanghai-south>

70. Jan Morris, 'Triumph of the capital', *Financial Times* (26 October 2007),.

71. 'Major new station opens in Berlin', BBC News Online, 27 May 2006 <http://news.bbc.co.uk/I/hi/world/europe/5022498.stm>

72. Richards and MacKenzie (1986), 103.

2 History

1. Gwendolyn Leick, *Mesopotamia: The Invention of the City* (London: Penguin, 2002), 1.

2. Charles Gates, *Ancient Cities: The Archaeology of Urban Life in the Ancient Near East and Egypt, Greece, and Rome* (London: Routledge, 2003), 29.

3. 'Introduction', tr. Andrew George, *The Epic of Gilgamesh* (London: Penguin, 2003), xvi. Mesopotamia comprised two regions: Sumer in the south and Akkad in the north. Akkadian was a Semitic language related to Hebrew and Arabic. Under the reign of King Sargon (2340–2284 BC) the Akkad state controlled the entire region, from the Gulf to Syria. The site of Sargon's capital of Akkad has never been found but is believed to be near Kish (Leick (2002), 93–5).

4. Marc van de Mieroop, *The Ancient Mesopotamian City* (Oxford: OUP, 1999), 23; cf. Guillermo Algaze, *Ancient Mesopotamia at the Dawn of Civilization: The Evolution of an Urban Landscape* (Chicago: University of Chicago Press, 2008).

5. Lewis Mumford, *The City in History: Its Origins, Its Transformations, and Its Prospects* (London: Secker & Warburg, 1961), 19.

6. Gates (2003), 18; J. G. D. Clark, *World Prehistory in New Perspective* (Cambridge: CUP, 1989), 49–55.

7. Aiden Southall, *The City in Time and Space* (Cambridge: CUP, 1998), 23.

8. See generally David Christian, *Maps of Time: An Introduction to Big History* (Berkeley: University of California Press, 2005), 267–71.

9. Southall (1998), 29; John Reader says eighty thousand (*Cities* (London: Heinemann, 2004), 39).

10. Leick (2002), 45.

11. Van de Mieroop (1999), 37; Gates (2003), 32.

12. Southall (1998), 28.

13. See Mumford (1961), 74.

14. Gates (2003), 24ff. For information on the continuing work at this remarkable site, see: <http://www.catalhoyuk.com/>

15. Mumford (1961), 33.

16. Reader (2004), 74.

17. Italo Calvino, *Invisible Cities*, tr. William Weaver (1972; London: Vintage, 1997), 44.

18. See Nancy Shatzman Steinhardt, *Chinese Imperial City Planning* (Honolulu: University of Hawaii Press, 1990), 6–8; cf. Southall (1998), 40.

19. Li'Chi, in Paul Wheatley, *The Pivot of the Four Quarters: A Preliminary Enquiry into the Origins and Character of the Ancient Chinese City* (Edinburgh: Edinburgh University Press, 1971), 418.

20. See Ezekiel, Chapters 40–48; on the shape of the Temple: Kings, I, 6: 16–20; Chronicles, II, 3: 8.

21. The Book of Revelation, 21: 2; 21: 11; 21: 18; see on this Helen Rosenau, *The Ideal City: Its Architectural Evolution in Europe* (1st 1959; London: Methuen, 1983), 18.

22. Rosenau (1983), 49.

23. Wolfgang Braunfels, tr. Kenneth J. Northcott, *Urban Design in Western Europe: Regime and Architecture, 900–1900* (1st 1976; Chicago: University of Chicago Press, 1990), 149.

24. Leonardo da Vinci, *Notebooks* (1st 1952; Oxford: OUP, 2008), 201–2.

25. Ian Tod and Michael Wheeler, *Utopia* (London: Orbis, 1978), 37; on the shape of the city: Sigfried Giedion, *Space, Time and Architecture: The Growth of a New Tradition* (1st 1941; Cambridge, Mass.: Harvard University Press, 2008), 46.

26. Rosenau (1983), 46.

27. Rosenau (1983), 49.

28. Braunfels (1990), 158.

29. Charles Nicholl, *Leonardo da Vinci: The Flights of the Mind* (London: Penguin, 2005), 202.

30. Leonardo da Vinci, *Notebooks* (2008), 357–8.

31. Rosenau (1983), 52.

32. Saint Thomas More, *Utopia* (London: Dent, 1978), 59–61.

33. Plato, *Timaeus and Critias* (Harmondsworth: Penguin, 1977), 38.

34. Thomas Campanella, tr. A. M. Elliot and R. Millner, *The City of the Sun* (Italian: La città del Sole; Latin: Civitas Solis; 1st 1623; London: Journeyman Press, 1981), 16. On Bruegel: Rosenau (1983), 78.

35. Mark Girouard, *Cities and People: A Social and Architectural History* (New Haven: Yale University Press, 1985), 352.

36. Braunfels (1990), 176.

37. See Spiro Kostof, *The City Shaped: Urban Patterns and Meanings Through History* (London: Thames & Hudson, 1991), 44ff. On the fractal structure of cities, see Michael Batty, 'The Size, Shape and Scale of Cities', *Science*, vol. 319 (8 February 2008), 769–71.

38. Deyan Sudjic, 'Theory, Policy and Practice', in Ricky Burdett and Deyan Sudjic, eds, *The Endless City* (London: Phaidon, 2007), 42–3.

39. Gates (2003), 60.

40. Hannah B. Higgins, *The Grid Book* (Cambridge, Mass.: MIT Press, 2009), 53.

41. Cited in Kostof (1991), 105. According to Mumford, Miletus was 'the first historic example of a deliberately fabricated neighbourhood unit', Mumford (1961), 193.

42. Cited in Higgins (2009), 59.

43. Higgins (2009), 59.

44. Cecilia Lindqvist, *China: Empire of Living Symbols* (1998; repr. Cambridge, Mass.: Da Capo, 2008), 154; on Suzhou see also Kostof (1991), 96.

45. Kostof (1991), 99.

46. See Kostof (1991), 107. On Roman army camps, see Gates (2003), 323.

47. Cited in Higgins (2009), 68–9.

48. Ric Burns and James Sanders, *New York: An Illustrated History* (New York: Knopf, 1999), 52.

49. Rem Koolhaas, *Delirious New York: A Retroactive Manifesto for Manhattan* (1978; repr. New York: Monacelli Press, 1994), 18–19.

50. Ebenezer Howard, *Garden Cities of To-morrow* (first pub. 1898 as *To-morrow: A Peaceful Path to Real Reform*; repr. Eastbourne: Attic Books, 1985), 11.

51. For a discussion of the international reach of the garden city idea, see Robert H. Kargon, and Arthur P. Molella, *Invented Edens: Techno-cities of the Twentieth Century* (Cambridge, Mass.: MIT Press, 2008).

52. Le Corbusier, cited in Geoffrey Broadbent, *Emerging Concepts in Urban Space Design* (London: Van Nostrand, 1990), 129.

53. See Witold Rybczynski, 'Master Builder', *New York Times* (7 December 2008) <http://www.nytimes.com/2008/12/07/books/review/Rybczynski-t.html>

54. Cited in Edwin Heathcote, 'Urban outfitters', *Financial Times* (29 June 2007).

55. Richard J. Williams, *Brazil* (London: Reaktion, 2009), 105.

56. Williams (2009), 110.

57. Cited in Benjamin Schwarz, 'A Vision in Concrete', *Atlantic Monthly* (July/August 2008) <http://www.theatlantic.com/doc/200807/editors-choice>

58. Richard Sennett, 'The Open City', in Burdett and Sudjic (2007), 290–92.

59. Sudjic, in Burdett and Sudjic (2007), 42.

60. Bryan Walsh, 'Desert Dreams', *Time* (25 February 2008), 37–41.

61. Sudjic, 'Cities on the edge of chaos', *Observer* (9 March 2008).

62. Eugène Toulouzé cited from Colin Jones, *Paris: Biography of a City* (London: Penguin, 2006), 15.

63. Mumford (1961), 7.

64. Cited from Liza Picard, *Restoration London: Everyday Life in London 1660–1670* (1997; repr. London: Phoenix, 2003), 13.

65. Cited from Picard (2003), 219.

66. Amanda Claridge, *Rome: An Oxford Archaeological Guide* (1998; repr. Oxford: OUP, 2010), 447.

67. G. W. Wallerston, 'Ornamental Graveyards', *Knickerbocker*, 7, no. 4 (April 1836), 376, cited from David Charles Sloane, *The Last Great Necessity: Cemeteries in American History* (Baltimore: Johns Hopkins University Press, 1991), 49.

68. See Jörg Vögele, *Urban Mortality Change in England and Germany, 1870–1913* (Liverpool: Liverpool University Press, 1998), 3.

69. Sloane (1991), 3.

70. John Loudon, cited from Hugh Meller, *London Cemeteries: An Illustrated Guide* (1981; repr. Aldershot: Scolar, 1994), 63. Abney Park was also influenced by the design of Mount Auburn Cemetery in America, as can be seen from the design of the Egyptian Revival-style gates.

71. Henry Arthur Bright, cited from Sloane (1991), 55–6.

72. Sloane (1991), 56, 71.

73. Hubert Eaton, 'The Builder's Creed' (1917), in Eaton, 'Creation of Forest Lawn', *Park and Cemetery*, 29 (September 1929), 209–10, cited from Sloane (1991), 167.

74. Yevgeny Zamyatin, *We*, tr. Bernard Guilbert Guerney (1924; Harmondsworth: Penguin, 1984), 99.

75. Mumford (1961), 45.

76. Plato, *The Laws*; cited from Mumford (1961), 51: although Mumford points out that Plato's ideal city didn't have a wall.

77. Richard Holmes, ed., *Battlefield: Decisive Conflicts in History* (Oxford: OUP, 2006), 3.

78. Jeffrey A. Lockwood, *Six-Legged Soldiers: Using Insects as Weapons of War* (New York: OUP, 2009), 18–21.

79. Holmes (2006), 4.

80. Higgins (2009), 19.

81. James W. P. Campbell and Will Pryce, *Brick: A World History* (London: Thames & Hudson, 2003), 33.

82. Van de Mieroop (1999), 37.

83. Mumford (1961), 67, citing contemporary text.

84. *The Epic of Gilgamesh*, Tablet 1, translated by E.A. Speiser, cited in Mumford (1961), 67.

85. Excavations suggest that Herodotus may have exaggerated. The true circuit of Babylon's walls was nearer eighteen kilometres, although it is possible he was describing another defensive structure. See Julian E. Reade, 'Early travellers on the wonders', in I. L. Finkel and M. J. Seymour, eds, *Babylon: Myth and Reality* (London: British Museum Press, 2008), 113–5.

86. *Herodotus*, tr. A.D. Godley (London: Heinemann, 1920), 4 vols, I, 223, 225.

87. *Cheng*, *du* and *jing* are the three most common Chinese terms translated into English as 'city' (Steinhardt (1990), 26). In some ancient texts the character for capital also means 'large granary'. This is because taxes were often paid in grain kept by the ruler in the imperial city where great quantities were stored. Lindqvist (2008), 285.

88. Steinhardt (1990), 36.

89. Steinhardt (1990), 57.

90. Lindqvist (2008), 281.

91. Lindqvist (2008), 283.

92. Lindqvist (2008), 280.

93. Steinhardt (1990), 13.

94. This is the latest and most accurate estimate of its length: <http://news.bbc.co.uk/1/hi/world/asia-pacific/8008108.stm> Accessed 20 April 2009.

95. Jonathan Barnett, *The Elusive City: Five Centuries of Design, Ambition and Miscalculation* (London: Herbert Press, 1987), 2.

96. Peter Clark, *European Cities and Towns, 400–2000* (Oxford: OUP, 2009), 12.

97. Clark (2009), 80.

98. Mumford (1961), 251.

99. Clark (2009), 195–6.

100. 'Kowloon Walled City', *Newsline*, University of Columbia: <http://www.arch.columbia.edu/gsap/21536>. See Greg Girard and Ian Lambot, *City of Darkness: Life in Kowloon Walled City* (Watermark, 1993).

101. Girard and Lambot (1993).

102. 'Bid to rescue Berlin Wall artwork', BBC News Online, 16 October 2008 <http://news.bbc.co.uk/go/pr/fr/-/1/hi/world/europe/7674135.stm>; see <http://www.eastsidegallery.com/>

3 Customs

1. Walter Ong, *Orality and Literacy* (1982; repr. New York: Routledge, 2002), 77.

2. Cited from Maryanne Wolf, *Proust and the Squid: The Story and Science of the Reading Brain* (Cambridge: Icon, 2008), 33.

3. Wolf (2008), 27; cf. Andrew Robinson, *The Story of Writing* (London: Thames & Hudson, 2007), 58–60.

4. John Reader, *Cities* (London: Heinemann, 2004), 40.

5. See Wolf (2008), 34–5.

6. See Reader (2004) for more on this. Among the remarkable details that have survived at Ur is a list of the materials needed to construct a ship, including 178 mature date palms and 17,644 bundles of reeds (pp. 40–41).

7. Cited in Lewis Mumford, *The City in History: Its Origins, Its Transformations, and Its Prospects* (London: Secker & Warburg, 1961), 78; see also the passages cited in Reader (2004), 38, and Robinson (2007), 90. When sent as letters, the tablet was encased in a clay envelope. The British Museum has such a letter, dated around 1850 BC, from Ashur-malik to his brother Ashur-idi complaining that, although winter has already come, he and his family have been left in Ashur in Assyria without food, clothes or fuel. Online here: <http://www.britishmuseum.org/explore/highlights/highlight_objects/me/c/cuneiform_tablet_and_envelope.aspx>

8. See Robinson (2007), 162.

9. Wolf (2008), 53.

10. Jonathan Taylor, 'Neo-Babylonian kings at Babylon', in I. L. Finkel and M. J. Seymour, eds, *Babylon: Myth and Reality* (London: British Museum Press, 2008), 68. Taylor uses the spelling 'Hammurapi'. A translation of the Code can be read online: <http://avalon.law.yale.edu/subject_menus/hammenu.asp>

11. Cited from Robinson (2007), 90. Punishments were harsher for those offending against an *awilum* (a person having full rights) than a *muškenum* (person with lesser rights). As far as the Code was concerned, a slave (*wardum*) had no rights and thus compensation for any injury was paid to the owner. (Gwendolyn Leick, *Mesopotamia: The Invention of the City* (London: Penguin, 2002), 186.)

12. Cited from Hannah B. Higgins, *The Grid Book* (Cambridge, Mass.: MIT Press, 2009), 41.

13. Wolf (2008), 53.

14. The Greek word for 'papyrus', or 'writing material', was also *byblos*, from which comes the later word *biblion*, book, and hence the Bible. (Gerhard Herm, tr. Caroline Hillier, *The Phoenicians: The Purple Empire of the Ancient World* (London: Futura, 1975), 27.)

15. Robinson (2007), 165; cf. Moscati Sabatino, tr. Alastair Hamilton, *The World of the Phoenicians* (1965; London: Sphere, 1973), 123.

16. Robinson (2007), 166.

17. '"Tit townies" struggle to be heard', BBC News Online, 3 June 2009 <http://news.bbc.co.uk/today/hi/today/newsid_8079000/8079780.stm>

18. Ronnie Ferguson, *A Linguistic History of Venice*, Biblioteca dell' 'Archivum Romanicum', Serie II: Linguistica (n.p.: Leo S. Olschki Editore, 2007), 34.

19. Peter Clark, *European Cities and Towns,*

400–2000 (Oxford: OUP, 2009), 186.

20. For the definitive study of 'venexian', see Ferguson (2007), 283–6. The Jewish Museum of Venice: <http://www.museoebraico.it/english/ghetto.html>

21. Julian Franklyn, *The Cockney: A Survey of London Life and Language* (London: André Deutsch, 1953), 47f.

22. William Matthews, *Cockney Past and Present: A Short History of the Dialect of London* (London: Routledge, 1938); cited in Peter Ackroyd, *London: The Biography* (London: Vintage, 2001), 159.

23. Franklyn (1953), 244.

24. *A Conference on the Teaching of English in Elementary Schools* (London County Council, 1909); cited in Franklyn (1953), 222.

25. Ackroyd (2001), 159.

26. See Liza Picard, *Restoration London: Everyday Life in London 1660–1670* (London: Phoenix, 2003), 198; Franklyn (1953), 231, 251ff.

27. Ackroyd (2001), 159.

28. Franklyn (1953), 278.

29. Walford's tube station in *EastEnders* is Walford East, which takes the place of the real Bromley-by-Bow station. See: <http://en.wikipedia.org/wiki/Walford_East>

30. Mian Ridge, 'Black slang in the pink', *Financial Times* (21 October 2005) <http://www.ft.com/cms/s/2/677d827a-411f-11da-a208-00000e2511c8.html>

31. See the frontispiece of *The Slang Dictionary; or, the Vulgar Words, Street Phrases and Fast Expression of High and Low Society* (London: John Camden Hotten, 1869): <http://www.archive.org/stream/slangdictionaryo00hottrich#page/n7/mode/2up>

32. Robert Reisner, *Graffiti: Two Thousand Years of Wall Writing* (New York: Cowles, 1971), 99.

33. Nigel Rees, *Phrases and Sayings* (London: Bloomsbury, 1995), 278. Kilroy has spread around the world, spotted everywhere from the very top of the Statue of Liberty's torch to the base of the Marco Polo Bridge in China. It even appeared in Stalin's bathroom at the 1945 Potsdam Conference. 'Who is Kilroy?' the Soviet leader was heard to ask. According to Peter Viereck's poem 'Kilroy' (1948), 'God is like Kilroy; He, too, sees it all.' (Reisner (1971), 14–17.)

34. Wildstyle is defined as 'an energetic interlocking construction of letters with arrows and other forms that signify movement and direction.' Henry Chalfant and Martha Cooper, *Subway Art* (London: Thames & Hudson, 1984); cited in 'Graffiti: Introduction', *Art Crime*: <http://www.graffiti.org/faq/graffiti_intro.html>

35. Mary Beard, *Pompeii: The Life of a Roman Town* (London: Profile Books, 2008), 59.

36. Beard (2008), 114, 183, 115.

37. Jeff Chang, 'American Graffiti', *The Village Voice* (10 September 2002) <http://www.villagevoice.com/2002-09-10/books/american-graffiti/1>

38. Sacha Jenkins, 'Introduction', in Jon Naar, *The Birth of Graffiti* (Munich: Prestel, 2007), 12.

39. 'Graffiti: Introduction', *Art Crime*: <http://www.graffiti.org/faq/graffiti_intro.html>

40. Jon Naar, 'On becoming a graffiti photographer', in Naar (2007), 18.

41. Bloomberg speaking in 2002; Chang (2002).

42. Brassaï was the pioneer of graffiti photography, working in Paris over thirty years. See his *Graffiti* (Stuttgart: Belser, 1960).

43. Naar, 'On becoming a graffiti photographer', in Naar (2007), 15–20.

44. Pichação (literally, 'trace' or 'stain') first appeared in São Paulo's streets in the 1980s. Stylistically it is inspired by the record sleeves of heavy metal bands like AC/DC and Slayer, as well as Brazilian bands such as Sepultura. Its angular, straight-letter style is reminiscent of runes. Office blocks rather than subway cars are the preferred target of pichadores. François Chastanet, 'Pichação', *Eye*, 56 (Summer 2005): <http://www.eyemagazine.com/feature.php?id=123&fid=540>

45. 'Street Art', Tate Modern, London, 21 May–25 August 2008, curated by Cedar Lewisohn. On Nunca's work: <http://www.lost.art.br/nunca.htm>. For more Brazilian street art, see: <http://www.lost.art.br/graff.htm>

46. Rebecca Solnit, *Wanderlust: A History of Walking* (London: Verso, 2002), 216.

47. Eric Hobsbawm, *The Age of Empire, 1875–1914*

(London: Weidenfeld & Nicolson, 1987; repr. 2002), 129.

48. Solnit (2002), 225–6. See also <http://en.wikipedia.org/wiki/Mothers_of_the_Plaza_de_Mayo>

49. *The Oxford English Dictionary* defines a demonstration as 'a public manifestation, by a number of persons, of interest in some public question, or sympathy with some political or other cause; usually taking the form of a procession and mass-meeting.' The first recorded usage in this sense is from 1839.

50. *The Times* (9 August 1872); cited from Donald C. Richter, *Riotous Victorians* (Athens: Ohio University Press, 1981), 87.

51. It is also enshrined in the Universal Declaration of Human Rights and the European Convention of Human Rights.

52. E. W. Kenworthy, '200,000 March for Civil Rights in Orderly Washington Rally', *New York Times* (29 August 1963), 1; cited in Simon Hall, 'Marching on Washington: The Civil Rights and Anti-War Movements of the 1960s', in Matthias Reiss, ed., *The Street as Stage: Protest Marches and Public Rallies since the Nineteenth Century* (Oxford: OUP, 2007), 215.

53. Norman Mailer, *The Armies of the Night: History as a Novel, the Novel as History* (New York: 1994), 119–20, 122–3; cited by Hall, 'Marching on Washington', in Reiss (2007), 225.

54. George Orwell, *The Road to Wigan Pier* (San Diego; n.d.), 86–7; cited in Matthias Reiss, 'Marching on the Capital: National Protest Marches of the British Unemployed in the 1920s and 1930s', in Reiss (2007), 168; on the Jarrow march, see ibid., 149.

55. In 2004, the Peace March was revived and, as in 1958, a rally was held in Trafalgar Square at the start before four hundred marchers walked to Aldermaston. See P. D. Smith, *Doomsday Men: The Real Dr Strangelove and the Dream of the Superweapon* (London: Penguin, 2007), 437.

56. VE Day was on 8 May 1945. On the CND demonstrations, see P. D. Smith, '"Gentlemen: You are mad!": Mutual Assured Destruction and Cold War Culture', in Dan Stone, ed., *The Oxford Handbook on Postwar European History* (Oxford: OUP, 2012).

57. 'Millions join global anti-war protests', BBC News Online, 17 February 2003 <http://news.bbc.co.uk/1/hi/world/europe/2765215.stm>

58. Cited in Reiss (2007), 15.

59. Nezar AlSayyad, *Cairo: Histories of a City* (Harvard: Belknap, 2011), 209.

60. Mohamed Elshahed, 'Tahrir Square: Social Media, Public Space', *Design Observer*, 27 February 2011: <http://places.designobserver.com/feature/tahrir-square-social-media-public-space/25108/>

61. Elshahed (2011).

62. Solnit (2002), 220–21. The streets of Paris have seen major insurrections in 1830, 1848, 1871, and 1968. Since the 1950s, demonstrations here have been called 'manifs' (short for 'manifestation'). Because of a rich tradition of street protest, the French authorities are very wary of demonstrations. Indeed, the French constitutions of the 1880s, 1946 and 1958 omitted the right to public demonstration. (Reiss (2007), 311.) See also Eric Hazan, *The Invention of Paris: A History in Footsteps*, tr. David Fernbach (London: Verso, 2010).

63. The remark is Victor Fournel's. Cited in Colin Jones, *Paris: Biography of a City* (London: Penguin, 2006), 366.

64. Solnit (2002), 225.

65. William R. Doerner et al., 'Our Time Has Come', *Time* (4 December 1989), 21 <http://www.time.com/time/magazine/article/0,9171,959148,00.html>

66. Solnit (2002), 230.

67. This idea is explored in Josef Reichholf, *Warum die Menschen sesshaft wurden: Das größte Rätsel unserer Geschichte* (Frankfurt am Main: Fischer, 2008).

68. Although Carnival can begin as early as Twelfth Night (6 January), the season generally starts on the Sunday before Ash Wednesday, known as Septuagesima.

69. Carnival began in Venice in the thirteenth century when the day before Lent became a holiday. In more recent years, there was a break of about two centuries when Carnival was not celebrated. But the city rediscovered it in 1980.

70. Tiziano Scarpa, *Venice Is a Fish: A Cultural Guide* (London: Serpent's Tail, 2009), 45.

71. Equally unusual is 'La Tomatina', a tomato fight festival held on the last Wednesday of August each year in the town of Buñol in the Valencia region of Spain.

72. See Robert H. Kargon and Arthur P. Molella, *Invented Edens: Techno-cities of the Twentieth Century* (Cambridge, Mass: MIT Press, 2008), 92ff.

73. Pierre Laszlo, *Citrus: A History* (Chicago: University of Chicago Press, 2007), 133–5; cf. 'Italy's Battle of the Oranges', *Spiegel* (8 June 2008): <http://www.spiegel.de/international/europe/0,1518,570471,00.html>

74. See <http://www.koelnerkarneval.de/> and <http://en.wikipedia.org/wiki/Cologne_carnival>

75. Trinidad and Tobago National Library: <http://www.nalis.gov.tt/carnival/carnival.htm>

76. Max Harris, *Carnival and Other Christian Festivals: Folk Theology and Folk Performance* (Austin: University of Texas Press, 2003), 201.

77. Harris (2003), 192.

78. Harris (2003), 195.

79. Harris (2003), 196.

80. Carol Flake, *New Orleans: Behind the Masks of America's Most Exotic City* (New York: Grove, 1994), 5; cited in Stephen Verderber, *Delirious New Orleans: Manifesto for an Extraordinary American City* (Austin: University of Texas Press, 2009), 146.

81. Verderber (2009), 145.

82. Verderber (2009), 148, 152.

83. In their architectural complexity, termite mounds resemble cities. See Jan Zalasiewicz, *The Earth After Us: What Legacy Will Humans Leave in the Rocks?* (Oxford: OUP, 2008), 171.

84. Bill Freund, *The African City: A History* (Cambridge: CUP, 2007), 12.

85. Finkel and Seymour, eds (2008), 126.

86. Ideal cities, such as Tommaso Campanella's *The City of the Sun* (1602), often developed this aspect of urban design.

87. Henri Stierlin describes it as 'a great cathedral-mosque … a work of dazzling splendour'. The Lutfullah Mosque was completed 1628, the year the Taj Mahal, at Agra, was begun. The architect of this mausoleum is unknown but Stierlin suggests he was influenced by this mosque. Henri Stierlin, *Islamic Art and Architecture* (London: Thames & Hudson, 2001), 142.

88. See Spiro Kostof, *The City Shaped: Urban Patterns and Meanings Through History* (London: Thames & Hudson, 1991), 172–3.

89. Le Corbusier, *Towards a New Architecture*; cited from Mary Beard, *The Parthenon* (London: Profile Books, 2002), 4.

90. Virginia Woolf visited twice, in 1906 and 1932. Beard (2002), 10.

91. Richard Sennett, *Flesh and Stone: The Body and the City in Western Civilization* (New York: Norton, 1997), 51; Beard (2002), 28, 73, 133–7.

92. See Beard (2002), 28. In Nashville, Tennessee (the Athens of the South), there is a replica of the Parthenon accurate to three millimetres. Originally built for the Tennessee Centennial Exposition, 1897, it was rebuilt in concrete in the 1920s. In 1990 a vast thirteen-metre statue of Athena was unveiled. It features in Robert Altman's 1975 film *Nashville*. (Beard (2002), 7.)

93. The eyewitness was Edward Dodwell; Beard (2002), 92.

94. Sennett (1994), 38. At one point during the restoration they considered enclosing the whole of the Acropolis beneath a Perspex dome. A fine museum has now been built on the slopes below the Parthenon.

95. F. E. Peters, *Jerusalem and Mecca: The Typology of the Holy City in the Near East* (New York: New York University Press, 1986), ix.

96. Mark Twain, *Following the Equator: A Journey Around the World* (1897; repr. New York: Dover, 1989): 'religious Vesuvius': 494; 'Benares is older': 480; 'Yes, the city': 484.

97. Cited in Ross E. Dudd, *The Adventures of Ibn Battuta: A Muslim Traveler of the 14th Century* (Berkeley: University of California Press, 1989), 65.

98. Dudd (1989), 69.

99. Muhammad ibn Ahmad Ibn Jubayr, *The Travels of Ibn Jubayr*, tr. R. J. C. Broadhurst (London, 1952), 80; cited in Dudd (1989), 72–3.

100. Richard Burton, *Personal Narrative of a Pilgrimage to El-Medinah and Mecca*, 2 vols

(New York, 1964), II, 161; cited in Dudd (1989), 73.

101. Augustine's *The City of God*, 14.1; see James Dougherty, *The Fivesquare City: The City in the Religious Imagination* (Notre Dame: University of Notre Dame Press, 1980), 25.

102. Dougherty (1980), 17.

103. Hebrews 13: 14; Dougherty (1980), 17.

104. Dougherty (1980), 48.

105. Peters (1986), 6.

106. Peters (1986), 93.

107. Peter Clark, *European Cities and Towns, 400–2000* (Oxford: OUP, 2009), 40.

108. Sigfried Giedion, *Space, Time and Architecture: The Growth of a New Tradition* (1941; repr. Cambridge, Mass.: Harvard University Press, 2008), 92. Sixtus's master plan of 1589 can be seen in Giedion, 83.

109. 'Lettre di Angelo Grillo, Venezia, 1612', in Antonio Muñoz, *Domenico Fontana* (Rome, 1944), 39; cited in Giedion (2008), 95.

110. Giedion (2008), 100.

4 Where to Stay

1. Witold Rybczynski, *City Life* (Toronto: Harper Perennial, 1996), 66.

2. Robert M. Fogelson, *Downtown: Its Rise and Fall, 1880–1950* (New Haven: Yale University Press, 2001), 10.

3. Herman Melville, *Moby-Dick* (1851), ch. 1, 'Loomings'.

4. Fogelson (2001), 11.

5. Fogelson (2001), 17. Unlike in New York, Chicago's downtown is actually at the east end of town.

6. Fogelson (2001), 12.

7. Julian Ralph, 'The City of Brooklyn', *Harper's New Monthly Magazine* (April 1893), 659–60; cited from Fogelson (2001), 15.

8. Jack Thomas, *Boston Globe* (11 February 1988); cited from Fogelson (2001), 2.

9. Fogelson (2001), 14.

10. Cited from Fogelson (2001), 13.

11. Cited from Fogelson (2001), 15.

12. *New York Herald* (1864); cited from Fogelson (2001), 45.

13. Fogelson notes that streetcars typically travelled at 4–6mph in normal conditions, but at only 1–2mph in heavy traffic (p. 45).

14. James Dabney McCabe, *New York by Sunlight and Gaslight* (New York, 1882), 143; cited from Fogelson (2001), 16.

15. Cited from Fogelson (2001), 19.

16. James Fullerton Muirhead, *America the Land of Contrasts* (Boston, 1898), 207; cited from Fogelson (2001), 20.

17. Fogelson (2001), 190.

18. Fogelson (2001), 198.

19. Joel Garreau, *Edge City: Life on the New Frontier* (New York: Doubleday, 1991), 104.

20. Joel Kotkin, *The City: A Global History* (London: Phoenix, 2005), 149.

21. An illustration by Louis Biedermann in the *New York World* (30 December 1900): 'New York as it Will Be in 1999', reproduced in Fogelson (2001), 38.

22. Tony Travers, 'Towards a Europe of cities', in Ricky Burdett and Deyan Sudjic, eds, *The Endless City* (London: Phaidon, 2007), 156.

23. Ricky Burdett and Philipp Rode, 'The Urban Age Project', in Burdett and Sudjic (2007), 11.

24. Edward Soja and Miguel Kanai, 'The Urbanization of the World', in Burdett and Sudjic (2007), 66.

25. Matthew Garrahan, 'A city rediscovers its heart', *Financial Times* (29 June 2007).

26. There were population gains in Atlanta, Chicago, Denver and Memphis in the 1990s. See Bruce Katz and Andy Altman, 'An Urban Age in a Suburban Nation?', in Burdett and Sudjic (2007), 98–100.

27. See Michael Scott, 'Downtown Central-Cities as Hubs of Civic Connection,' 8 March 2009 <http://www.newgeography.com/content/00946-downtown-central-cities-hubs-civic-connection>

28. Kotkin (2005), 152–3.

29. Deyan Sudjic, *The 100 Mile City* (London: André Deutsch, 1992), 305.

30. Edward Soja and Miguel Kanai, 'The Urbanization of the World', in Burdett and Sudjic (2007), 67; cf. Garreau (1991) and Sudjic (1992).

31. Martin L. Millspaugh, 'Waterfronts as catalysts for city renewal', in Richard Marshall, ed., *Waterfronts in Post-Industrial Cities* (London: Spon, 2001), 75.

32. Charles Warren Stoddard, *A Bit of Old China*

(1912), 2; cited from Yong Chen, *Chinese San Francisco, 1850–1943: A Trans-Pacific Community* (Stanford: Stanford University Press, 2000), 99.

33. Chen (2000), 261.

34. Chen (2000), 50.

35. Chen (2000), 56–7.

36. Helen F. Clark, 'The Chinese of New York contrasted with their Foreign Neighbors', *Century Illustrated Magazine*, 53 (November 1896), 110.

37. Chen (2000), 58–66.

38. Chen (2000), 74–5.

39. Clark (1896), 105.

40. Quotation from John L. Stoddard, *Portfolio of Photographs of Famous Scenes, Cities and Paintings* (Chicago: Werner, [n.d.]), n.p. On Chinese theatres, see Chen (2000), 90–94.

41. See 'Chinatown, the Death of Billie Carleton and the "Brilliant" Chang', <http://www.nickelinthemachine.com/2009/10/chinatown-the-death-of-billie-carleton-and-the-brilliant-chang/>. In 1955, the Situationists wrote a letter to *The Times* protesting against the clearance of Chinatown in the Limehouse area. (Tom McDonough, ed., *The Situationists and the City* (London: Verso, 2009), 52.)

42. See: Rachel Lichtenstein, *On Brick Lane* (London: Penguin, 2008) and Sukhdev Sandhu, 'Come hungry, leave edgy', *LRB* (9 October 2003) <http://www.lrb.co.uk/v25/n19/sand01_.html>

43. Jacob Riis, *How the Other Half Lives*, Hasia R. Diner, ed. (1890; New York: Norton, 2010), 18.

44. Mary Elizabeth Brown, *The Italians of the South Village* (New York: Greenwich Village Society for Historic Preservation, 2007), i.

45. H. C. Brunner, 'Jersey and Mulberry', *Scribner's Magazine*, 13, Number 5 (May 1893), 641–9; from Robert Zecker, *Metropolis: The American City in Popular Culture* (Westport: Praeger, 2008), 40.

46. Ric Burns and James Sanders, *New York: An Illustrated History* (New York: Knopf, 1999), 248.

47. *Harper's New Monthly Magazine*, 62 (371) (April 1881), 674–84; cited from Zecker (2008), 38.

48. South Village, the southern part of Greenwich Village below Washington Square Park, was also an important Italian area of Manhattan. Between the 1880s and 1920s, more than 50,000 Italians settled here in the new tenements and row houses. Many streets in South Village still look as they did a century ago. Fiorello Henry La Guardia, the first Italian-American mayor of New York City, was born to immigrant parents here. Many family businesses remain in the area including Faicco's Italian Sausage, Vesuvio Bakery, Florence Prime Meats. See Brown (2007).

49. Ronnie Ferguson, *A Linguistic History of Venice* ([n.p.]: Leo S. Olschki Editore, 2007), 285. On the etymology of 'ghetto' see Anatoly Liberman, 'Why Don't We Know the Origin of the Word Ghetto?', OUP blog, 4 March 2009: <http://blog.oup.com/2009/03/ghetto/>

50. Aiden Southall, *The City in Time and Space* (Cambridge: CUP, 1998), 390.

51. See Jenny Robertson's moving collection, *Ghetto: Poems of the Warsaw Ghetto 1939–43* (Lion: Oxford, 1989).

52. Burns and Sanders (1999), 323.

53. Claude McKay, *Harlem: Negro Metropolis* (New York: Dutton, 1940), 16.

54. Cited from Burns and Sanders (1999), 326.

55. Le Corbusier, *When the Cathedrals Were White* (1936; New York: Reynal and Hitchcock, 1947), 160.

56. Burns and Sanders (1999), 488.

57. See Alex Altman, 'Postcard: Harlem', *Time* (16 June 2008), 6.

58. *Demographia World Urban Areas (World Agglomerations): Population and Projections* (Demographia: Belleville, 2009). Figures for the populations of today's sprawling megacities vary, sometimes widely. This is partly due to the problem of defining the extent of a city but also due to inadequate statistics in the developing world. For up-to-date figures see especially Thomas Brinkhoff's site <http://www.citypopulation.de/>

59. Mahendra Kumar Singh, 'City of dreams? Over 8m slumdwellers in Mumbai by 2011', *Times of India* (15 November 2010) <http://articles.timesofindia.indiatimes.com/2010-11-15/mumbai/28263181_1_slum-population-rajiv-awas-yojana-urban-poverty-alleviation-min-

istry>. Forty-four per cent of all Indian urban households are classified as slums. In Haiti the figure is 76 per cent, in Pakistan 71.7 per cent and Brazil 34 per cent; UN-Habitat, *State of the World's Cities 2008/2009: Harmonious Cities* (London: Earthscan, 2008), 99, 102.

60. UN figures, from Randeep Ramesh, 'For India's real slumdogs, dream of a better life is not just something in the movies', *Guardian* (10 January 2009): <http://www.guardian.co.uk/world/2009/jan/10/slumdog-millionaire-reality-delhi-mumbai>

61. Jeb Brugmann, *Welcome to the Urban Revolution: How Cities Are Changing the World* (New York: Bloomsbury Press, 2009), 146.

62. 'A flourishing slum', *The Economist* (19 December 2007): <http://www.economist.com/world/asia/displaystory.cfm?story_id=10311293>; Simon Robinson, 'Remaking Mumbai', *Time* (17 March 2008), 49–50; Kevin McCloud, *Slumming It* (TV programme, Channel 4, January 2010).

63. 'Turning trash into treasure, and keeping it green in Cairo', *Independent*, 13 December 2009 <http://www.independent.co.uk/environment/turning-trash-into-treasure-and-keeping-it-green-in-cairo-1839549.html>; cf. Michael Slackman, 'Cleaning Cairo, but Taking a Livelihood', *New York Times* (24 May 2009) <http://www.nytimes.com/2009/05/25/world/middleeast/25oink.html>; Jasper Bouverie, 'Recycling in Cairo: a tale of rags to riches,' *New Scientist* (29 June 1991); Raghda El-Halawany, 'A landfill called Cairo', *Daily News Egypt* (7 September 2009) <http://www.thedailynewsegypt.com/article.aspx?ArticleID=24360>; all accessed January 2010.

64. Brugmann (2009) prefers migrant city to slum, and goes further, saying it is a 'world-class … residential-industrial city system' (134). For Robert Neuwirth, how such areas are described is important: '"Slum" is a problematic word – I try to avoid it. Its meaning is pejorative and it can mean dirty, criminal, ugly, depraved and violent, and that places the communities who live in slums in a different light. I prefer to use the words "squatter community".' Meena Menon, 'Squatters are

the largest builders of housing in the world', *Infochange*, June 2003 <http://infochangeindia.org/200306136092/Urban-India/Features/Squatters-are-the-largest-builders-of-housing-in-the-world.html>

65. Brugmann (2009), 141.

66. UN-Habitat, *Planning Sustainable Cities* (London: Earthscan, 2009), xxii.

67. Will Connors, 'Reclaiming Lagos', *Time* (6 October 2008), 103. Population figures: *Demographia* (2009); <http://www.citypopulation.de/Nigeria-Lagos.html>

68. Mike Davis, *Planet of Slums* (London: Verso, 2006), 14–15. Davis argues that globalisation, together with the policies of the wealthy nations and institutions such as the IMF, has encouraged economic liberalisation and deregulation, which have driven the rural poor off the land and into the urban slums.

69. Edward Soja and Miguel Kanai, 'The urbanization of the world', in Burdett and Sudjic (2007), 67.

70. Soja and Kanai (2007), 65–7.

71. Jerry White, *London in the Nineteenth Century: 'A Human Awful Wonder of God'* (London: Jonathan Cape, 2007), 31–2; cf. Engels' 1845 description of the St Giles Rookery in Jon E. Lewis, ed., *London: The Autobiography* (London: Constable & Robinson, 2008), 263–5.

72. Robert Neuwirth, *Shadow Cities* (2004), cited from Kevin Kelly, 'The Choice of Cities', 2 July 2009: <http://www.kk.org/thetechnium/archives/2009/07/the_choice_of_c.php>

73. Cited from Fogelson (2001), 322. See also New York's Tenement Museum at 97 Orchard Street: <http://www.tenement.org/>

74. See Peter Hall, *Cities of Tomorrow: An Intellectual History of Urban Planning and Design in the Twentieth Century* (1988; repr. Oxford: Blackwell, 1998), 19.

75. Walter Besant, 'Shadow and Sunlight in East London', *Century Illustrated Monthly Magazine*, 61 (NS 39) (1902), 409–10.

76. David Ward, *Poverty, Ethnicity and the American City 1840–1925: Changing Conceptions of the Slum and the Ghetto* (Cambridge: CUP, 1989), 88.

77. Fogelson (2001), 321. Roy Lubove (*The*

Progressives and the Slums: Tenement House Reform in New York City, 1890–1970 (Pittsburgh, 1962), 94) says there were 243,641 people per square kilometre in the most crowded area which is nearly 1,000 people per acre. The density of modern Manhattan is about 100 people per acre. The density of Dharavi is 82,000 people per square kilometre, but the densest part of Mumbai is Kamathipura at 121,312 people per square kilometre. See Ricky Burdett and Deyan Sudjic, eds, *Living in the Endless City* (London: Phaidon, 2011), 89, 294.

78. Jacob Riis, 'The battle with the slum', *Atlantic Monthly*, 83 (1899), 634; cited by Ward (1989), 73.

79. Sudjic (1992), 183–4. Yet even in 1979, the Greater London house condition survey revealed a quarter of houses unsatisfactory (some 640,000 homes) and 250,000 unfit for human habitation.

80. Fogelson (2001), 332.

81. Brugmann (2009), 142.

82. Kenneth T. Jackson, *Crabgrass Frontier: The Suburbanization of the United States* (New York: OUP, 1985), 8. Informal settlements are springing up in and around the world's rapidly expanding cities. The term 'favela' is used to describe them in Brazil and their occupants are known as 'favelados'. In Peru, such settlements are called 'barriadas'. In Argentina, 'villas miserias'; in San Salvador, 'tugúrius'; in Spain, 'chabolas'; in India, 'bustee'; in Uruguay, 'cantegriles'; in Mexico, 'colonias'; in Morocco, 'bidonvilles'; in Portugal, 'vilas de lata'; in Chile, 'callampas'; in Turkey, 'gecekondu'; and in Venezuela, 'ranchos'.

83. Richard J. Williams, *Brazil* (London: Reaktion, 2009), 237–8.

84. Howard Husock, 'Slums of Hope', *City Journal* (Winter 2009), 19, no. 1 <http://www.city-journal.org/2009/19_1_slums.html>

85. Husock (2009).

86. Rykwert (2004), 232.

87. Charles Dickens, 'Scotland-yard' (1836), in *Sketches by Boz* (1839; repr. London: Penguin, 1995), 89.

88. James Howard Kunstler, *The City in Mind: Meditations on the Urban Condition* (New York: Free Press, 2001), 220. Cf. Sudjic (1992), 195–6 and Sharon Zukin, *Naked City: The Death and Life of Authentic Urban Places* (Oxford: OUP, 2010).

89. Menon (2003).

90. Williams (2009), 161.

91. Urban Age, 'Cities and Social Equity: Inequality, Territory and Urban Form' (2009) <www.urban-age.net>; cf. Interview with Kees Christiaanse, 'Curating the Open City', 5 October 2009 <http://places.designobserver.com/entry.html?entry=10887>

92. Joseph Rykwert, *The Seduction of Place: The History and Future of the City* (2000; repr. Oxford: OUP, 2004), 177.

93. Rykwert (2004), 177. Originally the city was envisaged as having a population of no more than 500,000. In recent years, although the population of the city has been falling, that of the *Distrito Federal* has risen: 1.8 million by 1996 and growing.

94. The word 'conurbation' was coined in 1915 by Patrick Geddes, a disciple of Ebenezer Howard, to describe how towns expand to form a continuous built-up area, the result of urban sprawl.

95. Cited from Jackson (1985), 12.

96. Jackson (1985), 15.

97. Jackson (1985), 16.

98. See *Oxford English Dictionary*, online (2nd, 1989); Carolyn Whitzman, *Suburb, Slum, Urban Village: Transformations in Toronto's Parkdale Neighbourhood, 1875–2002* (Vancouver: University of British Columbia Press, 2009), 34.

99. Cited from Rykwert (2004), 161.

100. Rykwert (2004), 16. The French 'banlieue' comes from the Latin 'banlauca' or 'banleuca', meaning a 'distance of a league outside the limits of a town or monastery to which its rule, its "ban" would run' (Rykwert (2004), 161). In German, the word for suburb is 'die Vorstadt'.

101. See John Archer, 'Colonial Suburbs in South Asia, 1700–1850, and the Spaces of Modernity', in Roger Silverstone, ed., *Visions of Suburbia* (London: Routledge, 1997), 41–5, and Mark Girouard, *Cities and People: A Social*

and Architectural History (New Haven: Yale University Press, 1985), 242.

102. William Cowper, 'Retirement' (1780), cited from Girouard (1985), 274–5.

103. See Girouard (1985), 276–7.

104. In 1882, the Spaniard Arturo Soria y Mata came up with the idea of a linear city, or Ciudad Lineal, built along railroad lines and envisaged it stretching from 'Cadiz to St Petersburg'. (Ervin Y. Galantay, *New Towns: Antiquity to the Present* (New York: Braziller, 1975), 55.)

105. Cited from Jeffrey Richards and John M. MacKenzie, *The Railway Station: A Social History* (Oxford: OUP, 1986), 166.

106. Galantay (1975), 55.

107. Rykwert (2004), 115–16; cf. Christian Wolmar, *The Subterranean Railway: How the London Underground Was Built and How It Changed the City Forever* (London: Atlantic Books, 2005) 104–5.

108. Hippolyte Taine, *Notes on England*, tr. E. Hyams (London, 1957), 220; cited from Girouard (1985), 282.

109. Cited from Katz and Altman, 'An urban age in a suburban nation?', in Burdett and Sudjic (2007), 96.

110. Walt Whitman, *I Sit and Look Out* (New York, 1935), 145; cited from Jackson (1985), 27–8.

111. Olmsted cited from Fogelson (2001), 29.

112. Olmsted cited from Spiro Kostof, *The City Shaped: Urban Patterns and Meanings Through History* (London: Thames & Hudson, 1991), 74.

113. Fogelson (2001), 33.

114. Jackson (1985), 4.

115. Jackson (1985), 113.

116. Carey McWilliams, 'Look what's happened to California', *Harper's* (October 1949), 28; cited from Fogelson (2001), 394.

117. Cathy Ross and John Clark, *London: The Illustrated History* (London: Allen Lane, 2008), 209.

118. Jackson (1985), 15.

119. Richards and MacKenzie (1986), 170; Jerry White, *London in the Twentieth Century: A City and its People* (1st 2001; repr. London: Vintage, 2008), 30–32.

120. American Community Survey 2004, US Census Bureau <http://www.census.gov/Press-Release/www/releases/archives/american_community_survey_acs/001695.html> Accessed December 2009.

121. Donald N. Rothblatt and Daniel J. Garr, *Suburbia: An International Assessment* (London: Croom Helm, 1986), 2.

122. Lewis Mumford, *The City in History: Its Origins, Its Transformations, and Its Prospects* (London: Secker & Warburg, 1961), 486.

123. Richard Sennett, *The Uses of Disorder: Personal Identity and City Life* (1st 1970; repr. New Haven: Yale University Press, 2008), 72, xxii–xxiii.

124. George Orwell, *Coming Up for Air* (New York, 1950), 12; cited from Silverstone (1997), 111.

125. Joel Kotkin, 'America's (Sub)urban Future', *Forbes* (5 May 2009) <http://www.forbes.com/2009/05/05/state-of-the-city-opinions-columnists-suburban-future.html>

126. Tony Champion, 'Population Movement within the UK', Chapter 6 of *Focus on People and Migration* (Office of National Statistics, 2005), 102 <http://www.statistics.gov.uk/downloads/theme_compendia/fom2005/06_FOPM_MovesWithinUK.pdf>. About 80 per cent of the UK population is now urban, concentrated in a mere 9 per cent of the total land area.

127. Wendell Cox, 'Suburbs and Cities: The Unexpected Truth', *New Geography* (16 May 2009) <http://www.newgeography.com/content/00805-suburbs-and-cities-the-unexpected-truth>

128. In 1970, less than 20 per cent of Chinese lived in cities; now official figures show that 40 per cent do, a figure that is certainly an underestimation. Edward Soja and Miguel Kanai, 'The urbanization of the world', in Burdett and Sudjic (2007), 59.

129. Xiangming Chen, 'The urban laboratory', in Burdett and Sudjic (2007), 122.

130. See Bruce Katz and Andy Altman, 'An urban age in a suburban nation?', in Burdett and Sudjic (2007), 99.

131. R. E. Lang, Arthur C. Nelson and Rebecca R. Sohmer, 'Boomburb downtowns: the

next generation of urban centers', *Journal of Urbanism*, vol. 1 (March 2008), 78.

132. Lang et al. (2008), 79, 88.

133. Soja and Kanai (2007) refer to three types of urban areas: a city region, with more than a million inhabitants; megacity regions, with more than ten million inhabitants; and megalopolitan city regions which are quasi-continental metropolitan areas. 'The urbanization of the world', in Burdett and Sudjic (2007), 58–61.

134. P. Taylor and R. Lang, 'The Shock of the New: 100 Concepts describing Recent Urban Change', *Environment and Planning A*, 36 (2004), 951–8.

135. The words of David Ley, University of British Columbia; 'The in-between city slouches ahead', *Toronto Star* (21 November 2009) <http://www.thestar.com/news/insight/article/728286--the-in-between-city-slouches-ahead>

136. Kessler's 'Idyll of Venice' is described in: 'Lake in an Hotel', *St John Daily Sun* (2 September 1905); cf. Elaine Denby, *Grand Hotels: Reality and Illusion* (London: Reaktion, 1998), 292. A few years later Kessler celebrated Christmas at the Savoy by giving a North Pole dinner, with waiters dressed as Eskimos.

137. See Denby (1998), 11–13.

138. Denby (1998), 26.

139. Denby (1998), 21.

140. George Augustus Sala in *Temple Bar Magazine*, II (1866); cited from Girouard (1985), 302.

141. Denby (1998), 34.

142. Charles Dickens, *American Notes* (1842), cited from Denby (1998), 34. Dickens said that Barnum's in Baltimore (built 1825) was 'the most comfortable of all the hotels' he enjoyed in America.

143. Barnum's City Hotel, Baltimore (1825–6) had more than 200 beds. The St Charles, New Orleans (1837) had 600 and the Continental in Philadelphia (1858–60) accommodated as many as 900 people. See Girouard (1985), 302.

144. See Denby (1998), 58–9. There were lifts and electric lights in the entrance by 1879 (and in the whole building by 1888).

145. Paris already had a Grand Hôtel in the same quarter: the Grand Hôtel du Louvre, in the rue de Rivoli, was built to cater for visitors to the Exposition Universelle in 1855. It was far bigger than traditional English hotels (typically with 200–300 beds): it had 700 bedrooms and street frontage of 500 feet, the largest in Europe at the time. It boasted monumental staircases, galleries, a glass-roofed courtyard, a 133-foot-long salon, large billiard rooms, numerous bathrooms and twenty lavatories. Intended as a rendezvous for travellers from across the continent, it was – though luxurious – for 'toutes les classes de voyageurs'. However, it had a short life, becoming a department store by the 1880s. See Denby (1998), 84.

146. Denby (1998), 81–5. The Grand is now the Grand Hôtel InterContinental.

147. Denby (1998), 200.

148. Fogelson (2001), 383.

149. Opposite House: James Fallows, 'Beijing's Almost-Perfect Hotel', *Atlantic* (June 2009) <http://www.theatlantic.com/doc/200906/hotel-china>; Ryugyong Hotel: 'Will "Hotel of Doom" ever be finished?', BBC News Online, 15 October 2009, <http://news.bbc.co.uk/1/hi/8306697.stm>

150. Riazat Butt, 'Mecca super-hotel to offer spa, butler and a chocolate room', *Guardian* (15 October 2009) <http://www.guardian.co.uk/world/2009/oct/15/mecca-hotel-against-hajj-spirit>

151. Scott MacLeod, 'Grand Ambition', *Time* (1 December 2008), 47. Dubai is also home to the Burj Al Arab, completed in 2000, at 321 metres (1,050 feet), and the Rose Tower, a seventy-two-storey hotel which, at 333 metres (1,090 feet) high, is the world's tallest hotel. It opened in 2009.

152. Macleod (2008), 47.

153. Denby (1998), 22.

154. Denby (1998), 277.

155. Ronald Hayman, *Thomas Mann* (London: Bloomsbury, 1997), 248.

156. Hayman (1997), 226.

157. F. Scott Fitzgerald, *Tender Is the Night* (1934; Harmondsworth: Penguin, 1985), 11.

158. Thomas K. Grose, 'A Room with No View', *Time* (21 May 2007), 54–5.

159. See his website: <http://www.kisho.co.jp/page.

php/209>. During the most recent recession some Japanese have been living in capsule hotels, as the most economic way of remaining in the city: Hiroko Tabuchi, 'For Some in Japan, Home Is a Tiny Plastic Bunk', *New York Times* (1 January 2010): <http://www.nytimes.com/2010/01/02/business/global/02capsule.html> Accessed February 2010.

160. Lawrence Osborne, 'Sex And The City Of The Future', *Forbes* (9 February 2009) <http://www.forbes.com/2009/09/02/sex-future-asia-japan-opinions-21-century-cities-09-lawrence-osborne.html>; Roland Buerk, 'Love beats the recession in Japan', BBC News Online, 15 July 2009, <http://news.bbc.co.uk/1/hi/8137746.stm>

5 Getting Around

1. William Bittner, *Poe: A Biography* (London: Elek Books, 1963), 24–5.
2. Rebecca Solnit, *Wanderlust: A History of Walking* (London: Verso, 2002), 199.
3. Bittner (1963), 118.
4. Wordsworth writing in the Preface to the second edition of the *Lyrical Ballads* (1800); cited from Dana Brand, *The Spectator and the City in Nineteenth-Century American Literature* (Cambridge: CUP, 1991), 3–4. Brand comments: 'The lazy, passive modern imagination, Wordsworth suggests, is quintessentially urban' (p. 4).
5. Charles Baudelaire, 'The Painter of Modern Life' (1863), in Jonathan Mayne, ed. and tr., *The Painter of Life and Other Essays* (London: Phaidon, 1964), 9.
6. Mayne (1964), 9.
7. Mayne (1964), 13.
8. Walter Benjamin, *Charles Baudelaire: Lyric Poet in the Era of High Capitalism*, tr. Harry Zohn (London: New Left Books, 1973), 36; cited from Brand (1991), 6.
9. Virginia Woolf, *Mrs Dalloway* (1925; repr. London: Penguin, 1992), 6.
10. He walks for hours on end through the streets, 'filled with the longing to finally reach the place where what I'd forgotten would come back to me, I could not pass the smallest side street without entering it

and turning the corner at its end'. Siegfried Kracauer, 'Memory of a Paris Street', trans. from German by Ross Benjamin (2009), 'Erinnerung an eine Pariser Straße' (1930, from *Straßen in Berlin und anderswo*) <http://wordswithoutborders.org/article/memory-of-a-paris-street/>

11. See Jordan Sand, 'Street Observation Science and the Tokyo Economic Bubble', in Gyan Prakash and Kevin M. Kruse, eds, *The Spaces of the Modern City: Imaginaries, Politics, and Everyday Life* (Princeton: Princeton University Press, 2008), 373ff.
12. Donald Lupon, *London and the countrey carbonadoed and quartered into several characters* (1632); cited from Kate Newman, *Cultural Capitals: Early Modern London and Paris* (Princeton: Princeton University Press, 2007), 27.
13. Paul Auster, *City of Glass*, The New York Trilogy (1985; repr. London: Faber & Faber, 1987), 3–4.
14. In the US Boston has the highest percentage among large cities of employees who walk to work: 12.5 per cent; 32,000 people. In New York some 320,000 walk to work, 9 per cent of the population. The American Community Survey, U.S. Census Bureau, June 2007 (data for 2005).
15. Eric Bellman, 'Packed Streets Have a City of Walkers Looking Skyward for Answers', *Wall Street Journal* (19 January 2010) <http://online.wsj.com/article/SB10001424052748703837004575013193075912272.html> accessed 20 March 2010; cf. Ninad Siddhaye, 'Day after Ashok Chavan's promise, 16 skywalks nixed', *DNA India* (7 April 2010) <http://www.dnaindia.com/india/report_day-after-ashok-chavan-s-promise-16-skywalks-nixed_1368301> accessed 14 April 2010.
16. Michel de Certeau, *The Practice of Everyday Life* (1980), tr. Steven F. Rendall (Berkeley: University of California Press, 1988), 101.
17. See Newman (2007), 63–70.
18. Stow, cited from Newman (2007), 26.
19. William Blake, 'London', from *Songs of Experience* (1794).
20. Walter Benjamin, *The Arcades Project*, in Gary Bridge and Sophie Watson, eds, *The Blackwell*

City Reader (Oxford: Blackwell, 2002), 398.

21. Jérôme Carcopino, tr. E. O. Lorimer, *Daily Life in Ancient Rome: The People and the City at the Height of the Empire* (1941; repr. Harmondsworth: Penguin, 1956), 61–3.

22. Sigfried Giedion, *Space, Time and Architecture: The Growth of a New Tradition* (1941; Cambridge, Mass: Harvard University Press, 2008), 76; cf. Mark Girouard, *Cities and People: A Social and Architectural History* (New Haven: Yale University Press, 1985), 118–21.

23. Newman (2007), 73.

24. James Howell, an English traveller to Europe in the 1620s, cited from Newman (2007), 82.

25. Robert M. Fogelson, *Downtown: Its Rise and Fall, 1880–1950* (New Haven: Yale University Press, 2001), 253.

26. Fogelson (2001), 251.

27. Ernest Flagg, 'The Plan of New York and How to Improve It,' *Scribner's Magazine*, 36 (August 1904), 253-56 <http://www.library.cornell.edu/Reps/DOCS/flagg.htm>

28. See *Scientific American* (22 June 1907), in Fogelson (2001), 263.

29. First published 1964; repr. in Thomas M. Disch, ed., *The Ruins of Earth* (London: Arrow, 1975), 165.

30. Mimi Sheller and John Urry, 'The City and the Car' (*International Journal of Urban and Regional Research*, 2000); in Malcolm Miles et al., eds, *The City Cultures Reader* (London: Routledge, 2004), 202.

31. 2009 Urban Mobility Report, Texas Transportation Institute <http://mobility.tamu.edu/ums/report/>

32. Andrew Downie, 'Postcard: Brazil', *Time* (8 October 2007), 25.

33. Kai Strittmatter, tr. Stefan Tobler, *China A to Z: A User's Guide to the Next Global Superpower* (London: Haus, 2006), 296.

34. Hermann Knoflacher et al., 'How roads kill cities', in Ricky Burdett and Deyan Sudjic, eds, *The Endless City* (London: Phaidon, 2007), 340.

35. Cited from Fogelson (2001), 316.

36. Henri Lefebvre, *The Production of Space* (Oxford: Blackwell, 1991), cited from Sheller and Urry (2000); in Miles (2004), 206.

37. The World Health Organization and the World Bank, cited from 'Calming traffic on Bogotá's killing streets', *Science*, 319 (8 February 2008), 742–3.

38. Thanks to the car industry, Detroit grew from a city of 300,000 to nearly a million in the period 1900 to 1920, making it the fastest growing city in America at the time, after Los Angeles.

39. Sam Bass Warner, 'Learning from the Past: Services to Families', in Martin Wachs and Margaret Crawford, eds, *The Car and the City: The Automobile, the Built Environment and Daily Urban Life* (Ann Arbor: University of Michigan Press, 1992), 9. Before the automobile, Los Angeles had a light rail system known as the 'Yellow Cars'. Electric rail returned to Los Angeles in 1990 and there are plans for extending the network.

40. Jean Baudrillard, *America*, tr. Chris Turner (1986; repr. London: Verso, 2010), 54.

41. Barton Myers, 'Designing in Car-Oriented Cities: An Argument for Episodic Urban Congestion', in Wachs and Crawford (1992), 255.

42. Data for 2007: 2009 Urban Mobility Report, Texas Transportation Institute <http://mobility.tamu.edu/ums/report/>

43. Guy Debord, 'Situationist Positions on Traffic', *Internationale Situationniste*, 3 (December 1959), 36–7. Cited from McDonough (2009), 142.

44. See Ben Adler, 'A Tale of Two Exurbs', *The American Prospect* (27 April 2009) <http://www.prospect.org/cs/articles?article=a_tale_of_two_exurbs> Accessed 24 November 2009.

45. Fogelson (2001), 299.

46. Emily Pykett, 'Time not up yet as parking meters hit 50', *Scotsman* (11 June 2008) <http://news.scotsman.com/latestnews/Time-not-up-yet-.4171637.jp> Accessed 20 April 2010.

47. Sewell Chan, 'When Time Has Run Out for the Parking Meter, Not the Parked Car', *New York Times* (21 December 2006) <http://www.nytimes.com/2006/12/21/nyregion/21parking.html> Accessed 20 April 2010.

48. 'Annex – Managing car use in cities', in *Urban Age, Cities and Social Equity* (Urban Age/LSE, 2009), 166–8.

49. Ray LaHood, 'My view from atop the table

at the National Bike Summit', *Fast Lane* (15 March 2010) <http://fastlane.dot.gov/2010/03/my-view-from-atop-the-table-at-the-national-bike-summit.html> Accessed March 2010.

50. 'Annex – Managing car use in cities', in Urban Age, *Cities and Social Equity* (Urban Age/LSE, 2009), 166–8. The point is made by Enrique Peñalosa.

51. Collectif Argos, *Climate Refugees* (Cambridge, Mass.: MIT Press, 2010), 238.

52. Knoflacher et al. (2007), 345.

53. 'Mayor unveils programme to transform cycling and walking in London', Greater London Authority press release, 11 February 2008 <http://mayor.london.gov.uk/view_press_release.jsp?releaseid=15612> Accessed March 2010.

54. See 'How People Move', in Burdett and Sudjic (2007), 262, and 'Travelling to Work' in Ricky Burdett and Deyan Sudjic, *Living in the Endless City* (London: Phaidon, 2011), 288–9.

55. The number of cars driving down into Midtown is at its lowest level in nearly twenty years, thanks to increasing use of public transport. According to the *New York Times*, from November 2008 to October 2009, Thursday, 13 November was the slowest weekday of the year, with an average speed of 7.5mph, which is similar to the speed of a jogger in Central Park. The fastest weekday was Monday, 28 September with a speed of 11.7mph. Michael M. Grynbaum, 'Gridlock May Not Be Constant, but Slow Going Is Here to Stay', *New York Times* (23 March 2010) <http://www.nytimes.com/2010/03/24/nyregion/24traffic.html> Accessed March 2010.

56. See Chris Turner, 'Copenhagen, Melbourne and the Reconquest of the City', *Worldchanging* (18 December 2008) <http://www.worldchanging.com/local/canada/archives/009216.html> Accessed 17 April 2010.

57. See 'Annex – Managing car use in cities', in Urban Age, *Cities and Social Equity* (Urban Age/LSE, 2009), 166–8; Tristana Moore, 'Residents of Vauban', *Time* (5 October 2009), 78 <http://www.time.com/time/specials/packages/article/0,28804,1924149_1924154_1924430,00.

html> Accessed 20 April 2010.

58. Michael Brunton, 'Signal Failure', *Time* (30 January 2008), 35–6 <http://www.time.com/time/magazine/article/0,9171,1708116,00.html>

59. Simon Jenkins, 'Rip out the traffic lights and railings', *Guardian* (29 February 2008) <http://www.guardian.co.uk/commentisfree/2008/feb/29/guardiancolumnists> Accessed 20 April 2010.

60. 'Oxford Circus "X-crossing" opens', BBC News (2 November 2009) <http://news.bbc.co.uk/1/hi/8337341.stm> See also Laura Laker, 'DIY Streets: How locals transformed rat runs into public spaces', *Guardian* (25 November 2009) <http://www.guardian.co.uk/environment/green-living-blog/2009/nov/25/diy-streets-clapton-sustrans> Both accessed March 2010.

61. Michael M. Grynbaum, 'New York Traffic Experiment Gets Permanent Run', *New York Times* (11 February 2010) <http://www.nytimes.com/2010/02/12/nyregion/12broadway.html> Accessed March 2010.

62. John Lichfield, 'Paris plans new beach on riverbank', *Independent* (15 April 2010) <http://www.independent.co.uk/news/world/europe/paris-plans-new-beach-on-riverbank-1945231.html> Accessed 15 April 2010.

63. Neil Takemoto, 'Shanghai's eclectic new ped-only urban village', *Cool Town Studios* (20 October 2009) <http://www.cooltownstudios.com/site/shanghais-revitalized-ped-only-urban-village> Accessed 21 October 2009.

64. 'Calming traffic on Bogotá's killing streets', *Science*, 319 (8 February 2008), 742–3.

65. The American Community Survey, US Census Bureau, June 2007 (data for 2005).

66. Darryl D'Monte, 'Cities should be for people, not cars: Enrique Peñalosa', *Infochange* (December 2009) <http://infochangeindia.org/Environment/Eco-logic/Cities-should-be-for-people-not-cars-Enrique-Penalosa.html> Accessed 16 December 2009.

67. 'Annex – Managing car use in cities', in Urban Age, *Cities and Social Equity* (Urban Age/LSE, 2009), 166–8.

68. 'The Metropolitan Subterranean Railway,' *The Times* (30 November 1861), 5.

69. Christian Wolmar, *The Subterranean Railway: How the London Underground Was Built and How It Changed the City Forever* (London: Atlantic Books, 2005), 5.

70. Wolmar (2005), 5.

71. Some groups of shelterers produced their own newsletters. This is from the one for Swiss Cottage, amusingly called *De Profundis*; cited from Wolmar (2005), 286.

72. *The Times* (28 April 1897).

73. London Transport Museum. London's trams began to be electrified in 1900. Motorbus services were introduced from 1910. After 1931, London's trams were replaced with trolleybuses, which were powered by overhead cables.

74. Wolmar (2005), 41, 49, 54.

75. Henry Mayhew, *The Shops and Companies of London and the Trades and Manufactories of Great Britain* (Strand Printing and Publishing, 1865), 144–9; cited from Wolmar (2005), 58.

76. Fred T. Jane, 'Round the Underground on an Engine', *English Illustrated Magazine* (August 1893); cited from Martin Goodman, *Suffer and Survive: Gas Attacks, Miners' Canaries, Spacesuits and the Bends. The Extreme Life of Dr J. S. Haldane* (London: Simon & Schuster, 2007), 146.

77. Wolmar (2005), 66.

78. Wolmar (2005), 136.

79. *The Times* (4 November 1890); cited from Wolmar (2005), 136.

80. On Shanghai see <http://www.bricoleurban-ism.org/whimsicality/shanghais-metro-and-londons-tube-head-to-head/>; generally: Takao Okamoto and Norihisa Tadakoshi, 'Rail Transport in The World's Major Cities', *Japan Railway & Transport Review* (25 October 2000), 9, and <http://www.urbanrail.net/eu/mos/moskva.htm>

81. John Brownlee 'The Remains of Atlantis in Stockholm's Subways', *Wired* (1 May 2007) <http://www.wired.com/table_of_malcontents/2007/05/the_remains_of_/>

82. 'Transit City and Transit Cities', *Torontoist* (23 November 2009) <http://torontoist.com/2009/11/transit_city_and_transit_cities.php>

83. H. G. Wells, *The Sleeper Wakes* (1899; revised 1910; repr. London: Penguin, 2005), 42–3; 144; 168; 177.

84. Giedion (2008), 209.

85. Fogelson (2001), 115.

86. Peter Hall, *Cities in Civilization: Culture, Innovation, and Urban Order* (London: Phoenix, 1999), 773.

87. Ric Burns and James Sanders, *New York: An Illustrated History* (New York: Knopf, 1999), 232.

88. Girouard (1985), 319; cf. Thomas S. Hines, *Burnham of Chicago: Architect and Planner* (1974; repr. Chicago: University of Chicago Press, 2009), 61–4.

89. Corbett speaking in 1926, cited from Hall (1999), 772.

90. Gail Fenske, *The Skyscraper and the City: The Woolworth Building and the Making of Modern New York* (Chicago: University of Chicago Press, 2008), 54.

91. 'New York, the Unrivalled Business Center', *Harper's Weekly*, 46 (15 November 1902), 1673; cited from Fenske (2008), 54.

92. L. J. Horowitz and B. Sparkes, *The Towers of New York: The Memoirs of a Master-builder* (New York, 1937), 2, 118, cited from Girouard (1985), 322.

93. H. G. Wells, *The Future in America: A Search after Realities* (London: Granville, 1906; repr. 1987), 31.

94. Fogelson (2001), 9.

95. Fenske (2008), 11.

96. Fenske (2008), 3.

97. Spark, 'How Hugh McAtamney Put the Woolworth Building on the International Map', *Real Estate Magazine*, 2 (May 1913), 50, cited from Fenske (2008), 220.

98. Spark, cited from Fenske (2008), 220.

99. Cited from Fenske (2008), 216.

100. Lewis Mumford, *The City in History: Its Origins, Its Transformations, and Its Prospects* (London: Secker & Warburg, 1961), 220.

101. Mumford (1961), 221.

102. J. G. Ballard, *High-Rise* (1975; repr. London: Harper Perennial, 2006), 52.

103. Elizabeth Hawes, *New York, New York: How the Apartment House Transformed the Life of the City (1869–1930)* (New York: Owl/ Henry

Holt, 1994), 96, 99.

104. Girouard (1985), 315.

105. Rem Koolhaas, *Delirious New York: A Retroactive Manifesto for Manhattan* (1978; repr. New York: Monacelli Press, 1994), 89.

106. On the Burj see: Christopher Hawthorne, 'The Burj Dubai and architecture's vacant stare', *Los Angeles Times* (1 January 2010); Paul Goldberger, 'Castle in the Air', *New Yorker* (8 February 2010). <http://www.newyorker.com/arts/critics/skyline/2010/02/08/100208crsk_skyline_goldberger>; 'World's tallest building opens in Dubai', *BBC News* (4 January 2010) <http://news.bbc.co.uk/1/hi/world/middle_east/8439618.stm>

107. Data from Burdett and Sudjic (2007), 110, 252–3; also Deyan Sudjic, 'The Speed and the Friction', in Burdett and Sudjic (2007), 112–15; Xiangming Chen, 'The Urban Laboratory', in Burdett and Sudjic (2007), 118–25. On the loss of these traditional urban communities see Michael Sorkin, 'Learning from the Hutong of Beijing and the Lilong of Shanghai', *Architectural Record* (July 2008) <http://archrecord.construction.com/features/critique/0807critique-1.asp>

108. Adam Morton, 'China to get a "mini-Melbourne"', *The Age* (19 May 2010); The Skyscraper Museum, 'China Prophecy' exhibition <http://skyscraper.org/EXHIBITIONS/CHINA_PROPHECY/walkthrough_intro.php>

109. Norman Foster, '"Wir brauchen Hochhäuser"', *Die Zeit* (21 August 2008), author's translation <http://www.zeit.de/2008/35/FosterInterview>

6 Money

1. Cited from 'Romford: Economic history', in *A History of the County of Essex*, vol. 7, ed. W. R. Powell (Victoria County History, 1978), 72–6.

2. The market was demolished after Bowles wrote this and a new one built nearby. Paul Bowles, 'Worlds of Tangier', *Holiday* (March 1958); repr. Paul Bowles, *Travels: Collected Writings, 1950–93*, ed. Mark Ellingham (London: Sort Of, 2010), 232–3.

3. Edmund White, *The Flâneur: A Stroll Through the Paradoxes of Paris* (London: Bloomsbury, 2001; repr. 2008), 11.

4. See: <http://www.tsukiji-market.or.jp/youkoso/about_e.htm>

5. Harold Carter, *An Introduction to Urban Historical Geography* (London: Arnold, 1983), Joel Kotkin says the city traditionally performed three essential functions: the provision of sacred space (the temple), of security (the defensive wall) and as a locus for a commercial market. (Joel Kotkin, *The City: A Global History* (London: Phoenix, 2005), xvi.)

6. Lewis Mumford, *The City in History: Its Origins, Its Transformations, and Its Prospects* (London: Secker & Warburg, 1961), 72.

7. Mumford (1961), 72.

8. Kotkin (2005), 21.

9. Mumford (1961), 150–51.

10. Mumford (1961), 153.

11. By 1500 there were over a hundred cities larger than 20,000 people, twenty up to 100,000, with the most urbanised regions being in the Low Countries, Rhineland and northern Italy. (John Reader, *Cities* (London: Heinemann, 2004), 88.)

12. Robert Tittler, *Architecture and Power: The Town Hall and the English Urban Community c. 1500–1640* (Oxford: Clarendon, 1991), 133. During the Middle Ages, the largest cities were in the Islamic world, and, during the Renaissance, in China.

13. Mikhail Bakhtin, *Rabelais and His World* (Cambridge, Mass.: MIT Press, 1968), 154.

14. Niall Ferguson, *The Ascent of Money: A Financial History of the World* (London: Allen Lane, 2008), 27, 30, 31.

15. Ferguson (2008), 3.

16. Peter Clark, *European Cities and Towns, 400–2000* (Oxford: OUP, 2009), 274–5.

17. Peter Ackroyd, *London: The Biography* (London: Vintage, 2001), 329–32; cf. <http://www.cityoflondon.gov.uk/Corporation/LGNL_Services/Business/Markets/smithfield_meat_market.htm>

18. *Quarterly Review* (1854), cited from Reader (2004), 130.

19. Christopher Stocks, *Forgotten Fruits: The Stories Behind Britain's Traditional Fruit and*

Vegetables (London: Windmill, 2009), 216.

20. Jane Kirk Huntley, 'New York Women Liked Pushcart Tony's Good Opinions and Squashes and Regret the Abolition this Week of the Picturesque Markets', *Christian Science Monitor* (5 January 1940), 9; cited from Suzanne Wasserman, 'Hawkers and Gawkers', in Annie Hauck-Lawson and Jonathan Deutsch, eds, *Gastropolis: Food and New York City* (New York: Columbia University Press, 2009), 165–6.

21. Amélie Kuhrt, 'The Old Assyrian merchants', in Helen Parkins and Christopher Smith, eds, *Trade, Traders and the Ancient City* (London: Routledge, 1998), 23.

22. M. T. Larsen, 'Your Money or Your Life! A Portrait of an Assyrian Businessman', in M. A. Dandamayev et al., eds, *Societies and Languages of the Ancient Near East: Studies in Honour of I. M. Diakonoff* (Warminster: Aris & Phillips, 1982), 214.

23. Gerhard Herm, tr. Caroline Hillier, *The Phoenicians: The Purple Empire of the Ancient World* (London: Futura, 1975), 124–7; Ezekiel 27: 3–9, 28: 13–15.

24. Herm (1975), 126.

25. Richard Sennett, *Flesh and Stone: The Body and the City in Western Civilization* (1994; repr. New York: Norton, 1997), 198.

26. Sennett (1997), 199.

27. Geoffrey Parker, *Sovereign City: The City-State Through History* (London: Reaktion, 2004), 142.

28. See Sigfried Giedion, *Space, Time and Architecture: The Growth of a New Tradition* (1941; repr. Cambridge, Mass.: Harvard University Press, 2008), 249–55; Erik Mattie, *World's Fairs* (Princeton: Princeton Architectural Press, 1998), 11–15.

29. On Paris 1889, see: Giedion (2008), 268–71; Mattie (1998), 75–85; on the Eiffel Tower <http://www.tour-eiffel.fr/teiffel/uk/documentation/dossiers/page/debats.html>

30. 'China opens World Expo 2010 in Shanghai', BBC News Online (30 April 2010) <http://news.bbc.co.uk/1/hi/world/asia-pacific/8653426.stm>. Official website: <http://en.expo2015.org/ht/en/theme.html>

31. Parker (2004), 82.

32. William H. McNeill, *Venice: The Hinge of Europe, 1081–1797* (Chicago: University of Chicago Press, 1974).

33. William Shakespeare, *The Merchant of Venice* (1596–8), Act III, scene iii.

34. Clark (2009), 2.

35. Anne Goldgar, *Tulipmania: Money, Honor, and Knowledge in the Dutch Golden Age* (Chicago: University of Chicago Press, 2008), 10.

36. Cited from Kate Newman, *Cultural Capitals: Early Modern London and Paris* (Princeton: Princeton University Press, 2007), 23.

37. Syed Ali, *Dubai: Gilded Cage* (New Haven: Yale University Press, 2010), 44–6.

38. Geoffrey Blainey, *A History of Victoria* (Cambridge: CUP, 2006), 41.

39. Timothy J. Gilfoyle, *A Pickpocket's Tale: The Underworld of Nineteenth-Century New York* (New York: Norton, 2006), xiv, 23.

40. 1884 newspaper report; cited from Gilfoyle (2006), 24.

41. Jacob Riis, 'The Making of Thieves in New York', *Century Illustrated Monthly Magazine*, 49 (November 1894), 112.

42. David Robins, *Tarnished Vision: Crime and Conflict in the Inner City* (Oxford: OUP, 1992), 3.

43. Sennett (1997), 196.

44. The quotation is from the seventeenth-century historian of Paris, Henri Sauval, cited from Colin Jones, *Paris: Biography of a City* (London: Penguin, 2006), 190; cf. Newman (2007), 145.

45. Jones (2006), 191.

46. Robert Zecker, *Metropolis: The American City in Popular Culture* (Westport: Praeger, 2008), 12.

47. Zecker (2008), 15.

48. *New York Herald* (30 March 1859), cited from Gilfoyle (2006), 12.

49. Herbert Asbury, *The Gangs of New York* (1928), cited from Gilfoyle (2006), 185.

50. 1892 newspaper report, cited from Gilfoyle (2006), 189.

51. See: National Youth Gang Survey Analysis <http://www.nationalgangcenter.gov/About/Surveys-and-Analyses> Accessed 20 August 2010.

52. George L. Kelling and James Q. Wilson, 'Broken Windows: The police and neighborhood safety,' *Atlantic* (March 1982) <http://www.theatlantic.com/magazine/archive/1982/03/broken-windows/4465/>

53. Bernard E. Harcourt and Jens Ludwig, 'Broken Windows: New Evidence from New York City and a Five City Social Experiment', *University of Chicago Law Review*, 73 (2006), cited from Anna Minton, *Ground Control: Fear and Happiness in the Twenty-First-Century City* (London: Penguin, 2009), 146.

54. Jane Jacobs, *The Death and Life of Great American Cities* (1961; repr. Harmondsworth: Penguin, 1994), 42–7.

55. Paul Lewis, 'CCTV in the sky: police plan to use military-style spy drones', *Guardian* (23 January 2010); cf. Sophie Body-Gendrot, 'Confronting Fear', in Ricky Burdett and Deyan Sudjic, eds, *The Endless City* (London: Phaidon, 2007), 356, and Minton (2009), 31.

56. Tim Harford, *The Logic of Life* (London: Abacus, 2009), 135.

57. Mike Davis, *City of Quartz: Excavating the Future in Los Angeles* (London: Vintage, 1990), 226.

58. Richard Sennett, *The Uses of Disorder: Personal Identity and City Life* (1970; repr. New Haven: Yale University Press, 2008), n.p.

59. Burdett and Sudjic (2009), 181; cf. Ioan Grillo, 'Postcard: Culiacán', *Time* (29 December 2008), 6. Murder rates: Burdett and Sudjic (2009), 246.

60. Claudia Herrera-Pahl, 'Mexico City is a metastasis', *Deutsche Welle* (12 August 2010) <http://www.dw-world.de/dw/article/0,,5809384,00.html>

61. Richard J. Norton, 'Feral Cities', *Naval War College Review*, 56 (2003), 97–106, cited from Geoff Manaugh, 'Cities gone wild', in Nic Clear, ed., *Architectures of the Near Future*: *Architectural Design*, 79 (September 2009), 61.

62. 'Man "destroys" life for art', BBC News Online, 9 February 2001 <http://news.bbc.co.uk/1/hi/entertainment/1162348.stm>; Leo Walford, 'Burn what you love and love what you burn' <http://artcritical.com/blurbs/LWLandy.htm>; Evelyn Welch, *Shopping in the Renaissance: Consumer Cultures in Italy,* *1400–1600* (New Haven: Yale University Press, 2009), 1.

63. Jérôme Carcopino, tr. E. O. Lorimer, *Daily Life in Ancient Rome: The People and the City at the Height of the Empire* (1941; repr. Harmondsworth: Penguin, 1956), 198.

64. Rafik Schami and Marie Fadel, tr. Debra S. Marmor and Herbert A. Danner, *Damascus: Taste of a City* (2002; repr. London: Haus, 2010), 122–3.

65. Chardin, cited from Johann Friedrich Geiste, *Arcades: The History of a Building Type* (Cambridge, Mass.: MIT Press, 1983), 8; cf. Bill Freund, *The African City: A History* (Cambridge: CUP, 2007), 28, on Cairo and its shopping streets.

66. Clark (2009), 55.

67. Sharon Zukin, 'Shopping', in Ray Hutchison, ed., *Encyclopedia of Urban Studies* (Los Angeles: Sage, 2010), 710.

68. Clark (2009), 266.

69. Karl Baedeker, *London and Its Environs: Handbook for Traveller* (London: Dula, 1898), 23.

70. Marquis de Bombelles, *Journal*, C. Grassion and F. Durif, eds (1978–93), vol. 2, 206, cited from Jones (2006), 222.

71. Walter Benjamin, *The Arcades Project* (1927), in Gary Bridge and Sophie Watson, eds, *The Blackwell City Reader* (Oxford: Blackwell, 2002), 395.

72. Anon., *Hartly House, Calcutta* (London, 1789), vol. 1, 87–8, cited from Mark Girouard, *Cities and People: A Social and Architectural History* (New Haven: Yale University Press, 1985), 246.

73. Michael B. Miller, *The Bon Marché: Bourgeois Culture and the Department Store, 1896–1920* (London: Allen & Unwin, 1981), 29; cf. Dell Upton, *Another City: Urban Life and Urban Spaces in the New American Republic* (New Haven: Yale University Press, 2008), 177.

74. Geiste (1983), 74.

75. Geiste (1983), 49.

76. See Geoffrey Crossick and Serge Jaumain, 'The World of the Department Store: Distribution, Culture and Social Change', in Geoffrey Crossick and Serge Jaumain, eds, *Cathedrals of Consumption: The European*

Department Store, 1850–1939 (Aldershot: Ashgate, 1999), 27–9.

77. Émile Zola, *Au Bonheur des Dames* (1883), trans. as *The Ladies' Paradise* (Berkeley: University of California Press, 1992), cited from Crossick and Jaumain (1999), 3.

78. Victor Horta, *Mémoires*, ed. Cécile Dulière (Brussels, 1985), 103, 110–11, cited from Crossick and Jaumain (1999), 8.

79. Cited from Crossick and Jaumain (1999), 29.

80. Karl Marx, *Capital*, vol. 1, ch. 1, section 4, cited from Deborah Cohen, *Household Gods: The British and Their Possessions* (New Haven: Yale University Press, 2006), 18–19.

81. Pierre Giffard, *Les Grands Bazars* (1882), cited from Miller (1981), 192.

82. Richard Sennett, *The Fall of Public Man* (New York: Vintage, 1978), 144.

83. Miller (1981), 169.

84. Miller (1981), 49.

85. P. F. William Ryan, 'Scenes from Shop and Store London', in George R. Sims, ed., *Living London* (London: Cassell, 1903), 140, cited from Crossick and Jaumain (1999), 10.

86. *Scribner's* (1890), cited from Edwin G. Burrows and Mike Wallace, *Gotham: A History of New York City to 1898* (New York: OUP, 1999), 668.

87. H. G. Wells, *Anticipations of the Reactions of Mechanical and Scientific Progress upon Human Life and Thought* (1901), cited from Kotkin (2005), 151.

88. Seymour Buckner, 'The Independent Retailer – Downtown or Shopping Center' (1960), cited from Alison Isenberg, *Downtown America: A History of the Place and the People Who Made It* (Chicago: University of Chicago Press, 2004), 177.

7 Time Out

1. Cited from Lewis Mumford, *The City in History: Its Origins, Its Transformations, and Its Prospects* (London: Secker & Warburg, 1961), 111.

2. John T. Appleby, ed. and tr., *The Chronicle of Richard of Devizes of the Time of King Richard the First* (London: Nelson & Sons, 1963), 65–6, cited from Anne Lancashire, *London Civic Theatre: City Drama and Pageantry from*

Roman Times to 1558 (Cambridge: CUP, 2002), 32, 222n.

3. See: Margreta de Grazia and Stanley Wells, eds, *The Cambridge Companion to Shakespeare* (Cambridge: CUP, 2001), 99; Lucy Inglis, 'Shakespeare's First Theatre' <http://www.mymuseumoflondon.org.uk/blogs/blog/shakespeares-first-theatre/> Accessed 21 September 2010.

4. Christopher Hibbert, *Cities and Civilizations* (New York: Welcome Rain, 1996), 52.

5. See Cecilia Segawa Seigle, *Yoshiwara: The Glittering World of the Japanese Courtesan* (Hawaii: University of Hawaii Press, 1993).

6. Cited from Peter Hall, *Cities in Civilization: Culture, Innovation, and Urban Order* (London: Phoenix, 1999), 117.

7. Hall (1999), 137.

8. Hall (1999), 286.

9. Herbert Jhering, cited from Bärbel Schrader and Jürgen Schebera, *The 'Golden' Twenties: Art and Literature in the Weimar Republic* (New Haven: Yale University Press, 1988), 30.

10. Max Born, cited from P. D. Smith, *Einstein* (London: Haus, 2003), 89.

11. Stefan Zweig, *The World of Yesterday: An Autobiography* (London: Cassell & Co., 1943), 238.

12. On Döblin's *Berlin Alexanderplatz* and Berlin in this period, see P. D. Smith, 'Science and the city: Alfred Döblin's *Berlin Alexanderplatz*', *London Magazine*, 39 (April/May 2000), 27–36.

13. Justin Pollard and Howard Reid, *The Rise and Fall of Alexandria: Birthplace of the Modern Mind* (New York: Viking, 2006), 64.

14. Pollard and Reid (2006), 89.

15. Wendy Moore, *The Knife Man: The Extraordinary Life and Times of John Hunter, Father of Modern Surgery* (London: Bantam Press, 2005), 40.

16. Moore (2005), 353. His collection is now displayed in the Hunterian Museum <http://www.rcseng.ac.uk/museums>

17. Zaki Nusseibeh, the culture adviser to the Abu Dhabi Authority, cited in Georgina Adam, 'Abu Dhabi Guggenheim will have "potentially unlimited" budget', *The Art Newspaper*, 191 (May 2008): <http://www.

theartnewspaper.com/articles/Abu-Dhabi-Guggenheim-will-have-potentially-unlimited-budget/8439> Accessed 29 September 2010.

18. See *At the Instance of Benjamin Franklin: A Brief History of the Library Company of Philadelphia* (Philadelphia: Library Company of Philadelphia, 1995), online: <http://library-company.org/about/Instance.pdf> Accessed 29 September 2010.

19. The stated aims of the Edinburgh Working Men's Club and Institute which opened in 1864. 'The Working Men's Institutes': <http://historyshelf.org/shelf/learn/09.php> Accessed 29 September 2010.

20. Kai Strittmatter, tr. Stefan Tobler, *China A to Z: A User's Guide to the Next Global Superpower* (London: Haus, 2006), 130.

21. Strittmatter (2006), 87.

22. 'Street foods in developing countries: lessons from Asia' (UN, 1991); 'School kids and street food', *Spotlight* (FAO, February 2007): <http://www.fao.org/AG/magazine/0702sp1.htm> Accessed 4 October 2010; 'Street foods in Calcutta' (UN, 1996).

23. Rebecca Stott, *Oyster* (London: Reaktion, 2004), 61.

24. Stott (2004), 73.

25. George Makepeace Towle, *American Society* (London: Chapman & Hall, 1870), I: 272–3, cited from Andrew F. Smith, 'The Food and Drink of New York from 1624 to 1898', in Annie Hauck-Lawson and Jonathan Deutsch, eds, *Gastropolis: Food and New York City* (New York: Columbia University Press, 2009), 42.

26. Henry Mayhew, *London Labour and the London Poor: A Selected Edition*, ed. Robert Douglas-Fairhurst (Oxford: OUP, 2010), 51.

27. Henry Mayhew, *Mayhew's London: London Labour and the London Poor, Selections*, ed. Peter Quennell (1st 1951; London: Bracken, 1984), 127.

28. Mayhew (1984), 136.

29. Mayhew (1984), 140.

30. Mayhew (1984), 140.

31. Mayhew (2010), 53.

32. Mayhew (2010), 57.

33. Smith (2009), 35.

34. Jonathan Haynes, *The Humanist as Traveler: George Sandys's Relation of a Journey begun An.*

Dom. 1610 (Rutherford: Fairleigh Dickinson University Press, 1986), 18, cited from Markman Ellis, *The Coffee House: A Cultural History* (London: Weidenfeld & Nicolson, 2004), 8.

35. Laura Roberts, 'Fat cleared from London sewers will fill nine double-decker buses', *Daily Telegraph* (13 July 2010).

36. Donald G. Kyle, *Sport and Spectacle in the Ancient World* (Malden, Mass.: Blackwell, 2007), 26.

37. Kyle (2007), 7.

38. Kyle (2007), 8; 72–4; cf. Michael Silk, 'Sports Stadiums', in Ray Hutchison, ed., *Encyclopedia of Urban Studies*, 2 vols (Los Angeles: Sage, 2010), 762; Charles Gates, *Ancient Cities: The Archaeology of Urban Life in the Ancient Near East and Egypt, Greece, and Rome* (London: Routledge, 2003), 234ff.

39. Kyle (2007), 166.

40. Jérôme Carcopino, *Daily Life in Ancient Rome: The People and the City at the Height of the Empire* (1941; repr. Harmondsworth: Penguin, 1975), 242.

41. Carcopino (1975), 267.

42. Richard Tames, *Sporting London: A Race Through Time* (London: Historical Publications, 2005), 27.

43. Tames (2005), 87.

44. Iain Borden, 'Another Pavement, Another Beach', in Iain Borden et al., eds, *The Unknown City: Contesting Architecture and Social Space* (Cambridge, Mass.: MIT Press, 2001), 195.

45. Borden (2001), 182.

46. Iain Borden, 'Skateboarding', in Hutchison (2010), 730; cf. Iain Borden, 'A Performative Critique of the City: The Urban Practice of Skateboarding, 1958–1998', in Malcolm Miles, Tim Halla and Iain Borden, eds, *The City Cultures Reader* (1st 2000; repr. London: Routledge, 2004), 291–7.

47. Cited from Borden (2001), 190.

48. Jean Baudrillard, tr. Chris Turner, *America* (1st 1986; London: Verso, 2010), 19–21.

49. See: <http://www.kma.co.uk/>; <http://www.greatstreetgames.org.uk/>; <http://pruned.blogspot.com/2009/10/great-street-games.html> Accessed 14 October 2010.

50. Oli Mould, 'Parkour, the city, the event', *Environment and Planning D: Society and Space*, 27(4) (2009), 738–50.

51. Bruce Crumley, 'Leaps and Bounds', *Time* (30 June–7 July 2008), 83.

52. Sigfried Giedion, *Space, Time and Architecture: The Growth of a New Tradition* (1st 1941; Cambridge, Mass.: Harvard University Press, 2008), 724.

53. Both quotations cited from Lillian M. Li, Alison J. Dray-Novey and Haili Kong, *Beijing: From Imperial Capital to Olympic City* (New York: Palgrave Macmillan, 2007), 54.

54. M. L'Abbé Laugier, *Observations sur l'Architecture* (The Hague, 1765), 321ff, cited from Joseph Rykwert, *The Seduction of Place: The History and Future of the City* (Oxford: OUP, 2004), 49–50.

55. L'Abbé Laugier (1765), cited from Spiro Kostof, *The City Shaped: Urban Patterns and Meanings Through History* (London: Thames & Hudson, 1991), 226.

56. Madame van Muyden, ed. and tr., *A Foreign View of England in the Reign of George I and George II: The letters of Monsieur Cesar de Saussure to his family* (1902), 47–8, cited from Mark Girouard, *Cities and People: A Social and Architectural History* (New Haven: Yale University Press, 1985), 188.

57. Girouard (1985), 192. See also David Coke and Alan Borg, *Vauxhall Gardens: A History* (London: Yale, 2011).

58. Sir Roger de Coverley, a fictional character in the *Spectator*, cited from Dorothy Eagle and Hilary Carnell, eds, *The Oxford Illustrated Literary Guide to Great Britain and Ireland* (1st 1981; repr. London: Peerage, 1985), 178.

59. Jeremiah B. C. Axelrod, *Inventing Autopia: Dreams and Visions of the Modern Metropolis in Jazz Age Los Angeles* (Berkeley: University of California Press, 2009), 245.

60. Andrzej J. L. Zieleniec, 'Parks', in Hutchison (2010), 583. It is a phrase scorned by Jane Jacobs as 'science-fiction nonsense': *The Death and Life of Great American Cities* (1st 1961; repr. London: Penguin, 1994), 101.

61. Zieleniec, in Hutchison (2010), 583.

62. Zieleniec, in Hutchison (2010), 584.

63. Strabo cited from Michael Seymour, 'Classical Accounts', in I. L. Finkel and M. J. Seymour, eds, *Babylon: Myth and Reality* (London: British Museum Press, 2008), 107.

64. Quintus Curtius Rufus cited from Finkel and Seymour (2008), 107.

65. Frederick Law Olmsted, *Walks and Talks of an American Farmer in England* (New York: George Putnam, 1852), 79.

66. Rykwert, (2004), 192.

67. Frederick Law Olmsted, *Public Parks and the Enlargement of Towns* (Boston: American Social Science Association, 1870), 343, cited from Axelrod (2009), 248.

68. Rykwert (2004), 193.

69. Olmsted, cited from Leslie Day, *Field Guide to the Natural World of New York City* (Baltimore: Johns Hopkins University Press, 2007), 60.

70. Axelrod (2009), 249.

71. Clay McShane, *Down the Asphalt Path: The Automobile and the American City* (New York: Columbia University Press, 1994), 33.

72. Witold Rybczynski, *City Life* (Toronto: Harper Perennial, 1996), 126.

73. Jolanda Maas et al., 'Morbidity is related to a green living environment', *Journal of Epidemiology and Community Health* (15 October 2009; ref: jech.2008.079038v1); cf. Hannah Devlin, 'Urban residents living near parks are healthier and less depressed', *The Times* (16 October 2009).

74. See the research of Frances Kuo, director of the Landscape and Human Health Laboratory at the University of Illinois: 'How Cities use Parks to Create Safer Neighborhoods', *City Parks Forum Briefing Papers*, 4 (American Planning Association) <http://www.planning.org/cityparks/briefingpapers/saferneighborhoods.htm>; cf. Jonah Lehrer, 'How the City Hurts Your Brain ... And What You Can Do About It', *Boston Globe* (2 January 2009) <http://www.boston.com/bostonglobe/ideas/articles/2009/01/04/how_the_city_hurts_your_brain/?page=full>

8 Beyond the City

1. Stephen Halliday, *The Great Stink of London: Sir Joseph Bazalgette and the Cleansing of the*

Victorian Metropolis (Phoenix Mill: Sutton, 1999), 35.

2. Deborah Cadbury, *Seven Wonders of the Industrial World* (London: Harper Perennial, 2004), 189.

3. Jerry White, *London in the Nineteenth Century: 'A Human Awful Wonder of God'* (London: Jonathan Cape, 2007), 18.

4. See White (2007), 60; Mikael Hård and Thomas J. Misa, eds, *Urban Machinery: Inside Modern European Cities* (Cambridge, Mass.: MIT Press, 2010), 166.

5. *New York Herald* (5 September 1882), cited from Ric Burns and James Sanders, *New York: An Illustrated History* (New York: Knopf, 1999), 174.

6. Kate Ascher, *Anatomy of a City* (New York: Penguin, 2005), 91–3.

7. See Ascher (2005), 136–7; <http://de.wikipedia.org/wiki/Rohrpost_in_Berlin>; <http://en.wikipedia.org/wiki/Prague_pneumatic_post>

8. Aaron Renn, personal communication: November 2010.

9. From the invitation to IBM's PULSE 2010 event: Richard Adhikari, 'Cities of the Future, Part 1: The Self-Aware Metropolis', *TechNewsWorld* (23 March 2010) <http://www.technewsworld.com/story/69595.html?wlc=1282534243>

10. Greg Lindsay, 'Cisco's Big Bet on New Songdo: Creating Cities From Scratch', *Fast Company* (1 February 2010) <http://www.fastcompany.com/magazine/142/the-new-new-urbanism.html>

11. 'NASA Research Finds 2010 Tied for Warmest Year on Record': <http://www.nasa.gov/topics/earth/features/2010-warmest-year.html>

12. See David D. Kemp, 'Global warming', in David J. Cuff and Andrew S. Goudie, eds, *The Oxford Companion to Global Change* (Oxford: OUP, 2009), 295, 297–8; Richard Black, '2010 sets new temperature records', BBC News Online (2 December 2010): <http://www.bbc.co.uk/news/science-environment-11903397>

13. Gaia Vince, 'How to Survive the Coming Century', *New Scientist*, issue 2697 (25 February 2009), 28–33 <http://www.newscientist.com/article/mg20126971.700-how-to-survive-the-coming-century.html?full=true>

14. Bill McGuire, *Global Catastrophes* (Oxford: OUP, 2002), 12.

15. Philip R. Berke, 'Catastrophe', in Ray Hutchison, ed., *Encyclopedia of Urban Studies*, 2 vols (Los Angeles: Sage, 2010), 121; on flooding, cf. George Monbiot, *Heat: How to Stop the Planet Burning* (London: Allen Lane, 2006), 9; Kemp (2009), 356.

16. Rachel Warren et al., 'Impacts of Climate Change', in Cuff and Goudie (2009), 356.

17. McGuire (2002), 39.

18. Brian Fagan, *The Long Summer: How Climate Changed Civilization* (London: Granta, 2004), 138.

19. Fagan (2004), 140.

20. Andrew S. Goudie, 'Urban Climates', in Cuff and Goudie (2009), 607.

21. David Satterthwaite, 'Cities' Contribution to Global Warming: Notes on the Allocation of Greenhouse Gas Emissions', *Environment and Urbanization*, 20 (2008), 543.

22. David Dodman, 'Blaming cities for climate change? An analysis or urban greenhouse gas emissions inventories', *Environment and Urbanization*, 21 (2009), 188–91

23. Satterthwaite (2008), 547; cf. Dodman (2009), 191.

24. William Wiles, 'Urban Farming', *Icon*, 72 (June 2009), 73.

25. Klaus Töpfer, Executive Director of the UN Environment Programme (UNEP) in 2005; cited from David J. Cuff, 'Urban Trends', in Cuff and Goudie (2009), 608. Similarly: 'experts and policymakers increasingly recognize the potential value of cities to long-term sustainability. If cities create environmental problems, they also contain the solutions. The potential benefits of urbanization far outweigh the disadvantages: The challenge is in learning how to exploit its possibilities.' From *UNFPA State of World Population 2007: Unleashing the Potential of Urban Growth*, Introduction <http://www.unfpa.org/swp/2007/english/introduction.html>

26. 'Urban visionary', *Time* (25 February 2008), 39.

27. Herbert Girardet, *Creating Sustainable Cities* (Totnes: Green Books, 1999), 9.

28. Edwin Heathcote, 'Urban Evolution Adapting the City for the Future', *Financial Times* (7 September 2010) <http://www.ft.com/cms/s/0/9c365d34-b064-11df-8c04-00144feabdc0,dwp_uuid=05c2777c-38da-11df-9998-00144feabdc0.html>

29. Jeb Brugmann, *Welcome to the Urban Revolution: How Cities are Changing the World* (New York: Bloomsbury Press, 2009), 186.

30. Jon Turney, personal communication: November 2010.

31. Don Martindale, introduction to Max Weber's *The City* (1958), 62, cited from Andrew Blowers, Chris Hamnett and Philip Sarre, eds, *The Future of Cities* (London: Hutchinson Educational/Open University Press, 1974), 153.

32. 'Cities of Tomorrow', *Amazing* (1939), in Robert Sheckley, *Futuropolis* (London: Big O Publishing, 1979), illustration 28.

33. Ian Tod and Michael Wheeler, *Utopia* (London: Orbis, 1978), 133.

34. Antonio Sant'Elia, 'Manifesto of Futurist Architecture', *Lacerba* (1 August 1914), in Umbro Apollonio, ed., *Futurist Manifestos* (New York: Viking Press, 1973), 160–72.

35. Tod and Wheeler (1978), 136.

36. Yevgeny Zamyatin, tr. Bernard Guilbert Guerney, *We* (1st 1924; repr. Harmondsworth: Penguin, 1984), 23, 21.

37. Zamyatin (1984), 35.

38. Zamyatin (1984), 19.

39. Le Corbusier, *The City of Tomorrow and Its Planning* (London: John Rodker, 1929), tr. Frederick Etchells; cited from Tod and Wheeler (1978), 138–9.

40. Lang cited from James Sanders, *Celluloid Skyline: New York and the Movies* (London: Bloomsbury, 2002), 106.

41. H. G. Wells, *The Sleeper Awakes* (1899; revised 1910; repr. London: Penguin, 2005), 42.

42. Wells (2005), 71.

43. Norman M. Klein, *The History of Forgetting: Los Angeles and the Erasure of Memory* (1st 1997; repr. London: Verso, 2008), 95.

44. Jean Baudrillard, tr. Chris Turner, *America* (1st 1986; repr. London: Verso, 2010), 53–4.

45. Brian J. Robb, *Counterfeit Worlds: Philip K. Dick on Film* (London: Titan, 2006), 127.

46. Klein (2008), 97.

47. 'Designing Black Rock City' <http://www.burningman.com/whatisburningman/about_burningman/brc_growth.html> Accessed 8 December 2010.

48. Margaret Mead, 'Towards more vivid utopias', *Science*, 126 (1957), 958.

49. William Gibson, National Public Radio interview, *Talk of the Nation* (30 November 1999).

50. Arthur C. Clarke, *The City and the Stars* (1st 1956; repr. London: Gollancz, 2001), 16, 9.

51. Clarke (2001), 25.

52. Karl Marx, *The Communist Manifesto*, in Robert C. Tucker, ed., *The Marx-Engels Reader* (New York: Norton, 1978), 475–6, cited from Marshall Berman, *All That Is Solid Melts Into Air: The Experience of Modernity* (1st 1982; repr. London: Verso, 2010), 21.

53. Christopher Woodward, *In Ruins* (London: Vintage, 2002), 7.

54. Sanders (2002), 388.

55. H. G. Wells, *The War in the Air* (1st 1908; repr. Thirsk: House of Stratus, 2002), 155.

56. Doré's engraving appears in his book *London* (1872). On the history of the New Zealander visiting London's ruins, see: David Skilton, 'Contemplating the Ruins of London: Macaulay's New Zealander and Others' <http://homepages.gold.ac.uk/london-journal/march2004/skilton.html>

57. Richard Jefferies, *After London; Or, Wild England* (1st 1886; repr. Cirencester: Echo, 2005), 14.

58. Laura Spinney, 'Return to Paradise: If the People Flee, What Will Happen to the Seemingly Indestructible?', *New Scientist*, 2039 (20 July 1996), 30.

59. Spinney (1996), 30.

60. Jan Zalasiewicz, *The Earth After Us: What Legacy Will Humans Leave in the Rocks?* (Oxford: OUP, 2008), 189.

61. 'When History Has Forgotten New York', *New York Times* (31 May 1925), 12, cited from Nick Yablon, *Untimely Ruins: An Archaeology of American Urban Modernity, 1819–1919* (Chicago: University of Chicago Press, 2009), 2.

62. Kurt Vonnegut, cited from P. D. Smith,

Doomsday Men: The Real Dr Strangelove and the Dream of the Superweapon (London: Allen Lane, 2007), 319.

63. Vonnegut interview by James Naughtie, *The Culture Show* (BBC2, 2005).

64. Kurt Vonnegut, *Slaughterhouse-Five* (London: Vintage, 2000), 130.

65. Cited from Jeff Byles, *Rubble: Unearthing the History of Demolition* (New York: Harmony Books, 2005), 247.

66. Dan Hoffmann 'Erasing Detroit', *Architecture Studio: Cranbrook Academy of Art, 1986–93* (New York: Rizzoli, 1994), 28, cited from Byles (2005), 228.

67. Witold Rybczynski, 'Incredible Hulks: Exploring Detroit's Beautiful Ruins', *Slate* (18 March 2009) <http://www.slate.com/id/2213696/>

68. Brugmann (2009), 152.

69. Camilo José Vergara, 'Downtown Detroit,' *Metropolis*, 14 (April 1995), 33, cited from Byles (2005), 247–8.

70. Chan Davis, 'The Nightmare' (1946), in Gregory Benford and Martin Harry Greenberg, *Nuclear War* (New York: Ace, 1988), 15.

71. Stephen Vincent Benét, 'By the Waters of Babylon' (1937), in Walter J. Miller and Martin H. Greenberg, eds, *Beyond Armageddon: Twenty-One Sermons to the Dead* (New York: Donald I. Fine, Inc., 1985), 245.

72. Mike Davis, 'Dead Cities: A Natural History' (2001), in *Dead Cities and Other Tales* (New York: New Press, 2002), 386.

73. Davis (2002), 392.

74. Marshall Berman, 'Falling', in Matthew Beaumont and Gregory Dart, eds, *Restless Cities* (London: Verso, 2010), 124.

75. Beaumont and Dart (2010), 126.

76. Lamentations of Jeremiah, 1: 1, cited from Beaumont and Dart (2010), 128–9.

77. Beaumont and Dart (2010), 129.

Afterword

1. 'Megalopolis' was first used in urban studies by Jean Gottmann and is derived from the Greek for 'very large city'. See John Rennie Short's fascinating essay 'The Liquid City of Megalopolis', in Gary Bridge and Sophie Watson, eds, *The New Blackwell Companion to the City* (Chichester: Wiley-Blackwell, 2011), 26–37, and Richard Morrill, 'Megalopolis', in Ray Hutchison, ed, *Encyclopedia of Urban Studies*, 2 vols (Los Angeles: Sage, 2010), 498–502.

2. UN-Habitat, *State of the World's Cities 2008/2009: Harmonious Cities* (London: Earthscan, 2008), 11.

3. Tom MacInnes and Peter Kenway, *London's Poverty Profile* (London: City Parochial Foundation / New Policy Institute, 2009), 39, 23, online: <http://www.londonspovertyprofile.org.uk/>. Income is also more concentrated at the top than elsewhere in the country, with 20 per cent earning 60 per cent of the income. See also Susan Fainstein, Ian Gordon and Michael Harloe, 'Ups and Downs in the Global City: London and New York in the Twenty-First Century', in Bridge and Watson (2011), 43.

4. Richard Sennett, 'Boundaries and Borders', in Ricky Burdett and Deyan Sudjic, eds, *Living in the Endless City* (London: Phaidon, 2011), 324.

5. The phrase is Peter Droege's in 'One Hundred Tons to Armageddon: Cities Combat Carbon', Bridge and Watson (2011), 108.

Further Reading

General

Beaumont, Matthew, and Gregory Dart (eds), *Restless Cities* (London: Verso, 2010)

Borden, Iain, et al. (eds), *The Unknown City: Contesting Architecture and Social Space* (Cambridge, MA: MIT Press, 2001)

Bridge, Gary, and Sophie Watson (eds), *The Blackwell City Reader* (Oxford: Blackwell, 2002)

Burdett, Ricky, and Deyan Sudjic (eds), *The Endless City* (London: Phaidon, 2007)
—*Living in the Endless City* (London: Phaidon, 2011)

Chandler, Tertius, *Four Thousand Years of Urban Growth: An Historical Census* (New York: Edwin Mellen Press, 1987)

Clark, Peter, *European Cities and Towns, 400–2000* (Oxford: Oxford University Press, 2009)

Freund, Bill, *The African City: A History* (Cambridge: Cambridge University Press, 2007)

Hibbert, Christopher, *Cities and Civilizations* (New York: Welcome Rain, 1996)

Hutchison, Ray (ed.), *Encyclopedia of Urban Studies*, 2 vols (Los Angeles: Sage, 2010)

Kotkin, Joel, *The City: A Global History* (London: Phoenix, 2005)

Miles, Malcolm, Tim Hall and Iain Borden (eds), *The City Cultures Reader* (London: Routledge, 2004)

Mumford, Lewis, *The City in History: Its Origins, its Transformations, and its Prospects* (London: Secker & Warburg, 1961)

Norwich, John Julius (ed.), *The Great Cities in History* (London: Thames & Hudson, 2009)

Rybczynski, Witold, *City Life* (Toronto: HarperPerennial, 1996)

Rykwert, Joseph, *The Seduction of Place: The History and Future of the City* (Oxford: OUP, 2000; repr. 2004)

1 Arrival

Burns, Ric, and James Sanders, *New York: An Illustrated History* (New York: Knopf, 1999)

Díaz, Bernal, *The Conquest of New Spain*, tr. J. M. Cohen (Harmondsworth: Penguin, 1973)

Fenske, Gail, *The Skyscraper and the City: The Woolworth Building and the Making of Modern New York* (Chicago: University of Chicago Press, 2008)

Finkel, I. L., and M. J. Seymour (eds), *Babylon: Myth and Reality* (London: British Museum, 2008)

Mann, Charles C., *1491: New Revelations of the Americas before Columbus* (New York: Knopf, 2005)

Meeks, Carroll L.V., *The Railroad Station: An Architectural History* (New Haven: Yale University Press, 1956)

Pitkin, Thomas M., *Keepers of the Gate: A History of Ellis Island* (New York: New York University Press, 1975)

Richards, Jeffrey, and John M. MacKenzie, *The Railway Station: A Social History* (Oxford: Oxford University Press, 1986)

Sabloff, Jeremy A., *The Cities of Ancient Mexico: Reconstructing a Lost World* (London: Thames & Hudson, 1997)

Schwartz, Stuart B. (ed.) *Victors and Vanquished: Spanish and Nahua Views of the Conquest of Mexico* (Boston, MA: Bedford; Basingstoke: Macmillan, 2000)

Wolmar, Christian, *Fire and Steam: A New History of the Railways in Britain* (London: Atlantic Books, 2007)

2. History

Algaze, Guillermo, *Ancient Mesopotamia at the Dawn of Civilization: The Evolution of an Urban Landscape* (Chicago: University of Chicago Press, 2008)

Braunfels, Wolfgang, trs. Kenneth J. Northcott, *Urban Design in Western Europe: Regime and Architecture, 900–1900* (Chicago: University of Chicago Press, 1990)

Galantay, Ervin Y., *New Towns: Antiquity to the Present* (New York: Braziller, 1975)

Gates, Charles, *Ancient Cities: The Archaeology of Urban Life in the Ancient Near East and Egypt, Greece, and Rome* (London: Routledge, 2003)

Girard, Greg, and Ian Lambot, *City of Darkness: Life in Kowloon Walled City* (London: Watermark Publications, 1993)

Jones, Colin, *Paris: Biography of a City* (London: Penguin, 2006)

Kargon, Robert H., and Arthur P. Molella, *Invented Edens: Techno-cities of the Twentieth Century* (Cambridge, MA: MIT Press, 2008)

Kostof, Spiro, *The City Shaped: Urban Patterns and Meanings Through History* (London: Thames & Hudson, 1991)

Leick, Gwendolyn, *Mesopotamia: The Invention of the City* (London: Penguin, 2002)

Lindqvist, Cecilia, *China: Empire of Living Symbols* (Cambridge, MA: Da Capo, 2008)

Meller, Hugh, *London Cemeteries: An Illustrated Guide* (Aldershot: Scolar, 1994)

Mieroop, Marc van de, *The Ancient Mesopotamian City* (Oxford: Oxford University Press, 1999)

Rosenau, Helen, *The Ideal City: Its Architectural Evolution in Europe* (London: Methuen, 1983)

Sloane, David Charles, *The Last Great Necessity: Cemeteries in American History* (Baltimore: Johns Hopkins University Press, 1991)

Southall, Aiden, *The City in Time and Space* (Cambridge: Cambridge University Press, 1998)

Steinhardt, Nancy Shatzman, *Chinese Imperial City Planning* (Honolulu: University of Hawaii Press, 1990)

Williams, Richard J., *Brazil* (London: Reaktion, 2009)

Wheatley, Paul, *The Pivot of the Four Quarters: A Preliminary Enquiry into the Origins and Character of the Ancient Chinese City* (Edinburgh: Edinburgh University Press, 1971)

3 Customs

Beard, Mary, *The Parthenon* (London: Profile Books, 2002)   Ferguson, Ronnie, *A Linguistic History of Venice* (Florence: Leo S. Olschki Editore, 2007)

Dougherty, James, *The Fivesquare City: The City in the Religious Imagination* (Notre Dame: University of Notre Dame Press, 1980)

Dudd, Ross E., *The Adventures of Ibn Battuta: A Muslim Traveler of the 14th Century* (Berkeley: University of California Press, 1989)

Franklyn, Julian, *The Cockney: A Survey of London Life and Language* (London: André Deutsch, 1953)

Grévy, Fabienne, *Graffiti Paris* (New York: Abrams, 2008)

Harris, Max, *Carnival and Other Christian Festivals: Folk Theology and Folk Performance* (Austin: University of Texas Press, 2003)

Lilley, Keith D., *City and Cosmos: The Medieval World in Urban Form* (London: Reaktion, 2009)

Peters, F.E., *Jerusalem and Mecca: The Typology of the Holy City in the Near East* (New York: New York University Press, 1986)

Reisner, Robert, *Graffiti: Two Thousand Years of Wall Writing* (New York: Cowles, 1971)

Reiss, Matthias (ed.), *The Street as Stage: Protest Marches and Public Rallies since the Nineteenth Century* (Oxford: Oxford University Press, 2007)

Richie, Alexandra, *Faust's Metropolis: A History of Berlin* (London: HarperCollins, 1999)

Richter, Donald C., *Riotous Victorians* (Athens: Ohio University Press, 1981)

Robinson, Andrew, *The Story of Writing* (London: Thames & Hudson, 2007)

Naar, Jon, *The Birth of Graffiti* (Munich: Prestel, 2007)

Sennett, Richard, *Flesh and Stone: The Body and the City in Western Civilization* (New York: Norton, 1997)

Solnit, Rebecca, *Wanderlust: A History of Walking* (London: Verso, 2002)

Stierlin, Henri, *Islamic Art and Architecture* (London: Thames & Hudson, 2001)

Verderber, Stephen, *Delirious New Orleans: Manifesto for an Extraordinary American City* (Austin: University of Texas Press, 2009)

Wolf, Maryanne, *Proust and the Squid: The Story and Science of the Reading Brain* (Cambridge: Icon, 2008)

4 Where to Stay

Anderson, Jervis, *This Was Harlem: A Cultural Portrait, 1900–1950* (New York: Farrar, Straus & Giroux, 1982)

Brugmann, Jeb, *Welcome to the Urban Revolution: How Cities are Changing the World* (New York: Bloomsbury Press, 2009)

Chen, Yong, *Chinese San Francisco, 1850–1943: A Trans-Pacific Community* (Stanford: Stanford University Press, 2000)

Davis, Mike, *Planet of Slums* (London: Verso, 2006)

Denby, Elaine, *Grand Hotels: Reality and Illusion* (London: Reaktion, 1998)

Fogelson, Robert M., *Downtown: Its Rise and Fall, 1880–1950* (New Haven: Yale University Press, 2001)

Garreau, Joel, *Edge City: Life on the New Frontier* (New York: Doubleday, 1991)

Gray, Fred, *Designing the Seaside: Architecture, Society and Nature* (London: Reaktion, 2006) Hall, Peter, *Cities of Tomorrow: An Intellectual History of Urban Planning and Design in the Twentieth Century* (Oxford: Blackwell, 1998)

Isenberg, Alison, *Downtown America: A History of the Place and the People Who Made It* (Chicago: University of Chicago Press, 2004)

Jackson, Kenneth T., *Crabgrass Frontier: The Suburbanization of the United States* (New York: Oxford University Press, 1985)

Lichtenstein, Rachel, *On Brick Lane* (London: Penguin, 2008)

Riis, Jacob, *How the Other Half Lives*, ed. Hasia R. Diner (1890; repr. New York: Norton, 2010)

Rykwert, Joseph, *The Seduction of Place: The History and Future of the City* (Oxford: Oxford University Press, 2004)

Sennett, Richard, *The Uses of Disorder: Personal Identity and City Life* (New Haven: Yale University Press, 2008)

Silverstone, Roger (ed.), *Visions of Suburbia* (London: Routledge, 1997)

Sudjic, Deyan, *The 100 Mile City* (London: André Deutsch, 1992)

UN-Habitat, *State of the World's Cities 2008/2009: Harmonious Cities* (London: Earthscan, 2008)

Ward, David, *Poverty, Ethnicity and the American City 1840–1925: Changing Conceptions of the Slum and the Ghetto* (Cambridge: Cambridge University Press, 1989)

5 Getting Around

Amato, Joseph A., *On Foot: A History of Walking* (New York: New York University Press, 2004)

William Bittner, *Poe: A Biography* (London: Elek Books, 1963)

Brand, Dana, *The Spectator and the City in Nineteenth-Century American Literature* (Cambridge: Cambridge University Press, 1991)

Giedion, Sigfried, *Space, Time and Architecture: The Growth of a New Tradition* (Cambridge, MA: Harvard University Press, 2008) McDonough, Tom (ed.), *The Situationists and the City* (London: Verso, 2009)

Hawes, Elizabeth, *New York, New York: How the Apartment House Transformed the Life of the City (1869–1930)* (New York: Owl/ Henry Holt, 1994)

Hines, Thomas S., *Burnham of Chicago: Architect and Planner* (Chicago: University of Chicago Press, 2009)

Koolhaas, Rem, *Delirious New York: A Retroactive Manifesto for Manhattan* (New York: Monacelli Press, 1994)

Prakash, Gyan, and Kevin M. Kruse (eds), *The Spaces of the Modern City: Imaginaries, Politics, and Everday Life* (Princeton: Princeton University Press, 2008)

Roth, Ralf, and Marie-Noelle Polino (eds), *The City and the Railway in Europe* (Aldershot: Ashgate, 2003)

Vanderbilt, Tom, *Traffic: Why We Drive the Way We Do (and What It Says About Us)* (London: Penguin, 2009)

Wachs, Martin, and Margaret Crawford (eds), *The Car and the City: The Automobile, the Built Environment and Daily Urban Life* (Ann Arbor: University of Michigan Press, 1992)

Wolmar, Christian, *The Subterranean Railway: How the London Underground Was Built and How It Changed the City Forever* (London: Atlantic Books, 2005)

6 Money

Ali, Syed, *Dubai: Gilded Cage* (New Haven: Yale University Press, 2010)

Davis, Mike, *City of Quartz: Excavating the Future in Los Angeles* (London: Vintage, 1990)

Ferguson, Niall, *The Ascent of Money: A Financial History of the World* (London: Allen Lane, 2008)

Crossick, Geoffrey and Serge Jaumain (eds), *Cathedrals of Consumption: The European Department Store, 1850–1939* (Aldershot: Ashgate, 1999)

Geiste, Johann Friedrich, *Arcades: The History of a Building Type* (Cambridge, MA: MIT Press, 1983)

Gilfoyle, Timothy J., *A Pickpocket's Tale: The Underworld of 19th-century New York* (New York: Norton, 2006)

Mattie, Erik, *World's Fairs* (Princeton: Princeton Architectural Press, 1998)

Miller, Michael B., *The Bon Marché: Bourgeois Culture and the Department Store, 1896–1920* (London: Allen & Unwin, 1981)

Minton, Anna, *Ground Control: Fear and Happiness in the 21st-Century City* (London: Penguin, 2009)

Parker, Geoffrey, *Sovereign City: The City-State Through History* (London: Reaktion, 2004)

Parkins, Helen and Christopher Smith (eds), *Trade, Traders and the Ancient City* (London: Routledge, 1998)

Reader, John, *Cities* (London: Heinemann, 2004)

Scarpa, Tiziano, *Venice Is a Fish: A Cultural Guide* (London: Serpent's Tail, 2009)

Tittler, Robert, *Architecture and Power: The Town Hall and the English Urban Community c. 1500–1640* (Oxford: Clarendon, 1991)

Zecker, Robert, *Metropolis: The American City in Popular Culture* (Westport: Praeger, 2008)

7 Time Out

Berman, Marshall, *On the Town: One Hundred Years of Spectacle in Times Square* (London: Verso, 2009)

Carcopino, Jérôme, tr. E. O. Lorimer, *Daily Life in Ancient Rome: The People and the City at the Height of the Empire* (Harmondsworth: Penguin, 1975)

Cruickshank, Dan, *The Secret History of Georgian London: How the Wages of Sin Shaped the Capital* (London: Random House, 2009)

Ellis, Markman, *The Coffee House: A Cultural History* (London: Weidenfield & Nicolson, 2004)

Girouard, Mark, *Cities and People: A Social and Architectural History* (New Haven: Yale University Press, 1985)

Hall, Peter, *Cities in Civilization: Culture, Innovation, and Urban Order* (London: Phoenix, 1999)

Harvie, Jen, *Theatre and the City* (Houndmills: Palgrave, 2009)

Hauck-Lawson, Annie and Jonathan Deutsch (eds), *Gastropolis: Food and New York City* (New York: Columbia University Press, 2009)

Kostof, Spiro, *The City Shaped: Urban Patterns and Meanings Through History* (London: Thames & Hudson, 1991)

Kyle, Donald G., *Sport and Spectacle in the Ancient World* (Malden, MA: Blackwell, 2007)

Lancashire, Anne, *London Civic Theatre: City Drama and Pageantry from Roman Times to 1558* (Cambridge: Cambridge University Press, 2002)

Laurence, Ray, *Roman Passions: A History of Pleasure in Imperial Rome* (London: Continuum, 2009)

Mayhew, Henry, *London Labour and the London Poor: A Selected Edition*, ed. Robert Douglas-Fairhurst (Oxford: Oxford University Press, 2010)

Meller, H. E., *Leisure and the Changing City, 1870–1914* (London: Routledge, 1976)

Newman, Kate, *Cultural Capitals: Early Modern London and Paris* (Princeton: University of Princeton Press, 2007)

Pollard, Justin and Howard Reid *The Rise and Fall of Alexandria: Birthplace of the Modern Mind* (New York: Viking, 2006)

Rykwert, Joseph, *The Seduction of Place: The History and Future of the City* (Oxford: Oxford University Press, 2004)

Tames, Richard, *Sporting London: A Race Through Time* (London: Historical Publications, 2005)

8 Beyond the City

Alison, Jane, et al. (eds), *Future City: Experiment and Utopia in Architecture* (London: Thames & Hudson, 2006)

Ascher, Kate, *Anatomy of a City* (New York: Penguin, 2005)

Beard, Mary, *Pompeii: The Life of a Roman Town* (London: Profile Books, 2008)

Byles, Jeff, *Rubble: Unearthing the History of Demolition* (New York: Harmony Books, 2005)

Cadbury, Deborah, *Seven Wonders of the Industrial World* (London: Harper Perennial, 2004)

Chen, Katherine K., *Enabling Creative Chaos: The Organization Behind the Burning Man Event* (Chicago: University of Chicago Press, 2009)

Cuff, David J., and Andrew S. Goudie (eds), *The Oxford Companion to Global Change* (Oxford: Oxford University Press, 2009)

Davis, Mike, *Dead Cities and Other Tales* (New York: The New Press, 2002)

Fagan, Brian, *The Long Summer: How Climate Changed Civilization* (London: Granta, 2004)

Girardet, Herbert, *Creating Sustainable Cities* (Totnes: Green Books, 1999)

Granick, Harry, *Underneath New York* (New York: Fordham University Press, 1991)

Halliday, Stephen, *The Great Stink of London: Sir Joseph Bazalgette and the Cleansing of the Victorian Metropolis* (Phoenix Mill: Sutton, 1999),

Hård, Mikael and Thomas J. Misa (eds), *Urban Machinery: Inside Modern European Cities* (Cambridge, MA: MIT Press, 2010)

Johnson, Steven, *The Ghost Map: A Street, an Epidemic and the Hidden Power of Urban Networks* (London: Penguin, 2008)

Manaugh, Geoff, *The BLDGBLOG Book* (San Francisco: Chronicle, 2009)

Maslin, Mark, *Global Warming* (Oxford: Oxford University Press, 2009)

Pursell, Carroll, *The Machine in America: A Social History of Technology* (Baltimore: John Hopkins University Press, 2007)

Roberts, Peter, Joe Ravetz and Clive George, *Environment and the City* (Abingdon: Routledge, 2009)

Sanders, James, *Celluloid Skyline: New York and the Movies* (London: Bloomsbury, 2002)

Sheckley, Robert, *Futuropolis* (London: Big O Publishing Ltd, 1979)

Tod, Ian, and Micahel Wheeler, *Utopia* (London: Orbis, 1978)

UN-Habitat, *State of the World's Cities 2008/2009: Harmonious Cities* (London: Earthscan, 2008)

Upton, Dell, *Another City: Urban Life and Urban Spaces in the New American Republic* (New Haven: Yale University Press, 2008)

Woodward, Christopher, *In Ruins* (London: Vintage, 2002)

Yablon, Nick, *Untimely Ruins: An Archaeology of American Urban Modernity, 1819–1919* (Chicago: University of Chicago Press, 2009)

Picture Credits

Acknowledgements

I would like to thank my agent, Peter Tallack, whose enthusiasm and advice has been invaluable while writing *City*. Bill Swainson, at Bloomsbury, believed in the book from the beginning and shared my vision of what it could be. Everyone who worked on the book at Bloomsbury in the UK and in the US has been brilliant, particularly Emily Sweet, who was tireless in her efforts to track down the right images, but also Nick Humphrey, Polly Napper, Richard Collins, Peter Ginna and Pete Beatty.

I am very grateful to the Department of Science and Technology Studies at University College London for making me an Honorary Research Associate, a privilege that allows me to use the excellent libraries of the University of London.

Many people have been kind enough to offer information and advice during the writing of *City*, mostly via the dangerously distracting medium of Twitter. They include: Paul Bishop, Lewis Crofts, Steven Hall, Paul Halpern, Andrew Keen, Crystal Koo, Geoff Manaugh, Angela Meyer, Oli Mould, Maria Popova, Aaron M. Renn, Thomas Riepe, Jim Rossignol, Simon Sellars, Joel Toombs, Jon Turney, Will Wiles and Cindy Frewen Wuellner. Thanks to all of you.

Index

A note on the author

P. D. Smith is an independent researcher and writer. He has taught at University College London where he is an Honorary Research Associate in the Science and Technology Studies Department. He reviews regularly for the *Guardian* and the *Times Literary Supplement*, and has also contributed to other national publications including *The Times*, the *Independent* and the *Financial Times*. His books include *Doomsday Men: The Real Dr Strangelove and the Dream of the Superweapon* and a life of Einstein.

www.peterdsmith.com